Letters of Edna St. Vincent Millay

EDNA ST. VINCENT MILLAY
Bronze portrait head by Agnes Yarnall

Letters of
Edna St. Vincent Millay

Edited by

Allan Ross Macdougall

HARPER & BROTHERS, PUBLISHERS
New York

Library of Congress catalog card number: 52-7291

Contents

Acknowledgments

I wish, primarily, to express my thanks to my friend, Miss Norma Millay. In her capacity as the literary executor of Edna St. Vincent Millay, she has not only authorized this book of letters but has greatly contributed to it with material from the family papers, information, suggestions and comments. These have been most valuable and deeply appreciated.

Thanks are due also to Mrs. Franklin P. Adams, Miss Alice Blinn, Miss Margaret Cuthbert, and Mr. Edmund Wilson—all old friends of the poet—for their encouraging criticism and advice. For the information and advice of Mr. John S. Van E. Kohn, freely given, and for that of Mr. Robert W. Hill of the Manuscript Division of the New York Public Library, I also express my thanks.

For placing the Edna Millay files at my disposal, I am grateful to Mr. Cass Canfield, Chairman of the Board of Harper & Brothers. To Mrs. Arthur Davison Ficke I am also most grateful for making available to me material from the Arthur Davison Ficke Collection, now on deposit at the Sterling Memorial Library, Yale University. Miss Bernice Baumgarten of Brandt & Brandt made accessible the files of that literary agency and I would like to acknowledge her kindness and help.

To all the librarians of the various institutions who courteously answered my inquiries and sent me photostatic material for possible inclusion in this volume, I herewith express my obligation. I am especially obliged to Mr. Donald Gallup, Curator of the Collection of American Literature, Yale University Library. Miss Dorothy Plum of the Vassar College Library, and the librarians of the universities of Harvard, Chicago, and Buffalo, the Newberry Library in Chicago, and the New York Public Library were also most helpful. As for the many friends and correspondents of the late poet who sent me originals or copies of their precious letters—often with the addition of careful annotations—I have already thanked them all individually. They will, I am sure, understand that it is not discourtesy but reasons of space that

vii

Acknowledgments

prevent me from listing their names here. Reasons of space also prevent me from making use of all the interesting letters received.

Finally, in a special category, must go my thanks to Mrs. Beulah Hagen, Assistant to Cass Canfield, for her help with photostats and other preliminary details; to my friend, Ralph T. Ward, who helped me in the first months with the editorial chore of making clear transcriptions of the hundreds of letters and notes which came to me; and to Frances Park who labored over the final manuscript, putting it into shape for the publisher.

For permission to quote in the Foreword the excerpt from Mr. Deems Taylor's tribute to Edna St. Vincent Millay, I am indebted to the American Academy of Arts & Letters. The English renderings of the Latin quotations in letter No. 215 are from the translation of Virgil's *Aeneid* of Rolfe Humphries published by Charles Scribner's Sons (1951), and are reprinted with kind permission of Mr. Humphries and his publisher. The stanza from Elinor Wylie's poem, "Bronze Trumpets and Sea Water," from *Nets to Catch the Wind* (1921), is reprinted by permission of Harcourt, Brace & Company, Inc. Gerard Manley Hopkins' sonnet "In the Valley of the Elwy," from *Poems* (1948), is reprinted by permission of Oxford University Press.

A. R. M.

Foreword

Lovers of poetry everywhere have read the poems of Edna St. Vincent Millay. Perhaps they have also heard her read her own works in crowded auditoriums in this country, or over the radio. They do not have to be informed that she was a distinguished writer of poetry. That she had a way with words in prose should not come as any surprise to them. In the selected letters from her pen which follow, they will find more than a few examples of her word magic to cherish in their hearts with the lyrics and sonnets by which they now remember her.

Here they will learn of the poet's deep love for her family, her steadfast devotion to her friends, her profound concern for all poetry, and the meticulous self-criticism with which she approached even her slightest verse. They will admire the stand she took for causes she believed in; they will be touched by her humility; and if they have a feeling for music they will be moved by what she has to write of that sister art.

Looking back over the more than three decades to the night, in Christine's restaurant over the Provincetown Playhouse, when I first met Edna Millay, I remember her particular intensity. She was interested in some Scottish ballads I had sung and was eager to learn all the others I knew. She listened to what I had to say and sing with such grave concentration. Yes, I remember well her passionate interest, her intensity, her gravity; but I remember, too, her quick sense of fun, her wit, and her generosity. "Look what I have—and these are all for you."

Were I now—recollecting the poet's steady, gray-green eyes and her little girl's smile that lit her face in certain friendliness—to write out of my heart's love for my unforgettable friend, and set down my memories of the great poet whom I held in high esteem, I could doubtless fill many pages. This, however, is not the place for my personal recollections. My immediate task is to introduce the reader to these letters which I have had the honor to edit. Even in the least of her

ix

notes the poet speaks for herself with surer words and more sharply
minted phrases than any of mine.

Yet, before the reader settles down to the enjoyment of reading
these letters, I must make some necessary explanations. This book is a
selection from those letters of Edna St. Vincent Millay which during
the past year I have been able to collect. Lack of space has forced the
omission of many letters kindly sent in by friends and correspondents.
On the other hand, many I had hoped to include were unobtainable.
Some of these have been destroyed by fire; of those to her friend,
Elinor Wylie; to her first editor, Ferdinand Earle; to her sister Kathleen;
to her father; and to others mentioned in certain letters, it has been
impossible to learn the present whereabouts, if they still exist.

In the case of the poet's letters to her husband, Eugen Boissevain,
the reader will find only three in the year 1924, and one later one
written on Ragged Island. Until Mr. Boissevain's death in 1949 they
were rarely separated.

The comparatively few letters representing many of the latter
years can be partly accounted for by the fact that, after her marriage,
to leave the poet free for her work, Mr. Boissevain assumed much of
her correspondence. In other years, during the long illness following the
accident she describes, he not only answered letters from strangers, but
those from her family and intimate friends as well, although in these
cases Miss Millay often added a few words at the end. One outstanding
postscript addressed to the poet, Leonora Speyer, is included as letter
No. 235.

The telegraph, like the telephone, is a monstrous destroyer of
leisurely correspondence. In the last years Miss Millay frequently made
use of both these mechanisms instead of writing. The commissioning
and writing of "Poem and Prayer for an Invading Army," for example,
will not be found mentioned in any letter in this volume. The work,
written by Edna St. Vincent Millay for exclusive radio use by the
National Broadcasting Company, and read by Ronald Colman on
D-day—June 6, 1944—over the NBC network, was even proofread over
the telephone. According to Miss Margaret Cuthbert of NBC, there
were many long and arduous telephone conversations between herself
and Miss Millay before the poet, meticulous as always about the punctuation of her work, finally passed the script for the historic broadcast.

Deems Taylor, in a tribute written for the American Academy of
Arts and Letters, says of his friend and fellow-academician:

"She was ruthlessly self-critical, and would agonize for days over a single, imperfect line. This attitude, as well as her precarious health, accounts for the comparatively small bulk of her output. Even so, in a writing career of thirty-four years she turned out six plays, an opera libretto, and eleven volumes containing about five hundred poems, including upwards of one hundred and seventy sonnets, many of which, in the opinion of one reader at least, are the finest since those of Keats.

"She was generous in the extreme to the work of other poets. Professional jealousy was not in her. She had great admiration for Louise Bogan and Elinor Wylie, both of whom were close friends. It would be hard to find two poets who had less in common than Edna Millay and E. E. Cummings. Yet, when his application for a Guggenheim fellowship was referred to her, she wrote an exhaustive 3,000 word analysis of his work, recommending that he receive one."

Few of her admirers will ever know the long hours and mental energy which Miss Millay freely gave to these Guggenheim reports. Her editor at Harper & Brothers, the late Eugene Saxton, having been privileged to see some of these, wrote:

"I have not read anything as fine for a long time. For precision, ability to weigh particles and measure hairbreadths, they are models of what critical comment should be."

In editing these letters, I have kept the poet's own spelling and punctuation, except where it has been clear that there was an unconscious error. As the reader will see, the poet signed herself with a variety of names. As children, the three Millay girls, Edna, Norma and Kathleen, were known in the immediate family as Sefe, Hunk and Wump. In later years Miss Millay sometimes wrote to her sisters as Hunk and Wump and signed herself Sefe.

Where words or phrases in the original letters have been left out by the editor, the usual three dots . . . have been inserted to show this. Where more than a sentence has been omitted, this is shown by a row of asterisks: * * *. These, however, must not be confused with the long dashes across the page which the poet sometimes used, especially in handwritten letters, to indicate a division of paragraphs. In her handwritten letters, also, Miss Millay often used the & sign. This calligraphic preference has been followed in letters where it is so written. Editorial insertions of words, names or dates in the letters are all between brackets, thus: [ ]. Each correspondent has been briefly identified where it was thought necessary. The letters are printed in the order in which they were written, but the grouping in sections is somewhat arbitrary and done for the reader's convenience. Numbered notes will be found at the end of each letter. For the purpose of chronological orientation, I should mention that the poet was born on February 22, 1892, at Rockland, Maine, and that she died at Steepletop on October 19, 1950.

"Our letters are ourselves," said John Donne. Here then, is Edna St. Vincent Millay, herself.

ALLAN ROSS MACDOUGALL

May, 1952

I

Childhood and Youth in Maine
1900 – 1912

Rockport, Me.
Nov. 7, 1900.

Dear Mama:

I thought I would write to you and tell you how I am I am getting along all right in school but in my spelling-blank I had 10 and 10 and then 9 and I felt auful bad because I thought I would have a star I am getting along all right and so is Norma and Kathleens cold is better now I went to practice and a boy called me a little chamipion and I asked him what he ment and he said because I was the best singer and I thanked him. When teacher and I were alone I said you have not called on mama yet and she said she is away and then she asked me how you knew her and of course I had to tell her and I said I guess you used to go arond with George Keller[2] and she blused red as a June rose and then she asked me If I had ever rode in [h]is tire wagon an[d] I said I knew she had and she said oh yes. here I will write you a peace that I am going to speak Thanksgiving

On Thanksgiving Day little Dorothy said,
With many a nod of her wise curly head,
The cook is as busy as busy can be,
And very good to for 'tis easy to see
She gives us our Thanksgiving Dinner[3]

* * *

I do not know the other verses so good. lots of love to you your loving daughter Vincent

[1] Mrs. Millay was out of town on a case.
[2] Mrs. Millay's cousin.
[3] There followed three more stanzas of this poem her teacher had given her to memorize and recite.

Salisbury
Feb. 12, 1902

Harper & Brothers
322 Pearl St.
New York.

Gentlemen I wish to subscribe for
"Harpers young People" and here en
close $2.00 for that purpose. I wish to
begin with the next number and
so have written, as soon as I found your
residence by reading one of your bo
oks.

Respectfully yours.
E. Vincent Millay.

2   TO HARPER & BROTHERS[4]

Salisbury, Mass.
Feb. 12, 1902

Harper & Brothers
322 Pearl St.
New York.

Gentlemen:—I wish to subscribe for "Harpers Young People" and here enclose $2.00 for that purpose. I wish to begin with the next number and so have written as soon as I found your residence by reading one of your books.

Respectfully yours.
E. Vincent Millay.

[4] The businesslike letter, written by her daughter in the fourth grade at the age of nine, interested Mrs. Millay enough for her to save it. Her interest would not have been lessened could she have known at the time that it was addressed to her child's future publishers. The date is repeated on the back, followed by "4 Grade" and "Miss Vincent Millay, Salisbury, Mass."

3   TO NORMA and KATHLEEN MILLAY[5]

This is such a big letter that I have to put it in two envelopes. Read your letters together, as they come. Read this first.

Chelmsford, Mass.
Aug. 9, 1909

Dear old girls—

It is too hot to get my hands all ink and have to wash them. I intended to write you yesterday—Sunday—but it was even hotter than it is today, hotter than I ever saw it before. The thermometer was 96° in the shade yesterday afternoon and not a breath of air anywhere. Aunt Georgia made some dandy ice-cream and it tasted just about right. We all went to Lake View Park last Friday and saw King and Queen, the same diving horses that we saw at Salisbury Beach and whose pictures were once in St. Nicholas. Uncle Curt and the two boys and I rode on the flying horses, the ones that rear up and buck down, you know. Oh dear, they were almost real. We also had a ride on the roller coaster. Did you ever see one? It must be something like the shoot-the-chute, and the loop-the-loop. I will try and tell you what it is.

There is a space cleared for it about as big around as a circus tent. Around this space is built a track just big enough for the car to run in with a little room on each side. There is a fence and railing all the way. Above this is another track and so on for four stories. Each track is far enough above the one below so that it seems quite a distance looking up. The whole thing is made of white-washed boards and all open in through. The four stories are arranged cork-screw fashion. You start at the bottom in a bright red plush and gilt car—bright enough to look very pretty as it whirls along the white-washed track. The car has two seats and will hold four. Uncle Curt and the boys and I went at one time. The man behind gives you a push—the car slides around a curve and starts to climb—by machinery—a steep straight track to the very top of the whole business. All the way you will see these signs—Hang on to your hat!—Sit still!—Don't stand up! etc. When you get to the top—whoosh!—you go down the other side a little way—whish! up again! spin along about a second lickety larrup—then—bang around a corner—hold your breath & down—gasp and you're up—whack! 'round a corner and up against the side of the car—and all the time screeching and laughing with your hair-pins falling out, your hat over one ear—every now and then catching a glimpse down through the trees of people walking around eating pop-corn and ice-cream—and over through the trees the flying horses going at full tilt. And so you go slamming down the   track,—whirr—whizz—bang—slam—whack—spud—whisk—thump—tumble—holler—screech—yell—laugh—with your feet banging through first one side of the car and then the other. At last you get down to the ground floor and are beginning to think it is all over—just when you have hauled in your feet and have adjusted your hat—then—whackety—bangety—slam!!! you bump into the side of the railing once more and worse than ever before. Then before you have time to catch your breath the car glides serenely down the track to its starting place and delivers its passengers to the gaping crowd,—any side up—with no care whatsoever.

So much for the joys and sorrows of roller-coasting. I expect you'll be whizzing through space on a shooting star in your dreams tonight. Did you ride in the "Lovers' Tub" before the merry-go-round left? Or did you decide it was too sticky? I am anxious to know.

We are all going to Canobie Lake some day. That is the biggest summer amusement park around here. I expect to have some more thrilling experiences. One more Lake View surprise I'll tell you about. It wasn't very thrilling but it was rather odd. While we sat on the bench by the flying horses waiting for the boys who wanted to ride forever, I noticed a little girl sitting two or three seats away. In one hand she held a dark blue cone—something like the ice-cream cones, only larger. Wound loosely around this was a great, soft, cloud-like ball of something which I would have sworn to be pink absorbent cotton. While I was watching her curiously—wondering whether the poor child had a broken leg or a tooth-ache, I was much surprised to see the young lady pull off a piece of the cloud and eat it. For a moment it seemed to me that the little girl must either shoot up to the ceiling or dwindle down to the floor, like Alice in Wonderland after eating the funny cake. But nothing happened, and I made up my mind that, although Revere Beach was quite a way off and I was certainly not in "Wonderland" still Lake View might have something in it I had never seen before. So I turned to Aunt Georgia and inquired very calmly, "Excuse me, mum," —sez I—"Is there anything the matter with my lamps?"—sez I—"or is that kid follerin' after the instincts of its kind . . . (This is the second part of Norma's letter—put the two together and read them as they come.)

. . . and chewin' up the inside of a bed quilt?!!"—sez I (mebbe that wan't jest 'zactly whot I sez, but anyhaow it's near enuff).

Aunt Georgia replies very cool-like, much as if she was sayin' as haow the little gal was eatin' a 'lasses cooky her granny jest baked— "Why, the chee-ild is merely eatin' sea-foam."

* * *

To come back to earth. The pink absorbent cotton cloud is really nothing but tinted sugar spun by electricity. I went down and watched the thing work. There is a kettle about the size of a dish-pan with a tube standing up in the middle making it look like a big doughtnut-cutter upside down. The pink sugar is put into the tube—the electricity is started underneath it and gradually as the tube turns faster and faster until at last you can't see it at all, a pink mist arises in the pan. As this rises it is taken out one cloud at a time and wound around the blue cone. I had some. It was just nothing but a sweet browned sugar taste and if you should put a great big piece in your mouth and leave it a minute there would be nothing left in it but a sweet taste. I am beginning to believe that it's "the stuff that dreams are made of."

Norma and Kathleen, take the front seats and recite your lesson. Norma, where is situated the city of Tease-Your-Sister? Ans. In Norma's head.—Correct—Kathleen, where is the unpleasant valley called

Raise-your-Sister's-expectations-only-to-let-them-drop? Ans. In Kathleen's head. Correct. Question. Who are the two most provoking little brats in the world? Ans. Hans and Fritz Katzenjammer—alias—Norma and Kathleen Millay. In other words, girls, aren't you just too mean to exist? Why under the vaulted heavens did you say anything about any old prize? Why under the azure canopy can't you send it to me? Why under the celestial firmament don't you tell me what it is?[6] Why under the arched dome of the sky does mama let you two run around loose? ? ? ? Answer me that, young man! ! ! ! ! ! !

I wonder how many green peas you have eaten, Wump, since you got well. What a little fool you were! I hope you are all of you well now. It will be lovely for you to have a chance to earn some money, Norma.

* * *

Now I'm going to answer questions.

1. I am very well, thank you. I haven't eaten any green peas.
2. We have had some blue-berry pies.
3. I think it very likely that I may come home although it is not decided. If I could plan to come home on a day when Uncle Curt was going to Boston it would be very simple.
4. Papa sent me $2.00.
5. Howard has not wet my brown suit at all. He doesn't require much holding and when he does I'm not the holder.
6. I don't expect to go to Uncle Charlie's. If I go home by boat I couldn't but if by train I might possibly stop over.
7. I don't know when I'm coming home.
8. I don't have any idea when I'm coming home.

Now for Items.

1. I am awfully sorry Wump has been sick.
2. I saw Percy Buzzel at Salisbury Beach. He sends love.
3. I've been to two plays, or rather musical comedies, "The Brinkley Girl" and "The Crazy House."
4. Give my love to Aunt Ida and Benitz.
5. It is too bad the three cases had to all come on one day.
6. I hope Wump will have lots of fun at Mrs. Sherman's.
7. I am glad Bonny Boy is such a favorite and I am sure he deserves it.
8. I am glad Kitty is fat and amusing.

9. I am glad mama is not sick.

10. I am glad you have such a nice chance to ride in the auto.

11. I'm glad you're not here, Norma, so that I'd have to show you I'm neither a pickled lime nor a pants-button.

12. I'm glad this is the last page.

13. I'm glad that instead of being two hectors like Norma and Kathleen I am just

Your loving sister,
Vincent.

[5] With the prize she received at her high school graduation for her poem, "La Joie de Vivre," Miss Millay traveled to Massachusetts to visit her mother's family. She is writing from the home of Mrs. Curtis J. Holt, her mother's youngest sister.

[6] Silver Badge from the St. Nicholas League.

4   TO *St. Nicholas Magazine*[7]

Camden, Me.
[Summer, 1910]

Dear St. Nicholas:

I am writing to thank you for my cash prize and to say good-by, for "Friends" was my last contribution. I am going to buy with my five dollars a beautiful copy of "Browning," whom I admire so much that my prize will give me more pleasure in that form than in any other.

Although I shall never write for the League again, I shall not allow myself to become a stranger to it. You have been a great help and a great encouragement to me, and I am sorry to grow up and leave you.

Your loving graduate,
Edna Vincent Millay

[7] Like all eagerly literate children in America during the latter part of the 19th century and the beginning of the 20th, the three Millay girls were avid readers of *St. Nicholas Magazine*. In the summer of 1906, E. Vincent Millay, as she signed her work then, sent to the St. Nicholas League a poem called "Forest Trees." It was published in the October issue of the magazine. The following year she had the pleasure of having three of her poems accepted: "The Land of Romance" (for which she received the Gold Badge of the St. Nicholas League); "After the Celebration (as told by the Firecracker)"; and "Vacation Song." The first appeared in the March, 1907, number, the second in the July and the last in

the August. In 1908, "Life" was published in the April number
and "Day's Rest-Time" in that of November. Only one poem
appeared the following year: "Young Mother Hubbard,"
which was published in the August number, 1909, for which
she received the Silver Badge. Finally, in 1910, approaching
the age limit of eighteen, she sent in "Friends," which was
printed in the May issue and won the prize which she ac-
knowledges in this, her farewell letter to *St. Nicholas.*

5   TO MRS. CORA B. MILLAY

Camden, Me.
July 7, 1911.

Mother Dear,—

I am so sorry and ashamed about things. I started out with the idea
that I was an invalid and unable to do a thing. I really did feel pretty
bum, but I might have kept things going. I am feeling fine now and
I have been doing well at home lately. I baked the most delicious bread
Friday. It was just perfect. I shall put up bread tonight or tomorrow.
Saturday we had baked beans and I had awfully good luck with them.
I have made pies, cakes and doughnuts and we are living almost wholly
from home cooking.

Pascal's bill is enclosed. The extra pound of butter was an error
which he readily corrected when I gave him the money order. Does
that sound satirical? I didn't mean it that way.

Yesterday I was one of a party in Mr. Elwell's big motorboat, the
"Inda," Mr. Knight hired the boat for the day, and took, besides his
whole family, Corinne, Gladys, myself, and that crowd. There were
fourteen of us not counting Mr. and Mrs. Elwell, Hazel Hall is here
and she went too. We started at 8 A.M. and didn't get home till 11 P.M.,
went all around in and out through the islands to Pulpit Harbor where
we landed, on a little uninhabited island. I felt like Robinson Crusoe.
Fun? Believe me, kid! And eat! I never ate so much in all my life. We
had twenty-three different things to eat. We had fish chowder on the
boat before we landed; then we had baked clams and boiled lobsters
on shore: all kinds of sandwiches and cake: plums, peaches, and pears;
and an enormous watermelon to eat on the way home: salted almonds,
chocolates, wafers, gum; and mercy knows what we didn't have. We
caught the fish for the chowder way out in the bay before we went into
Pulpit Harbor, mostly cod. Gladys caught one dandy haddock and

Jake a great pollock nearly a yard long. We had two hooks on each line and we had to let it down what seemed like miles and miles until it stopped going. Then it had struck bottom and we had to haul it up about three feet. Martha & I each caught two good-sized cod; then Martha caught two at once so of course I was crazy to. After much waiting my prayer was answered and I hauled in a double catch—only to find that one was a dog-fish and the other a sculpin. Roars of derision greeted my exploit and I sank onto a camp stool and simply howled. Mr. Knight kindly unhooked them both—with much care since dog-fish are poison and sculpins, to say the least, unattractive— and threw them overboard for me. I haven't stopped laughing yet. Jake & Martha both took cameras and we took a number of pictures that ought to be awfully good. There were seven girls of us all in middy blouses and farmer hats and we had one taken lying flat on our stomachs facing the camera, elbows on the ground, chins in hands and feet in air. We are going to call it "We Are Seven".

In the order which came today there was the most ridiculous error on the part of the postmaster in Rockland, which necessitates a slight delay—until tomorrow afternoon, in cashing. In place of my name as payee he had written "Camden, Me." My name was nowhere to be found on the order though the address "40 Chestnut" was carefully inscribed. Mr. Miller laughed when I showed it to him. He has to send them word of the mistake with the number of the order. They consult their books and give him the name of the payee and after that I get the money. Evidently your errand-girl isn't much of a business woman else she would have noticed it. It strikes me screaming funny. In order to have got the money today I would have had to sign myself "Camden, Maine" which would have rendered me liable to imprisonment for forgery, as I am no Camden Maine. Isn't it killing?

O, I'm having some perfectly great times this summer! A crowd of us took James[8] over on Sherman's Point one night in Jake's motor boat "The Frolic." We did him up very carefully in a hat-box. Arrived over there we concocted a delicious shrimp wiggle on the shore.———— I just interrupted this discourse by an hour's jaunt over town listening to a band concert.—There were five of us that night; Ethel, Martha, Norma, Emma, and I. Jake left us and came over later after us. Norma & Emma walked over and Jake towed them home in the tender. The phosphorus was dazzling: there were spots of it as big as saltines. It was beautiful. We had a great time. James enjoyed himself very much. Norma requested me to say that she & Emma rowed over, not walked.

I beg their several pardons. Can one say "several" when speaking of two?

Well, dear I really must go to bed. I am a little tired after yesterday. Lots of love from your three girlies.

Vincent.

[8] Miss Millay's name for her chafing-dish.

6   TO MRS. CORA B. MILLAY

Camden——Me.
Aug. 20, 1911.

Dear Mother,—

The dash between "Camden" and "Me." is to indicate a brief period during which Mr. Jones called and was informed as to your whereabouts. He's a nice little man.

How did you like our alphabetical epistle? You must have been reading it just as we were reading yours, or perhaps the deliverys are not at the same time. We got the money all right this time and without delay. And what do you think we did the very first thing? I am sure you would have wanted us to if you had been here. We all went to see "The Man On The Box." Marion Johnquest played in it—the same one that played in it last year—and I wouldn't have missed it for anything. She is perfectly beautiful and perfectly great. It seemed pretty hard to cut our allowances in two the very first thing—the seats were fifty cents—but we might never have a chance to see her again. Her costumes were simply wonderful. Not flashy or stagey, you know, but perfectly correct and the very latest thing. Oh, she is a darling. We are all determined that she is a society girl gone on the stage for fun. It's just like peeking in someone's window to watch her move about, she's so natural. Perhaps we oughtn't to have done it but Kathleen said she would put off getting her corsets—much as she wants them—till you could send her another dollar, we wanted to go so bad.

* * *

Mother, I can swim lots better than I could last year. We've been in lots of times. I swam a real long swim a few days ago down on the shore below the lime-kiln. Did you know that Dr. Hooper told me it was perfectly all right down there? I am going down in a few minutes to measure the distance. It is quite low tide so I can walk out there.

Wump and I have just been down to the shore. The tide was way out and we could walk out beyond the two points of our swim—Norma and I both did it, you know. One is a white slab stuck in a barrel of rocks and the other is a big black boulder; the water covers them both at high tide. We swam out to the white slab at about three-quarter tide and then from there up along the shore to the black rock. Guess how far! You never would believe it! Seventy-five feet! Just plain breast-stroke and without even turning over to float. What do you think of that? I want to do one hundred feet before the summer is over. Kathleen is going to try it the next time she goes down. Just think of it, moth, your girls can really swim! Not very well, of course, but it's fine to swim even that much. Isn't it? It was seventy-five just from the slab to the rock, you know, not counting swimming out to the slab because we rested there. Aren't you proud of us?

Love from us all,
Vincent.

7   TO MRS. CORA B. MILLAY

Mon. Mar. 4, 1912
Kingman. [Maine]

Dear Mother:—

Papa is better and they think he will get well.[9] I have been too tired and too busy to write before and now I haven't time to write much of anything but it is certainly time I wrote. I don't know just what has been the matter with papa. He's had pneumonia I guess, and asthma and a bad heart and Friday I think they didn't expect him to live through the day. Dr. Somerville says his recovery is marvellous—I don't know whether that's spelt right—

I have lots of pleasant things to tell you but I can only tell you a few now;—Mr. Dunton[10] has invited me to visit them on my way back, and has promised to take me driving all over the city behind his pair of light chestnuts—which papa tells me are the best span in Bangor—Think of it! Gee! Doctor takes me driving every day. On one of our drives I pointed to a big snowy mountain and asked what it was and Doctor told me it was Mt. Katahdin. Yes sir, I've seen it! Beautiful! I've been sleighing right straight up the Mattawamkeag River to Spragues' Mills and saw a deer hanging to a tree. They said it was killed by a bob-cat. Papa says that now a bob-cat is the only thing that can legally kill deer. He seemed rather skeptical. I showed him the Post that had your verses in it. He thinks they're great. They have a nice nurse from Bangor. I have to run on like this because I'm in a hurry. Dr. S. is a Scotchman and looks exactly like Andrew Carnegie, he wears a cap just like those C. wears in the pictures you see. He has the twinkliest blue eyes you ever saw. There's been a young minister here over Sunday—at the Somervilles'—he is a tiny Scotchman and Ella & I call him the Little Minister. He's awfully funny. I'll tell you about him later, Ella is Dr. S.'s daughter.

I see Papa twice a day. We can't talk very much but he loves to have me with him. Of course too much talking would tire him. Mr. Dunton calls up every day from B. to inquire. I never in my life heard so many people inquire for one man. All festivities here are post-poned until he recovers. An M.D. and an L.L.D. from somewhere around here came in on the train today just to see him a minute—great friends of his.

I'll write later, home,

Love,
Vincent.

⁹ While the Millay girls were still young, their parents were divorced. The relations between Henry Tolman Millay and the family, however, were always friendly; and he on his side followed with proud interest their varying fortunes. When her father fell seriously ill in the spring of 1912, Edna Millay went from Camden to be with him at Kingman, Maine, where he was superintendent of schools and chairman of the board of selectmen.

¹⁰ Head of the insurance company of Bangor with which H. T. M. was connected for years.

8   TO CAROLINE B. DOW¹¹

Camden, Me.
Oct. 23, 1912

Dear Miss Dow,—

I am enclosing a list of my courses when in school; the only other courses provided that might be of use to me I think are Physics and Solid Geometry. I could take them up next term, if you think best. I have, myself, very little idea of the Vassar entrance requirements.

The principal of the High School here has been helping me hunt up the files; he will be very willing to get for me any further information you may need.

I will give you now a rough list of authors and books, the principal ones; without attempt at classification:

Authors with whom I am very well acquainted:—Shakspere, Dickens, Eliot, Scott, Tennyson, Milton, Wordsworth. Also Ibsen, Arnold Bennett, and Robert Hichens.

Well acquainted with:

—Hawthorne, Browning, Kipling, Barrie, Mark Twain, Elbert Hubbard.

Slightly acquainted with:

—Bacon, Addison, Lamb, Macauley, Burke, Ruskin, Richard Jefferies, Thoreau, Mabie,—and Josephus.

Have read:

—Tolstoi, Anna Karenina; Kingsley, Hypathia; Holmes, Elsie Venner, and Autocrat of the Breakfast Table; Chas. Reade, Cloister and the Hearth; Swift, Gulliver's Travels; Defoe, Robinson Crusoe; Carlyle, Sartor Resartus; Cervantes, Don Quixote; Bunyan, Pilgrim's Progress; Brontë, Jane Eyre; Blackmore, Lorna Doone; Dumas, Black Tulip, and Count of Monte Cristo; Stevenson, Jekyll & Hyde, and Treasure Island; Amelie Rives, The Quick or the Dead, and Dione; Goldsmith, Vicar of Wakefield, She Stoops to Conquer, and others; Saint-Pierre, Paul & Virginia; Hughes, Tom Brown; Mulock, John Halifax, Gentleman; Wilkie Collins, The Moonstone; John Watson, Beside the Bonnie Brier Bush; Sienkiewicz, Quo Vadis; Von Hutton, Pam, and Pam Decides; Rostand, Chantecler; Marguerite Audoux, Marie-Clair, Maeterlinck, Mary Magdalene.

This list must seem awfully crazy to you. I've really read so much that I hardly know what to pick out.

Believe me, I will do my very best at whatever you think best for me to do. And believe, too, that I quite understand and deeply appreciate what you are trying to do for me.

I will type-write the little poem and send it to you.

Very sincerely,
Vincent Millay.

[11] Head of the National Training School of The Young Women's Christian Association in New York City. At a party given at the summer hotel, Whitehall, in Camden, Maine, during the season of 1912, Miss Dow heard the young poet read "Renascence" and sing some of the songs which

she had composed. Becoming interested in the poet, Miss Dow suggested that she apply for a scholarship at Vassar. She undertook to help her in this to provide funds for necessary expenses, and arranged for her to take some preliminary courses at Barnard College, Columbia, before entering Vassar in the fall of 1913. Miss Millay's volume, *Second April*, is dedicated "To my beloved friend Caroline B. Dow."

The year 1912 was an important one in the history of American poetry. In the fall of that year there was issued in Chicago the first number of *Poetry, A Magazine of Verse*, conceived and edited by Miss Harriet Monroe. Some weeks later, in New York, appeared a book called *The Lyric Year*, the first and only number of what its editor, Ferdinand Earle, had planned to be a yearly anthology of the best in this country's contemporary poetry. Long before its publication great excitement was caused by the announcement that Earle was donating three prizes totaling $1,000. These would be given, he said, to the three poets whose work was adjudged best by himself and two other judges: Edward J. Wheeler, editor of *Current Opinion* and president of the recently founded Poetry Society of America, and William Stanley Braithwaite, poetry editor of the Boston *Transcript*.

The announcement of the proposed anthology appeared in 1911. Manuscripts immediately began to roll into the office of Mitchell Kennerley, who was to publish the volume. Up in Maine, Cora B. Millay, during a long night watch in a patient's room picked up a discarded magazine and read the announcement. She wrote to her daughter in Kingman and urged her to return home and submit some of her recent work.

In a letter written a few months before his death in 1951, Mr. Earle tells how he and a friend, Professor Donner, passed one week end at his country place in Monroe, N. Y., examining scores of manuscripts forwarded there by Kennerley.

". . . it was Mr. Donner who happened to open Miss Millay's two contributions. We were silently unsealing the piles of envelopes and casting the discards into two tall waste baskets. I heard the thud of a manuscript hit the bottom of Donner's basket as he gave a chuckle.

" 'What's so amusing?' I queried. Still chuckling, Mr. Donner fished a long envelope out and began reading:

'RENAISSANCE [*sic*]
'All I could see from where I stood
Was three long mountains and a wood;

I turned and looked another way,
And saw three islands in a bay . . .'

" 'Ha, ha, ha!' And again I heard the thud of the manuscript falling into the basket!

" 'Hey! That sounds good!' I exclaimed. And Donner once more fished it out and began reading: 'The world stands out on either side/ No wider than the heart is wide'; etc., the closing passage of the poem.

" 'It doesn't sound so bad after all!' Donner admitted freely, and turned to the start of the piece and read it through, twice! We both agreed that it was tops."

Misled by the maturity and finish of the poem and the signature which followed it, Earle says he immediately wrote to the poet in Camden, Maine. "E. St. Vincent Millay, Esq., Dear Sir: . . ." telling of his enthusiasm. Unfortunately Mr. Earle's enthusiasm ran away with him. Without waiting to learn the conclusions of his fellow judges, he brashly announced to the young poet that he expected her to receive the first prize of $500. But, as is now literary history, the other two critics did not agree, and not only refused "Renascence" the first prize but did not consider it worthy of either the second or the third.

"Before I had selected the 'best' 100 poems out of over 10,000 mediocre manuscripts, most of them insipid and drivelling nonsense, it was like a shot in the arm to receive a letter from Miss Millay . . ." says Mr. Earle in the letter previously referred to. He continued corresponding with the poet, coyly keeping her guessing as to the sex and identity of her "Dear Editor." Unhappily it has been impossible to find the fifteen or so letters which the young poet, in her excitement over his appreciation and acclaim, wrote to Ferdinand Earle from Camden. In them she had told him of the genesis of the poem, her feelings about poetry, and also of a desire, according to Earle, that her poem, "Interim," and not "Renascence" (she had accepted his editorial suggestion that the title be anglicized), be the one chosen for inclusion in the 100 poems.

When the volume was finally published in November, 1912, Edna St. Vincent Millay's "Renascence"—though voted first by the editor—came out fourth and without award. The laureates were Orrick Johns, T. A. Daly, and George Sterling. The storm that broke about their heads overwhelmed them and their judges. Orrick Johns in his autobiography tells of receiving:

". . . the news that 'Second Avenue' had won the Lyric Year first prize of $500. Nothing had been further from my expectations, and when the book arrived I realized that it was an unmerited award. The outstanding poem in that book was 'Renascence' by Edna St. Vincent Millay, immediately acknowledged by every authoritative critic as such. The award was as much an embarrassment to me as a triumph."

Today that first and only volume of *The Lyric Year* is a collector's item. Not for any of the prize-winning poems, however, but because it contains the first printing of "Renascence."

Among the poets who appeared in *The Lyric Year* were Arthur Davison Ficke and Witter Bynner. They had been classmates at Harvard and had both published distinguished verse in popular magazines and in book form. When Ficke's advance copy of *The Lyric Year* reached him, Bynner was visiting him in Davenport, Iowa. In Arthur Ficke's notes he tells how, as they were walking home from his law office, Bynner, who had been leafing through the book, came upon "Renascence" and was so moved by this work that he felt he must read it to his fellow poet. They sat down at the base of the Soldier's Monument and there, on Thanksgiving Day, 1912, Bynner read the poem aloud. Later, together with Mrs. Ficke, they sent a letter to its author saying: "This is Thanksgiving Day and we thank you. . . ."

In a letter to Miss Millay dated December 3, 1912, Mr. Earle wrote: "Here is a quotation from Mr. Arthur Davison Ficke's letter to me, which you yourself must answer:

'. . . The thing that has moved me, personally, into wanting to write to you is your choice of Miss Millay's poem for the first prize. And the other judges passed it by!! . . . Witter Bynner, who is visiting me, and I read through most of the book. We grew somewhat downhearted over most of the poems, . . . including our own. And suddenly we stumbled on this one, which really lights up the whole book. It seems to both of us a real vision, such as Coleridge might have seen. Are you at liberty to name the author? The little item about her in the back of the book is a marvel of humor. No sweet young thing of twenty ever ended a poem precisely where this one ends: it takes a brawny male of forty-five to do that. Don't, however, fear that Bynner and I are going about budmouthed with dark suspicions; if it's a real secret, we respect the writer of such a poem far too much to want to plague "her" . . .'

Will you drop Mr. Ficke, please, a line . . . and thank him for the remarkable compliment, at the same time convincing him of his error, which is very amusing?"

Camden, Maine, Dec. 5, '12.

To Mr. and Mrs. Arthur Davison Ficke
and to Witter Bynner: ——

You are there
dear people. This is
Thanksgiving Day, too.
and I thank you.

Very truly yours

Edna St. Vincent Millay.

9   TO MR. and MRS. ARTHUR DAVISON FICKE and WITTER BYNNER

Camden, Maine.
Dec. 5, 1912.

To Mr. and Mrs. Arthur Davison Ficke and to Witter Bynner:—

You are three dear people. This is Thanksgiving Day, too, and I thank you.

Very truly yours,
Edna St. Vincent Millay.

To Mr. Ficke and Mr. Bynner:

Mr. Earle has acquainted me with your wild surmises. Gentlemen: I must convince you of your error; my reputation is at stake. I simply will not be a "brawny male." Not that I have an aversion to brawny males; *au contraire, au contraire.* But I cling to my femininity!

Is it that you consider brain and brawn so inseparable?—I have thought otherwise. Still, that is all a matter of personal opinion. But, gentlemen: when a woman insists that she is twenty, you must not, must not call her forty-five. That is more than wicked; it is indiscreet.

Mr. Ficke, you are a lawyer. I am very much afraid of lawyers. Spare me, kind sir! Take into consideration my youth—for I am indeed but twenty—and my fragility—for "I do protest I am a maid"—and—sleuth me no sleuths!

Seriously: I thank you also for the compliment you have unwittingly given me. For tho I do not yet aspire to be forty-five and brawny, if my verse so represents me, I am more gratified than I can say. When I was a little girl, this is what I thought and wrote:

> Let me not shout into the world's great ear
> Ere I have something for the world to hear.
> Then let my message like an arrow dart
> And pierce a way into the world's great heart.

You cannot know how much I appreciate what you have said about my *Renascence.*

If you should care to look up the April, 1907 number of *Current Literature,* you would find a review of my *Land of Romance,* (near a review of Mr. Bynner's *Fair of my Fancy.*) And you might be interested in Mr. Edward Wheeler's comment: "The poem which follows (by E. St. Vincent Millay) seems to me to be phenomenal. The author, whether boy or girl we do not know, is just fourteen years of age."

E. St. V. M.

P.S. The brawny male sends his picture. I *have* to laugh.

10   TO LOUIS UNTERMEYER[12]

Camden, Maine,
Dec. 5, 1912.

Dear Mr. Untermeyer,—

I was especially glad to get a note from you. Your verses are among the first in the book to me. There is a twist to them, whimsical, daredevil and pathetic combined, which particularly appeals to me. Please don't think I am just "hitting back."

I am glad you like *Renascence* so well. If you do indeed review the book as you spoke of doing, will you send me a copy of the paper, please? I should not be likely to see it otherwise, and I shall wish to.

Very truly,
Edna St. Vincent Millay.

[12] Louis Untermeyer, in a review in the Chicago *Post*, was one of the first to praise "Renascence" in print.

11   TO MR. ARTHUR DAVISON FICKE

Camden, Me.,
Dec. 15, 1912

My dear Mr. Ficke:

Ever the "dulcet phrases!" You deserve them. And I make it a point always to "gie the deil his due." I can with impunity, since you have called me "the limit," say that you are a ridiculous thing; and I will add that your home-life is mild in comparison to what I had imagined it, and that Mr. Metcalf's portrait of you is no doubt a flattering likeness,—but I must, out of justice, admit that I love the little book. Indeed, I cannot tell you how much! But I can and will tell you the things in it that I like best. First of all what *The Other Sculptor* says. That is one of the very finest things I ever read. It seems to me quite perfect. And its simplicity is breath-taking. Then the shepherd's song. Did you ever hear sheep, Mr. Ficke? I do not see how otherwise you could have done it.—"This year winter was not bad," and "Such a pair as thee and me," and this, loveliest of all "Many a day and many a day." I truly do not see how I ever got along without the Shepherd-song! And I love the page beginning "I will remain till my last line is writ." And, oh, the first stanza of that "Monday in April"! You need not wish to be a painter, my friend; you are one. And truly a poet. I am very glad you wrote me. And very, very glad to have "The Earth Passion."¹³ The earth passion! I have always had that. Perhaps that is why I love the book so well. I thank you for it— and for the scribble on the fly-leaf.

If by "Do you read Coleridge?" you mean, "Is *Renascence* done in imitation of *The Ancient Mariner*—no, it is not. I have read Coleridge, of course; but not for years. And I never even heard of William Blake. (Should I admit it, I wonder?)

As to the line you speak of—"Did you get it from a book?" indeed! I'll slap your face. I never get anything from a book. I see things with my own eyes, just as if they were the first eyes that ever saw, and then I set about to tell, as best I can, just what I see.

And I have an idea that there are vastly fewer "accidents of com-position" than one might think.

But I will answer honestly, as you bade me. I did see it, yes. I saw it all, more vividly than you may suppose. It was almost an experience. And it is one of the things I don't talk about easily. All of my poems are very real to me, and take a great deal out of me. I am possessed of a masterful and often a cruel imagination.

All this is just the wee-est bit confidential, you know, and just because you asked me to be honest.

When I bring out a volume (save the mark) you shall certainly know.

I was interested in your book's dedication. "Cambridge days and *nights!*" T.N.M. is of course Mr. Metcalf. And is Witter Bynner H.W.B. or W.H.L.B.? If the former, I am convinced that his first name is Hezekiah. If, as you predict, you fail to get back the snap, I will send you another.

I wonder if I may be remembered to Mrs. Ficke?

Sincerely,

Edna St. Vincent Millay.

¹³ Arthur Davison Ficke had already published two books of poems, *The Happy Princess* (1907) and *The Earth Passion* (1908).

12   TO ARTHUR DAVISON FICKE

Camden, Me.
Dec. 27, 1912

My dear Mr. Ficke,—

The little book of Blake has come.¹⁴ And I take it all back, just as you said I would, about slapping your face. I haven't the heart. I am going to like him as well as even you could wish. And strangely enough, I find that I have always known and liked one little song of his without even knowing that he wrote it. It is the first of the *Songs of Innocence*, the one that begins "Piping down the valleys wild," you know. And the music is by a Mr. Gilchrist who is, I suppose, that very Mr. Gilchrist who is spoken of so often in the introduction. Now isn't that interesting? Did you know it had been set to notes?

The lines I like best in it so far, (in the book, I mean) even better than *Sunflower*, are these, the fourth stanza of *The Birds*:—

> "Dost thou truly long for me?
> And am I thus sweet to thee?
> Sorrow now is at an end,
> O my lover and my friend!"

Now I truly and absolutely love that. Do you? And I love the little song in the front of the book beginning "How sweet I roamed from field to field." Especially the last:—he "*stretches out my golden wing*, and mocks my loss of liberty."
Can't you *see* that? The picture is perfect in my mind.

I have had very little time to read since the books came. But I have, of course, *skum* them. (Forgive me! That isn't just the way I do it; but the word is *so* expressive.)

There are two and a half lines in *The Happy Princess* that I wish to speak of right this minute.

> ". . . I will not press
> On you one breath of its great tenderness
> If thus it stirs your pitiful sweet tears."

I think you have said that wonderfully well. It is so simple, yet somehow so *big*. You might have dedicated to me *The Poet Yoshi*, for indeed your songs have found in me a heart that loves them. But then of course a great many people must do that, despite your suggestions to the contrary.

You may have another sheet of paper this time. This isn't Christmas stock.

I am enclosing two or three manuscripts that I happened to have on hand. Don't hesitate to tell me you don't like them; there is every possibility that you won't; they are very unlike *Renascence*. But don't be afraid to tell me. I shall bear up wonderfully well under the shock. That word is "shock"—mercy, I can't write it. I always want to put a "c" in the first part. Shock; shock; an electric thrill. There. Please criticize frankly. I want you to. They're not my best things. They're just "something I wrote" . . . This letter is a sight. I'm scribbling terribly and can't seem to stop.

Please tell me the top-notch line that owes that quality to an accident.

And please reassure Mrs. Ficke as to her doubt as to my doubt as to your sanity,—(example of a periodic sentence!) I am sure that you are quite, quite sane,—in so far, that is, as a poet can be sane, for the poetic temperament is a kind of monomania, I think. The unspeakable "gifts", even, caused me nary a shiver,—I could understand so perfectly the mood which caused you to send them. You are unconditionally forgiven. But are you seized often by those spells? For I imagine that people who did not understand might be very much offended, and then you *would* get your face slapped.

I do not go to school, old man. I was honorably graduated from the Camden High School nearly four years ago. It is only because you are so very old that I seem to you a child, old man. But even if I were still attending, and should be late subsequent to the perusal of your epistle, (keep it up, dear, you're doing fine!) even then you need not feel no compunctions, for I should without the slightest doubt have been late anyway.

* * *

This letter is too incoherent even for the fact of *me* to excuse it.
I am nevertheless,
Sincerely yours,
Edna St. Vincent Millay.

P.S.   This very minute the P.S. of A.[15] is vivisecting my verses! Happy thought to go to bed on. "Sleep well, sweet angel!"

[14] The "little book of Blake" which Ficke sent was one of the small pocket volumes of the Walter Scott Company's "Canterbury Poets" which the poet cherished all her life and finally took to Ragged Island, Maine, to be part of the small library there.

[15] The Poetry Society of America.

[Camden, Maine
Dec. 29, 1912]
Saturday night.

Dear Sir: Behold me walking into your parlor for legal advice. I am in receipt of a letter from a lunatic who wishes my autograph on the one-eighty-eighth page of his copy of *The Lyric Year*. Keep's a'! Are you in receipt of a similar request and what are you going to do about it? They won't do it, will they? He seems quite sure of my acquiescence —perhaps because he thinks I will be flattered by his request—and he encloses a stamp and a somewhat premature thank-you. Do you remember in the *Mikado*, "the literary nuisances who write for autographs"? I never got a letter just like it before. Is it usual? Do be indulgent and explain. There are more things than William Blake that I never heard of. I am a dreadful bother, I know. If your *other* clients clamor too clamorously postpone me, do. But don't waste-basket me, please, for I am in earnest. (I am not so afraid of lawyers as I used to be. They are lambs in wolves' clothing.)

—E. St. V. M.

II

College Years, Barnard and Vassar

1913 – 1917

[Camden, Maine
Jan. 6, 1913]
Saturday evening.

Dear Mother,

We are *so* glad you like there. We fret terribly about letting you go, because you seemed to dread it so. But perhaps it won't be so awfully bad, after all. Though it *is* quite a responsibility to be the only night nurse.

* * *

I got a Vassar catalogue from someone today. Miss Dow must have asked them to send it, as it came direct from Poughkeepsie. I've had lots of fun looking up names, in that and in the Smith catalogue.

* * *

In Vassar now there are four girls from Persia, two from Syria, two from Japan, one from India, one from Berlin, Germany, and one or two others from "across the water." The Japanese girls' names are Nabe Amagasu and Koto Yamada. Wouldn't it be great to know them? There isn't one "furriner" in Smith. Lots of Maine girls go to Smith; very few to Vassar. I'd rather go to Vassar. I must hunt up things in the catalogue and begin to study, I suppose. "I don't know where I'm going but I'm on my way."

* * *

Love from us all, Vincent.

15 TO MRS. CORA B. MILLAY

[1913]
Friday Morning

Dear Mother,—

This is a hurry-up note.

* * *

O, what do you think!—I've got another letter from Louis Untermeyer, and he's sent me a copy of the volume "First Love" that you've heard

29

me speak of. I'm *crazy* about his poems!—He's married, and invites me to call on them when I come to New York. There's *another* place. And, oh, mother, he wrote on the fly-leaf "To (me) With the intense admiration and best wishes of (him)." What do you know about that?— Mary Emery has just been here. She brought a friend, a Mrs. Getchill, with her. Have you met her?—She's awfully nice. Went to Colby. Awfully interested in Vassar. Has been there visiting a Vassar friend. Most beautiful place she ever saw. *Swell!* She's crazy about it. You can bet I had a lot to tell and a lot to show.—I found the *dearest* shoes at Haskell's. Perfect loves,—tan, lace, broad soles, sensible heels, high ones,—but the smallest he had was a 2½ and they were too big, so I had him send for a pair of twos. They'll probably be here tomorrow. He was awfully nice.

Haven't heard yet from Kingman. Or from Miss Dow. The *sweetest* letter from Miss Bannon. Glad I'm to go to college even if it's not to be Smith,—"much love" to me—*and*, if anything should happen even now that I can't go to Vassar, to write to her at once and she will be my friend again—and again. If that isn't being a friend, then I don't know. She's wonderful. Lovely letter from Mr. Donner.—Have written two perfectly darling verses,—finished them yesterday. You shall hear them Sunday,—*ole dear!*

I got an invitation to the Poetry Society dinner. Wish I could *go!* Why *don't* they send back my Mss.? Love from us all,

Vincent.

16 TO ARTHUR DAVISON FICKE

Camden, Me.
Jan. 12, 1913

My dear Mr. Ficke,—

Your unstinted admiration of my Escaped-nun stationery has led me to submit to you a second specimen.— You described the other as "a nun in a diamond dog-collar." Very well, I raise you one. *This* severe white envelope with its brazen border represents the Mother Superior—with *"an edge on!"*

Don't let anyone who's the least bit respectable know that I said that, will you?—As far as yourself is concerned,—after that comic-Valentine episode of our early correspondence, *you* are not in a position to say a word!

It is quite true that I have yet to learn the ABC's of my art. I am

hoping that college will help me;—but if I should come back a suf-
fragette instead of a poet wouldn't it be dreadful?

(I am not sure whether it is Vassar or Smith to which I am going.
If I were your grand-child, say,—now which do you think you would
prefer for me?)

Potpourri belongs in that division of my verse which I classify as
"bull-doggerel"; that is to say, "I was *determined* to write a sonnet."
"The Little Bush" needs pruning. (But I am much too busy in another
part of my garden to bother with it now. It will doubtless die for want
of attention.) "Tiny Bird" was pure inspiration.—I had no typed copies
on hand, you must remember, of the things I would have liked best to
send you. They have not even yet been returned from the P.S. of A.
(You didn't really think, did you, that I, myself, was going to read
them aloud to the assembled deities? Keep's a'!—O, my fluttering heart!
I am quite content for a while yet to be nothing but just "The Littlest
Member." I imagine it will be some time yet before I get right up and
"speak in meetin' ". When I get them back, I am, with your august
permission, going to send you something else. I have gratefully absorbed
into my system all you said about the others.—And I hope they didn't
spoil your smoke!

I thank you very much for sending me Mr. Untermeyer's review
in the Chicago Evening Post. My appreciation of your kindness is in
no wise dimmed by the fact that I had already—and now don't be getting jealous, will you?—had already received a copy from Mr. Untermeyer himself, with whom I am also corresponding. I saw your little
mark under *Blake*. It *is* funny. I see, too, that Wm. Marion Reedy[1] and
Miss Rittenhouse (Secretary of the P.S. of A.) have both likened my
style to that of John Masefield. And *that's* funny. Dead funny. Do you
suppose he would feel even—even mildly amused if he knew it?

(You were disappointed in my manuscripts, weren't you? I knew
you would be. And I don't know why I sent them—I knew they were
inferior. But think of the atrocious puns and all the ungramaticisms of
Shakespere, and the many many times when Browning stoops to
vaudeville stunts—and don't quite lose faith in me!)

"Queen Mab in the Village" is indeed charming. Somehow, I can't
tell why, the lines I like best in it are these two, near the end, "Bowing
to a maiden in a pansy-velvet gown." Somehow that—that just "gets
me"! The whole thing is bewitching—I wouldn't dare to read it on
Hallowe'en just before going to bed! So it was Mr. [Vachel] Lindsay's
thumb-print on the envelope,—*not* yours! I wondered.—I have found

Miss Blunt[2] in my Vassar Bulletin,—Miss Katherine Blunt, Ph.D.—
Dr. Blunt! What is Mrs. Ficke's name, *please* tell me? It's not *Helen,* is
it? *Please* tell me.

Sincerely,
Vincent Millay

[1] Editor of *Reedy's Mirror.*
[2] Sister-in-law of Arthur D. Ficke.

17   TO THE MILLAY FAMILY

135 East 52nd Street[3]
New York City,
Feb. 6, 1913

Dear Mother and Girls,

This is the first chance I've had to write, and I can't write very
much now, because I'm tired and I have to get up early in the morning
to go to school. Yes, *so* quick! Miss Doerin took me over to Columbia
this afternoon to see a professor and he sent me to the registrar at
Barnard (with a note) and she sent me to the bursar with a slip, and
we went to see the Dean and she was at a committee meeting, so we'll
have to see her tomorrow, and I'm all registered, and I have a class
("English 24," they call it) at 10 in the morning. I am in room No. 840,
on the eighth floor of the National Training School—the loveliest place
and one of the biggest I ever saw almost, that is,—I've seen some
pretty big ones already . . . We have dinner at night, on the eleventh
floor. I sit at Miss Dow's left at the head table. She's "de hull ting" here
and lovely to me. She's the busiest woman I ever saw. I probably shall
be here only a week or two. We've begun already to make investiga-
tions concerning a dormitory, Brooks Hall or Whittier Hall it will be.
We shall perhaps know tomorrow.

From my window in the daytime I can see *everything,*—just
buildings, tho, it is buildings everywhere, seven & eight stories to million
and billion stories, washing drying on the roofs and on lines strung
between the houses, way up in the air;—they flap and *flap!* Children
on roller skates playing tag on the sidewalks, smokestacks *and* smokestacks, and windows and windows, and signs way up high on the tops
of factories and cars and taxicabs,—and *noise,* yes, in New York you
can *see* the noise. We took a subway car twice today; and the first
time Miss Doerin said, "This is the noisiest place in New York.["] I

don't mind the noise a bit; I can sleep better for it. I rested beautifully in my berth last night. (I tipped the porter, too, this morning, a dime) The train was an hour and a half late. In the night we stopped somewhere and I reached out and raised the shade a little so as to peak and leaned on my elbow and looked and saw a big sign all lighted up on a big dark factory—"Brockton Die Company", I think it was. We stopped there a long while. George[4] met me at Portland and carried my bag and got my sleeper berth (lower 10 in *A*) and came down with me afterwards. Just think, I traveled Pullman all the way. It didn't seem very long, I was so lovely and comfortable. This morning . . . they made me go to bed when I got here and after a while a maid came in with my breakfast on a tray and raised the shade and told me what time it was and went out and I had more fun. I'll bet when the chambermaid put away my kimono & slippers and cap she thought they were cute. I found the kimono on a hanger in the closet and the slippers under it and the cap over the corner of the mirror. Send my comb along will you?—I forgot it and have had to borrow one.

I haven't seen Mr. Monroe yet.

I think I'll send some cards tomorrow.

I'll write you whenever I have time but I guess I'm going to be awfully busy.

Must go to bed now. Just basketfuls of love,

Bincent.

[3] The Residence of The National Training School of the Y.W.C.A.
[4] George Ricker, her cousin.

18 TO ARTHUR DAVISON FICKE

[135 E. 52 St.]
New York City.
Feb. 9, 1913

My dear Mr. Ficke,—

Shall I give your regards to Broadway,—now that I am here within hailing distance of it? To any question that you might raise concerning my presence in this locality I could only answer, "I'm here because I'm here because I'm here." And I might add that I expect to take a few courses at Columbia this semester.

Yesterday I got a note from Sara Teasdale, inviting me to take tea with her. Whaddayouknowaboutthat! The news of my arrival has *sprud clean* from here to East 29th Street!

How do I like New York? O, inexpressibly! Yes, the Public Library is! No, the subway *isn't*! O, the St. Patrick Cathedral!—Quite too sweet, I assure you! And the view—charming, charming! So many roofs and things, you know; warships, and chimneys, and brewery signs—*so* inspiring! Yes, to the Madison Avenue Presbyterian! Dr. Coffin is *wonderful*. O, my *dear*,—tre*men*dous!

———————————

I have learned to glare with a wild hunted expression all about me at a corner, to elbow fiercely on occasion those fellow creatures whom I love as myself, and to run and grab,—literally *grab* a street-car! I have been here since Wednesday and I am become a hardened citizen of a heartless metropolis.

Adamantinely,
Vincent Millay

P.S. That is the name I am called by. I didn't think how odd it would seem to you. V.M.

19　TO ARTHUR DAVISON FICKE

[135 East 52nd St.]
New York City.
Mar. 6, 1913.

Dear Mr. Ficke,

I think you are very, very nice. And I wish very much that you were here in New York and that some of the people who are here were out in Iowa.

I am not being a Bohemian. I am not so Bohemian by half as I was when I came. You see, here one has to be one thing or the other, whereas at home one could be a little of both. And whereas heretofore I have amused myself in idle moments by the diffusing of indiscreet letters which I would now give the half of my kingdom to recall, I am at present (unless indeed that confession has made this letter also indiscreet) prudent to the point of Jane Austen. I left all my bad habits at home,—bridge-pad, cigarette-case, and cocktail-shaker. I brought with me all my good habits,—diary, rubbers, and darning-cotton.

This is not intended to be humorous. So please believe that this whole page is true, and take it seriously.

Tuesday, at the luncheon given by the Poetry Society to Alfred Noyes, I met, among others, our friend Witter Bynner. He was one of the speakers, and he spoke very well.

What do you think of Anna Hempstead Branch[5] (if that's the way to spell it)?

Miss Rittenhouse[6] is to have a Literary Evening (don't you hate the expression!) Sunday. I'll tell you about it later perhaps,—it may be a lot later, you understand. I am sure that no one in New York has time to write letters. This is quite an effusion for me now. I hope you didn't ask me any questions.

I am quite settled down. I run in my rut now like a well-directed wheel. Sometimes, it is true, I feel that I am exceeding the speed-limit. But I seldom skid, and when I do there is very little splash.

Please give me some good advice in your next letter. I promise not to follow it.

Very sincerely,
Vincent Millay

[5] Anna Hempstead Branch, poet [1875–1937].
[6] Miss Rittenhouse was Jessie B. Rittenhouse, Secretary of the recently founded Poetry Society of America, a poet and critic who was one of Miss Millay's earliest admirers.

20 TO THE MILLAY FAMILY

New York City,
Mar. 13, '13

Dear Family,—

I don't think I've written you a really truly letter since a week ago yesterday,—and that was a small one, wasn't it? So I'm going to start in with March the fifth and tell you a little of what I've been doing since

* * *

Saturday—Went to International Art Exhibition. Impressionistic school, you know, and perfectly unintelligible things done by people they call the "Cubists" because they work in cube-shaped effects. Everything they do looks like piles of shingles. I'll get some postals of the pictures, I think—especially the one called "Nude descending the stairs", and if you can find the figure, outline it in ink and send it back to me.

* * *

Sunday—*My* party at Miss Rittenhouse's. She told them they were there to meet me. There were present (it was just a small party) Mr. & Mrs. Edwin Markham, Dr. & Mrs. Rolf-Wheeler, Mr. & Mrs. Louis V. Ledoux (he's charming), Sara Teasdale, Anna Branch, Edith M. Thomas (tell Mother to hunt her up in *those Atlantic Monthlys* . . .), Gertrude Hall, three or four others, Witter Bynner, and Dugal Walker (a young artist that Miss Branch is very anxious to have fall in love with me and me with him. She doesn't suspect that I know it. But you should hear her talk about him to me. I can't help wondering if she says the same kind of things about me to him.) She's to have him and me up to tea with her some afternoon. Just him & me. Isn't it delicious? —He's really a darling, too, but Sunday night I was very much taken up with Witter Bynner, with whom I had a long chat; and Mr. Walker, early in the evening, was lassoed and tripped and thrown by a sweet young thing from boarding-school who came with Miss Thomas and who—and who is so exactly like Josephine Hobbs in every way you can think of that it's absolutely startling. So that Mr. Walker & I have not yet "gone on", as it were.

Yes, I have seen and talked with Witter Bynner. He has said to me "Do you mind if I smoke?" and I have said to him, "Not in the least." He has proffered me his cigarette case and I have said, "No, thank you." He has raised his eyebrows and said, "O, you don't smoke?" And I have replied, "Not here, certainly."

He.—Then you have no prejudice against it.

I.—None whatever.

He.—I'm glad of that. My sister used to think it dreadful, but now she smokes more than I do.

(Did you ever think of Witter Bynner as having a sister?— I never did.)

We talked a long time. And later in the evening he read *Renascence* aloud. He has a beautiful voice, and he reads beautifully. It was truly wonderful to hear it like that. He's crazy about it anyway.

I suppose he's gone back to New Hampshire now. He lives right on the border between N.H. and Vermont. (O, Mr. & Mrs. Dawson— he's the Pres. of the P.S. of A.—were there too. And Mrs. Trowbridge went with me. You can't go across the street alone at night, you know.)

Monday.—That letter you forwarded from Texas was from the craziest kid you ever heard of. He sent me some of his verses, "To a Spring Flower." I was hysterical the rest of the day.

* * *

Lots of love,
Vincent.

21   TO THE MILLAY FAMILY

135 East 52nd Street
New York City
Tuesday Morning
[April 8, 1913]

Dearest Darlings—

I just this minute got a check for twenty-five dollars from Mitchell Kennerly for two little poems I sent him. I am going to indorse it and send it home after I've looked at it a little while. He says "I am delighted to have them and shall print them in early numbers of the *Forum*. I should like to talk to you about your work, and hope you will come to see me."

Have just got a letter from some of you but haven't had time to read it.

O, Mother and girls!—Vincent.

22   TO MRS. CORA B. MILLAY

Friday Morning
[April 11, 1913]

Mother,—

Promise me, please, that with some of this you'll do something to make something easier for yourself. Shoes, dear,—or have your glasses fixed if they're not just right. Please, please, do something like that. And I'd like it so much if each one of you would get some little tiny silly thing that she could always keep. But that's just a whim; the other isn't.

O, Mother, when I opened that letter and saw that pinky-lavender slip! I had read of finding pinky-lavender slips in letters, but—goodness! It's indorsed all right, isn't it? There won't be any trouble about it, will there?

It seems as if this had broken my hoodoo of "all praise and no profit." The two poems were the one beginning "O, world, I cannot hold thee close enough" and the one called "Journey." Louis Untermeyer and Sara Teasdale are crazy about them both. William Rose Benét of the *Century* told me that there were some things in them he should hate to have the *Century* lose, but that there were several obscurities in them that I'll have to clear up a bit, and as some of the obscurities happened to be the best things in them, I sent them off just as they were to the *Forum*, so the *Century* has lost them for good. . . .

23   TO ARTHUR DAVISON FICKE

[135 East 52nd St.]
New York City.
April 12, 1913.

Dear Spiritual Advisor,—

O, thank you!—such a beautiful, beautiful book, inside & out![7] You are very nice, I think, Mr. Ficke; doesn't your family think so?

I must tell you some of the things I like especially; some, not all—because to tell you all of the things I like especially I should have to send back the book. And that *would* be a mess. But just a few things that I notice in skimming through—"To strew with little waves the deep," "Lightning of unleashed desires"—*that* is simply terrific; so too is this, "A fury tracking toward some shaken mind." (If you will excuse my saying so, there are four reels of moving-pictures in that last.) In the first two lines of your "Two Women" on page seven, I get a wonderful picture, tho perhaps not the one you intended:—a wide, wide marble court, and, out beyond, the widest bluest sky that ever was, with swallows not too small, and very black. Of course the women are in the court, but I cannot seem to make them Japanese. In my picture they are Greek. "Some thin branch where the Spring is green," that is perfect. Tho of course it is more beautiful because of the "tall form" behind it—a white form, I am sure—and the "wistful eyes," that, I am sure, are gray.

Right here, and apropos of "The Birds and Flowers of Hiroshige," which I love best of all, and with which I am drunk at this moment, right here let me say that you are the only person I know whose poems about flowers and birds and skies and things, filled as they are with your own so evident Earth-Ecstasy, quite satisfy my Earth-Ecstatic soul. The colors in that poem make me fairly stagger. And, oh, your wonderful birds! The pheasant with its "snow-clogged feet", the "wild geese that rush across the moon," the kingfisher "over the reeds of the lagoon," the crane under the sunset!

There, there. This is a debauch. I must read a nice cool little poem. Where is the "Grecian Urn"?

I have two poems coming out in the *Forum* soon.[8] I don't know just when. I hope you'll like them.

_____

Heavens! The dinner gong! Ten minutes to dress. And my hair!— if only I hadn't torn it so feverishly. Really, in places like this, one shouldn't take time to orgify.

Honorable sir, I am as ever your unworthy slave,—

The Spirituelle Advised.

[7] *Twelve Japanese Painters.* This book of poems about the Ukioye School of Painters was issued in a finely printed limited edition of 250 copies by Ralph Fletcher Seymour of Chicago. Besides being a lawyer and a poet, Ficke was a collector of Japanese prints and an authority on the subject.

[8] "Journey" and "God's World." The first was published in the May issue of the magazine; the second in the July issue. Later, "God's World" was included in the volume called *Renascence* and "Journey" in *Second April.*

24 TO THE MILLAY FAMILY

New York City,
Friday,
April 18, 1913.

Dear Old Folks at Home,—

You've given me such a scare this last week. Was there or wasn't there a stamp on the letter that had my check in it?

* * *

I didn't see how I *could* talk to Mr. Kennerley[9] about my poem all the time thinking that check was lost, and I had an appointment with him for this morning. But, oh joy, I got mother's letter before I had to go. So it's all past & over & I'm just horribly thankful. I'll bet I'll never mail another letter without being *sure* about the stamp. There *wasn't* a stamp on it *was* there?

Mr. Kennerley (I went down alone & all by myself; I don't have any trouble now about finding my way) is lovely. He's invited me out to see them some Sunday as soon as I can—they live in a suburb about twenty miles out—and pick flowers. He's not old at all, as I thought he would be, about thirty-five or under, & he's a dear, and I'll bet she's a dear, and there are two kiddies.

* * *

Mr. Kennerley wants me to let him publish a volume of my stuff but I don't believe that's a very wise thing. I got the proof of one poem the other day, "Journey"; it's to come out in the next, May, number. He says he was scared to death to read them, but is delighted with them. He gave me a book by an Englishman[10] on Shakespeare that he was very anxious for me to have. A lovely book, says "$2.50 net" on the paper cover thing. People have the funniest habit of giving me books, don't they?

* * *

I have written Dad, And I had *too* written him after I got his present. He's dippy.

* * *

Lots of love to you all.
Vincent.

[9] Mitchell Kennerley, owner of the *Forum Magazine* and founder and head of the publishing house bearing his name.
[10] Frank Harris. The book was *The Man Shakespeare*, which Kennerley had published in 1909.

25 TO ARTHUR DAVISON FICKE

[135 East 52nd St.]
New York City,
May 7, 1913

Dear Mr. Ficke,—
You speak of my recklessness in telling you which of your poems I like best quite as if I had chosen those for which you do not care at all. Now that's a bluff, and I call it. There is no doubt at all that every poem I like you like, because you were pretty well satisfied with the whole book before you ever let it go to press. Go to! Get thee to a hermitage!

Can you change your mind to the extent of thinking that Witter Bynner's "Tiger" in the last *Forum* is good?[11] I think it tremendous. And if you say it's because I'm young that I like it, I'll say it's because you're young that you pretend not to. And you might tell me what you think of my "Journey" in the same number. It is neither sublime nor rotten, so there is a middle ground. But you needn't try to get out of it by saying "Fair-to-middlin' ". It isn't eccentric never to tell a poet which of his poems you like best, it's just plain lazy. I beg your pardon if I've said anything rude and hope I have.

For goodness sake send me the photograph you spoke of. Have you no personal pride? Just recollect the hideous images you sent me as a prologue to our correspondence, and fancy, if you can, the horrible picture of you I am carrying in my mind at the moment. You owe it to yourself. As for me,—please. (And isn't there a weeny snap of Mrs. Ficke and Stanhope I might have? I want it awfully bad.—I suppose if I told you I want that more than the other you would be mean and not let me have either. The masculine mind moves in a straight line; it is easy to track it.)

I am learning Russian. There are one hundred copecks in one rouble, and Anna Karenina isn't pronounced that way.

If the prophecy contained in your last letter has been fulfilled you are by now lying stark. If so, peace be to your ashes.

But if not, "Serus in caelum redeas."

Sincerely,
Vincent Millay.

[11] A one-act play on the subject of the White Slave Traffic.

26 TO THE MILLAY FAMILY

[135 East 52nd St.
New York City]
Thurs. 8 of May, '13.

Dear Family,—

I'm feeling awful tickled about something. It isn't that I have another poem accepted. Don't jump at any conclusions. It just has to do with Barnard. Last week, being hard up for a theme to send in, I dug out *Interim* & submitted that. I hated to, because Mr. Brewster[12] usually reads the verse themes (he picks out three or four themes with a gentle cynicism which would spoil even good verse and is especially hard on middle-class. If he takes a dislike to anything he delivers it accordingly & I was scared to death for fear he would read it & I should be obliged to go up and take it away from him.)

So this morning, after reading two rather indifferent short poems on *Spring*, he picked up my *Interim*, and I felt a pang. "Gosh," I said to the girl at my right, "I wish he wouldn't read that. He reads verse so *wretchedly*." "Yes, doesn't he?" she agreed, and he began.

"Here," he said, "is a very interesting piece of verse that I want to read to you, that is well worth reading."—I noticed that there wasn't even the twitch of a twinkle in his eye, and you may be sure I was watching for it. "It is called *Interim*," he said, and he didn't even smile at the odd title, "and I'll tell you a little about it, tho its easy enough to understand. It's supposed to be the thoughts of a man about the woman he loved who has died very unexpectedly & very recently. The attitude is naturally rather tense. It is written in blank verse.—Well,— it is called *Interim* then," and he began.

He read it beautifully. I was never so astonished in my life. He had really got hold at last of something he liked, and he was a changed man. He seemed to understand every bit of it. Nothing struck him funny. Even the *Santa Claus* figure at the end and which some people have thought ridiculous, you know, he read with understanding, and when he stumbled over one line (it was a sixth or seventh carbon, & very faint) he went back and did the whole paragraph over.

When he had finished he asked, as usual, "Any comment on this theme?" (The girls, by the way, are crazy about it, of which more anon)—and when somebody suggested, "Well, it certainly isn't very amateurish," he said "It isn't amateurish at all." Then he went on, "No, it is a very remarkable production for a girl in college. The verse is very smooth, and there are a great many striking figures. For instance, this,—" and he read over the part about the planets spinning "like tops across a table".

"I want you to notice," he said, "the great number of *words* that are employed. There are a great many words here;—a great command of language.—I notice that some of the critics say that the theme is noticeable for its sincerity. Now it is very obvious that the theme cannot be sincere, since a woman is writing it and a man is supposed to be speaking. It is not sincerity,—it is imagination."

That's about all he said about it, but of course he gave me an A on it. And then after he'd got through reading that, which he had saved over from last week for the purpose, what do you suppose he did?—Why, he picked up my this week's theme, a short story,[13] and a pretty good one if I do say it as shouldn't, and said, "Now I'll read you a theme which was very popular with the critics,—they all liked it.["] (You know the way we do, Tuesday when we hand in our themes he shuffles 'em and hands 'em out to the class and we read & swap & a slip of paper goes around with each theme and each critic affixes her little criticism to that,—see?) Well then he said, "I'll read the criticisms. The first one says 'This is an adorable story,' etc. The second one says 'The girl is made so attractive that one understands why the man asks her to marry him so many times.'—I suppose", interpolated Mr. Brewster, "that the critic means by that he asks her so many times to marry him." And then he read it, and read it well, especially one beautiful "damn" which, as we sometimes say of a song, needs a man's voice on it. I wish I could reproduce his tone when he said it, something of this inflection, "But—but—*damn* it, I," you know. It was very convincing.

The girls are all crazy about that story. One of them asked, rather doubtfully, if I'd let her have it for the *Barnard Bear* and when I said "No, I guess I'll keep it", she grinned, understandingly. She wants a copy of *Interim*, really wants it, you know, and I told her that when I type it again I'll put in a carbon for her, *provided* she promise that under no conditions it should get into print.[14] Isn't that rich?—And it wasn't even funny. Nobody laughed. One of the girls says she loves my story so she's ashamed of herself. And Mr. Brewster says it is noticeable that I have no trouble at all with the dialogue, which is usually the stumbling block. This is the way my story begins.

I found Barbara sitting on the beach, delectable in white icing, her quite unbelievable hair shining in the sun, and her rather sizable but very graceful feet crossed in front of her.

"How do you do, Barbara?" said I, not throwing away my cigar. "Do you love me today, Barbara?"

"No, Peter," said the girl of my heart, "no indeed, Peter. But I think you're very nice-looking."

Don't you wish you knew the rest of it?

You needn't bother to send the *Forum;* I've seen it in the college library. Have you read Witter Bynner's tremendous *Tiger* in the same number. It isn't a very pleasant thing, but it is, I think, wonderful. We out here are really face to face with the terrible conditions which he describes. None of us girls dares go alone to the corner of the street after dark for fear of being kidnapped. There was a wonderful statuette called "The White Slave" in the International Art Exhibit here a little while ago. But it is not a pleasant subject.

I went to Ellis Island last week. It is the most enthrallingly interesting place I was ever in. Can't tell you about it till I get home.

Nom will be tickled to know that when I was singing to myself in the living-room this afternoon the girls came in and made me keep on and I did & sang some of my own cunning little songs and they all love 'em and wonder why on earth I haven't sung before. I'm glad I didn't, tho. Because now I have a sure-enough good chance to be really modest, and for the first time in my life, I think.

You didn't tell me if you like my poem.[15] I don't think you do. It isn't anything great, I know. But Miss Rittenhouse says it is nothing I need be ashamed of even if tho it does come after *Renascence*, that some of it is wonderful and a lot of it is lovely and it's all good. So there now. And I got a letter from a *Princeton* man, whether student or instructor I do not know, congratulating me on my "articulation of a mood essentially inarticulate," if you please. I haven't answered him because I haven't had time, and I guess I won't anyway; I've too much to do to bother with men.

I'm joking. I know you read my poem before I came out here. But you might have said something. Bincent is 'coldin'.

* * *

Did I tell you how I was very informally invited to luncheon with Miss Kissell, a girl in my theme class, and when I got there I was let in by a butler & ushered & announced!—and how there were two butlers to serve the luncheon,—one to waltz and one to juggle?—No?—O, well.—I was so nervous that I couldn't hold anything in my fork, but I could manage a knife real skilful so I buttered my muffin & ate that & drank thirstily of water (and by the way, remind me to tell you a joke later; that made me think of it)—and so help me that's all I could get, but I strategized & "toyed with my food," and anyway its classy not to eat any-thing—*but it was chicken*, Darn it all! Makes me sick. I had wonderful voice control, and talked pleasantly, and rather wittily, in a soft, slow way that was not the least bit hysterical you know. Even the butlers couldn't have guessed—er—my condition, which is to say that I was not myself—unless they had seen my hand shake—and that *would* have told on me. I didn't spill anything or put anything where it didn't belong,—and there was an awful good chance, too, and I didn't grab the dishes in my left hand while I helped myself to things with my right either. *That's* one sure sign of a greenie—to help the butler hold it, you know. Gee, tho, but I was sick when I got home, weak as a kitten, had to go right to bed.

Gosh, there goes a German band under the window, playing the kind of schottishe you walk, (ask Hunk). How's a feller going to write to his family? I'll tell you that joke some other time.—If there's a question I haven't answered, just remind me of it in your next.

—Gosh, goodbye,

Vincent.

[12] William Tenny Brewster, then Professor of English at Columbia and Provost of Barnard from 1910 to 1923. He was well-known as the author of many books on English prose, poetry, composition, and style.

[13] The story "Barbara on the Beach" was published in the *Smart Set* November, 1914.

[14] Later, at Vassar, having won a prize, "Interim" was published in *The Vassar Miscellany* for July, 1914. It was also published in the *Forum* for September of the same year before being included in Miss Millay's *Renascence*.

[15] "Journey" in the May *Forum*.

27 TO MILLAY FAMILY

[May 9, 1913]

Oh, Girls, I can't wait to tell you—I have seen

Sarah Bernhardt

in

Camille!

Just came back, and I'm all gone to pieces, but, oh, my soul.—She only did one act—the last—she is in vaudeville, you know and there were a half-dozen other things beside her. But oh, when I can tell you, when I can tell you!—V.

28 TO ARTHUR DAVISON FICKE

Camden [Maine]

July 8, 1913

Dear Mr. Ficke,—

If you hadn't written to me for as long as I haven't written to you I should be feeling bad just about now, thinking I had lost a friend.

Probably men are different, and you haven't noticed. I hope so. You see, it was that picture, the other one, the one I was to send back,—I have started to do it a hundred times, and then somehow haven't, and I've packed it and unpacked it, and carried it around with me for years and years—it's been a veritable Flying Dutchman that just couldn't get to port, you know, a thing bewitched and unholy, its influence over me has been hellish and horrible beyond expression,—and now, *take it!* I have sent it home! Yes, I have. Don't ask me how I did it. I don't know.

You'll find a little tear at the bottom. I'm sorry. I didn't do it. Both were that way when I got them. There was a little notice on the outside saying "Received in the New York office in bad condition." But I'm sorry just the same.

The one I've kept I think the more like you. Anyway, it is the one I like to think is the more like you. Tho the one I am returning is not without interest.

You didn't know that Andrew Marvel is an old love of mine and that his *Coy Mistress* is one of my favorites. He's great, I think,—not a great poet, you know, I don't mean that,—just *great*.

You were mistaken in thinking I'd disagree with you about Mr. Bynner's little poem in the *Smart Set*. I agree perfectly. He spoiled it when he changed it, and he ought to be ashamed.[16]

Aren't you going to send me a snap of *Her* and *It*? *Please*, and forgive me for being so stupid about the picture. I do hope you get it all right.

Read me in the July *Forum*[17] and see if you don't like me a little.

I've had a wonderful time with the Kennerleys this spring. They live about twenty miles out from New York. Mr. Bynner was out on Sunday. And Herbert Kaufman once. What an unusual man,—and *why* does he try to write verse![18]

It's Vassar for me next fall, I think,—and Latin Prose all summer. But there's *got* to be a little time for paddling. Do you know anything about a canoe? Someday I shall *live* in one, just *live* in it. And then I shall be happy. I'm to have one of my almost own all summer, if you know what that means. It means I can paddle *bow* all I like.

Such a crazy letter!
Sincerely your friend,
Vincent Millay.

[16] The Bynner poem referred to is "Union Square" which,

according to Ficke, was changed back to the original form
when published later in *Greenstone Poems*.
[17] "God's World."
[18] A well-known journalist and the author of a small volume,
Poems, Printed for private circulation only, 1910.

29   TO ARTHUR DAVISON FICKE

"My Native Heath"
July 12, 1913

Dear Mr. Ficke,

Your letter got stuck in the box and I have just found it. Of
course by this time you know that I am back in Camden and that it is
"all off" but I thought you would appreciate a word of condolence.
This is it. I have been back and forth about New York so much for the
last few months that it doesn't seem possible I'm really not to see you,
that I can't just run in and be there, you know. It would have been
fine to see you. I'm sorry.

But why on earth didn't you come on a little sooner? I've only
been home about two weeks now.

I have a fearful amount of study ahead for this summer. I must
pass examinations in mathematics and American History, and I always
just—just—*skun*, as you might say, through algebra, and all I know
about American History is one verse of the Star Spangled Banner. It's
really horrible, when you stop and think, which I'm taking pains not
to do. I'm stealing time for this letter. I hope you appreciate it.

Fannie Stearns Davis[19] has just written me. Do you like her stuff?
—I love it.

Now I really must stop. Write me when you get to New York.
It's a lot different from Iowa to me now,—just across the yard, you
know, in everything but distance.

Sincerely,
Vincent Millay.

[19] Contemporary poet.

From the summer of 1913 on, with the entrance to Vassar
in view, Miss Millay applied herself to her studies. She was
being tutored in Latin by correspondence with the Professor
of Latin at Vassar, Elizabeth E. Haight, and at the same time

cramming up on other subjects in order to prepare for the entrance examinations.

As Professor Haight says in *Vincent at Vassar*, a memoir written after the death of her friend and former pupil: "The college then set exacting conditions for the B.A. degree: required year courses in English, one Classical Language, one modern (French or German), History, Mathematics, Physics or Chemistry, half a year of Philosophy, and students had to take 14 or 15 hours of class work for three years, 12 to 15 in the last year. Vincent fulfilled all these conditions and then built her course around her own interest. English studies were its foundation, and they included a wide range and great teachers: Old English and Chaucer with Christabel Fiske, Nineteenth Century Poetry, and Later Victorian Poetry, an advanced writing course with Katherine Taylor, English Drama with Henry Noble Mac-Cracken, the Techniques of the Drama with Gertrude Buck. . . . Then she enriched her knowledge of literature by many courses in foreign languages: both Greek and Latin, French, German, Italian, and Spanish. Besides the course in General European History, she elected Lucy Maynard Salmon's course in 'Periodic Literature: Its Use as Historical Material.' And she had a semester in Modern Art . . . one in Social Psychology . . . one in Music."

30   TO ARTHUR DAVISON FICKE

[Vassar College
Poughkeepsie, N. Y.
1914]

Go to!—Would you have me write you an *im*proper letter?—Upon my soul I half believe you would! And I am not yet so Vassarized but that such a thing is still possible. But I should never send it, you know,—so what would be the use?

Let me tell you, something: Don't worry about my little songs with wings; or about any of my startling & original characteristics concerning which you ought to worry, an you be my friend, for quite a different reason.

I hate this pink-and-gray college. If there had been a college in *Alice in Wonderland* it would be this college. Every morning when I awake I swear, I say, "Damn this pink-and-gray college!"

It *isn't* on the Hudson. They lied to me. It isn't anywhere near the Hudson. Every path in Poughkeepsie ends in a heap of cans and rubbish.

They treat us like an orphan asylum. They impose on us in a hundred ways and then bring on ice-cream.—And I hate ice-cream.

They trust us with everything but men,—and they let us see it, so that it's worse than not trusting us at all. We can go into the candy-kitchen & take what we like and pay or not, and nobody is there to know. But a man is forbidden as if he were an apple.

Oh, dear. I said that if I should write an improper letter I should never send it, but I'm going to do just that thing. And it's your own fault.

Mr. Ficke, are you fond of truncated prisms?—If you are I will ship you a box. This is where they grow.

I don't wonder Miss Blunt went to the University of Chicago. I am thinking seriously of going to the University of Moscow, and taking a course in Polite Anarchy & Murder as a Fine Art.

But, there!—You will wish you hadn't stirred me up.

I am, if you prefer an unseemly abandon to a "seemly reserve,"

Yours irrevocably,
Vincent Millay.

31 TO MRS. CORA B. MILLAY

Vassar College
Poughkeepsie, N. Y.
[Feb. 24, 1914]
Monday Night.

Dear Mother,—

Will you lend me, and send to me, your Bible?—I think I am old enough now to read it; too grown-up to be any longer bitter and scoffing and sceptical about it all, and so lose all the loveliness there is in it.—No, I've not "got religion", and I don't have much time to read, goodness knows, but it really is, isn't it, sort of heathenish, with all the books I have, not to have a Bible?—You know it by heart, so you don't need it. But I really do need it, Mother dear, and want it a whole lot, and especially your own Bible, if I may borrow it.—Moral support, perhaps. Anyway, I want it in my room.

You'll all think I'm crazy. Everbody here does. Because tonight, at ten o'clock, Kim, and Bee, and Harry and I all had a prayer-meeting in Harry's room.—Just for a few minutes, you know, and no hymns— we really are grown-up, and have a little sense—but Kim, who's a dear & whom we always poke fun at because she's so devout on Sundays & will study till one o'clock Saturday night but not on any account Sunday morning, Kim led the meeting, just read three short psalms that we asked for, in her soft Southern voice, and then I read two little things I'd copied from a calendar & talked about them a minute, and then we all said the Lord's Prayer together and meeting was over.

I don't know how it started. But after dinner tonight a few of us were talking & making fun of Kim—calling her a missionary—and Kim called me a heathen & then somehow the thing just grew. And we're going to do it every night, but if anybody's away of course it doesn't matter,—just those who want to, come to Harry's room at ten. It's very simple. And the truth of it is we need it. We hate to go to chapel, & cut whenever we can, and we *do* miss something, tho I couldn't for the life of me say what, that we ought to have. We've got so sort of sceptic & scoffy here that if anybody has a real thought she's ashamed of it & keeps it to herself & we don't get to know each other's best. With me it's something like drinking malted milk, this ten o'clock togetherness is,—I like it twice because I know it's good for me.—But of course everybody thinks we're crazy. Dorothea came in tonight with a novel to read if things were dull, and we sent her out. I never saw anybody so surprised in my life.—Don't think I don't know just how screamingly funny it is.—I do know, but I don't care.

> —Your loving daughter,
> Vincent.

32   TO THE MILLAY FAMILY

> Vassar College,
> Poughkeepsie, N. Y.
> Saturday [1914]

Dearest Family,—

These are my parting words. Next week is mid-years and if I perish I perish. I shall flunk everything but French and that only because no one in the French department would have the nerve to flunk me,—after promoting me & putting [me] into the French Club & having me write poems for them and a' that.—Last week they asked me to write a little farewell song to Miss Conrow who is to be gone next semester, & I did, to the tune of "Au Clair de la Lune"—it's *Little Friend Pierrot* in the school song-book—& they sang it & everybody was crazy about it, they told me, (I was tired and didn't go) and Agnes Rogers told me that M. Bracq said "C'est exquis!"—I'll write

it on the opposite page & Wump can translate it for you. Remember
that in singing the final e's are pronounced: "O, Journée obscur-e"
e—*uh*

> "O, journée obscure!
>   L'Adorée s'en va!
> Comme la vie est dure
>   De tous ici-bas!
> Ce qu'on beaucoup aime,
>   Ce qu'on veut garder,
> —Toujours c'est le même—
>   Ce ne veut rester.
>
> Paix!—O, Coeur qui pousse
>   Un tel grand soupir!
> Pense à l'heure douce
>   Où elle va revenir.
> O, toi que j'adore,
>   On ne doit pleurer;
> Pour venir encore
>   Il faut s'en aller."

Isn't it *sweet?*—It goes darling with the notes.

O, about flunking my exams,—I shall flunk History & probably
Geometry, and I may pass German and possibly Old English. That's
the way I stand at present. I'm going to cram some, but, darn it, I'm
tired. If I flunk 'em all they won't send me home, because two of 'em
are Sophomore courses and oh, well, they wouldn't.

Love,
Vincent.

33 TO MRS. CORA B. MILLAY

Vassar College
Poughkeepsie, N. Y.
[May 7, 1914]
Wednesday.

Dear Mother,—

I love you. In a few minutes I'm going to be home. We've drawn
lots for next year's rooms, & I have a perfectly wonderful single in
North, a corner room with two windows & lots of room for every-

thing. North was the most popular hall. Catherine Filene & Harry are right down stairs from me, & Margaret & Kim down below them. (Catherine & Harry are in here & they both send you their love.)

I shall have the cutest room. I'm going to get me a little alcohol tea-kettle so I can have tea, & bring back my lovely tea-set for show, & use my cute one. I'm going to subscribe for a couple of good magazines & a newspaper, so the room'll look alive, so to speak. And I'm going to try most always to have a flower. I'll have to buy a little furniture—we get it here second-hand from the seniors. Desk & extra cot, etc.

O, I'm so crazy to get home!—Seems to me I can't wait, tho I'm crazy about the college & everything.—My history teacher who is perfectly dear but very dignified & has never unbent the least little bit before today, said this morning, àpropos of my absentminded disregard of a certain hard & fast rule, "Well, why *didn't* you think, you naughty little thing?"

Was that a scolding,—or not?

Four weeks from tomorrow I take my last exam. Martha Bull wants me to stay over for Commencement,—the 10th, but I can't. Couldn't stand it.

It's lovely weather here now. That helps. But I tell you I'm all ready to be home.—What a wonderful summer we'll have, 'spite of Latin Prose, & all the rest!—Please make 'em plant some pansies, if nuffin' else.

Yo' lovin' chile,
Vincent.

34   TO NORMA MILLAY

[Vassar College
Poughkeepsie, N. Y.
May 10, 1915]

Dear Hunk,—

* * *

My Marching Song was accepted & day before yesterday was Sophomore Tree Ceremonies—I'll send you a program (I was on the committee, you know, and wrote all the words—to Grieg & Tschaiwoski (!) tunes) and after the ceremonies, the best they ever had here, people say, the class marched all around campus for hours singing their Marching Song for the first time. It's a custom. Everybody's mad about it. (It isn't to the tune I told you. That's hard to sing. But I made up a brand new one you'll hear it—*in a few days!* God help me in my exams. I haven't opened a book since "My Freshman Year."

Love to you all,

Vincent.

Will write again soon & send you "Candida".[20]

> [20] She played the role of the poet, Marchbanks, in the production of Shaw's *Candida*, March 5, 1915.

35   TO MRS. CORA B. MILLAY

Vassar College

Poughkeepsie, N. Y.

May 21, 1915

Beloved, beautiful, sad, sick Mother,—

I love you, I love you. Don't be sad any more. I'll take care of you, way from here. I remember how you used to rock me and sing to me when I was sick and sad. And now I'm going to make you better by telling you some lovely things all about yourself.

First:—Of all the songs I sing,—and I sing often now to crowds of people who love my little songs—the one they seem to love best is your beautiful "I may not dream again." Miss Landon, the Spoken English teacher, is just mad about it. She appreciates every little lovely thing about it.

Second: I'm just beginning to really appreciate at last the twenty-five red books full of knowledge that you gave me once. Now I'm really reading them a lot. Elaine has found that some of them are just what she needs for her biology courses and is using them, too. She said, "Who gave them to you?" and I said, "My mother." And she said, "That's what I call a present. That's a wonderful present to give."

I'll save other nice things to tell you in another letter, dear.

Next fall is Vassar's 50th anniversary. We have a tremendous celebration. And your daughter has made the part of Marie de France in the pageant, a lovely part.

I have sent some poems to the *Atlantic Monthly*. Here's hopin'.

Give my love to my sisters, my mother.

Your daughter,

Vincent.

36   TO ARTHUR DAVISON FICKE

[Vassar College]
October, 1915

Dear Mr. Ficke,—

I have just come across & reread two letters that I received from you last spring, and I remember now how very nice you are, and think with chagrin how you will probably never write to me any more.

Do you recall writing to me last April, saying that you were coming to New York, & inviting me to an ice-cream soda?—I can't for the life of me think why I didn't answer that letter. It couldn't have been because I loathe ice-cream sodas,—for I must have realized, even as long ago as April, that you would make it something else, if requested,—a whiskey & soda, for instance. The reason might have been examinations,—the reason often is, up here.

Anyway, I am become superstitious about you. I think it is fated that we shall never meet.—And possibly that is just as well;—I might be terribly disappointed in you.—(You see I feel perfectly sure that you would like me.)

So you have forgotten telling me that your son's name is Stanhope. —Think of this:—You may have told me a hundred things that you fancy still secreted in your esoteric heart!—Doesn't that make you awfully nervous?

_____

Sometime when you are in New York you might run up to see me. —Mightn't you?—Or mightn't you?—I suppose you mightn't.—But then, again, you might.

—Very truly,
Vincent Millay.

P.S.—That you should _see_ any "reserve" in my signing myself "Yours truly" is a matter of interest.

37   TO ARTHUR DAVISON FICKE

Vassar College,
Poughkeepsie, N. Y.
October the Nineteenth
_1915_

Dear Mr. Ficke,—

So you went through Poughkeepsie & didn't come to see me!— _How could_ you?—The thought that I was probably not here at the time does not lessen my grief, or my annoyance.

I am not a forward miss, and since you yourself are so retiring,—
I fear we shall remain strangers.

Mr. Bynner, if he remembers me at all, will not give you a glowing
account of me. But never mind. Although I would have chosen somebody else to "put you wise" to me.

———————

I love the little Japanese picture. It gives me a want-to-be-there
feeling.

———————

I don't know if I shall ever get out a book.—If you have, as you
say, issued three in twelve months, and do *not* stop forever, you should
be forced to.

Although I do like the things you write.

I don't know what has happened to my handwriting.[21]—I cross
my hands differently, too,—with the right thumb outside, now, instead
of the left.—I don't know whether it means a change of character, or
simply an increase of it.—What do you think?

Is it Mrs. Ficke who writes like me?—the one that you say came
to a bad, esoteric & delightful end?

I have to go to a class now.—Does that strike you as silly?—Sometimes it seems to me very silly indeed,—not the fact that there is a
class,—or that I go to it,—but that I *have to*!

I am glad you didn't return my letter unanswered.

Sincerely,

Vincent Millay.

[21] Her correspondent had commented on the fact that her
handwriting had changed. See facsimile letters, 1912 and
later.

---

38 TO DR. HENRY NOBLE MAC CRACKEN

Vassar College
Poughkeepsie, N. Y.
November the seventeenth
1915

My dear Dr. MacCracken,—

I have written to my mother, telling her what you said to me
yesterday about the possibility of Kathleen's coming here. Kathleen
herself is not at home now, and unless Mother is able to get together the
information you want, I may not be able to get it to you until some
time after Thanksgiving.

It may be that yesterday you made it seem quite too possible to me, for I find that my heart is set upon her coming here next year—my last year here—and it seems to me now that if she doesn't come back with me then, I shall not care if *I* don't come back.

If the entrance requirements are made as sympathetic to my sister as they were made to myself—then there will be no doubt about her preparation to enter next fall. I had my arms full of conditions when they let me in,—but they are all gone now—except that I flunked gym last spring!—If they will only be as nice to her—after she is once *in* here there will be no question about her suitability—as her high school record will show you.

I am neglecting my Spanish to write this—just one thing more to interfere with my lessons, Dr. MacCracken!

Very truly,
Edna St. Vincent Millay.

P.S.—I do so *hope* it may come true.

39   TO NORMA MILLAY

Vassar—
Sunday, Nov. 26
'16

Dear Sister,—

Indeed you almost never write to me.—A letter from you is an event.—We should write oftener, I think, if only for the pleasure that the letters give—(for of course, whether we ever write or not, we are sure that we love each other just the same.)—It is very sad, about Helen Rittenbush.[22] (I felt strange when I wrote the name, thinking that it was a meaningless thing, that name, no longer signifying anything at all.) Of course I couldn't help thinking when I read you letter—"If it had been you—or I—or Kathleen".—I wish you were with me now, sweetheart. Kathleen will be with me Wednesday night—I feel as if I should add "God willing".—I love you both so very much.—I can't help wondering what happens to Love when people die,—if I should die—what would happen to my love for you & Kathleen & mother.—It's queer, isn't it?—*Hello, dear.*

I wish you could see 1st Hall Play. We are giving three one-act plays, in one of which Frances, my room-mate, has a big part, & in another of which, Masefield's *Locked Chest*, I play Vigdis,[23] the best part.—It comes off the 9th of December.—I may be home in less than a month!

It is possible that Kathleen can come up again for the play.

Did I tell you that Salomón[24] is teaching the Spanish language at *Williams College*? And that Prof. & Mrs. Rice, great friends of Salomón, have invited me up for the week-end of the 1st of December? I hope I can go.—Miss Palmer, the head warden, says it is very hard to get off for that week-end—because on account of Thanksgiving holiday— one day!—they have switched Thursday classes to Friday & Friday classes to Saturday!—I could oath!

Mother has been so darling to me, sending me beautiful towels, & a fir pillow, & *fresh butter*, perfectly delicious—from Belfast.

Where's that cake, old top?

Dear, did you ever find the negative of that snap of me looking through the curtains?—I feel *terribly* about it.—I wish you would try again to find it.

* * *

Dear, I must stop.—This is *so* pleasant—I would like to keep on for an hour—talking to you—*my darling*—but I have to study.

Goodbye.

Write me soon again, 'lovèd.

Vincent.

P.S.—Miss McCaleb told me that Miss Hartridge wrote her, saying "I am *so* glad you sent me the little Millay girl.[25]—She is a dear!" Isn't that glorious news? V.

[22] A school friend in Camden, Maine.

[23] In 1915 Miss Millay had played Sylvette in the French Club's production of Edmond Rostand's *Les Romanesques*. This was followed by her acting the role of Marchbanks in Shaw's *Candida* and a spectacular appearance in Hazel MacKaye's *Pageant of Athena* when, as Marie de France, she greatly moved the audience by reciting "The Lay of the Honeysuckle." She also played Deirdre in Synge's *Deirdre of the Sorrows* and took part in Selma Lagerlof's *The Christmas Guest*, both of which were produced in 1916. In her last year at Vassar, she played the leading role in her own poetic play *The Princess Marries the Page*. She wrote another one-act play, *The Wall of Dominoes*, which was published in

The Vassar Miscellany Monthly, May, 1917, but never re-
published in book form.
[24] Salomón de la Selva, a Nicaraguan poet.
[25] Her sister Kathleen was attending The Hartridge School in
Plainfield, New Jersey, in preparation for college.

40   TO NORMA MILLAY

[Vassar College
Poughkeepsie, N. Y.]
In my Sitting-room
Tuesday Morning.
[Dec. 5th, 1916]

My darling sister,—
We shall be together very soon now—all of us.—Kathleen & I had
such a happy time Thanksgiving.—We didn't see so very much of each
other, because I had to keep trying on costumes & practicing for the
skating dance we did Thursday night. K. couldn't stay for the real
event but she saw the dress-rehearsal—which was rotten.—Thursday
night our dance went off wonderfully.—We ended up by standing on
one leg with the other out behind us in skating attitude—facing the
audience—with our arms across each other's bodies, you know—while
slowly–slowly the curtains closed.—It was *such* fun—we didn't even
wiggle.—
Saturday morning I went to Williamstown—to visit Prof. & Mrs.
Rice & to see Salomón. Did I tell you about them?—how Salomón,
who is now teaching the Castilian tongue in Williams, talked so
extravagantly of me to Prof. Rice, who teaches Spanish also I think,
& to his wife, that they wrote me & asked me to visit them—& I went?—
I had the most beautiful time. Williamstown is up in the Berkshires—
& you know how lovely in winter many blue hills are all together. We
heard a very excellent concert Saturday night & Sunday afternoon Mrs.
Taylor, the wife of the head of the romance language department, who
plays almost as well as Paderewski—I say that to let you know that she
really plays wonderfully—played for us a long long time, Bach, &
Schumann, & much Chopin.—Judge if I was happy!

* * *

I get darling letters every little while from Harrison Dowd.—Do
you remember about him—the Andover boy?
Next Saturday night is First Hall Play—I told you that I have a

very good part, I think,—one of the most interesting I ever had—& most difficult.

I have sold some poems to Harriet Monroe of the *Poetry Magazine* for which she is going to pay me sixteen dollars—as soon as I write & tell her *yes it is all right. Kin to Sorrow, Tavern* & *Afternoon on a Hill.*[26] She would have taken *October-November* (which by the way Salomón *adores*—he says over to himself "*October-November*"— & then "*October-November—Ah, Ednah!* That is *marvelous!*") She liked it very much, as I was saying—but would have to wait *until next November* to print it!—so sent it back!—Oh, heaven, the stupidity of that!—I told Salomón that it is as insulting as *illustrating* verse—to print it in season! Exactly the same.

Never mind, sixteen dollars aren't many dollars—but oh, I can *use* them all right!—This room of ours has cost awfully—I have to write many more poems before I am straight—& be very sparing from now on—else I shall find myself in wrong.

* * *

I have to go to a class, 'lovèd.—Goodbye.

Vincent.

[26] These poems were published in the August, 1917, number of *Poetry*.

41   TO THE MILLAY FAMILY

[Vassar College
Poughkeepsie, N. Y.
Jan. 29, 1917]

Darlings,—

Excuse everything.—I am cramming as I have never crammed before in all my crammous days for my baby Italian exam.—I am actually learning the whole grammar by heart.—The three o'clock bell has just rung,—& my mind is on you—I shall be with you—but do you mind if under these most 'straordinary scumstances I study in your presence?

I have something nice to tell you—I had a letter a few days ago from no less a person than John Masefield—he says that a great many of his friends have written him, telling him how wonderful I was as Vigdis & he wishes he could have been here. He says I am the first person ever to have played Vigdis—it is quite new, you know.—He is going to send me a copy of the book as soon as it is published in England.

Mrs. Reed, whom I met after the play here, a very good friend of Aunt Calline's,—writes me that she has written to Mr. Masefield that I write poems & that he says "Tell Vigdis to send me some of her work,"—so I am going to at once—my very best—you may be sure.[27]

The letter was so exciting. It said "Opened by Censor" on it.

Mme. Homer sang here at college Friday night.—I wish Norma might have heard it. She was wonderful,—and so beautifully gowned & so beautiful to look at generally—& oh, to listen to!

I must write Wump a weeny note & then study.

Lots of love & thanks for dollar. Will really answer letters after Thursday—

Vincent.

[27] The following summer Miss Millay wrote to her mother: "I had a letter from John Masefield yesterday; isn't *that* nice? Says he likes my poetry very much, that I have a 'quite rare personal gift.' "

42 TO THE MILLAY FAMILY

[135 East 52nd Street
New York City.
March 24, 1917.]
Saturday

Dear Family,—

Probably this will be too late to instruct the addressing of your Sunday mail, & I shan't get your letters for nearly two weeks!—Oh, dear!—It serves me right for not telling you before when I was going to come here.—I am spending the holidays with Aunt Calline, or rather, at the training school,—Aunt C. having just run over to Omaha for a few days. I shall not see her. In a way, though I am sorry not to see her, I am glad she is not here, for I am to have an interview with the manager of the Washington Square Players, whose theatre is just now *The Comedy* here in town, with a view to being with them next year. Aunt Calline would object as little to them as to any company, but she would object all right, & it would make it very hard for me, even though the matter is so very tentative. I wrote Mr. Roeder, one of the company, whom I met through Salomón, & he writes back that he will arrange for me an interview with Mr. Goodman, & that he hopes I may be one of the company next season. Of course Mr. Goodman may not like me,—but personal interviews are my longest & strongest suit, & Mr. Roeder didn't speak as if the company were too full to admit another.

I got a personal letter from the *Atlantic Monthly* a few days ago,—to wit:

"There are arresting lines in this unusual sonnet, & we return it to you only after serious consideration." I felt pretty pleased at that from the old *"Family Reunion"*,—though they are publishing things every day that I could have written with one hand tied behind me—(preferably my left hand)!—I am sending the sonnet in question—a new one —to another magazine—soon I will send you a copy.

I wish I had some money,—this year is driving me crazy. Everything costs so much,—I'm scared to death,—so I *must* sell some poems, —& I'm going to.—I've *got* to get my bills paid.

Norma, my hat is just the cutest thing,—everybody *adores* it. They really do—they mention it themselves,—and, baby, old blond plumblossom, if I get a good job here sometime in the near future you're coming out here & get a job & study at the School of Design, because it's wicked for you not to. You're the most talented one of us all, & you've got to have your chance, too. Of course Mother must come & we'd just have to leave Camden forever, I suppose, which seems sad. When we get rich, though, (in a few months, of course) we'd all go back for the summers. We could have a little place just outside, & commute, that is, you and I could, come in on the train every day,— but if I were acting, I couldn't go out at night,—I suppose I'd have to have a little place in town—a room in someone's garret would be fine. We couldn't be in the city all summer,—we'd die—and it's bad enough in the suburbs.—Well, I'm just thinking in ink—will talk it all over when I come home in the spring.

I expect to see Wump & go to see the *Yellow Jacket* with her, if possible, next Saturday.—I wish you two could see that play—it's Chinese, & queer, & absurd, & beautiful, & sad, & altogether ravishing.— Much love to you both & Wuzzy.

Vincent.

43   TO THE MILLAY FAMILY

> [Vassar College
> Poughkeepsie, N. Y.
> May 21, 1917.]
> Saturday.

Dear Family,—

*   *   *

A week from next Thursday our exams begin!—*Whoops,* my dear!—All to the merry!

It's beautifully warm here at last.—We wear *thin* things.—As all my things are in that condition by now it's fine weather for me.

Had a beautiful motor trip yesterday & today,—50 miles today— don't know how far yesterday. *Beautiful.*—Some friends of Charlie's,[28] —girls. Four of us in a little Saxon—stayed all night at the house of one of them,—dinner today at the house of the other—*such* good food.

Norma,—I am *crazy* about that black hat.—It is exceedingly becoming to me. *What* is it?—I recognize the white cemetery-wreath sea-weed decorations; but *what* is the hat itself?—Is it new?—*Tell* I!— I *love* it.—It is stunning.

I must go to bed.—Excuse this for not being in the afternoon. I was motoring.

> Much, much love,
> Vincent.

[28] Charlotte Babcock, her roommate.

44   TO THE MILLAY FAMILY

> Vassar College
> Poughkeepsie, N. Y.
> June 6, 1917

Dear Mother & Sister,—
    In a few days now I shall write myself
                    A. B.
& send home my sheepskin for you to frame & hang up unesthetically in a conspicuous position. Everything is all right. My bills are paid.

But I must tell you something unpleasant but quite unimportant which has just occurred.—Because I was absent-minded & stayed away out of town with three other girls one night, forgetting until it was too late that I had no right to be there because I had already lost my privileges for staying a couple of days in New York to go to the Opera,—the Faculty has taken away from me my part in Commencement.—That doesn't mean just what it says, because my part in Commencement will go on without me,—Baccalaureate Hymn, for instance, or the words of Tree Ceremonies, which we repeat—& all the songs & our Marching Song which will grace the final activities,—no one really has a speech or anything in Commencement.

What I mean is this,—I can't stay here at all for Commencement: I can't graduate with the class,—my diploma will be shipped to me, as I told Miss Haight, "like a codfish"—& it all seems pretty shabby, of course, after all that I have done for the college, that it should turn me out at the end with scarcely enough time to pack and, as you might say, sort of "without a character."—The class is exceedingly indignant, bless 'em, & is busy sending in petitions signed by scores of names, & letters from representative people, & all that. It will do no good. But it is a splendid row.

I always said, you remember, that I had come in over the fence & would probably leave the same way.—Well, that's what I'm doing.

I don't pretend that I don't feel badly. I do.—I have wept gallons, —all over everybody.—Terribly nervous, you know, because I had sat up three whole nights during exams, to get my topics done,—& no sleep in the day-time. I don't want Wump to know until after she is through there, if we can help it.—This will make no difference about her. If she passes her exams she has next year here sure. I have seen about her room, at McGlynns, where I was Freshman year. And Miss McCaleb tells me that the money is all here for her for next year. It isn't a disgrace, you see, folks,—it's just a darned unpleasant penalty for carelessness of college rules, occurring at a darned unfortunate time.

But I never knew before that I had so many friends.—Everybody is wonderful.

Now listen,—wonderful news, maybe. Edith Wynne Matthison— who, by the way, is Mrs. Kennedy—not Mrs. Matthison, writes that she thinks she has an opening for me. It may mean my going to Milwaukee for eight weeks this summer, beginning sometime in July. In which case I should be home only a week or two,—& possibly not at all.—Mrs. Kennedy has shown some of my poems to Mr. Platt, & told him about me. Mr. Platt is the man who produced *The Blue Bird* in New York.—He is going west this summer & play wonderful plays,—

some of Synge,—who wrote Deirdre, and I am to see him, & perhaps will get the chance to go.—I never was so happy, in spite of my trouble. —I am not sending cameo. (Never mind heap inappropriate Commencement gift.)

Love,
Vincent.

45   TO NORMA MILLAY

New York
Sunday.

Dear Norma,—

Tell Mother it is all right,—the class made such a fuss that they let me come back, & I graduated in my cap & gown along with the rest. Tell her it had nothing to do with money;—all my bills have been settled for some time.—Commencement went off beautifully & I had a wonderful time. Tell her this at once if you can. I didn't get the Milwaukee season, so I'm staying here & just looking around for a job. If I get one soon enough, & it doesn't begin for a short time perhaps I shall come home when Kathleen does, but otherwise I shall just stay on here until I get something to do, probably. You see I have to start right in working as soon as I can get a job,—& I may not be able to come home at all. We mustn't be foolish about these things.

———————

I have sold *October-November* to *The Yale Review*, a fine magazine.

If I got an engagement for the fall then I could come home & do some writing, which I am very anxious to do, this summer. But I *can't* come home unless I have something sure here to come back to,—you understand.

* * *

I am feeling much rested,—& all keyed up to go to work—but, oh, I am so *homesick* to see you, dear, & Mother,—& the garden & everything!—Never mind, if I have good luck I shall come home,—unless I have to begin work at once.

* * *

Please write my darling, darling, darling, sister.

Vincent.

(Edna St. Vincent Millay A.B.!)

III

Post-College Years
June, 1917, to end of 1920

[New York, N. Y.
June 20, 1917.]

Norma, dear,—

I have about decided to come home instead of staying on here. Kathleen and I shall probably leave here next Friday night and get home Saturday night, (a week from this Friday. See P.S.) in time for baked beans. I am enclosing $2. to make sure of the baked beans. Probably that old box of books caused you no end of trouble; I am sorry. I just neglected to send you the money for it. I have had so many things to think of I have been on the verge of insanity.

I have decided to come home for several reasons: because this is rather a bad time to look for a job, and it will be awfully expensive staying here while I'm looking, and it is going to be no end hot in a few days,—it is hot already; and then, I need very much to look over my clothes and mend and make over, and I have a tremendous washing to do which would cost me a great deal to have done here; then, I have some writing which I ought to do, and home is the best place to do that; I could write in the summer, and perhaps sell something, and then come back in the fall, whether I have a job or not, and hunt around for a job and take what I could get at first. I wish you could come back with me. But that would leave mother alone. I want very much to have you here, sister. We could have such a good time if we had some tiny dirty uncomfortable room somewhere down in the disreputable district where Cutie Smith lives: that's where I'm staying now,—way down on West 4th Street. (I'm doing this typewriting, however, uptown, in Mr. Kennerley's office.)

Dear, cheer mother up about my commencement; I went off in a cloud of glory. It was wonderful fun. I thought mother would feel rather badly if I didn't come home, if only for a little while,—and I sorter wanted to see you all myself,—(which, as you have probably guessed long ere this, is not the least of my reasons for coming home.)

If I am at home I shall work very hard this summer, at something or other,—I have a perfect passion for earning money, don't care much how I earn it, just feel I have to hurry around all the time and make money. Darling, I wish we could arrange it so that you could be here with me next winter. Don't you suppose we can? There's nothing for you there at all, and I've always wanted to bring you out here with me. I'm sure we can fix it up in some way. Don't you suppose mother could get a job editing some dum page in some newspaper?—she might. She writes such beautiful English and she's so funny. She could try. At least there's no reason for sticking in Camden,—except that it *is* nice in the summer,—oh, I'm so crazy to get home and see you all!

With all my love,

Vincent.

P.S. I have just found out that Charlotte Carr, (V.C. '14) is not going to be using her little apartment down here for the next two weeks, so I think I shall get Wump to stay there with me at least a part of that time, while I look for a job. It is just around the corner from Cutie's. Then we shall come home. But it is too wonderful a chance not to take advantage of.

V.

47   TO CHARLOTTE N. BABCOCK

Camden, Maine

[July – 1917]

Charlie,—

You are my dear sister,—and I love you. You know how beautiful I want it all to be for you & Mac, I think.—I wish I might be there Thursday—you will be so lovely to see—but I shall be thinking of you and imagining how you look. Probably Anne or Fran will be keeping at you all the time to tuck in or ease out somewhere.

—I wish I could be there!—But I sometimes think that it is only the guests at a wedding who really notice whether they are there or not.

I am sending you my whole heart in love, dear,—and, (don't faint) —the *tea-ball*!

Yes, I am!

Someday I will give you something real,—but in the meantime I thought you wouldn't mind the tea-ball.

* * *

—Vincent.

Dear Charlie

When you think of me,
Blow in a cup, & make some tea!

Rotten bad form although it be,
Blow in a cup, & make some tea.
This kind of tea ball—open wide—
Will not become mildewed inside,
And when you use it—think of me,
Blow in a cup & make some tea!

48 TO EDITH WYNNE MATTHISON[1]
[Mrs. Charles Rann Kennedy]

Camden, Maine
July the Sixth
1917

Dear Mrs. Kennedy,—

I have fled to Maine.—It is your fault, entirely. You see, you told Miss Haight to tell me to "wear my prettiest frock"—and that terrified me—because everything I had was in tatters—and when I found by telephoning that Mr. Milton was out of town for a week,—I just suddenly got on a train and came home, because it's only at home that one can work & iron & mend & sew on buttons & run in ribbons & make window curtains into hats,—isn't that true?—I am coming back as soon as I have something pretty to wear,—but I know it would have been silly to stay, & I must have seemed a dismal outlook to any theatrical manager.

——————

You wrote me a beautiful letter,—I wonder if you meant it to be as beautiful as it was.—I think you did; for somehow I know that your feeling for me, however slight it is, is of the nature of love. I was sure of that the night of my play. I like to think that it is true,—and nothing that has happened to me for a long time has made me so happy as I shall be to visit you sometime.—You must not forget that you spoke of that,—because it would disappoint me cruelly.

——————

Listen; if ever in my letters to you, or in my conversation, you see a candor that seems almost crude,—please know that it is because when I think of you I think of real things, & become honest,—and quibbling and circumvention seem very inconsiderable.

Thank you for the letters.[2] They will still be in time when I get back to New York, will they not?

Your husband was so cute to put a post-script to your letter,—it made me feel so friendly with you both!—I shall write him one.

Yours very sincerely,
Vincent Millay.

P.S. Thank you, Mr. Kennedy.—I shall be severe & uncompromising with Mr. Tyler; if he assays procrastination, I shall bring him sharply to account.—V.M.

¹ One of the important friendships of her life and one which began at Vassar, was with the distinguished actress, Edith Wynne Matthison who was famous for her beauty and rich, warm voice. She was married to Charles Rann Kennedy in whose plays she acted. Miss Millay wrote of Miss Matthison:

If I should lose my hearing, I
Two senses would have lost thereby,
There having passed beyond my reach
At once my hearing and your speech.

When Miss Millay met the Kennedys they were both associated with the Bennett School at Milbrook, N. Y., and occasionally visited Vassar. Among the plays they produced at the Bennett School was *The Princess Marries the Page*, which the author later dedicated to Miss Matthison in the published version in 1932.

² Letters of introduction to New York theatrical managers: George C. Tyler, Winthrop Ames, and others.

49 TO EDITH WYNNE MATTHISON

Camden, Maine,
July 28, 1917.

Dear Mrs. Kennedy:

Camden is about one hundred miles from Kennebunkport; I just asked "Information." Are you coming up to see me?—I wish you would; you would like it here; it is beautiful. Norma will let you pick the peas; we have the first ones tomorrow, and I am going out to pick them right after I finish this letter. Please come up here to see me. Then we can all come back—I mean go back—together. That means that I am inviting Mr. Kennedy, too. *I want so much to see you.*

I can come before August 13—indeed, I *will* come whenever you want me—I will do whatever you want me to do—but it would be better, because of many things, if I could go back with you when you go back from Kennebunkport. One reason why it would be better later is that I am doing quite a bit of tutoring now and quite a bit of type-writing. I will do whatever you tell me to do, however. I am beginning by writing you by return mail,—the first thing you have asked me to do. Love me, please; I love you; I can bear to be your friend. So ask of me anything, and hurt me whenever you must; but never be "tolerant", or "kind". And never say to me again,—don't dare to say to me again—"Anyway, you can make a trial" of being friends with you! Because I can't do things in that way; I am not a tentative person. Whatever I do, I give up my whole self to it; and it may be a trial—of course, most things are, I suppose—but I never am conscious of making a trial; I am conscious only of doing the thing that I love to do,—that I *have* to do—and I *have* to be your friend. It may seem to to you that it is only a trial, but I can't think that you meant that. Didn't you just say that to frighten me into consciousness of the enormity of being friends with you?—But enormity does not frighten me; it is only among tremendous things that I feel happy and at ease; I would not say this, perhaps, except that, as I told you, I do not trouble to lie to you.

"So *that's* all right, Best Belovèd,—do you see?"

Yes, your typing *is* rather rotten, I am enchanted to be able to say. My own is rather admirable, don't you think?

No, I don't mind wearing other people's things,—I had five roommates last year at Vassar—because if they are things I like I always feel myself into them until I forget that they actually "belong" to anybody at all,—a dangerous propensity, you will say, and one with an imminence toward kleptomania! But I shall try to bring a few quite nice things with me; I will get together all that I can, and then when you tell me to come, I will come, by the next train, just as I am. This is not meekness, be assured; I do not come naturally by meekness; know that it is a proud surrender to You; I don't talk like that to many people.

With love,
Vincent Millay.

50 TO EDITH WYNNE MATTHISON

Camden, Maine,
August 27, 1917.

Dear Mrs. Kennedy:

At last I am sending you some more poems; I hope it is not too late for you to read some of them to Miss Gage,—you said you wished to do that. I have been unable to send them before; when I see you I will

explain. But I am very sorry. Some of the poems—I am thinking especially of the sonnets—I read to you at Miss Haight's that morning when
we breakfasted together; perhaps you will remember them. But I think
most of them are new. They are rather rottenly typed; I did them in
the almost complete darkness last night, and I need a new ribbon. (That
sounds like "He promised to buy me", etc,—doesn't it? If I were a
parodist I should put this vulgarly new wine into that old bottle.)

Tell Mr. Kennedy, before he has time to remark the fact himself,
that I know very well the sonnets of the incomplete sequence are not
perfect sonnets,—I made the fourteenth line an alexandrine purposely,
somehow they had to be ended in that way. Remind him also, if he
refuses to read them open-mindedly (Mr. Masefield told me that he
does not like Interim *because he does not like blank* verse) that Mere-
dith made some rather nice poems of sixteen lines each which we
permit to be called sonnets. (This is all very inconsequential; it is, as
you doubtless have guessed, just by way of sending my regards to
Mr. Kennedy.)

I will meet you at the South Station Friday, just before train-time.

With love,

Vincent.

51   TO THE MILLAY FAMILY

[New Hartford, Conn.
September 3, 1917]

Beloved Family,—

I am having the most wonderful time,—oh, *wonderful*! And they
are arranging for me to do some readings later this fall,—trying to
arrange,—& I think they will.

I am sitting on the porch now. Rann is up in his little house in the
field working on his new play, *The Army With Banners*, in which one
line—such fun!—was suggested to him by me. Edith is up in the
garden,—you see, they don't fuss all the time about *me*.

I recited *Renascence* to them & some other people Saturday. None
of them had seen it. Rann says it is one of the great poems of all time in
any language. I am encouraged for my book.—It will take me only a
few days on a typewriter here to get all my stuff ready for Mitchell.
I have just written him telling him to send mother that Lyric Year I
left in his office. Hope he doesn't forget.

I have learned to speak English: "Really, you know, when you consider the beastly pen & the filthy ghastly (pron. like grass) paper, its rather footling to attempt a letter. Such infernal, blasted weather, too, you know! Amusing, isn't it?—One becomes so bored. And everybody seems such a filthy rotter."

That's it. That really is the way Rann Kennedy talks. And Edith, too. I wish you could see them about the house. (She said to me on the train, all of a sudden: "You can smoke everywhere except in your bedroom." She is afraid of fire.) He is a great big gruffey man with a childlike smile & eagerness,—he wears an enormous yellow smock which reaches to his knees,—& that is *all*—excepting a pair of sneakers, & drawers whose cunning hems sometimes show when he puts a book on a high shelf. Imagine—bare legs—long, grey hair—& a face like a child's! Oh, he is so sweet!—and she is beautiful—in her blue linen smock & bloomers. We have a wonderful time together.

Will write more when I can. Have met & am just going over to call on Laura Hope Crews, who played a big part in Peter Ibbetson. Have fallen deeply in love with another woman's husband who lives down the road.

Please write. How is Wumps getting on?

Vincent.

---

52   TO MRS. CORA B. MILLAY and NORMA MILLAY

257 West 86th Street
[New York City]
Sunday, Sept. 22, '17

Dear Mother & Norma,—

I have all the will in the world to write you a very long letter— but the flesh is weak. I am in bed with a curiously upset tummy. What *did* I eat?—If you want to hear a nasty, unpleasant story, just listen to the recital of what a perfect lady of your acquaintance did last Friday night, vis. to wit, as follows:

* * *

Dinner, with Mitchell & Helen at the Plaza, and after that the theatre & after that, T H I S!

We were standing on the corner of 5th Avenue & 50th Street, waiting for a bus. We had walked up from the theatre a way to get the air. But there *is* no air on 5th Avenue, there is nothing but oil & old gasoline & new gasoline—there is never one breath of pure air—nothing but gas, gas, gas—but people who live in New York walk there to get the air. Probably they do get it—all of it—& that's why it blows to me so scummily. Well, this is what I did: I had been feeling rarely funny all day, but didn't know just what ailed me. But all of a sudden the thought came to me, "*What* if I should have to up-swallow right here?" and I nearly died at the thought, but got a sort of control of myself & said to myself with shaky reassurance, "Ah, no, people don't do such things!" but then I thought, "Well, what if I *had* to?—then I guess I would!" and I felt very ill. Also I felt very weak & dizzy & queer & I began to lean on Helen & say, "I feel ill. I feel very ill. I am sorry," and I saw the machines going down the Avenue & up & smelled by the quart "That Good Gulf Gasolene" & saw Mitchell signal a taxi which did not see him but kept on going down the Avenue, & then there began to strike down into my mind the most beautiful streaks of colored light & I had the same wonderful dreams that I have when I take gas at the dentists (I *had taken gas*!) & I kept thinking, "Oh, how beautiful! If I can only remember this to write it up!" & so I dreamed for what seemed quite a long while, and then, way, way off somewhere I heard two men speaking. One of them was saying, "There, that's right. Careful. Lift her up a little." And the other one said, "Yes, sir. Where to, sir?" or something like that. And I thought, "Wonder who's ill?—Poor girl. She must have fainted. Wonder who she is—why, it's I, that's who it is! It's my own self! That's what all those colored lights & dreams meant,—I was unconscious, I really fainted—oh, how wonderful—I'm so glad—now at last I know how it feels!" because you see I had sort of flopped over once or twice but I had always kept my head clear & could hear & see; I had never lost consciousness. This was very different, & it's comical to consider how happy I was about it.—For one thing, of course, I didn't feel ill any more, because only my mind had become awake; I was quite oblivious of my whole body. It was *so* beautiful & comfortable! I had even forgotten for a few blissful moments that I had a stomach.—But in a little while I heard some funny little sounds, little regular moans "Like mother used to make" (forgive me, but I'm not very well yet,—and they did sound so much the way mother sounded when she used to feel faint!) And then I heard Mitchell & Helen talking & realized that we were in a taxi & that Mitchell was holding me in his arms like an infant with my head back on his shoulder. Next I remembered that I had a hand, a left hand—& I thought I'd like to move it—but I couldn't remember where it was. I thought I'd like to open my eyes & look about for it, but I didn't feel like opening my eyes. Then I became conscious of a queer cold lump on my legs, ice-cold, & very heavy, & suddenly little horrid tingles began to rush through it & I knew it was my hand. And I thought "so *this* is the way it feels—cold, & dead & tingly—I'm glad I know—like when your foot's asleep, only colder, & more belonging-to-somcone-else," and I made the most prodigious attempts—awful *pushes* with my mind, to lift that hand, & I might just as well have tried to lift Mitchell's hand just by thinking of it. But after many determined attempts it must be that it made some movement because Mitchell suddenly caught it in his & held it very hard & rubbed it & then it felt oh, so funny & after a while it was all right.

All this time, I hadn't thought of my tummy. But we stopped at a drug-store, & Helen got out & came back with some smelling-salts & they propped me up & I smelled & began to get back *all* my senses & the taxi went bumping & lurching on & oh, Lord! All at once I *knew!* & so did Mitchell, for he put his handkerchief into my hand, & said, "Stick your head out of the window, dear," & I did—& oh, Mother & Norma—it was Fifth Avenue, darlings, with thousands of people & millions of lights, but I didn't seem to care at all, I was only happy that things had been decided for me. Only I *did* try to avoid the policemen. —And nobody knew me. There is a beautiful anonymity about life in New York. And even at the time I thought, "I'll bet people think here's one young sport that's been on a beautiful party!" And the joke was on them, because I hadn't had a swallow,—excepting only a very little very good beer—not half so much as I had had with Rann every night at New Hartford.

When I got out of the taxi at Helen's, tenderly supported by Mitchell, who had been *such* a darling, not seeming to mind at all, I looked about on the wreckage I had wrought & turned to the astonished cabby & said, "Oh, I'm *so* sorry!" whereat he smiled in a most friendly kind way & said, "Why, you can't help *that*, Miss!" & I got into the house and proceeded to have a chill—I've seen Nazimova do it when recovering from stage-faint, & now I can do it every bit as well. So Mitchell carried me upstairs & laid me on a bed & went out to help the poor cabby, & Helen undressed me & put me to bed—and *berlieve muh* —I slept!

It's a ghastly loathsome tale, isn't it? But doesn't it make a good story? I had to tell it all to someone,—"& it might as well be you," poor suffering family.

* * *

Next Thursday I see Mr. George C. Tyler of the New Amsterdam theatre, who is a very good friend of the Kennedys, & have a promise of an appointment with Winthrop Ames. Also, Laura Hope Crews, the actress, whom I saw in *Peter Ibbetson*, & who lives near Edith in the summer in New H. has spoken of me to the managers, notably the Selwyns, & Mr. Carpenter, who wrote a last season's success, *The Cinderella Man*, & who says he would give me a secondary part in *his* play except that my hair is too near the color of the lead's, has also spoken of me to the Selwyns & will give me a letter to them. Seems as if *somewhere* there ought to be something for me, doesn't it? Meanwhile, my money is holding out very decently, what with all this dining out & having to pay nothing for the apartment. And I am going to make some money pretty soon giving readings. I told you I gave one (of just some of my poems) at Mrs. Hooker's in Greenwich Monday. She is a very wealthy woman & a friend of Miss Haight, who got the job for me. Mrs. Hooker did not pay me for that reading because it was only a preliminary, as she said, to some others she wants me to give, probably this week. She liked it *very* much. My trunk hadn't come & so she dressed me up in something of hers, a gown with a train & hanging about six inches on the floor all around, made out of three rainbow colored scarfs. And, family, I discover that I have nothing to give readings in, I *must* have long dresses, trailing ones. The short ones won't do. If Norma hasn't yet done anything to the greenish chiffon & rose scarf then *that* dress ought to be made up very long & drapy—more like a negligée than a dress, really—very graceful & floaty.—If she's cut that up short I'll have to get me some scarfs & make me one—Edith is arranging with her friend Miss Bennett, of the Bennett school near Vassar, to have me give some readings there. I may get quite a number to do & if so I shall have to arrange for some more dresses. I wish Hunk were right here this meenit to help fix me up. If I get the 500 simoleons for my book *then* she shall come out anyway whether or not she has the slightest prospect of a job—& stay till she gets one.

* * *

I have seen the fac-simile of the title-page of my book—did I tell you?—never mind if I did. It is all—the whole book—going to be printed on that beautiful, very rough, very torn-edgy paper, like my

Modern Love—do you remember.—I said to Mitchell concerning this matter—"Won't it be terribly expensive? to print the whole book on such wonderful paper?" & he said "Oh, well,—you *promised* me, Edna, it was to be a very small book!"—and so it is—lovely & thin—only the very best—& bound in black with gold letters. Mitchell does get out the prettiest books!—It ought to sell well for Christmas presents— shouldn't you think Jess Hosmer would want some? (It's so funny for me to think of the business end of it—but I want it to be read—it's that more than the disgusting money—the dirty necessary money!)

* * *

Mrs. Thompson, a lovely woman who helped put me through col- lege wants me to come & be her secretary for a while—she believes in me as a poet & would even pamper me in order not to interfere with my writing & she would pay me a salary & her place is out in the beautiful country & everything would be lovely & Aunt Calline is exceedingly anxious to have me do it—but I just *don' wanna!*—Edith has been kind to me too, & I can't just stick all her letters to managers in the waste-basket & break all my dates & say "I'm going up to Sparkhill to be private secretary to a beautiful woman of fashion." She *is* lovely to look at, is Mrs. Thompson. Of course, I feel like the underneath of a toad not to do what she wants me to do—but I *can't* make up my mind to address envelopes & make out card catalogues all fall—& then if I had time to write—which I know she intends me to have—nevertheless be always conscious that I may be called on to answer the telephone & make appointments & reject invites. I might have been governess to the Aults, except for a similar feeling about my independence. I shall write to Mrs. Thompson & tell her how kind I think she is, & explain that I have gone too far in this other business to be able to come back now— unless it all comes to nothing.

* * *

Goodbye, & please write,
Much love, Vincent.

P.S.   I have just finished numbering the pages. "Lak a Mercy on me, this is none of I!"—V.

Am sending you a dollar 'cause have feeling you may need it. Am shipping proof of title-page for you to see & send back soon—Must have something to live on till book is pub.—V.

53   TO MRS. CORA B. MILLAY and NORMA MILLAY

At Mrs. Thompson's—
Monday Oct. 27, '17.

Dear Mother & Sister,—

This is my annual letter home. I am a beast;—but od's my life! it is a beast of burden that I am!—Yet after this I shall write you often, whether I have time to say anything or not,—(and see how you like that!) I feel now upon me the onerous (?—is that spelled?) necessity of telling you everything that has happened to me in three weeks.

Le *voici*! (& don't mind the cigarette ashes I spill on the page);

It is eleven o'clock in the morning. I am still in bed. At nine o'clock Anna, my personal maid—(for all I ever see her doing for anyone else) awakened me with my breakfast. She came in with the tray—silver coffee-things, & fruit, & bacon and an egg—(God forgive me if you are even now hungry!—I will send you five no, *one* dollars I wish I could send ten)—and little sticks of toast rolled up in an embroidered napkin, & a vase of hot-house flowers. This she set down on the bed. Then she closed the windows, saw that the register was open, brought me my negligee & helped me into it, propped pillows behind my back, brought two hair-pins from the bureau for me to pin back my hair with, put my cigarette-case, holder, & matches within easy reach—all this without a word from me except Good-morning—then asked me if there were anything I would like, & left me, softly closing the door behind her.— I swear to you I am not inventing a word of it; & that is the way it happens every morning!

You see, when I got out here, after having spent a few days at the Kennerley's upon leaving Edith's & Rann's apartment—(for it *was* theirs—I thought I had told you)—it was in the evening; and before going to bed I said to Mrs. Thompson, "Will you tell me what you want me to do in the morning, so I can get about it early?"—whereat she replied as follows :"There is nothing for you to do, my dear; you may, if you like, help Jean arrange the flowers,—(Jean is her daughter). I asked you to come out here so that you might rest, & have a chance to write.—At what time would you like your breakfast sent up?"— The whole house, I later discovered, has its breakfast in bed, & no one expects nor desires to look upon another human countenance before luncheon time.—Everybody does just as he pleases,—except that Mrs. Thompson does not like the smell of cigarettes, so Dora, her other daughter, who is just about my age, & I confine our smoking to the third floor, which we share, having our separate rooms, but sharing a bath-room. The day before I went to Milbrook, having quite forgotten to send my laundry for three weeks, & consequently having a terrible wash, Dora & I, after the house was asleep, sat up half the night, padding about in our tucked-up nighties & smoking our heads off, I washing, in the bath-tub, she rinsing in the bowl, & hanging up on door-knobs, chair-backs, coat-hangers & suspended lingerie-ribbons & corset-strings, until we had about fifty pieces nicely drying—it was wonderful. She was such a peach—insisted on doing it—she never goes to bed, anyway—The next morning I ironed them—oh, no, I ironed all day—& it was the day after that I went to Milbrook.—Anna, while she was packing my suit-case—(You might just as well let 'em do it, I have found—they don't understand at all if you do the least little thing for yourself, these Annas & Suzannes & Mathildes,—they think you suspect their honesty if you so much as stick in a shoe-tree for yourself)—So I dumped a pile of stuff on the bed & told her it all had to go,—which made her perfectly happy; she brought in a ream of tissue-paper & did a beautiful & scientific job of it,—things were planted in so tight I could scarcely get 'em out—My little rubber-boots, of course, were among the pile; with all gravity she wrapped them up & tucked them in.—She made one remark during the process of packing,—to the effect that I iron exceedingly well—yes, she says, I really do, it is not flattery. When she was finished with the suit-case I sent her in search of a bodkin & set her to running ribbons in the lingerie I was going to wear.—Then I asked her in German if she were not tired,—& she was so pleased!— You see, she is Austrian,—and Mrs. Thompson talks to her in French, which must, I should think, make a dubious hit.

I went into New York early the next morning—ten something! & had the day in town, going up to Milbrook in the late afternoon.

* * *

Then I called up Mrs. Schauffler[3]—have I told you about her?—I think I did—she's the one who has all the soldier sons—(& don't let me forget to tell you the cute thing Bennet did) & I took her down to the St. Andrew for luncheon, because it was near Helen's & it would not take me long to get back for my appointment.—I see a great deal of the Schaufflers,—was there last night.

Harrison [Dowd] was waiting for me when I got back; Helen had gone out & we had the drawing-room to ourselves. He is a darling,— very shy, with a curious bold sort of shyness, the kind that tells you analytically just how shy it is & wherefore.—I made him play for me—

he knows whole opera scores nearly by heart—it is quite remarkable—
he has set some of [*A*] *Shropshire Lad* to notes—very understandingly
—he is quite a wonderful kid—very poor, trying to live on nothing at
all, pauvre petit,—he said to me suddenly, turning from the piano,—
"How does it feel to be a success?"—bless the baby!—But, darlings,
I do think I am going to get on. Miss Bennett has just sent me fifty
dollars for my week at the Bennett School in Milbrook—I gave a reading one evening, & helped coach the plays[4]—& I have three more readings to give, I don't know just when,—but they are reasonably sure.
And there may be quite a bit from my book. All the Bennett School &
about all Vassar is going to give it to each other for Christmas, I understand! There are to be ten volumes in Japanese vellum at ten dollars
each,—& Hilda Strouse has already ordered one!—*Oh*, my Lord!

The theatrical business is not yet booming, which troubles me not
at all,—if I can get readings to give I would quite as soon wait a bit.—
I am going to put fifty dollars in a sort of bank at Aunt Calline's, where
I shall go from here in a few days,—& try to keep it.—If ever you
want it—wire me.—I gave Wump five dollars when I was at Vassar.—
I went over from Milbrook to see her.—Dr. & Mrs. MacCracken, Miss
Haight, Miss Yost, & Miss Thallon—& Kathleen, were sent for by Miss
Bennett's private limousine the night of the production of my plays.—
I wish I could take the time to tell you how beautifully they were done
& how everybody loved them.—Sweet Dr. MacCracken whom, as you
know, I adore,—came up to me afterwards, holding out his hands—we
had not seen each other since he shied my sheep-skin at me in the spring
—& said, "Oh, you're a wonder!"—them was his actual woids.—He
loves me dearly, I know,—& is quite convinced I can do whatever I
like with the world. I spent a very happy evening with him & Mrs.
MacCracken the night before I came back here from college.—Do you
know, he is only thirty-six years old,—the sweet baby?

* * *

Oh, dear, I wish you were here! I have so many things to tell you
that I can't write, because it takes so long, & for other reasons—about
Salomón & me & how we raise the devil, for one thing!—I've seen quite
a bit of him lately—He and I took Mrs. Schauffler to the Poetry Society
last Thursday after having dinner at Henri's,—I was to meet them there
& just before I got to the door—dressed so pretty in my green blouse &
wisteria velvet skirt & wearing a big bunch of tiny yellow roses—a man
& a woman who were passing turned & half-stopped, & I looked at them

& we all stopped—it was Helen Westley of the *Washington Square Players* & that darling Ralph Roeder—such fun to just plain meet them on the street—& last night, while I was sitting in the Thompsons' big Packard outside the Plaza waiting for the rest of the crowd to assemble who should come strolling along, swinging his silver-handled stick, but Mitchell,—Oh, things are so funny!—I feel really at home in New York now,—the man in the *Information Booth* in the Grand Central Station knows me & nods & smiles when I come up for a time-table or something—I never really lose time-tables but I have an unfortunate habit of keeping them in the bottom of my trunk, you know.

Did I tell you about the day I went into the Grand Central Subway Station to take an up-town train & discovered that I had left from my shopping only a couple of pennies & a couple of two-cent stamps?—Well, Hunk, the sweet man behind the wicket, in that one of the seven busiest places on earth, took the two stamps & a penny & smiled at me & gave me a ticket—whaddayou-know!—Oh, I do have such a good time in New York—it's such fun to treat people as if they were human beings just like yourself! They always like it & come right back at you with it.—I picked up a spilled bundle for a woman the other day—her arms were so full she could hardly bend—& carried it for her a couple of blocks—& she blessed me as if I were an angel—kept saying how kind I was—& that it was things like that, happening once or twice in a lifetime, that made life worth living.—I wish you were with me, Hunk —but you will be later!—Are you studying stenography, at all?—or have you followed up that friend of Bertha's?—tell me, dear.—I want to get you out here.

This is the cute thing Bennet Schauffler did. He is the sailor son of the five.—I wrote him a note one day telling him I should be in New York in a few days & to call me up as soon as he got the note: Some days later there was a long-distance call for me. I went & answered & it was Bennet, away off somewhere, I could scarcely hear him.—"Bennet" I said, "Where on earth are you?"—"I'm down at Annapolis," he replied; "You told me to call you up as soon as I got your note, & I just got it." —He had been made an ensign & sent to Annapolis & the letter had just reached him, forwarded from New York.—Wasn't that the kind of thing you have always thought you would do if you were a man?— *Oh*, he's such a dear,—a great big, handsome dark-eyed thing of twenty-four—too cute for words in his sailor-suit & stunning in evening-things

—we went to the theatre one evening before he was called away.—I had an appointment to meet him one day at the McAlpin.—He was late, & there were crowds of people there, & after a while I could see they were imagining to themselves the sort of person I was waiting for —you know how you would—& I was so glad when he did come that he was so darned good-looking!—you know how you would be!—

Tuesday Morning

I think I shall send this Special Delivery, because I have more stamps than I need—(that is somewhat reminiscent of a poem I once wrote, isn't it?) & tomorrow is the last of October, & after that I believe one has to use three-cent stamps.

Did I tell you I heard Kreisler yesterday—I mean Sunday?—There is no one like him—but he doesn't know how to make up a program. I think he has improved since I last heard him. Tonight I'm going to another concert—going all alone & secretly,—it is an adventure. One day a few weeks ago, as I was coming in from Long Island on the train, where I had been to see the big Rosemary Red Cross Pageant— in which Edith played—I sat down beside a young man, because there were only single seats,—I have told you I always pick a man under those circumstances, because if they talk to you it is either interesting & you are glad they did, or rude & you can shut them up,—but women always talk & you can't do a thing about it—well, Aunt Calline was only four seats in front of us—thank chance it was in *front*—but I became suddenly very well acquainted with the young man, a Polish musician named Edward Kreiner who had been in the Pageant Orchestra.—We had a wonderful time,—oh, you can scarcely believe it could happen so—this is how I knew he was wonderful—we in some way got to speaking of books & things & what we liked best,—& I said that I never knew who was my favorite writer, "It is so stupid," I said, "to ask you what poet you like best,—or what flower,"—& he added—oh, the daring of him & me returning from a patriotic Red Cross American Pageant!—softly, but with complete understanding he added, "—or what country."—Well Hunk!—We got on all right after that.—He is extremely well-educated, aged twenty-eight, married & has a little girl named Edda.—And tonight he is to play as one of a string-quartet composed of one of the great disbanded Kneisels & himself & two others,— & I promised to go & hear him & to go behind & speak to him afterwards. —And it is pouring, & I was to go in in the motor—dog-gone!—But I'm going anyhow.

I must bring this to its formal close.—If there's anything I've done which I have kept from you, remind me of it & I'll tell you in my next! —Next time I'll try to answer some questions.

Berlieve muh, Hi ham

Has Hever,

Your obedient & humble servant

Sefe.

[3] Mrs. C. E. Schauffler, a close friend during her early days in New York.
[4] *Two Slatterns and a King, The Princess Marries the Page.*

54   TO NORMA MILLAY

135 East 52nd Street
New York City.
[November 24, 1917]

Dear,—

Am sending you twenty dollars. If you can't make that do all right, telegraph me—or, no, Hunk, I'll just send you twenty-five instead, & let you save all you can of it. It's going to be hard, baby,— we'll probably want money pretty bad pretty often,—but no unworthy girl ever had so many friends as I have, & we shan't starve, because we *can* borrow.—I'm as crazy to see you as if I were going to be married to you—no one is such good pals as we are—I want you to bum around with—to cook breakfasts with.—I am hunting rooms & on the track of a job.—If you can get the movie job, by all means take it. Be sure at the last moment before leaving the house that you have Tim's address in your pocket-book.—You'll probably need two or three things to wear when you get here—I haven't much money but I can help get you looking fit—& what I can't buy I can lend.—Come to Uncle Charlie's for Thanksgiving,—that is right—although if Mrs. Simpson knew you were near she would want you there. Still, one can't do those things. Then by that time—say Saturday after Thanksgiving come in town & stay with me over Sunday,—I'll have some kind of diggings or we can sleep on a park bench—weather's mild now.—We're bound to succeed —can't keep us down—I'm all enthusiasm & good courage about it. So come on out, my dear old sweet Sister,—& we'll open our oysters together.—You've heard that "The world's your oyster", I suppose.—

Love, Sefe.

Having found a small room in the heart of Greenwich Village, Miss Millay and her younger sister, Norma, began the year 1918 earnestly prying open their oysters. In his *Love in Greenwich Village,* Floyd Dell, who himself had migrated from the Middle West a few years before seeking success as a writer, gives a pen-picture of the young poet:

"When the Provincetown Players were starting their venture, and a play of mine was to be given, I remember how, in response to a call for some girl to play the ingenue part, a slender little girl with red-gold hair came to the greenroom over the stable, and read the lines of *Annabelle* in "The Angel Intrudes." She looked her frivolous part to perfection, and read the lines so winningly that she was at once engaged—at a salary of nothing at all. . . . She left her name and address as she was departing, and when she was gone we read the name and were puzzled, for it was 'Edna Millay.' We wondered if she could possibly be Edna St. Vincent Millay, the author of that beautiful and astonishing poem 'Renascence.'

"And indeed she was. Having just been graduated from Vassar, she had come to New York to seek fame not as a poet, but as an actress: for who could expect to make a living at writing poetry? She acted in several plays at our theatre, and put on some of her own, including the tremendously impressive 'Aria da Capo.' But the stage, as it turned out, could offer even more meager rewards than poetry, and so Edna Millay turned back to her first Muse, fortunately for American literature. She lived one icebound, dreadful winter in a tiny room on Waverly Place, a few doors from the house where Poe wrote 'Ligeia.' The house she lived in may one day be known as the place where 'She Is Overheard Singing' and 'Oh, think not I am faithful to a vow!' were written. . . ."

55   TO ISOBEL SIMPSON[5]

139 Waverly Place
New York
[Jan. 30, '18]

Isobel, dear,

Someday I shall write a great poem to you, so great that I shall make you famous in history, or dedicate a book to you, or collect a fortune & die & leave it to you,—or perhaps, more than all of these, I shall write you a letter, thanking you as nearly adequately as ever may be, for service done me or some lovely gift—,some whole garden of lovely gifts—sent me on no occasion whatever & for no reason at all. Meanwhile I shall probably go on as I have done,—thinking of you in the day-time & wondering where my pen is & did I bust the point in removing the stopper from the sulpho-napthol?—& at night dreaming suggestive dreams of telegraph-blanks & telephone-booths & corner letter-drops,—all respectable or accepted means of interborough communication.

The scarf did come,—thank you—so did the roses or orchids or other trifling flora. God forgive me my silence.

Vincent.

⁵ The friendship of the poet and Miss Simpson began at Vassar.

56 TO HARRIET MONROE

139 Waverly Place,
New York City.
March 1st, 1918.

Dear Harriet Monroe,—

Spring is here,—and I could be very happy, except that I am broke. Would you mind paying me *now* instead of on publication for those so stunning verses of mine which you have?⁶ I am become very, very thin, and have taken to smoking Virginia tobacco.

Wistfully yours,
Edna St. Vincent Millay.

P.S.   I am *awfully* broke. Would you mind paying me a lot?

⁶ A group called "Figs from Thistles" which were published in *Poetry* of June, 1918, and were later to form the basis of a much larger group which comprised the whole of the first and only number of the chapbook, *Salvo*, published in November, 1920. The group in *Poetry* consisted of five light verses: "First Fig" (the candle one, surely the most quoted and mis-quoted quatrain in America), "Second Fig," "The Unexplorer," "Thursday," "The Penitent."

57 TO MARGUERITE WILKINSON

25 Charlton St.,
N. Y. C.

My dear Mrs. Wilkinson:

I don't understand Mr. Kennerley's refusal to let you reprint the whole of Renascence in your book. I am writing to him about it, and I feel sure that he will decide to let you have it. As for my own consent, you have that already; I am only too glad that someone wishes to do something with it which will help to circulate it in England. Salomón de la Selva wrote me a short time ago that he had tried all over London to get the book and no one seemed ever to have heard of it there,—which answers another question of yours—no, it has not been published abroad.

I think we shall be able to arrange this all right. I will let you know what I hear from Mr. Kennerley, and if you get word from him please write me.[7]

Sincerely yours,
Edna St. Vincent Millay

[7] Permission seems to have been received from Mr. Kennerley. *New Voices, an Introduction to Contemporary Poetry*, by Marguerite Wilkinson, appeared in the summer of 1919 with "Renascence" printed in full. There was, however, no commentary on the poet's work, though contributors long since forgotten were sometimes dealt with at length.

58　　TO MRS. CHARLOTTE BABCOCK SILLS

25 Charlton Street
October the eleventh
[1918]

Charlie, *NO!*—

Why didn't you tell me when you were here, old darling?—as a matter of fact I had not heard from anybody else, but its a great wonder—why didn't you wait until the sweet little beast was all grown up before you told your friends & room-mates & 'dopted sisters?—

Mother says she's *crazy* to have a grandchild, & you are her only hope, as far as she can see!

I am writing all the time, most; I send you some poems.—Have enough for another book, Charlie,—isn't that stupendous?—Some of my poems will be coming out in *Ainslee's* soon—also in *The Dial*.

I had a sweet letter from Anne [Gardner] this morning.—She is doing something arts & craft-y for the government, going to teach the soldiers how to crochet & cream shrimps, as I understand it, but probably she has explained it to you long ere this, she having been mad at me lo! these many moons—but now so no more. (all 'cause I di'n't write—oh, dear!)

Norma has a job, making air-planes,—she doesn't make quite all of them—just the screws, I guess, on maturer thought.

Have you-all had the "Flu" yet?—We escaped it—but we all had colds & ear-ache or jaundice & string-halt & housemaid's knee, etc.

The best good luck to you, darling, & *please* let me know how you are, whenever you can,—& believe me, I send a whole heartful of love to the three of you!

—Vince—

59   TO MRS. CHARLOTTE BABCOCK SILLS

[Dec. 18, 1918]

Charlie, dear sister,—

Of course I couldn't do the right thing like a Christian girl & write to you the minute I heard your wonderful news—I never have stamps —or else I don't have paper—or else I have just tipped over the ink— *you* remember *me*—Vince, the ne'erdo well of college days—but I'm terribly glad just the same & probably a person that has a new baby doesn't even notice, anyway, who's written & who hasn't.—Well, I'm the one that hasn't, darling,—forgive me, can you?—I really care—& love you very much.—I enclose a letter I wrote you ages ago & the poems I *didn't* enclose then.

Much love to you, dear.

Vincent.

P.S.—The other letter was long before *IT* happened, you see. "The three of you" was a little joke!—V.

60   TO W. ADOLPHE ROBERTS[8]

[West 19th Street
Early Jan., 1919]

Dear Mr. Roberts,—

Here is the sonnet you wanted. I had to make you a special copy because I couldn't find it anywhere among my manuscripts—and my typewriter ribbon is rotten,—literally so, I mean. I'm sorry. If you can't make it out, call me up and I'll declaim it to you over the wire.

I can sing a Japanese song now, for all the world as if I had been born in Nikko, and my eyes are slowly beginning to turn up at the corners—from sitting on a cushion all day. Soon I shall look like a wood-blocked Outomaro, with the colors put on a little bit wrong, that's all. Don't forget you are coming to see me,—the 17th.[9]

E. St. V. M.

[8] Walter Adolphe Roberts, an author then editor of *Ainslee's Magazine*, was one of Miss Millay's earliest admirers. Through the years 1918 to 1921 he bought for this magazine many of her poems and stories. In 1919, in each monthly issue there appeared a Millay lyric or sonnet, and in the May, July, September, October, and December issues also appeared stories and sketches, some of the first to be signed with her pseudonym, Nancy Boyd. Except for the two poems spoken of in letter No. 61, all her published work of this year was in *Ainslee's*.

[9] Playing the Japanese girl, Tama, in Rita Wellman's *The String of the Samisen* at the Provincetown Playhouse.

During this year, besides her preoccupation with her literary work, she was busy acting in various bills staged at the Playhouse in Macdougal Street by the Provincetown Players group: Susan Glaspell, George Cram Cook, Eugene O'Neill, Ida Rauh, Djuna Barnes, Floyd Dell, and others. She also appeared in the spring of 1919 in the first bill of the newly formed Theatre Guild at the Garrick Theatre. Playing the role of Columbine in *Bonds of Interest*, she made a handsome picture in the seventeenth-century Spanish costume.

61　TO HARRIET MONROE

449 West 19th St.
N. Y. C.
March, 1919

Dear Harriet Monroe:

This is to remind you that if you don't find a place for those poems of Edna's very soon, you gotta return 'em to her. There are two of them—Recuerdo; and She Is Overheard Singing; stunning things, both.[10] You are committing a bitter and a presumptuous folly in thus long keeping them from the world. If you don't look out I'll just tell the world all about it, and then where will you be?

Lovingly,
Edna St. Vincent Millay

[10] Both poems were printed in the May, 1919, number of *Poetry*. They were later included in the volume, *A Few Figs from Thistles*.

62 TO W. ADOLPHE ROBERTS[11]

[July 12, 1919]

Dear Walter—

I have made good my escape with two petty thefts,—one, the little picture you gave me of the Shakespearean theatre; the other, the cigarette-case of Salomón de la Selva. As to this latter robbery, if you can give me any satisfactory explanation of its presence in your apartment, that is to say, if Sal simply forgot it and left it there, or if he has given it to Mrs. Roberts, very well, I will return it. But on no other grounds, that is to say, you cannot have it, my friend. Sal gave it to me first, a long time ago, except that I wouldn't take it, because it was new, and I thought he must want it himself;—but if he's around giving it away, la, la! that's a different matter!—The little bijou which was inside I've put beside your ink-well on the writing-table.

I've not finished the ode[12]—though I've done a good bit on it and some other things besides—you bum, the people downstairs do play the piano!—It's as bad as 19th Street for a truly music-loving population.— "I shall hate sweet music my whole life long"!

I have read *Bubu-de-Montparnasse*—why did he call it that?— Seems to me little Berthe was the principal actor in the little commedia del' arte. I don't like your Charles-Louis Philippe so darned much. He's such a self-conscious cuss—loves to think he's a stylist, makes me sick, you bum. Though some of the stuff is quite fine in spite of his panting efforts,—and on the whole it's a very pathetic little tale.

Also I read *Le Journal d'une Femme de Chambre*. [By Octave Mirbeau] There's an amusing book—a lovely book! So much better than *Le Jardin des Supplices*—though he neglected to clear up what gave the lady such a pain in the upper leg and lower intestine during the first part of the story. I couldn't make out for a long time whether she had swallowed a pin or been careless in some other way,—and Mr. Mirbeau forgot to explain. Perhaps he thinks he's going to get the beanless public to pay itself a sequel!

I learned no end of disgusting French expletives that Pete[13] will not let me use—he said: "How would you like to have me going around saying '———' and '———', and '———,' etc.?"—the dashes indicating atrocious English expressions which every nice girl would pretend she had never even *overheard*,—whereupon I swooned, saying, "Oh, damitall, have it your own way, camel!"

This isn't to say that Pete has been living up here with me—I came up here to work—but I *have* permitted him the dubious pleasure of taking me out and feeding me up once in a while.

Thanks a heap for letting me have the place, Walter—I haven't smashed anything, or torn anything, or spilled the ink.—I have merely slightly stolen, as I say.

Edna.

[11] Returning from a vacation, during which he had loaned his apartment to Miss Millay, Mr. Roberts found this letter awaiting him.

[12] The "Ode to Silence," later published in *Second April*.

[13] Rollo Peters, scenic artist, actor, and one of the founders of the Theatre Guild.

63 TO MRS. CORA B. MILLAY

[November, 1919]

Dearest Mother,

We're not going to let you stay away from home much longer, little old Irish devil!—This nonsense has gone just about far enough!—Sweetheart, truly we are as homesick for you as can be.—We haven't been very good girls about writing, I know, but see what I have done, dear, I have actually written the *Aria da Capo* play & finished it,[14] you know the one, Pierrot & Columbine & the shepherds & the spirit of Tragedy.—Well, it's a peach,—one of the best things I've ever done, & the Provincetown Players are going to produce it in the next bill, about three weeks. (You must come home in time to see it, dear, surely.) Norma is going to play Columbine, & Charlie one of the shepherds. Charlie is going to paint the set. They are very keen about it at the theatre.

Norma has just gone up to see *Tom Shea*, of all people,—Gil Patten[15] took her up to see him. She may get a shot at vaudeville!

I am enclosing a clipping of the last bill. They liked both myself & Norma, apparently. Isn't it a stunning clipping. Please take very good care of it & bring it carefully home with you; I took it out of my scrap-book to send you.

Must go down to the theatre now.

Financially, dear, I need to get bucked up a bit before I can send you the money to come home with. I've been giving all my time to this play, you see, & now I have to hurry up & get a story off to Ainslee's. In a couple of weeks I will send it. Is that all right?—If you're homesick, dear, & just want to come home, I think I could borrow the money, perhaps, but I'd rather not unless I have to.

Love to Uncle Albert & Aunt Clem[16] & heaps of love to your own self, dearest.

—Vincent.

[14] Her one-act play, *Aria da Capo*, which she herself directed, and for which the artist, Charles Ellis, designed the costumes and settings, was given its first performance on December 5, 1919, at the Provincetown Playhouse. Her sister Norma played the part of Columbine, and Harrison Dowd was the Pierrot. Charles Ellis and James Light played the two shepherds; while the role of Cothurnus was taken by the artist, Hugh Ferris.

[15] Gilbert Patten, who wrote under the name of Bert L. Standish, was an old friend from Camden, Maine.

[16] Mrs. Millay was visiting her sister, Mrs. Albert W. Parsons, in Newburyport, Mass.

64 TO ARTHUR DAVISON FICKE

[October 1919]

Arthur, you sweet old thing,—

You were quite right about your sonnet sequence having become a weight on my chest. But only because I *cannot* parcel-post parcels! The very thought of it prostrates me for days.—As for the poems themselves,—I have loved them—not all of them, but, oh, so much of them—& I am reluctant to return them to you.—I had read & re-read them many times before you ever even began to think I was keeping them a rather long time.

When are you coming on to New York?—You said "January",— but I am afraid you have changed your mind, oh, cherished friend, & I have so wished to see you.—I am right in believing, am I not, that you will not be in town without at least calling me up?—I am in the telephone directory.

My prose name is Nancy Boyd. I have a story, I think, in the present, in the immediately preceding, & in the about-to-appear, issues of *Ainslee's* magazine.—No, I am not getting rich,—but I could, if I had the slightest iota of business sense.—Some of my stories are good, some are bad,—almost invariably they are beautifully written, after a flippant fashion.

No, I have not read the book of de Gourmont that you mention,—
mebbe I will.—Have you read Barbusse's *L'Enfer?*—a beautiful, terrible
book.

I am sending you a clipping in which you may be interested. If I
can find a copy of the play I will send you that,—in which case: *you
need never return it.*—(in testimony whereof witness my hand & seal,
whatever that may mean.)—with love

Vincent.—

I marked the sonnets all up. I hope you meant me to. The remarks,
footling as you may think, were not appended thoughtlessly to impress
you with my serious interest. I have really *thought* about the doggone
pomes.—V.

65   TO ISOBEL SIMPSON

[Jan. 9, 1920]

Dearest Little Sphinx,—

Edna never wrote her own true love at all to thank her for lovely
Christmas gift—Edna is a *Pig who walks by Himself.*

It is such a lovely little lacquer chest, dear—quite beautiful—it
looks charming on my desk—on my lacquer tray by the tea-things, &
also on the dressing-table, to hold exquisite, exotic, poisonous perfumed
jewelry which I aint got at all!—

This is not half as nice a letter, belovèd child, as I wish to write
you,—but I am so tired these days—working terribly, terribly hard—&
I write you stupidly, dear, do you see, rather than wait & not be
writing you at all.

With how much love you know,

Vincent.

Thursday night

66   TO ALLAN ROSS MACDOUGALL

449 West 19th Street
New York City.
April 7, 1920.

Dear li'l' Alling:

I didn't get my proofs until about two weeks after you sailed, so
all the mean things you've been thinking about me aren't true at all.

Also, I'm having a sort of nervous break-down, which interferes a bit with my keeping my promises and getting my business attended to on time. I hope you have got the manuscript long before this; and that you didn't need it too badly before I could get it to you.

I sent the first page-proofs back to Mitchell Kennerley yesterday; and the book, which I call simply POEMS, ought to be out in two or three weeks. Mr. Kennerley is going to bring out my ARIA DA CAPO in a little book, too, this spring. And I have decided to let him have the FIGS FROM THISTLES,—thus confining my publishing to one publisher, which I have decided is the best thing to do. What do you think, I wonder, of finding my little pome to your own se'f in the Personalities?[17]

Best of luck to you, dear boy. Keep a list of all the folks that sass you, and I'll come over there and beat 'em up.

Lovingly,
Edna.

[17] About to sail for Europe in March of 1920, this correspondent suggested to Miss Millay that he take some of her poems along to try to place them in English magazines. It was also decided that he take *Aria da Capo* in the hope of finding a theatrical producer as well as a publisher. As there was no script available, one was sent on later, together with a group of poems under the heading of *Personalities*. Some of these, later published in different volumes, were one to her sister Kathleen; the Columbine sonnet to her sister Norma; the one to Scudder Middleton, "If he should lie a-dying"; and the one about Rollo Peters, the boy who was "born in Paris, France." The others have never been published: the quatrain to Edith Wynne Matthison, quoted in the note to letter No. 48; a poem to Ralph Roeder; one to Arthur Ficke; and the "little pome" printed here:

Blessing on the Head of A.R.M.
(On the occasion of his going abroad a-minstrelling)

Allin dear, li'l' wisdim toot',
Spirit uv eternil yout',
Bless you up and bless you down,
Bless you into London town;
Bless you round and round about,
Bless you into France and out;
Let your sayin' an' your singin'
Set the bells o' London ringin',
Let your singin' an' your sayin'

Set the beads o' Paris prayin';
Let the sun and rain so sweet
Bless the road before your feet,
Bless the ditch you lay your head in,
Bless the weeds will be your beddin';
Allin dear, li'l' wisdim toot',
Edna luvs you,—thet's the trut'.

67   TO ARTHUR DAVISON FICKE

449 West 19th St.
N. Y. C.   [1920]

Dear Arthur,—

You must by all means send me the sonnets. I am eager to see them. You should always write in the sonnet form,—letters even.

As for your selling your beloved prints,—it is an overwhelming pity. Were I a wealthy dowager, or even a wealthy debutante, I would be your patron,—& you should never do it.—

My second book of poems, *A Stalk of Fennel*,[18] will be published this fall. There are some very good things in it,—one group especially, a group of elegies,[19] I am anxious to have you see;—but I think I will wait & send you the book instead, when it is "released."

* * *

I am earning a creditable living by writing short stories under an assumed name. Just sold one for four hundred dollars. Now I am negotiating with a moving picture company concerning it.—Incredible!

So you have been reading old letters. I must do that, too.—Consider, old friend, that someday our letters may be published in print! At least, it would need nothing more than a premature death or two!

I want to see the sonnets very soon.

As for the prints,—I am heart-broken for you.

Vincent.

---

[18] This book, which the poet had first called "Poems," was published under the title of *Second April*.
[19] "Memorial to D.C."

68 TO WITTER BYNNER

> 449 West 19th St.
> New York City.
> [Spring 1920]

Hal, dear,—

You have by this time, I think, the proof of my two books, but I am not sure that you have a copy of *Aria da Capo*, so that I send you this, clipped from *Reedy's Mirror* of March 18. It is an unconscionable bunch of stuff to be wishing on a man, but it's *your* obsequies,—I hope you were not intoxicated when you wired.

My heart is breaking with envy of you. The day you sail I'm going down to Chinatown and get a job in the *Oriental*, scrubbing chow-mein off teakwood tables with Old Dutch Cleanser. Ah, me.—and if Arthur goes with you there is only one thing left: I shall asphyxiate myself in Pell Street punk-smoke.

Good friend, write me sometime. It would afford me no end of innocent girlish pleasure. And forbear to let the yaller petticoats and little green eyes crowd me entirely from your heart.

And yet perhaps my dearest wish for you would be that you might forget all of us here, and everything, and rest.—Because you told me you are very tired.—

Wherefore, for a year, dear Hal, be faithless as a god to all mortals!

> Edna

69 TO ARTHUR DAVISON FICKE

> [1920]

Arthur, dear,—

Please don't think me negligent or rude. I am both, in effect, of course, but please don't think me either.—My mind is full of pounding steam, like a radiator. And I am sodden with melancholy.

However, I should not be saying such things to you, who have arrived quite honestly & even meritoriously at your wits' end; my own progress, while by no means vicarious, is rather piffling.

I shall send back the sonnets in a day or two. I had to keep them a long time, or my judgment on them would have been worthless. In order to understand them sufficiently to criticize them, I have been obliged to live so closely with them as to make it seem I had written them myself.—The first time I read them I didn't like them. They struck me as wanting beauty, which seemed important to me, & besides that, they oppressed me vaguely. It is true that they haven't, except very sparsely, the actually material beauty of color & sound which we tend to consider as immaterial, a spiritual beauty. But the second time I read them I recognized that they have much beauty, & that it is of a nature truly spiritual. They weighed me down as before, but no longer like a cloud,—like a great stone, rather. It is their intellectual integrity which weighs the most, although the harsh & sombre restraint of your manner of treatment is extremely telling.—I am scribbling the margins of the sonnets with my separate, respective reactions to them. Once in a while, not often, I feel you do something for an easy, & so unworthy, reason; but for the most part I think the sequence is a very fine & beautiful piece of work.

Your little note was heart-wringing.—It saddens me, too, person-ally, of course, to look into your mind through these sonnets, my dear friend,—though, naturally, I forget you quite in reading them, as you would wish me to do.—It is a pity you are so far away. There are so few people in the world to whom one has a word to say, Arthur!

Write me sometimes.—I shall always care for what you are thinking.

—Vincent.

70 TO W. ADOLPHE ROBERTS

North Truro,
Mass.
[Summer 1920]

Dear Walter,—

Heavens! An issue of Ainslee's without a pome by me? I feel that if such a calamity should come to pass it would be necessary to run a blank page in that number, with my name signed to it—don't you? I hasten to send you several.

I can get no information as to people in this vicinity who let rooms, and so forth, but a very good place to put up, they tell me, is the Gifford House in Provincetown. The Atlantic House is also possible; and the Red Inn is the grandest, swellest and most expensive. The only place in Truro is a horrible place one passes on the way to the railway station, to which I would ship blindfolded not even my woist enemy. I'm awfully glad you like "Mr. Dallas".[20] I was sure you would.

Some blurb about me for the August number! And I got the slick little knock, too, about my promising to do the darned thing and "evading the issue." Walter, I swear to Gawd I meant to do it. But you know how it is. Life, and all that sort of thing, does take up one's time so!

As ever,
Edna

[20] "Mr. Dallas Larabee, Sinner," a Nancy Boyd piece which appeared in the October, 1920, issue of the magazine. In the August number first appeared also the two-stanza tribute to her sister Kathleen.

71 TO ALLAN ROSS MACDOUGALL

T'Other Hollow, Old King's Road,
Truro, Mass.
[Summer 1920]

Allan, dear, my sweet friend,

I am distressed and ashamed that I did not answer your letter the moment it came, such a beautiful letter, and so full of good news, and other good things! I was not neglectful of it. It happened that it came at a time so very busy,—what with moving the four of us from New York to Cape Cod for the summer, and storing all our worldly goods in another place—such a terrific amount of work and worry that I am shattered by it for the time being—that although I might have been able to find a minute to write you a note, I had not the time to read the contract carefully and to give you sensible decisions on the other matters as well, so that I have waited until now. And I am afraid, dear li'l' Alling, that you will think me neglectful, or uninterested, or some other thing which I am not at all. I think you are doing wonderful things, and I am as thrilled as a child about it all, thrilled to see my poems in an English paper,[21] and thrilled to get an English checque, and thrilled by the things you tell me in your letters about Aria da Capo and all the rest.

* * *

Alling, li'l' switheart, we have all come to a dear little house on a windy hill in Truro, which is nine miles from Provincetown, to spend at least five months and possibly six, and we wish youse was here. It is a mile and a half only to the outside surfy sea, a lonesome beach where you never see anybody but sandpipers. There are whip-poor-wills which not infrequently keep one awake all night, but nobody cares much, it's such a sweet sound, and there are millions of mosquitoes sometimes, but most of the time, as for instance, right now, none at all. The wind blows a gale about this cottage all the time, and smells so sweet of the little pine woods that is up behind the house, and the hills all around are nothing but over-grown sand-dunes with a bit o' green on, and the sand showing through in bald patches. If you get back to New York before the end of the summer, you must come up and see us. We have your Victrola here, and I do all my work to the tune of the Fifth Symphony.

Do forgive li'l' Edna, darlink, for being so slow in writing; truly I couldn't help it, I have been sore tried these last few weeks! I hope the delay has not mattered too sadly.

I am glad you have seen something of Pete. He is a lovely person. I am sorry about Harrison. Poor baby!

Do write me as soon as you have time, that will be the true forgiveness. And tell me not only what you are doing for me, but what you are doing for yourself, what you are liking and what you are hating, and how things are generally,—which matters will ever be of the extremest interest to

> Your loving friend,
> Edna.

[21] *The Nation,* a literary and political weekly.

72   TO EDMUND WILSON[22]

[Truro, Aug. 3, 1920]

I don't know what to write you, either,—what you would like me to write, or what you would hate me for writing.—I feel that you rather hate me, as it is.—Which is false of you, Bunny.

The note you sent to 4th Street was forwarded to me here. Otherwise I should surely have seen you again before I left. Twice I started to call you up, anyway, but thought that perhaps you would not want me to.

I don't know just when I shall be in New York again. I am going to the Adirondacks a week from today to spend about a fortnight, & after that to Woodstock for a few days, & on my way back from Woodstock I may stop in New York a day or two.—But that won't be for a month, or nearly.

I don't suppose you can get away from the office during the week, & especially now that John [Peale Bishop] is away. But could you get away Thursday or Friday of this week, do you think?—Then you could go with me Sunday or Monday as far as Boston, on my way to Lake Placid.—If you can make it, please do come.

I have thought of you often, Bunny, & wondered if you think of me with bitterness.

Edna.

My sister is amused & disgusted by my lewd portrait of myself.[23] At her suggestion, which I now feel to be a wise one, I beg you not to circulate it. If you have not shown it to Mr. Crowninshield,[24] please don't. If you have, it doesn't matter, but do shatter at once, in that case, any illusion he may have as to publishing it.

E.

[22] Edmund Wilson, writer and critic, then on the staff of *Vanity Fair*.
[23] Miss Millay and her two friends, John Peale Bishop and Edmund Wilson, had amused themselves one evening writing poetic self-portraits. Hers follows.

E. St. V. M.
Hair which she still devoutly trusts is red.
Colorless eyes, employing
A childish wonder
To which they have no statistic
Title.
A large mouth,
Lascivious,
Aceticized by blasphemies.
A long throat,
Which will someday
Be strangled.

Thin arms,
In the summer-time leopard
With freckles.
A small body,
Unexclamatory,
But which,
Were it the fashion to wear no clothes,
Would be as well-dressed
As any.

[24] Frank Crowninshield, editor of *Vanity Fair*.

73 TO ALLAN ROSS MACDOUGALL

77 West 12th Street,
New York City.
September 11th. 1920.

Dearest li'l' Alling,

Long time ago I wrote you a big big lovely letter, but it never got mailed at all, because in it I told you exactly what to do about Mr. Macdermott and Aria da Capo, and immediately afterwards I was advised by Susan Glaspell not to sign his contract, as she was not going to do so and Gene O'Neill had not done so,—so that put me all off again and I didn't know what to say, so I never said nuthin'. And there you is. The letter is all lost now, I suppose, and it was a pearly letter. I am back in New York again, as you see, and have a lovely room at this address which Gawd he knoweth how I am to pay for. You must have had a most beautiful time walking and motoring about France. Wouldn't it be wonderful if we, you and I, could go back there next year, and go to those places you spoke of? Oh, Lud! Have you noticed how Vanity Fair is featuring me of late?[25] They just can't seem to go to print without me. And the New Republic is writing to me in long-hand begging for a crumb of verse. Aint it wondafil? Allan, I do wish Mr. Macdermott would see the light and send me a more reasonable and decent contract, asking for only one year instead of three years monopoly on my play. I want him to play the play, but I hate to sign such a doggone document, so learned and legal and whereasinine, generally. (Isn't that a lovely silly joke? It just occurred to me!) Yon damfool contract, Alling, is almost as long as the play, which don't seem reasonable nor fitting. When you get back to England, if you get in touch with him, can't you put the fear of Moloch in his heart?

Rollo [Peters] is here in town, they tell me, but I just got back, so

I haven't yet seen him, the Lord bless and keep him, the darling. I have met a handsome and perfidious Don Giovanni of an Italian baritone and am learning to speak Italian. He sings the solo baritone parts of the Metropolitan Opera Company in Bohême and Butterfly and Faust and Pagliacci, etc. From the point of view of character and personality, he is just a sweet and friendly fellow, not so deep as a well nor so broad as a church-door, but oh, how he doth sing! He was spending three weeks in Woodstock while I was spending three weeks in Woodstock. And I learned a lot of Italian. His name is Luigi Mario Laurenti, —possibly you have heard him sing. (The important part of the preceding disquisition being that I am actually learning a new language. I can read it, I find, almost as easily as French, which is to say, almost as easily as English. And in a short time I could speak it, were I in Firenze, let us say, or had I an uncle that kept a fruit store.)

Did you know, li'l' wisdim toot', that li'l' aingil had had her hair bobbed? 'Sawful cute. I look, when I am blessed with health, approximately twelve years old. Don't cry, Alling, for Edna's pretty hair. She was so tired of putting the pins in. I'm wondering what Rollo will say. He will think he is sorry, but he won't be, really.

I have enjoyed the Victrola so much! I can whistle almost the whole of the Fifth Symphony, all four movements, and with it I have solaced many a whining hour to sleep. It answers all my questions, the noble, mighty thing, it is "green pastures and still waters" to my soul. Indeed, without music I should wish to die. Even poetry, Sweet Patron Muse forgive me the words, is not what music is. I find that lately more and more my fingers itch for a piano, and I shall not spend another winter without one. Last night I played for about two hours, the first time in a year, I think, and though most everything is gone enough remains to make me realize I could get it back if I had the guts. People are so dam lazy, aren't they? Ten years I have been forgetting all I learned so lovingly about music, and just because I am a boob. All that remains is Bach. I find that I never lose Bach. I don't know why I have always loved him so. Except that he is so pure, so relentless and incorruptible, like a principal of geometry. Did you know I had written a sonnet to Euclid?[26] Does it strike you as funny? It isn't funny, really. Unless, perhaps, I am funny,—which is just possible.

Allan, that letter which went astray and was returned to you, was it returned to Mr. Wisdim Toot? I thought I should expire when I looked at the return address. How funny that that particular letter should be the one which went astray!

Well, li'l' Agint, this is a long letter when one considers that it is single-spaced.

Is you lonsim, Ignatz? Nivva mindt, youse will be home in the swit bye end bye, end will tell Krazy all youse edvintures, end thet will be wondafil![27]

I bet you know some new songs, the wedding ceremonial chants of the Igaroots, or some such darned thing, ol' dear.

Lots of love, li'l' Alling, till I see you again, which will be soon now.

                                                    Edna.

P.S. I know "rue" should be written with a little *r*—but wot the 'ell— you'll get it just the same.

> [25] The July, August, and September numbers of *Vanity Fair* each had a poem by Miss Millay and the editor was preparing for the November, 1920, issue a full page with four lyrics, four sonnets and a photograph.
> [26] Published in *Reedy's Mirror* May 20, 1920.
> [27] Miss Millay and this correspondent were among the many admirers of Herriman's endearing creation, Krazy Kat.

74   TO WITTER BYNNER

                                        77 West 12th Street,
                                        New York City.
                                        October 29, 1920

Dear Hal,—

When are you two boys coming back here? Where you used to be, there is a hole in the world, which I find myself constantly walking around in the day-time, and falling into at night. I miss you like hell.

But aside from that, I'm having a terribly nice time. I met a member of the Metropolitan Opera Company this summer, an Italian tenor, a thin one,—and now I can speak Italian. The absurdities of life are not without their little compensations.

Also, I am becoming very famous. The current Vanity Fair has a whole page of my poems, and a photograph of me that looks about as much like me as it does like Arnold Bennett. And there have been three reviews of something I wrote, in New York newspapers, in the last week alone. I am so incorrigibly ingenuous that these things mean just as much to me as ever. Besides, I just got a prize of a hundred dollars in Poetry, for the Beanstalk. And I'm spending it all on clothes. I've the sweetest new evening gown you ever saw, and shoes with straps across them, and stockings with embroidery up the front. I wish you were here. We'd go on a swell party together.

My book isn't out yet. It's dreadful. I write Mitchell all the time, and he won't answer my letters; and every time I call up the office they tell me he is out, and I know dam well he is so near the telephone all the time that I hear his breathing. I have had no communication from him whatsoever since the last of May. Isn't it frightful? This is one big reason why I wish you were in town. You are both so much bigger than he is, it would be a great comfort to me, somehow, even if you should think it advisable not to beat him up. And besides, Arthur used to be a lawyer, he always told me. I am going to see Knopf about it, I think. Although I don't see what he could do. Maybe there'll be a law-suit, 'n everything. I wish I'd taken it to Knopf in the first place, as you advised me to do, Hal. I know better now. Henceforth I am wax in your hands.

I am reading the poems of Leopardi, in the Italian. Beautiful, some of them; do you know them? Like Heine, sometimes.

* * *

I'm getting awfully tired of James Branch Cabell, sentimental old cock. His books are all alike,—the pent-up drool of a long and timorous adolescence. Page after page after page of "Whereupon he knelt upon the ground and busied himself for a few moments with . . ." and "At night upon retiring it was her curious custom . . ."—page after page of "Droll practices" chucklingly contrived and recorded, to tickle the fishy blood-circulation of the amorously introspective and intro-active. Bah! It bores me to death, lascivious old impotent! I started out to like him, you see, for some passages of real beauty. And I'm so irritated. Such a cheap trick to use to stir up nervous tension among one's readers. Anyone can cut a sentence in two and string along a row of periods at the end of it. And the result is almost automatic. Cheap vaudeville trick.

But there, my dear friends!

A great deal of what Arthur wrote on the margins of the Ode to Silence is perfectly true. But it's too late to change it now. You see, I can't get in touch with Mitchell. And when he gets ready to print it, he'll go ahead and print it, without consulting me at all. However, the most of those poems you advised me to leave out, Hal, were not going into the book anyway. I just happened to send them along. Many of them will be collected, eventually, into the volume I am going to call

Figs from Thistles. I am going to call this book "Second April," if I can get the change made.

I am enclosing some new poems.

Hal, dear, when you and Arthur come back, you must each bring me a whatever is the Chinese equivalent for kimono. Not a nice one, just a sort of cheese-cloth one, you know. But you mustn't forget to. And you mustn't neglect it till you get back here, and then try to fool me with some batiked dish-towelling from Vantine's. I love kimonos. I just adore them. I would like to wear them all the time. I've made me two, myself,—and really made them right, too, studying the Japanese ones very carefully. Now please, old Hal and old Arthur. This is the very first thing I ever asked of either of you. And don't go scorning my childish request just because I don't happen to be your idiot cousin or your divorced wife or somebody else with a rightful claim.

Thank you, Hal, for the little snap of Arthur. But isn't there one of you, too? Are you trying to lead me on?

* * *

The Poetry Society of America is raising its dues. I dare say many people are indignant. But as for me, I take it in a very equable frame of mind. Big or little, it's all the same to me, since I don't pay them anyway.

The people of this country are just electing a new Sacred Goat.

I have a lovely place to live in now, a big room and everything, just not quite a block from Fifth Avenue. I have my own furniture and stuff, and it is beautiful, almost as Chinese as China. This is my way of following you out there. Oh, if you were only here at this moment, how nice it would be! Wouldn't it?

Love to you both, my dears.

Vincent.

It is a very silly letter I have written, I see now, reading it over. It is not at all what I want to say to you, my cherished friends. But you will not be angry with me?—Perhaps you would as soon have me silly as sad—and I am sad so much of the time, no matter what sort of letter I write.

Of the poems you sent me, Hal, I like particularly the *Mountain in China* (though not the close of it so much) and *The Dragon-Fly*. *The Dragon-Fly* is beautiful. And it is very impressive. It gets into one. —Tell Arthur I am particularly keen about the *Marcia* sonnet—the final couplet is exquisite.

Goodnight—and forgive my chattering.

Edna.

75   TO ARTHUR DAVISON FICKE

> 77 West 12th Street
> New York City.
> October 29, 1920.

Arthur,—

I love you, too, my dear, and shall always, just as I did the first moment I saw you. You are a part of Loveliness to me.—Sometimes at night, when you were in France, I would read over the sonnets you had sent me—just as you have been doing now with mine—& long for you in an anguish of sweet memory, & send all my spirit out to you in passion.—It seemed incredible you were not in the room with me, you were so much nearer than anything else, nearer than the dress I was wearing.—It doesn't matter at all that we never see each other, & that we write so seldom. We shall never escape from each other.

It is very dear to me to know that you love me, Arthur,—just as I love you, quietly, quietly, yet with all your strength, & with a strength greater than your own that drives you towards me like a wind. It is a thing that exists, simply, like a sapphire, like anything roundly beautiful; there is nothing to be done about it,—& nothing one would wish to do. —There are moments, of course, when I am with you, that it is different. One's body, too, is so lonely. And then, too, it is as if I knew of a swamp of violets, & wanted to take you there, & share them with you, because you are my friend.—But all that is the least of it, my dear.—And you must never think that I don't understand.—

You will never grow old to me, or die, or be lost in any way.

> —Vincent.

76   TO MRS. CORA B. MILLAY

> [77 West 12th Street
> New York City.]
> Monday night, Dec. 20,
> 1920

Dearest, beloved Mother,—

The reason why I have not written you for so long is because I have been sick. I am all right again now, but I have been quite sick, almost ever since I moved in here,—bronchitis for a while, & another small nervous breakdown after that. I didn't want you to know, for fear you would worry.—But now that I am all right again I have decided that the thing for me to do is to have a change,—change of everything,—so I am going to travel.

The editor of Vanity Fair has a scheme which calls for my doing two articles a month for the Magazine, one under my own name & one under Nancy Boyd. So I am going to Europe, technically as "foreign correspondent" for Vanity Fair, although the articles need not necessarily be foreign articles,—probably most of them will be. This is the thing I have always wanted to do, you know how much, dearest,—& my work, more than anything else, my poetry, I mean, needs fresh grass to feed on. I am becoming sterile here; I have known it would be, & I see it approaching if I stay here.—Also, New York life is getting too congested for me,—too many people; I get no time to work. Over there I shall be entirely alone, except for a few people to whom Mr. Crowninshield & some of my friends here will give me letters. And I need to be alone for a while. I shall come back a fine strong woman.

Now, darling, it is needless to say that I cannot possibly go without seeing you. And I am sailing on the 4th of January, two weeks from tomorrow. I have made all arrangements about my passport, etc. & have bought my passage, & have my stateroom, on the "Rochambeau." Some people I know are going over on this boat, which is why I chose it; for I am so unacquainted with such matters that it will be much better if I know somebody to instruct me a little. But after I get to Paris I shall be alone. And I shall be perfectly happy, & perfectly safe, because I speak French, & because I am a very capable & sensible woman, when left to myself. You know that, dear.—

I send you for your very own—not to give away, because it is just an extra one—one of the pictures I had to have taken to go on my passport. In some ways I think it one of the most remarkable photographs I have ever seen,—no retouching, no shadows, no flattery—just stark me. I hope you will like it, mother.

Sweetheart, could you come as far as Aunt Georgie's, or perhaps even Uncle Charlie's, in about a week, do you think?—Then I will come to see you. As things are here now, with Kay just married & everything, its all a mess. I shall be giving up my room & bunking in with Norma, & it will be the most sensible thing, since you are planning to visit Aunt Georgie & Aunt Jennie, if I can come to see you there, for just a day or so.—You see I have made up my mind so suddenly to take Mr. Crowninshield's offer, & go, that I have very little time.

Can you write me at once, Mother, & suggest what we shall do? —I couldn't come so far as Aunt Clem's, because it's such an expense, besides the time it takes.

Mother, dear, this is the whole thing, just as I've told it. It has nothing to do with any love affair, past or present. What the future may bring I don't know, maybe something more satisfactory than I've had so far. But that is not even on the horizon. I'm going as a free woman, a business woman, & because I want to travel.

Write me, dear. And will you forgive me for not writing before? I have been sick, you see.

Your devoted daughter,
Vincent.

VI

Steepletop

1926 – 1930

A Bord le "Rochambeau"
le 13 Janvier, 1921

Dearest Mother,—

It is about eight-thirty of Thursday, my ninth day on the ocean, & we are almost into Havre. By noon we will be off the boat & on the train to Paris. We are now in the English Channel, which the French call "La Manche", which means *sleeve*. I was awake long before dawn this morning—at four-thirty, & couldn't get to sleep for excitement. I kept running out & looking through the port-hole to see if the sky was getting grey, & at six o'clock I dressed & went up on deck, the slippery, wet, deserted deck, with all the deck-chairs in rows with their knees up under their chins,—to see the sun over France. And the darned sun didn't rise at all, because it was raining.—But I didn't care. It began to get lighter & lighter. At first all I could see was the revolving flash of a light-house, then presently I could see the rock that it was on—*Land*! And after a while a big island loomed up, with another light on it & lots of great queer-shaped rocks, just a deeper grey under the grey sky—beautiful.—The cabin steward came out just then, & saw me huddled in my great white Hudson Bay blanket that Bill sent me from Canada & asked if I wasn't cold & I said I didn't care if I was, & he told me about the places that we passed, all islands at first.—And I asked him a lot of questions & he explained so nicely—(all in French, of course—the servants speak almost no English, the whole boat is French & almost all the passengers. I've spoken scarcely a word of English since I came aboard—once in a while some Yankee cuss-word to Laurence[1] when they would tell us we wouldn't get in till Friday or something; but Laurence speaks French better than he does English,—so I almost think in French now)—but to resume: all at once the steward pointed to a shadowy grey bluff off the starboard bow & said, "Voilà, Mademoiselle, la terre de France!" And I just stared at it for a long time, not even thinking, just staring, & I didn't care whether it rained or what the hell it did.—(Besides, I have a beautiful new dark-blue silk umbrella, a departure present.)—We are now passing the islands of Jersey & Guernsey. Last night on deck Laurence pointed to some lights & said, "Those are light-houses on the coast of Cornwall; we are now just between Cornwall & Brittany." And I thought I should die, thinking of Tristan and Isolde. We had just passed Ireland, but too far north to see. I thought of how Tristan brought Isolde from Ireland to Cornwall in a great ship to be the bride of King Mark, & how they two fell in love & King Mark came home early from the hunt & found them together, & how Tristan crossed the channel—crossing just where I was at that moment, maybe—to Brittany, & lay all day sick & wounded, looking towards Cornwall, looking for a sail which should bring Isolde. —Oh, mother, I've been so thrilled these last two days!—It was very monotonous for a while, the ocean—not a thing in sight for eight days, except one day a steamer on the horizon. I wasn't sick at all, though a great many people have been, & Laurence who has crossed the ocean about eleven times was sick one day. I didn't take any of those darned remedies that I had bought at people's suggestion, either. I had some sea-sick remedy pills to be taken as soon as the boat started, & I couldn't make up my mind to take them. Whatever it might be—& I was looking forward to something awful, because I had been sick in my stomach for a week from actual excitement—I wanted the whole of it. —I wanted every bit of the experience, & no dope. (Like you, when I was going to be born.)—But it was not for nothing this chile was brought up on the water-front! I have been the marvel even of the ship's doctor, who says I am an extraordinarily good sailor.—Dearest, I must go up on deck now & see the boats & the harbor & things as we pass them. (I am sitting in my berth, writing this.)—Love to Aunt Clem & Uncle Albert & Randolph & Emery, & oh, so much to yourself!

> Your devoted daughter,
> Vincent.

Will write soon again, when I get a permanent address.

[1] Laurence Vail, a writer.

78   TO NORMA MILLAY

> [Paris]
> Jan. 20, 1921.

Dearest Normie,—

* * *

—How are you, child?—Write & tell sister all about it.— How's the play going, & are you getting any returns from your speculation?— Do tell me.—Me, I'm finishing up now a couple of articles for *Vanity*

Fair. I went to see the French editor yesterday, & he's perfectly adorable. We had such a nice talk.—And I'm going to have luncheon with him tomorrow. (Don't die,—as Alice Tufts would say.)

I do an awful lot of walking here, which is, of course, very good for me. I go out nearly every afternoon & walk miles & miles. It is so fascinating, when I once get started, that I can't stop. Usually, as I wrote Wumps, I walk until I can't lift a foot, & then fall into a taxi & come back to the hotel.—But last night I found my way back all by myself. —You know, it's amazing how well I know the city from studying the map the way I did. I feel perfectly at home everywhere.

Give my love to Charlie, & remember me to little [Cleon] Throckmorton.

> So much love to you, dear.
> Your big sister,
> Vincent.

79   TO EDMUND WILSON

> Hôtel des Saints Pères
> 65, rue des Saints Pères
> Paris.
> [January 20, 1921.]

Dear Bunny,—

I can never thank you enough for the beautiful Verlaine.—The *Manon* hurt me a little, of course, but it doesn't matter.—Such a lovely book,—what does it matter?—I am not really like that girl,—but I can understand that it seems so to you.—Poor Bunny—it will never be right between us, will it, my dear?—I have wronged you greatly. I know that. Whatever my motives may have been, as far as you are concerned it is all a great wrong.—However, I shall try to do better in the future,—(as the wits have it).

I wrote a little poem today, of which I send you a copy.[2] It is not for publication, because I may want to change it, when I look it over later.—It is of no importance, of course, anyway.

It is beautiful here even now. What will the spring be?—

> —Edna.

[2] "Sheep." Later titled "Nuit Blanche," published in *Vanity Fair*, November, 1922, and later in *The Harp-Weaver and Other Poems*.

80   TO NORMA MILLAY

[Paris, March 18, 1921]

Darling,

Do you remember how we worked finishing up *The Seventh Stair*?[3]—I am slaving now to typewrite & ship off my Vassar play, *Snow White & Rose Red*,[4] which I have just finished, and as I was putting in the carbon sheets, I remembered how you would have them all ready for me to stick into the machine the minute I took the other out, & I wished you were with me now, old girl.—How we worked!—And what a brick mother was!—I am sending Kay a copy of it, because we worked out the idea together. And she will let you read it.—But don't let any of the *Provincetown Players* get hold of it to read. I mean this most seriously. They would hate it, & make fun of it, & old Djuna Barnes would rag you about it, hoping it would get to me.—Of course, you kids will understand about it.—It's written in the first place for Vassar College, in the second place it's written to be played out of doors, as spectacularly as possible, & in a foreign country & medieval times because in that way you can use more brilliant costumes, in the third place I haven't had time to work it over at all, in the fourth place it's full of anachronisms which I haven't had time to look up & put right, & in the fifth place it's a frank shameless imitation of the Elizabethan dramas, in style, conversation & everything, & of course does not show up so darn well in comparison.—You'll think from all this that it's a bum play. You're wrong.—I expect the darned thing to make a great hit.—There is a lot of fine stuff in it, too,—but some pretty ragged spots. Don't let it get out of your hands. And while you have it in your hands, don't let anybody read it over your shoulder.—Chas. [Ellis] can read it if he does it in your room. Don't let him take it away.

* * *

Love,
Bincent.

[3] A novelette, the third Nancy Boyd piece to be published in *Ainslee's* magazine in 1919.
[4] Later titled *The Lamp and the Bell*.

81   TO NORMA MILLAY

Hôtel de L'Intendance
50, rue de L'Université
Paris.
[May 25, 1921]

Dearest Darling Baby Sister 'Lovèd Hunk,—

* * *

—I am working like the devil, which is why I don't write more letters—& I suppose you are, too—which is why you don't write more letters,—but it does seem a long long time, little sweet sing, since us heard from each other!—I have your beautiful photograph right up in front of me on my work table, & as I do a lot of work, I just naturally has to look at it, whether I want to or not, but the joke is on it, because I allus wants to!

Sweetheart, this is a silly letter for one grown-up sister to write another grown-up sister, but maybe it will express as well as a sensible letter how much I love you, & how often I miss you.

Won't you write old Sefe, sometime, Normie, & tell her how you're getting on & all about everything?—Maybe you think I don't wonder about you, dear, & worry, & want to know just how you're making out!

I heard a Negro orchestra & quartette the other night, supposed to be excellent, & it made me homesick for you & Wump & our baby that does so need a new pair of shoes[5]—we three can sing so much better harmony & agony than those four!—We'll do it again sometime, darling, with Mother along, too, to put in once in a while a beautiful rich deep absolutely certain & right bass note!

Write sister, 'lovèd!

Eddyner.

[5] "My baby needs a new pair of shoes—" one of the songs the sisters sang.

Hôtel de l'Intendance
50, rue de l'Université,
Paris. [June 15, 1921]

Dearly Beloved:

* * *

I have been doing a lot of work lately, and I have sent word to Mr. Crowninshield to send a cheque for a hundred dollars to Kathleen; it is for you, dear, but I didn't know your new address, and besides you might have trouble in cashing a cheque in a new place, and such a little place. I have not yet got the work done for the Metropolitan but I have written them about it, so they understand.

Darling, I am so excited about the Chore-Boy,[6] and all the rest of the wonderful news! Whether or not the Pictorial Review woman can do with it what she wants to do, never mind, the thing is started, and oh, my sweetheart, I am happy, happy, happy! And I am tickled to death that you've had your old cute head bobbed. I know it is adorable. You have such pretty, wavy hair, and so much of it. It must look very thick now. And you were determined you would do it, you sly old thing. I am all the time talking about you, and bragging, to one person or another. I am like the Ancient Mariner, who had a tale in his heart he must unfold to all. I am always button-holing somebody and saying, "Someday you must meet my mother." And then I am off. And nothing stops me till the waiters close up the café. I do love you so much, my mother.

* * *

It is nearly six months now since I saw you. A long time. Mother, do you know, almost all people love their mothers, but I have never met anybody in my life, I think, who loved his mother as much as I love you. I don't believe there ever was anybody who did, quite so much, and quite in so many wonderful ways. I was telling somebody yesterday that the reason I am a poet is entirely because you wanted me to be and intended I should be, even from the very first. You brought me up in the tradition of poetry, and everything I did you encouraged. I can not remember once in my life when you were not interested in what I was working on, or even suggested that I should put it aside for something else. Some parents of children that are "different" have so much to reproach themselves with. But not you, Great Spirit.

I hope you will write me as soon as you get this. If you only knew what it means to me to get letters from any of you three over there. Because no matter how interesting it all is, and how beautiful, and how happy I am, and how much work I get done, I am nevertheless away from home,—home being somewhere near where you are, mother dear.

If I didn't keep calling you mother, anybody reading this would think I was writing to my sweetheart. And he would be quite right.

It's a shame Norma isn't being sent to London, poor little girl. She would love so to get over here, and I know she would like to see me, and London is only seven hours from Paris! Not that I wouldn't like to see her, too, but I was thinking of her end of it.

Allan Macdougall is doing very well over here. He is editing a column rather on the style of F.P.A.'s in the Paris edition of the Chicago Tribune, and people are very enthusiastic about it. I just got a letter from Harrison Dowd, who also is doing very well, playing the piano in a jazz orchestra, which he does inimitably well, in Berlin.

Dearest, it was dreadful that you didn't hear a word from me on your birthday. But I didn't notice it was so near the 10th till too late to get a letter to you, and I couldn't cable you, because I had no idea of your address. Sweetheart, if you expected a cable, and were disappointed, I shall just die. Answer me this, if you were all alone on your birthday, and were lonely. Please tell me about it.

I am sending you a little Paris flower, which is just an old-fashioned pink, isn't it? It smells very sweet now, but will have no odor, I am afraid, by the time it gets to you. It is one of a handful which I bought today of a little tiny girl outside the Café des Deux Magots on the Boulevard St. Germain. I paid ten sous for the bunch, which is to say in ordinary times about two cents, but now less than a cent. These little bits of girls are always going around the cafés selling little bunches of flowers from baskets which they carry on their arms. They always say when asked the price, "Dix sous," and then one always gives them a whole franc, and they smile shyly with self-controlled pleasure.

Well, dear, this is enough for now. I will write again soon. And you write me. And believe me to be as ever, honored parent, your most obedient humble servant and devoted daughter,

Vincent.

---

6 Story by Cora B. Millay.

83 TO MRS. CORA B. MILLAY

> Hôtel de l'Intendance
> 50, rue de l'Université
> Paris. [July 23, 1921]

Dearest Mother,—

You do write the sweetest and the most wonderful letters! They are so lovely that very often I read parts of them aloud to people, just as literature. It was delicious what you told me about the turtle,—you are so gentle and kind to everything, dear—and all the things you write about birds and animals I love. Thanks for the little flower. I never saw one like it, either.

I am going to the sea-shore in about five days now, and I am crazy with excitement. I am going with about five other people, painters and writers, whom I met here. I know how much you long for it, too, dear, and wish you were here, or I were there, so that we could be at the sea-shore. Only I must not come back to America until I have been to more of the places which are so near to France and so far from America. Next fall I shall go to Italy and to Egypt, I think, very possibly to Germany, and back to England, where I spent only a week before.

And, sweetheart, how would you like, in place of the birthday present I did not send you for the 10th of June, sometime in the late fall or winter, depending on how much money I can make between now and then, to come over here, and play around with your eldest daughter a while in Europe? We could go to Italy and Switzerland, and to England and Scotland, and, if there are not too many riots and street fights there at the time,—mavourneen, we would go to Ireland!

It would take a lot of money, but Otto's having sold Sentimental Solon[7] gives me a lot of hope. I will write a lot more stories, and let him place them, and then, my Best Beloved, you and I will just have ourselves a little honey-moon.

> With all the love of my heart,
> Vincent.

P.S.—Do you suppose, when you & I are dead, dear, they will publish the *Love Letters of Edna St. Vincent Millay & her Mother?*

P.P.S. I am sending you a poem I just wrote.—Show it to the girls, too, darling. —V.

---

[7] A Nancy Boyd story, sold by the literary agent, Otto Liveright, to *The Metropolitan Magazine* and printed in the

October, 1921, issue. This work and the novelette *The Seventh Stair*, previously mentioned, were the result of a collaboration of Edna St. Vincent Millay and her sister Norma.

84 TO NORMA MILLAY

Paris
July 24, 1921.

Dear Hunk,—

Whatever you ever have done or ever will do to me, I will forgive, for the sake of that letter about the party given on my birthday, which you and Chas concocted together. I never in my life read anything so funny. I nearly had convulsions over it. I howled and yelled over it. I made such a noise that I fully expected to get put out of the hotel immediately after luncheon. It cleared all my mental atmosphere in such a way that there can not possibly appear a cloud on my horizon for a long, long time. Darling, it was too lovely. That long list of names, and the screaming juxtaposition of them, the description of the Rev. Mr. Dell and the Chinese Nightingale—these nearly killed me, also the insertion of the name of Mrs. S——!

Yes, once I was a child, and I played a mean trick on you, dear. I stuffed your mouth full of geranium leaves and sought earnestly to suffocate you. I am glad I did not succeed. Because you are a very amusing young woman, and deserve to live.

Otto will pay you half the proceeds of *Sentimental Solon*, sister. I hear that you are living in great luxury. Nevertheless, it may come in handy, for Christmas presents to your butler's wife and children.

I saw Peggy Johns Cowley. She says that you are looking perfectly beautiful, and like a million dollars plus war-tax, or words to that effect. As a matter of fact, I believe that is an expression I got from Starkie. Bunny Wilson is at a hotel just around the corner from me. I haven't seen Djuna, but have had a note from her, and am going to look her up. Have you seen my Greek Dance article, in the last Vanity Fair? I think it very funny.

Oh, honey, your little friend John Coggeshall has been around to see me a couple of times, and I went on a jazz-party one night with him and Starkie and Pete Chambers. It was terribly funny. Starkie told me afterwards that Pete had said to him when they were getting up the party—which was to include several other kids and some kid girls, besides—"Can Vincent dance?" And Starkie had replied, "Oh, no, I don't believe so. Probably not a bit. You couldn't expect her to. She's probably awful. And Pete, you take her on, because you lead better than I do. I don't dare try her out." So that night, when I appeared in my most beautiful evening gown,—a Poiret gown, by the way, which I bought at a place where they sell the gowns which have been worn by the models—we all motored up to the Acacias, and the jazz-band jazzed,—and Pete "took me on." Really, darling, it was a scream. Of course, he didn't say a word, but his face was actually stupid with astonishment. Naturally, I didn't know about the conversation which had taken place before, but I had a hunch that they probably thought I couldn't dance very well, and I outdid myself. I never danced more beautifully. It was too comical for anything. Pete dances extremely well, and it was a lot of fun. Of course, after that, everybody "took me on." Pete had tipped them off, as Starkie told me later, to the fact that "Vince is wonderful!" This is a silly little story, but I think it will amuse you. 'Member how you and me used ter dance together?

Johnnie Coggeshall is a dear kid, isn't he? He talks about you, and how he and his father and sister are all crazy about you. He behaves a little bit silly about me, too, as you knew he would, of course, but I hold him sternly in check. For heaven's sake don't let him know I said this, it would so terribly wound that adolescent pride, which is such a delicate thing to deal with. He belongs to the most beautiful type of characteristically American youth, I think.

If you see Henrik van Loon, give him my love. The drawing was very amusing. I adore it. How one does enjoy something sublimely silly, like that,—that enormous bunch of flowers, and the Arc de Triomphe in the distance, to show that it is Paris!

I am so happy about the music, my lovely Normie, my childhood's friend!

Love-love-love-From-Bincent.

85   TO MRS. CORA B. MILLAY

Chalet du Nord, Pourville,
Dieppe. September 5, 1921.

Dearest Mother,—

It seems ages since I have heard from you, and I suppose it seems ages since I have written. Everybody has left this place several days ago, except for one other girl and myself who are staying on for a few weeks more, because the weather is still beautiful and it seems such a pity to go back to the city. (poem!) Mother, the flowers here are almost all entirely different from those at home. Butter-and-eggs is about the only one I have seen about that I recognize, that and yarrow and what they call wild parsley, which is about the same as what we call Queen Anne's lace. Everywhere you see a wheat field you see thousands of red poppies, single poppies, and have seen them growing, too, in a field, an immense field, of yellow mustard, a wonderful sight. Isn't there something about that combination in Chesterton's Napoleon of Notting Hill?—the colors of Nicaragua, or something to that effect. And all along in front of the Tuilleries in Paris are long beds of culti-vated daisies, such as both the English and the French call marguerites, but which are almost precisely the same as your own common field daisy, which does not grow wild here at all. It is so amusing to see poppies, which we plant and thin out and weed with such diligence in little beds, growing wild all through the country; and daisies, which our farmers plough up and try their best to kill, so carefully tended and watered and fostered, along a crowded street in the very heart of Paris. One of the men who were here told me the names of fifty-four wild flowers which I did not know at all, except, in the case of some, like vetches and broom, which I had come upon in poems. Such names as milk-wort, willow-herb, campion, hound's-tongue, flea-bane, ladies'-bed-straw, sweet-agrimony, rest-harrow, hard-head, bird's-foot-tre-foil, dead-nettle, silver-weed, and scabius. The *a* in scabius is long, as in lady. Rest-harrow gets its name from the fact that it is found for the most part around the edge of the ploughed land, where they *rest* their *harrows*. I thought at once of you when he told me that, knowing you would enjoy it. Some of the peasants still make brooms for sweeping from the long fronts of the yellow broom bush. I don't know whether the broom was named for the bush or the bush for the broom.

A few days ago I went down to Rouen, the old town where Joan of Arc was imprisoned and later burned at the stake. The tower is still there where she was kept. A lot of streets and shops and things are named after her. And there is a sort of shrine to her in the great cathedral,—she is a saint now. Isn't life funny? The cathedral is extraor-dinarily beautiful, in parts. The old part of the front is too lovely for words. And there are some magnificent tall stained glass windows, the colors mostly blue and red and purple, which date back to the thirteenth century, and are extremely beautiful. The stained glass was all removed from the cathedral and hidden away during the recent war, and has just been put back into the window-frames. One of the principal streets in Rouen is called "la rue de la grosse Horloge," the street of the Big Clock,—forgive me for translating it, darling, I didn't realize how plain it must be to you. Half way along this street one has to pass beneath a low arch on which, all gold and scarlet and black, is the big clock itself, a very handsome old thing, which still tells time. On the clock and under the arch and in fact all over the town one sees a device of a little white lamb stuck about, apparently the device of the arms of Rouen. (The name Rouen is pronounced very much like this: Roo-on, —except the final *n* is merely suggested; it is as if you started to say *on* and stopped yourself before you said the *n*.)

I expect to go down to Rome when I leave here, about the first of October, probably. John Carter, a youth whom I met in Paris, who was Steve Benét's room-mate at Yale, and is now connected in some way with the American Embassy in Rome, has written to me suggesting that I come down. He says Richard[8] and Mrs. Child are very anxious to see me, and that this is undoubtedly the auspicious moment for me to come. I ought to have a beautiful time in Italy with the Childs and this boy who knows the place very well and is all excited about giving me a wonderful time. So I guess I'll go. I intended to go a long time ago, but now I'm glad I didn't. When I come back I shall go to London for part of the winter, maybe the whole winter, and then I shall probably come home. Though now that I have found how easy it is to get about the world I shall probably never stay in one place long.

Darling, you apparently didn't get a letter which I wrote you a long time ago. Because if you had got it you surely would have replied to it. In it I asked you how you would like to come over here, provided I could get the money together, late this fall or next spring— probably next spring, as my finances look now—and play around Europe with Bincent a little, maybe go to Ireland, for one thing, if they've stopped shooting by that time, and then you and me go home together to the States, and get a little cottage some where for the summer, and you and me and Wumps and Hunks and Howid[9] all live together in a little crooked house for a little crooked while. I wrote you such a booful letter about this, mothie, you would have loved it. I sent it off by the same post in which I sent a letter to Otto Liveright which he apparently never received, ages ago. But anyhow, here is the proposition, dear. Of course I'll have to stop gadding around and begin to save centimes. But if I do that there's no reason why it shouldn't come true. And you may go right ahead and tell anybody you like that you're coming over here and join me later and look over the place a bit before I go back. See?

I hope you are well, sweetheart. I worry about you a little when you don't write. Though of course you have Wumps and Normie dropping in rather often, if anything were really the matter. I miss you tremendously, too. You know that. And I miss the kids. But when we get together again it will be all the more wonderful. I've been gone over eight months now. Think over our lovely plan, darling. And tell anybody you like.

Your adoring daughter,
Vincent.

[8] Richard Washburn Child, writer and friend of Miss Millay, was at that period American Ambassador to Italy.
[9] Howard Irving Young, playwright, husband of Kathleen Millay.

86 TO NORMA MILLAY

> [Les Algues,
> Pourville, Dieppe.
> France.
> September 8, 1921]

Listen, Hunk, I know the greatest joke on the French people,—they don't eat blackberries; they think they are poison. They eat every dam thing you can imagine and many dam things you can't imagine, frogs, mussels, periwinkles, snails, every kind of grass that grows, etc. but they are convinced that blackberries are poison, and they never touch them. The blackberries, however, having not yet been informed that they are considered poisonous and undesirable, still grow in great plenty about these parts, the roads are lined with them, and there are great thickets of them on the bluffs over the sea, just getting ripe now. And since nearly all the English and Americans have gone back to town in the last few days, as far as I can see all the blackberries in northern France are living and having their being and ripening in the sun for my personal delectation. Isn't that amusing?

And speaking of blackberries, you might write me a letter once in a while, I should think. How about it? What if your fountain-pen is lost or busted or stolen or something else as good as dead, and you can never find a pencil with a point, and mother has the Fox, and the only scrap of paper you can find is the back of a bill from L. P. Hollander or the margin of an invitation to tea from Davy Belasco, and you can never remember how much the postage is to France, anyhow, and besides you never have a stamp, anyhow, and there's never any place to rest your elbow whilst you write except in a pot of massage cream, and the only envelope you can possibly find in the whole goddam flat, besides those that are sketched over with obelisks and church-steeples and muscular undressed hussies, is the one that you have already addressed to Riegie and then decided not to write him after all,—nevertheless how about it? Rise on your legs, you poor piece of imitation Camembert, and write your loving sister a little note. See?

   And that's that.

As ever, your childhood's friend,
Sefe.

87   TO MRS. CORA B. MILLAY

37 Broadwater Avenue,
Letchworth, Hertfordshire,
England
[Sept. 14, 1921]

Dearest Mother,

   Here I am in a little English town, visiting the daughter of an English rector in her home. It is not a rectory, because the rector is dead now, and they are living in a house; but it is much more like a rectory than the houses in which I usually visit, you may be sure. We have just had tea. I was out for a walk with Judy, my friend, who was with me at Pourville, and her sister, and suddenly they put their noses to the wind and began streaking it for home,—tea-time! The tea was poured when we got to the table, and there was milk in it, for everybody, without a question asked. I drank it, of course, and do you know, rather liked it. I remember you used to take it that way, mother, when I was a little child, very hot, and with milk in it, and I used to come to you with a hard, round, "common" cracker, and beg to soak it in your cup, after which I would butter it and eat it. Oh, the butter melted so quickly, and slid all around, usually dripping on me before I could prevent it, I remember, and nothing was ever so good! The next time I see you, you shall have a cup of tea with milk in, and I shall soak my common-cracker in it, and butter it, and eat it, and we shall be very gay.

We walked past a place where there was a deep gully, where once the Romans pitched their camp. We walked past hawthorn bushes, bright with red haws, and past very high-climbing hedge rose-bushes, bright with red hips,—"hips and haws",—it always thrills me; and through a wood where ivy was growing all over the ground. The fields were all enclosed by hedges, instead of fences; and at the back of the garden at Judy's house (here where I am writing) is a privet-hedge,— just a hedge of high bushes not very interesting in appearance. We are only about twenty-five miles from Cambridge, and are going to bicycle there one day next week, and come back by train. (I just noticed that I said "one day next week" instead of "some day next week",—isn't that ridiculous?—it's the English way of saying it, and I've been with nothing but English people constantly for the past seven weeks. Their idioms for almost everything are so different from ours that it consti- tutes a foreign language. I'm going to make that fact the basis of one of my articles for Vanity Fair.

Crossing the Channel yesterday was a great experience. I had always heard that it was very rough and that everybody was always seasick. But both the times I had crossed it before—(from Calais to Dover and back—a trip of an hour and a half) it had been perfectly smooth, like a lake, almost. Well, night before last Judy and I were awakened, like Annie and Rhoda, by the sound of the rain, and the ramp and roar of wild wave climbing a rocky shore, or however the thing went we used to be so keen on when we were kids. The little inn where we were staying, after the crowd had left the big villa and we were forced to find some other place if we wished to stay on a while, was just across the road from the beach, and we simply couldn't sleep, for the howling and banging and pounding and swishing of the storm. "I hope you'll have a pleasant crossing tomorrow, Miss Hutton," and "Oh, go to hell!" was the gist of our conversation for a time. My stomach had been rather upset for several days previous, and for the last two days madame had conceived the bright idea of buying up a hog and "going the whole hog" (!) by way of the menu, pork-chops, pork this, pork that, but mostly hot roast pork. As a consequence of which my innards were not feeling too happy. Fine situation, and we about to embark on a floating see-saw at eleven the next day. Well, we started (from Dieppe). And the minute we had got out of the harbor the little old packet put her nose down, lifted her hind legs in the air, and reared. We arranged to get two steamer-chairs on the upper deck, just amidships, (I had tried to make the steward stick them right up in the bow, but he laughed at me and refused to do so.) It was to be a three hour journey. We had not been out of the harbor five minutes when, as we were sitting calmly there like the couple of ladies that we are, with gloves on and hats, and our purses and hand-bags on our stomachs, when, as I said before, the English Channel came right aboard the boat in back of us, fell over us with a tremendous swish and splash, and we were drenched to the skin. Of course, the boat was not really shipping water on the top deck, but there was such a wind and such a sea running that when a wave struck the side it came with tremendous force, and sent up into the air a shower of spray which came down over the passengers. There was no way of telling that it was spray and not a wave, except that when one got the water out of ones eyes and looked at the rail one saw that the sea was not actually coming in over it. This went on for three hours, wave after wave after wave of spray breaking over our backs, umbrellas floating about on the deck, deck-chairs blowing down with a crash, sailors rushing about shouting, all dressed in oilskins and rubber-boots and souwesters—though it was a fine day, mind you, blue sky, white clouds, bright sunshine,—we were just having a shower on deck, nowhere else. We could of course have gone inside, but we didn't relish the idea of sitting in an air-tight saloon with a lot of people packed in like herrings, very green about the gills and shaky about the knees, and leaning over the yellow earthen basins we had long ago spied thoughtfully deposited for the use of the guests at intervals of a yard or two everywhere aboard. So we stayed. There was nobody at all on that part of the deck where we were except the two of us and one young man who became gradually more and more the color of a Roquefort cheese.

* * *

Well, as for me, I was never so desolately uncomfortable in my life. The first sea that came aboard had drenched me to the corset. Judy had on a raincoat, but I was wearing only my grey cloak outside my checked skirt and blue jacket. For three solid hours I sat in that chair, frozen, dripping, and under constant inundation, with my poor weak stomach on which nothing had sat steady for over a week. It was really dreadful. If it had not been salt water I should probably have got my death, for when we got ashore my grey cloak was just a soggy dripping mass and my shoes sklugged when I walked, and my corset is hanging over the back of a chair now, not dry yet. But I seem to be experiencing no ill effects whatsoever. I haven't even caught the least bit of cold. We saw in the paper this morning that the storm which had wakened us the eve of our voyage was the worst storm in London since 1913, or something to that effect, and that the gentle zephyr which had so playfully spattered the spray on us in our crossing was a forty-mile gale, on land,—heaven knows what it was at sea! I think I may safely boast that I am a pretty good sailor.

This is a long and ridiculous letter, but I know it is fun to hear what people really are doing. Mitchell Kennerley, or his secretary, has sent me a great sheaf of clippings, reviews of *Second April*, exceedingly good. They have received the book very well, much to my astonishment. It is not so good as it should have been, actually. I think, personally, they are giving it more than it deserves. But I am glad, as long as I myself am not taken in, that it is selling, and pleasing, and that I shall not be in disfavor at the time of the appearance of my next book, which is going to be dam good.

* * *

A train just passed, in sight of the house,—the Cambridge Express.

Lots of love, my dearest one.

Vincent

88   TO MRS. CORA B. MILLAY

[England
September, 1921]

Mumsie, dear,—

Maybe *you* will dig out from Wumps the information, whether or not when they played *The Lamp & the Bell* at Vassar they used my music for the minstrel's lyrics.—I have asked everybody, I have tried desperately to find out, because I worked so hard over the dam songs, & got Hi Moderwell, who is a very good musician, & was in Paris at the time, to harmonize them for me, & paid thirty-five francs to a French music-copyist to make them all plain & beautiful & just like real music!—and then sent them off myself all insured & everything but a little bit late in the day, & have been worrying over the business, off & on, ever since. They should have got the music by the tenth, & since the performance was not until the eighteenth, they really would have had time. But I never even heard if they received the music, & I keep asking everybody to tell me how the music went & who sang it & everything, & nobody will tell me a single kind friendly word & I'm 'scouraged—Ya-ah-ah-ah!

Lub,
Bincent.

P.S. Another thing, lost in the shuffle of the international post, is a lovely poem of mine, called *The Ballad of the Harp-Weaver.* I sent a copy of it to you a long time ago, & I think if you had received it you would surely have spoken of it.—I send you another copy of it now. It is practically the only poem I have written since I left America.—That was just what I wanted, you know, not to write a word of poetry for a year. When it begins to get a little *easy*, or one begins to write in certain forms almost from habit, it is time to stop for a while, I think, & almost forget that one is a poet—become a prose-writer, for instance —& then let it all come back to one later, fresh, & possibly in a newer form.—The next thing I hope to do is to finish the long sonnet sequence about the New England woman. My next book may be composed entirely of sonnets, & after that I may never write a sonnet again—or if I do, it will be a big one, & inevitable.—I am looking forward already to my next book.

I hope you will like this poem, darling. It is dedicated to you, of course, as may be seen at a glance.

Much love, mother dear,—
Vincent.

89   TO MRS. CORA B. MILLAY

Letchworth, Hertfordshire,
England
Sept. 23, 1921

Dearest Mother,

I am sending you a bit of English sweet-clover, which is just exactly the same as American sweet-clover, or rather, perhaps, New-English sweet-clover; also, an English poppy, such as grows wild in all the grain fields, and an English purple vetch; the poppy is scarlet now, but when it gets to you will be very faded, I'm afraid.

* * *

Dearest, I *can't* think why you don't write me, but I suppose there is some good reason, you are writing furiously, or packing up, getting ready to go back to town. I do hope it is not the best reason,—that you are ill and can't write. You must send me a word at least as soon as you get this, letting me know how you are. Address it to the Intendance, and it will be forwarded to me in Rome.

Judy and I passed a cottage the other day when we were out walking, called REST HARROW. You remember I told you about the flower of that name, and explained the derivation of it to you. A place where you may rest your harrow—it really is a beautiful name for a home.

I carry my typewriter all over the world with me, the little Corona Jim gave me. He was a sweet boy, mother. I loved him very much. And still do, whenever I think of him, though it was all nonsense, of course, and I wouldn't want him back. Only I like to think about him sometimes. You were wonderful, mother, about him and me. I realized afterwards how terrible it must have been for you. But you never hurt me in any way.

I have a curious feeling that someday I shall marry, and have a son; and that my husband will die; and that you and I and my little boy will all live together on a farm.

No, I'm not out of my mind, darling, or morbid, or anything of the sort. I am feeling very well, and standing very straight, and spend most of my time out of doors. It's only that more and more in my letters to you I feel a desire to write not only the things that I do but also the things that I think.

* * *

By the time you get this, I shall have been gone about nine months, longer than we ever were separated before. It doesn't seem so long as that, really, that I came to see you and say goodbye to you at Aunt Clem's. I am going to write her a letter in a day or two, so she won't think that the only reason I ever wrote her was because you were there. Sweet Aunt Clem. I wouldn't hurt her for anything. And I do love her quite for her own self. Only I haven't much time for anybody but you and the girls. I am awfully faithful to my immediate family.

Do write me, sweetheart. If you knew what your letters mean to me!

As ever your loving daughter,
Vincent

[Albania]
Care of American Embassy
Rome.
[October, 1921]

Arthur, my dearest,

I must write you, or you will think I did not get your letters. But when I start to write you all I can think of to say to you is—Why aren't you here? Oh, why aren't you here?—And I have written that to you before.—I have no news, you see.—Or rather, there is news enough, but when I try to write it, it all goes from my mind, & I have nothing to say but that I long to see you.—I take the photograph with me everywhere, the big one. I love it.—Arthur, I have no good photograph of myself, but if when you are in New York you should call to see my sister Kathleen, who is now Mrs. Howard Young, and lives at 184 West 4th Street, she would either give you or tell you where you could get one that is not so very bad. I will send you some snap-shots, too, as soon as I get them developed.

Dear, when I come back to the States, won't you come east to see me?—I know you can't come to Europe, but you could come to New York, because you often do, to see Hal, or somebody, & don't you love me most as much as you love Hal?—I think we might have a few days together that would be entirely lovely. We are not children, or fools, we are mad. And we of all people should be able to do the mad thing well. If each of us is afraid to see the other, that is only one more sympathy we have. If each of us is anguished lest we lose one another through some folly, then we are more deeply bound than any folly can undo.

———————

Doubtless all this reasoning resolves itself into one pitiful female cry,—what ever happens, I want to see you again!—But oh, my dear, I know what my heart wants of you,—it is not the things that other men can give.

Do you remember that poem in *Second April* which says, "Life is a quest & love a quarrel, Here is a place for me to lie!"?—That is what I want of you—out of the sight & sound of other people, to lie close to you & let the world rush by. To watch with you suns rising & moons rising in that purple edge outside most people's vision—to hear high music that only birds can hear—oh, my dearest, dearest, would it not be wonderful, just once to be together again for a little while?

(Just as I wrote those last words the muezzin began to cry his prayer from the little white minaret—he is still singing—)

One is so silly, isn't one?—Listening to him it seemed that he was calling us to worship—heaven knows what—something that we both hold dear.

————————

Arthur, I am glad that you love me. Your letters have hurt me & healed me. Such sweetness, to be loved like that. But to be loved like that by you,—how shaking & terrible besides.

————————

That sonnet you asked me about—the one, "There is no shelter in you anywhere"—was written both about you & about myself—we were both like that—but are not any more. The "golden vessel of great song", also was written to you. My time, in those awful days after you went away to France, was a mist of thinking about you & writing sonnets to you.—You were spending your time in the same way, I believe.—That day before you sailed,—I shall never forget it. You were the first man I ever kissed without first thinking that I should be sorry about it afterwards. There has been only one other, a boy I truly loved, in a simpler way.

————————

Arthur, it is wicked & useless,—all these months & months apart from you, all these years with only a glimpse of you in the face of everybody.—I tell you I must see you again.—

Edna.

91   TO MRS. CORA B. MILLAY

Palace Hotel, Rome
Nov. 13, 1921

Dearest Mother,—

I've been getting a lot of letters from you lately, and if you want to know how glad I was to get them, just figure to yourself how you would feel if you had not heard a word from *me* in three months and then all of a sudden did. I have received from you six in all, I think; and Vanity Fair has written saying that they have a letter from you to me which they do not wish to forward until they have my permanent address, so that makes seven,—although I believe you said something about the Vanity Fair one being a duplicate of one you were sending to another address, so that I have probably already received it, or its carbon copy. Vanity Fair wrote me as follows: "Dear Miss Millay,—A letter has arrived at this office from your mother, in which she complains of your not keeping in touch with her with sufficient regularity. Etc. etc." !!!!! Oh, injustice, injustice! It seemed to me that was about the last straw. When I had been deluging you with letters from every port where the boat touched, so to speak, and you had been neglecting me entirely! Naturally they took it for granted that it was I who was not writing; I, the wild young poet over in Europe on her own, had forgotten all about my family and home and mother, whilst my distracted family and home and mother was writing me tearful epistles by every outbound mail!—which apparently I was not receiving, since I never replied! Little did they know the 'orrid truth. Well, anyhow, the above will be my address for a while, as long as I can pay the bill, which is fairly steep. All the cheaper hotels have fleas, or are likely to have. And speaking of fleas, which is a pretty subject and one not sufficiently discussed, how I did git et in Albania! When the fleas got full-up the sofa-birds started in. But in spite of all the hardships and inconveniences of traveling in a country with no railroads or public conveyances of any kind, as a matter of fact for the most part no roads at all except a bridle path through the mountains, no plumbing, no butter, no coffee except Turkish coffee which is made with sugar, and other such-like lacks, seeing Albania—and also Montenegro, where we traveled for a couple of days only—has been my most thrilling experience so far from the point of view of "seeing the world." I would write you all about it, but I am going to write it up for the Metropolitan, which I should think would be very glad to have it, and when it is done I will send you a carbon copy. One thing only I will tell you now, apropos of the little flowers I am sending, which are called in Albanian "lulet", at least, that is the general name for flowers, and in Serbian, (Montenegro is a Serbian country) "koshuta." Of course in both cases the spelling is my own; I have no idea how they should be spelled. Well, as I was going to tell you. The first day we rode through the mountains was from Tirana to Elbasan in Albania. Tirana is the capital of the country and Elbasan is one of the principal cities, and the only way to get from one to the other is over this road through the mountains, passable only to donkeys and mountain horses, which are surefooted and accustomed to carrying packs and people up and down stairs without dropping them. Just as a matter of possible interest, I was ten hours in the saddle that day, and it was the second time in my life I was ever on a horse, the first time being for half an hour or so at

Woodstock, as Hunk will remember, on Lawrence Langner's "Billy".
Well, as we were riding along, myself, John Carter, the boy from the
Embassy who was traveling with me—(this Albanian trip was Dick
Child's idea)—our interpreter, who spoke no English, but very good
Italian; the man who owned the horses, an Albanian peasant, who
looked as if he never had owned anything but the rags which covered
him, and rode a pack-horse on top of the pack, sidewise, exactly as if
he were sitting in a rocking chair; and two guards, with their rifles
ready across the saddle, because the day before on this trail an
Albanian had been shot in a feud,—as we were riding along, I saw some
beautiful little lavender flowers such as I had never seen before in the
bushes by the road. I asked what they were and was told they were
"lulet." I wanted very much to dismount and gather some, but rea-
soned with myself that I should probably see plenty of them while I
was in Albania and that it would be a bad idea to stop the whole
cortege for anything which would seem to them so silly. So I said
nothing about it. Three days later, on the road from Elbasan to Cavaja,
—a fourteen hours' journey, twelve hours on horseback; we started in
the starlight before dawn, under the moon and the morning star, and
did not arrive until the evening starlight—on this road again I saw these
beautiful little flowers, and was dying to get off and gather some, for
they were like no flowers I had ever seen, and I could not bear to pass
them without looking at them more closely; but it was a long journey,
and it seemed even sillier than before to stop the whole procession for
such a trifle, so I said nothing. About ten days later we left Albania for
good and boarded the boat which crossed the lake of Scutari to Rieca
in Montenegro. And perhaps my one regret in leaving the country,
for we had seen the things we came to see and were going on to things
equally interesting, was that I was going away without once having
held in my fingers the beautiful strange Albanian "lulet." We arrived
in Rieca after a day's journey by boat, a little Austrian gun-boat made
over, a journey made harrowing and deafening by the Serbian soldiers
aboard who spent most of the day shooting with their long rifles at the
wild duck which were everywhere on the water about us; as part of the
trip was up a river shut in by high cliffs on both sides you can imagine
what the echoing and reverberation and general hell-of-a-racket was
like. When we got to Rieca we were able to get a little open carriage
drawn by two horses and driven by an old Montenegran to take us to
Cetinje, the capital of the country, over a beautiful smooth white road
cut for miles along the face of the mountains, ten thousand feet in the

air,—that is to say, ten thousand feet above sea level, not ten thousand feet above the isolated farms and sparse, infrequent gardens which we glimpsed below us in the growing darkness, although sometimes it seemed so, it was a long, long, long look down. We spent that night in Cetinje, and the next day went on to Cattaro, the sea-port town where we were to take the boat back to Italy. This ride from Cetinje to Cattaro is the most wonderful experience I ever had, and it would be difficult to do anything more beautiful or more thrilling. It was over a road much like the road we had traveled the night before, excepting that it was made up entirely of what is known as "hair-pin curves", and that we traveled it not in a slow-going carriage but in a touring-car at the rate of about forty miles an hour. After this trip a roller-coaster would seem about as hazardous and exciting as a rocking-chair. But this is what I was going to tell you. As we were racing along I noticed that we passed some people, I saw them from the tail of my eye, not clearly. And just then something was hurled into the car from the road, a small, light object. The man who was beside me, a charming old Serb, stooped and picked up the object and handed it to me with a bow. No, not a bomb, dear, but a small, carefully-tied fresh nosegay of lavender flowers, my "lulet" at last, tossed by some Montenegran child in greeting to the unknown travelers.

Well, that's my little story. It's a pretty one, isn't it? I am sending you a few of the flowers, and I shall keep a few myself. Later I may be able to send you a picture of a part of the road, if it comes out well, the most incredible sight.

I love the little pressed mushrooms, and should imagine that panels made of them would be really beautiful,—sort of Arthur-Rackham-beautiful.

I am so pleased about Hunk and Charlie. Of course I am writing to her, too. In fact, I may as well admit that I am writing to my whole dam fam'ly, because I want to thank Wumps first-hand for her booful photograph. I got my letters from you three, about ten in all, all in a bunch, for I was in Albania nearly four weeks, with no possibility of having my mail forwarded, and it was all waiting for me when I got back to Rome. I felt like I was twins and it was my birthday!

Tell you what, mother, would you like a good modern map of the city of London? Or have you one? You seem to know so much about it, that I rather feel you may have. But if you haven't and would like one to play with I will send you mine, which I never have time to look at. And you can learn all about the dam place so that you can pilot me about it when we get there. See? Also, if Howard still has a map of Paris, make him lend it to you. See? Love, Sefe. (Also, if you come across anybody who has a loose map of Mandelay, Tahiti, or Yucatan, you'd better keep it around where you can lay your hand on it at a moment's notice. Because you never can tell. *See?*)

—Bincent

92   TO NORMA MILLAY

Palace Hotel, Rome.
November 13, 1921.

Darling Sister,—

I am so glad about you and Charlie! Now I have two bruvvers! And two such nice bruvvers. I couldn't have picked me nicer ones. Charlie knows I love him, unless he has lost his memory, but tell him anyway that I love him very much, and that I think he is a great actor and has a very handsome nose, and that I am proud and happy to have him in my immediate family.

And how *good* to have a lovely apartment all your own, dear. Oh, I am so glad about it all. Mother in all her letters this summer and in the ones I have just received speaks of you, how much good it has done you, and of Charlie, how fond she is of him and how sweet he is to her. Well, both my little sisters are young married women, and me, I am just about three months from being an old maid. . . .

Sister will get Normie her long tortoise-shell ear-rings just as soon as the transportation strike is over and it is possible to get a taxi. Sister will send them to her by Mr. John Carter, a nice and amusing American kid who was Steve Benét's room-mate at Yale, and who is leaving the American Embassy here to return to the States on the twentieth of this month. So *that's all* right, best belovèd, do you see?

Do you know, I thought it might be Charlie, even before you told me. Isn't that funny?

* * *

Well, darling, all the sweet things in the world sister would say to him if sister only could express herself better.

As it is, love and kisses, to both you and Chas, and I do hope you'll go ahead and have a baby. If you can't suppose it, I will.

As ever, the companion of your middle age, the friend of your declining years, the old woman who'll sit before the fire with you fifty years from now and knit the left stocking while you knit the right,

Edna.

It was so sweet & such a happy omen, dear, that in your letter to me in which you announced your marriage, three times you misspelled the word "separate."

93   TO ELINOR WYLIE

Palace Hotel, Rome
November 27, 1921.

Dear Elinor Wylie:[10]

I have read with keen delight your beautiful *Nets to Catch the Wind*, of which I am writing a review for the *New York Evening Post*. Not since I discovered Ralph Hodgson have I had such happiness in a new volume of poems.

Keep well and strong. Do not suffer your foot to be moved.—A thousand people will be waiting, as I shall be waiting, with assurance, for your next fine book.

Wishing you all good things and the success which you so unquestionably merit, I am,

Most heartily yours,
Edna St. Vincent Millay.

[10] This was the poet's first contact with Elinor Wylie. The review appeared in the *New York Evening Post* Literary Review of January 28, 1922. It was the first and only review of a book of poetry she ever published. The following year the two poets were introduced to each other by Edmund Wilson and became warm friends. When *The King's Henchman* was published in book form, Miss Wylie wrote a front page review of it for the New York *Herald Tribune's* Book Section, February 20, 1927.

94   TO ARTHUR DAVISON FICKE

Grand Hotel, Vienna
Dec. 10, 1921

Dear Arthur:

This is where I am now, & your print[11] is in my trunk in Paris. I can't go to Paris to get it, because I haven't the money:—I can't have the trunk sent here, because, owing to the street rioting & general unsettled condition of this city just now, personal property runs a great risk of being either lost or stolen.—I am dreadfully sorry you are worried about it. I swear to you that it is quite safe, & that I will get it to you just as soon as I can.—If I had had the money I should have gone to Paris the moment I received your letter & sent the print off to you in some way.—But I can't leave Vienna probably for several months yet. I am here because it is the cheapest place in the world to live just now, & I am in one of my periodic states of being entirely busted.—So please forgive me if it is some time before I can get it to you.—I am very, very sorry.

As for myself, I shall be quite all right, unless I lose my head, which I don't intend to do.—And as for you, don't you dare breathe to a soul that I am hard-up. Because I have no business to be & I am frightfully ashamed of it, and I don't want anybody to be getting worried about me & sending me money to help me out. (As they say in the *No Admittance* signs: THIS MEANS YOU.)

I wonder if you have got any of my letters.—Not that it matters very much.

It seems a long time since I have seen anybody I cared anything about.

Edna.

[11] A rare Japanese color print he had loaned Miss Millay.

---

95 TO WITTER BYNNER

7 Floragasse, Vienna
Dec. 23, 1921.

Dearest Hal,—

I never received your letter of which Arthur speaks.—So that his crazy card-index note, and your post-script, are all I have to tell me what is in your mind.—Do you really want me to marry you?—Because if you really want me to, I will. I have thought for a long time that someday I should marry you.

Of course I can't write to you about it, you must see that, my dear, not knowing what was in your letter. Whatever I say would be perhaps the wrong thing to say.—And perhaps you will understand that I would give much if you were here at this moment.

You have known me since I was a little girl. It is curious to think of that. As little as we have seen of one another, yet you are bound in the memories of my childhood.

Dear Hal, there are thoughts in my head that I must not tell you now, particularly one of them. Because all this may not be true at all, may be just a dream that you had a month ago, and that I am having tonight.—Yet this I will say, that if it is a dream I am sorry.

I wish you could come here. It is not so very far, and I feel I must see you, and I can't come there. But I suppose you have duties now from which you cannot be released—even for me. (It is amusing and pleasant to say to you: even for me.) In any case, I wish you could come, and wanted to.

You will let me hear from you at once, Hal, won't you? Oh, if you knew the comical state my mind is in! What a *ridiculous* person you are!

Edna.

96   TO ANNE GARDNER LYNCH[12]

7 Floragasse,
Vienna, Austria.
Dec. 23, 1921.

Anne, darling,—

I have just got your letter. Oh, if I could just get my arms about you!—And stay with you like that for hours, telling you so many things, & listening to all that you must have to say.—I love you very much, dear Anne, & I always shall.—Ours was a perfect friendship—I knew it at the time—and it is still just as true. I would do anything in the world for you, & I know that you would for me.—And it doesn't matter if we never write, and never see each other, it is just the same,—except that it would be so nice to see each other!

I have thought of you a thousand times, & wondered, wondered acutely, with anxiety & such deep well-wishing!—how you were getting on. A dozen times I have started to write you. The little card that came with your wedding announcement & had your New York address on it, has travelled about with me everywhere, because I was always on the point of writing & I wanted your street & number where I could lay my hands on them.

Dear, by the time you get this letter your baby will be very near to life. If you want to know how I am feeling about you, & all I am wishing for you, & how my heart will be with you from this time on until I hear from you again, you have only to imagine to yourself just how, in the same circumstances, you would be feeling about me.

Also, may its sex, temper, & general topography be what you prefer! Also, may it wait & be born on the 22nd of February, which is my birthday, & I will be its god-mother.

* * *

Dear, there's no room here for more than a word. All that you told me is in my heart & on my mind. And I shall go through it all with you as surely as if you were clinging to my hand.

—Your Vince.

¹² A college friend.

97 TO WITTER BYNNER

Floragasse 7
Wien IV
Jan. 23, 1922

Hal, dear,—

I have just got your note, with the poems, which are lovely— especially *Web*—that is very beautiful. My dear—and the one about *Moonlight* and the *Chinese Scholar*.

As for your note itself—well, you have by this time received my letter, which seems to you, perhaps, a silly letter, and you know, if not how I feel about you, at least how I feel about us, as possible companions.—You wrote me once, "We are too much alike, you and I, for any earthly marriage." I believe that to be nonsense,—not as regards you and me, particularly, but as regards everybody. Why it should be thought a good thing for people to spend their lives, which might otherwise not impossibly be used to some purpose, in a series of disagreements, misunderstandings, adjustments, ill-adjustments, and readjustments, I have never been able to see.

But Hal, if there is something else, if you are sorry now that you asked me to marry you; if you have changed your mind, and don't want to marry at all; if you have suddenly decided that you would prefer to marry somebody else; if for some reason you were not yourself when you wrote me—if some unhappiness or disappointment had weakened you and made you lonely, or if you were intoxicated at the time (always a possibility, which people too seldom take into account!); or even if it was all just a roaring joke, which I for the moment was too earnest and stupid to see—oh, my dear, if for any reason at all you feel you made a mistake, that it is not I, after all, that you need and want—why then, you must just write and tell me so, quite plainly, and I shall understand; and you and I will be but friends again.

At any rate, I am glad you are coming to Europe.—I was always happy to be with you; and shall be no less so now, no matter what we do, or don't do.

Of course, I see from your note one thing which troubles you. And I want to speak to you about that.

It is true that I love Arthur. But we have all known that for some time,—haven't we?—I shall love him always. He is something to me that nobody else is. But why should that trouble you, Hal? Don't you love him, too? Don't you love several people?—If you loved me, I should not want you to love only me. I should think less highly of you if you did. For surely, one must be either undiscerning, or frightened, to love only one person, when the world is so full of gracious and noble spirits.

Besides, I should not wish to marry Arthur, even if it were possible, —so it is not because you are free and he is not, Hal, as may have come into your mind.

As for you,—if I loved you more than the apples at the end of the bough, I should not tell you; for I have shared too much with you already, and you with me nothing, saving your misgivings.

Oh, well—why be so serious, about a trifle! You'll think I've lost my sense of laughter,—but it's not so.—If you think for a moment I don't see the idiotic side of this nefarious business—just wait till you see my quivering smile.

Oh, Hal, do come soon, darn you!—And write me a word when you get this letter—if it's nothing but a cuss-word.

Edna.

Your little note hurt, hurt, hurt me, my dear, I don't mind saying.—I had been waiting for it—don't you see at all?—But it doesn't matter. Bless you anyway, mad sweet thing.

98   TO ARTHUR DAVISON FICKE

7 Floragasse, Vienna IV
January 24, 1922.

Dear Arthur:

I am writing you on the type-writer, because I want to write you a long letter, and I hold a very nervous pen lately. Does your hand get that way sometimes, so that you want to dig in the earth with it, or whittle it, or thrust it into a broad fat back,—anything but write with it?

Your letters of December the 19th and 27th have just reached me, forwarded from Rome. The others came some time ago; I believe I have received them all. You do not know how much they mean to me, my dear friend. You must never tear them up. Sometimes they have thrust loveliness back into my life, where there seemed almost no place for it. I am living curious and difficult days in this grey city where there is never a shred of sunlight. Outside my window is a great grey wall flattened against it like a hand; it is so near the window it is almost in the room; I have to keep the light burning all day long. I smoke too many cigarettes, and the German food nearly kills me—hot bread and cabbage and grease, when what I want is a bowl of plain rice and an apple. Fortunately I have to exercise, because I can't afford taxis, and I loathe streetcars.

* * *

Well, so much for that. But when I tell you that I am lonely, and want a friend to talk with, you will believe me.

I am not getting much work done. I might as well try to work on a ship-wrecked raft, in sound of the dice which are to determine which is to be et.

My dear, I knew all about the girl in New York, long before you told me. At least, of course I knew nothing at all about her, but I knew what had happened. I knew when you were to be in New York, and while you were there I thought of you, and I said to myself, "He is falling in love with some girl there." Then, you see, you didn't write me while you were there, and after you went back to Davenport your letters were different, a little, little bit. Anyway, I knew. It doesn't matter. Except that if she is hurt, it is too bad. How fortunate she was to be with you, to be where she could talk with you. But as for the rest, it doesn't matter with whom you fall in love, nor how often, nor how sweetly. All that has nothing to do with what we are to each other, nothing at all to do with You and Me.

Arthur, dear, I think I am going to marry Hal. He is coming over here in the spring. Of course we may do nothing about it. But I rather feel we shall. Would you be sorry or glad if I did? Tell me seriously, dear, what you feel about it. Of course, there is every geometrical reason why I should. We should make such a beautiful design, don't you see,—Hal and you and I. Three variable and incommensurate souls automatically resolved into two right angles, and no nonsense about it. Of course, it's not so simple as that. But there's something very pleasing about that aspect of it.

Do you remember when I said I was going to wait for you and Hal? How funny it all is.

Hal, poor fellow, is very much troubled about my feeling for you. At least, I don't think he would mind, except that he feels I care more for you than I do for him. I just got a note from him, in which I saw that plainly. That letter of mine to you, which he opened by mistake, was the devil, wasn't it?

Well, there's no denying that I love you, my dear. I have never denied it for a moment, since the first time I saw you, whether to myself or to anybody else who seemed interested. When people ask me if I know you I say, "Yes, I know him." Then if they ask me if I like you, I say, "I love him." And that's all there is to that. And they can shut up, or go on asking questions, or talk it over among themselves.

You, best of all, know how I feel about you, and always shall. No one can ever take your place with me. We know each other in such a terrible, certain, windless way. You and I have almost achieved that which is never achieved: we sit in each other's souls.

But that's no reason why I couldn't marry Hal, and be happy with him. I love him, too. In a different way.

Well, enough of that.—It was like you, generous and comical, to send me your reverend father's impeccable paternal checque. I accept it quite humbly and gratefully, in spite of all my man-sized talk. (Oh, Arthur, you are so sweet, *so* sweet!)

* * *

I am glad you like the Lamp and the Bell. I know it has beauty in it. Someday, perhaps, I shall take it apart and make a really fine play of it through-out. I wrote it last February, under pressure of great hurry, and of course there are holes in it. I heard they produced it magnificently at Vassar. The copy you have is full of little typographical slurrings and misunderstandings which make it a little muddy in places, but which will be corrected in the next edition.

The sonnets about me in Seven Years are beautiful. I have just been reading them over again. And you must by all means add the one which begins, "In times hereafter". But I think you should not say "*flee* to worlds where only shadows move." For surely people as proud as the people you tell of do not *flee* from anything; they move, they turn, they go,—but they do not flee. (Now tell me to mind my business. I shall bend my glance downward and reply with serene arrogance that it *is* my business, I am one of the people.) The first Girl Beside Pool is very, very lovely.[13] I hope the public *will* know it is I,—I shall be happy to have them know, to have everybody know, when they read your book, that you love me like that. Almost everybody, to be sure, is mortal, but the gods should worry.

I am sending you some new sonnets of mine.

Arthur, dearest, I feel quite gay and risible, having got all this pifflous bunk off my chest and onto yours. Next best to talking with you, after all, is writing to you. This dam letter seems to be full of *after alls*. Makes me think of a little French poem I wrote once, and had forgotten:

> Et après tout qu'est-ce qu'on a fait
> Pour la beauté, qu'on aime tant?—
> Tout simplement, un cri ou deux;
> C'est tout ce qu'on peut, pour la beauté.

Well, goodbye. I shall now issue forth and fodder my bewildered Muse on Wiener schnitzel, Brussels sprouts and beer.

Here's to crime. May the lowliest live to commit it.

With love,
Vincent.

Write me and do not tear them up. For God's sake, post them.—I am suffering in this place.

---

[13] Two sonnets by Ficke published later in his book, *Out of Silence*, and titled: 1. "Go," 2. "Stay." Other sonnets in the same volume, such as "To a Girl Singer," were also inspired by Miss Millay.

Hotel Ritz
Budapest
February 22, 1922

Poor boy,—*did* Edna write him solemn letters from German cities and frighten him almost to death?

Oh, Hal, you abysmal nut!

As I sit in my small but costly apartment looking out upon the Danube, the thought of you hits me on the head like a piece of lead pipe.

Oh, Lord—oh, Lord—Oh, *Hal!*

Apoplectically yours,
Edna

I am now going under the divan and have a fit.

Ritz Hotel, Budapest
March 1, 1922

Beloved Sister:

Bless you forever and ever for your letter. If ever a girl needed a letter, I was that girl, and yours was that letter. You see, it put some things straight in my mind that had been a little cluttered before. Your telling me that mother had been sick, and all that,—*you* know—made me realize that nothing in the world is important beside getting mother over here with me. At least, of course the Russian famine is important, and a few other things like that, but nothing in my life, at least, is important in comparison to this thing. A possible marriage, for instance, is not important beside it. Anybody can get married. It happens all the time. But not everybody, after the life we have had, can bring her mother to Europe. Besides, any marriage that could be upset by such a circumstance is not a marriage worth having. I was a little panic-stricken, and confused, when I wrote that letter about postponing mother's coming,—*you* know, darling,—a bee was chasing me! But now my mind is clear again, after an aberration that was beginning to be more than temporary, and I know what I want, and I want just one thing, and that thing is to get mother over here, and I'm going to do it.

I am cabling her today to get ready, and fortunately having just this morning, in the same mail with your letter, received my five hundred dollar checque from Liveright, advance on my novel, "Hardigut", I am able to send mother the money at once to come. I shall send it tomorrow, as it is too late today to get into the banks, and I shall have a lot of business to go through with, getting it off. I can't take time to tell you about the novel, dear, because what time I have to give to it I must spend in writing it. It has to be done by early fall. This morning in the same post with the money from Liveright and your letter, came a checque for fifteen dollars from the Literary Supplement of the New York Evening Post for my review of Elinor Wylie's book—I wonder if you saw it—and also a cable from Henry Holt & Co., saying they hear I am writing a novel which is not yet placed, and offering me five hundred dollars advance on it! On the whole, it was a very good morning I had. No, you don't have to beg me to "bear wiv you" in order to have me read your letters through to the end. I devour them. They don't come very often, but when they do come, I take a day off and run up all my flags. No, you did not ask me to get you the ear-rings in the same letter in which you announced your marriage. But you might just as well have, and you know darned well it just happened that you didn't, and that you're not at all sure whether you did or not! You sweet old ninny! No, this was how it was. I had not received word from you for months, for half a year, for a life-time, not a word, not a sound. I might be dead,—you should worry. You might be dead, and I thought very likely you were, though I hoped you were not. Then one day I get a letter, and I think, "Aha! From Norma! All the news from home! Explanations of long silence! Inquiries as to my health! Assurances as to hers! Apologies! Vows of eternal what-you-may-call-it!"— Not at all. Not on your life. Thus it ran: "Dear Sister I want some Ear-rings some long ones They say they have lovely ones in Rome tortuss-shel I gotta have some I just gotta Do get me some darling Sister Yours Normie." That is not exactly word for word, but it's pretty damn near. Well, I want to tell you that I never laughed so much in my life. And I spent half an hour loving you so hard that I near bust. After which I marches out to the joolry store, and standin' serene and unafraid in the midst of the infernal glitter, I says to the man, I says, "What have you in the way of ear-rings?"

Well, I am glad you like them, sweetheart. I knew you would take the onyx ones. I could just imagine how sweet they would look under your silly yellow hair. And it is true that John [Carter] really preferred the round ones to both the others. He told me here that he hoped you would not take the round ones. And I replied, "That's all very well, Carter, but if you do one single thing to prejudice her, if you so much as bat an eye, I'll never speak to you again, so that's that." You see how fierce I am when my children are attacked! But it turned out just right for everybody.

How wonderful it is about Charlie. I met some people in Vienna who were talking about Gene O'Neill's plays and they said they had seen "Diff'rent" and spoke of the wonderful acting in it, particularly that of the young soldier, and I said with pride, "That man is my brother-in-law." I was very distressed when I saw that "Ambush" was taken off, and now am so happy about "The Deluge." I remember when it was played before, although I didn't see it. I hope that since you wrote me, things have gone well, that nothing unfortunate will happen to this play; I do wish him all the luck in the world, the darling boy. He is a fine actor, and he deserves it. Just remind him when you see him (joke—because you is married to him!) just remind him that I love him. He knows it already.

* * *

It is interesting that you know Donald Ogden Stewart. I used to hear Steve Benét and Henry Carter talk about him. Of course I read his stuff in Vanity Fair. It is delightful. Mother writes me that he and his mother may be coming to Europe in April. If they are really coming, and on a not too expensive boat, it would be wonderful if mother could come with them. I hate to think of the little old Irish devil stepping out alone. Especially as it is likely to be stormy at this time of year. Though perhaps April is as good a time as any, because the winter storms will be over, and the ice-bergs not yet floating south. Of course, thousands of people are crossing all the time, every boat, the year around. If it were myself, I wouldn't think twice. But you know how it is when you're planning for somebody else,—and especially when that somebody is your only mother. Don't put any of these ideas into her sweet old head. Anyhow, I suppose any boat that Donald Stewart will be taking *his* mother on, will be as safe as any for *my* mother. I do hope they can arrange to come together. But if it means postponing it after she is ready, she would better just climb aboard something that looks as if it were about to shove off, and come on over.

I can't have any more of this postponing stuff. I've been going around all the morning, saying aloud in a clear firm voice, "They can all go to hell 'cept just my mummie!" Norma, sweetheart, you will do all you can, I know, to help her get ready. I am sorry I can't send more money. She must need lots of things. And I feel very disappointed about not being able to pay up the Camden bills. But after all, they can wait a while longer. And she can't wait a while longer. I know that Charlie will be too busy to arrange the business details for her, about her passport and her passage and everything. And I suppose Howard is very busy, too. I am going to write to John [Peale] Bishop, who is my good friend and will do anything for me, and ask him to see about those things for her. I am mailing her only three hundred dollars tomorrow, but shall be sending in the same mail an article to Vanity Fair, which is all finished but the typing, and ask Mr. Crowninshield to send the hundred for that to her. It seems to me she should be able to manage with four hundred, unless prices have gone up enormously since I sailed, and I see no reason why they should have done. As for me, I shall be a pretty busy girl from now on, what with writing my novel, and making a lot of money besides to show mother a swell time with when I get her over here. Anyhow, two can live as cheaply as one, I've always heard, and I shall be so happy and excited all the time she's here that I shan't be able to eat, and that will be a saving. I just happened to think, John Bishop won't be able to do all those things for mother, because she will get my cable in a day or two, and the minute she gets it will want to set about getting ready, while John won't get my letter for three weeks at least. So she'll just have to manage the best she can. There'll probably be dozens of people eager to help her in every way, she's such a sweet thing, and everybody loves her. It was wonderful what you told me, Normie, about how sick she was, and how she kept crying and everything. God! When I think of her going through the streets, and not being able to keep from crying! Isn't it terrible, the way it makes you feel, when you think of it? I suppose my last letter, in which I said I must postpone her trip, nearly killed her. She sent me such a brave cable on my birthday—POSTPONED TRIP UNDERSTOOD HAPPY BIRTHDAY LOVE MOTHER.—But even before I got your letter I was troubled by that cablegram. There seemed to be in it an undertone almost of tragedy. Well, by now she has got my cable, and is busy getting ready to come. And everything is going to be all right.

As for my getting married, I may and I may not. You know who the man is, Norma. At least you could guess. Do you remember one day in Truro, you and I were walking to the station together, and I had a letter with me which I was reading, and I said, "I think I shall marry this man some day"—do you remember? Well, if you don't remember, you don't deserve to know. And if you do remember, don't breathe it to a soul. Because it very likely will never happen. But it may.

I shall be here until April, and very likely shall go back to Paris just in time to get rooms in some hotel and then rush up to Havre or Cherbourg, wherever she docks, to meet mother's boat.

You were so cute to try to cable me roses. It was so like you. You have no sense. Only feeling. You is a littil idjit.

Lord knows what mother will do for trunks and things like that. But you must think up some dodge, Hunk, and manage somehow. Nothing must stand in the way now. At least, I don't advise anything to stand in the way, unless it wants to get stepped on!

Well, I must now dress to go out. I am having tea this afternoon with some charming Hungarian people. Did I write you that I saw Liliom here and was crazy about it? I feel I may have written that to mother. Tell mother for god's sake to bring over some books.

* * *

Goodbye, darling. So much love. And love to my bruvver Chas. And to Kay and Howid. Tell Kay I'm going to write her a letter in a minute. And if you catch a glimpse of Mrs. Cora Buzzing Millay (I'll bet this is a good name for her since she got my cable) tell her to keep cool and make good use of that famous head of hers for a month or two, at the end of which time her and me will be sitting cozy in a Paris taxi, going round and round and round the Place de la Concorde on one red wheel.

As ever, your obedient servant,
Sefe.

101   TO NORMA and KATHLEEN MILLAY

Café de la Rotonde
[Paris]
Tues. Apr. 25, [1922]

Dearest Kids,—

Here are your mother and sister sitting with Margot Schuyler at the famous sink of corruption (see above) of the Latin Quarter.—

Mother has a cold & is imbibing a Grog Américain, which is to say a hot rum with sugar & lemon.

Me, I have been sick in bed about all the time since mother came—the weather is frightful here, it has rained every day for nearly three months. But in spite of hell, we have had a swell time together.—Mother is so wonderful, & she enjoys every minute of it. I take her everywhere, on all my rough parties, & she is always the best sport present—everybody loves her & is crazy about her.—We have moved from the Intendance because it is so cust expensive, & are now in a cheap but not a very clean hotel on the Boulevard du Montparnasse two minutes from this bleeding kafe & just around the corner from the beautiful Luxembourg Gardens. We found a little grocery store on our way home in the shower this morning, & bought a whole lot of fruit & dates & little crackers, & little cheeses, & had such fun eating in our room. We have rooms right side by side (must eat my soup before it gets cold, mother says—forgot to say we are having dinner in the Rotonde Grill Room, a new addition to this emporium).

(Later.—Have et my soup,—am using the wine-list, spread open before me, as a writing desk.—Now to the business of this letter: I can never tell you, Normie, how beautiful I think the hat you made me. Every little thing about it is perfect, & oh, it is so beautifully made—you are really a genius, dear.—When I think of your little nervous fingers pinching and tweaking at that ribbon I could cry. (Margot now says I must eat my noix de veau braisé aux endives while it is hot.)

The meat is now et, & I am doing as well as may be expected.

Wumps, dear, the little bag is the sweetest little bag Sefe ever saw—I am trazy about it.—And I am trazy about Mummie's, too.—The most amusing thing happened.—One night I was carrying my little bag—I had carried it about three times already, & I remembered to my horror that I had neglected to provide myself with a handkerchief. I looked everywhere. I found none. I was desperate. At last I dug deep into the bag & brought up—your sweet little silk handkerchief—I had never seen it before that moment!—

Griffin & Curtis Moffet who have just come in say that I must eat my tarte aux cerises while it is cold!—Love, & thank you so much, darlings.

Sefe.

102   TO NORMA MILLAY

Hotel Venetia
159 B'd Montparnasse
Paris 6.
May 11, 1922.

Dearest Hunk,—

Am having a fine time wish you was here.—Why the devil don't you write to your mother? Of course, she is almost perfectly happy to be here with me, but she still remembers you & Wumps, & watches the mails quite pathetically. She has seen more of Paris in the five weeks she has been here than I saw in five months. We're doing the whole darned town, like a couple of flat-footed tourists, museums, churches, everything. The only thing that has saved me from an early grave, is the fact that she has just acquired a small blister on her heel, & is content with doing not more than twelve miles an afternoon.—She is so cute. The first thing she did was to run into a small lending library & take out a book on Paris!—And whenever we go she gives me paragraph after paragraph of profound information concerning that particular spot.

Darling, mummie—that is to say, mummie and Sefe—are sending you a birfday present now, because we didn't send you any on your birfday—it is really mummie who is sending it, & Wumps', too; but I want to feel in on it because it's so pitty. We're not telling you what it is. We had to tell Wumps, because she must know on her birthday, or thereabouts, but youse kin be kep in suspinse a little whiles lungir.

Mummie & I about live in this here kafe. We feed on *choucroute garnie*, which is fried sauerkraut trimmed with boiled potatoes, a large slice of ham & a fat hot dog,—yum, yum, werry excillint. That's about all they serve here in the café—that and onion soup & sandwiches. And mummie & I come here every day & eat the stinkin' stuff, & all our friends hold their noses & pass us by till we've finished. A few of them are getting inured & acquiring a taste for it.—Today they burned it a little, & it was great.—We are having the most beautiful time together. Isn't it wonderful, sweetheart, that I really did it &—here she is!—And it was all due to you, Normie, that I had her come so soon.

She is the sweetest looking thing, & you have no idea how everybody looks at her, & how everybody loves her.—She's sitting right here at my right hand & has no idea I am writing all this about her.

A man I met the other night, named the "Baron du Puget" has just come up & asked if he may sculp me. I don't know whether or not he's a good sculptor, but if he is, I'd certainly love to be sculped.—Well, my pen is running dry!—And I think it's time mother & I had a drink.—So goodby, sweet chuck, for the nonce.

Your affectionate sister & obedient servant,

Sefe.

103 TO EDMUND WILSON

Shillingstone, Dorset,
July 20, 1922.

Bunny, I adored your drunken letter. Never be sober again, oh, lofty one, O Centaur with song in his heart and burrs in his tail, O half a maudlin god! The moment I heard from you, I sat down to write a canto in reply, but as it was just on the eve of my departure from Paris to London, I was obliged to defer same and pack my trunks (Eng. *boxes*), buy my tickets (Eng. *book passage*), check my baggage (Eng. *register luggage*), and board the Calais steamer (Eng. *Dover packet*), for Great Britain (Eng. *U.K.*). In its unfinished and formless state I enclose my immediate reaction to your letter.[14]

I am alone with my mother in this lovely town in Dorset. We live in a little thatched house in the village, board there, but I have a hut off in a field in view of the down but out of sight of everything else, where I can be by myself all day. That's where I am now. The hut is white-washed and has clean straw on the floor. I have a table and chair in it and a rope hammock, and that's all. The place is beautiful, not so barren as Truro. I love it. You would probably hate it. I have been sick as a dog for months, and so entirely convinced of the elaborate uselessness of everything, that there was nothing in the situation to get dramatic about and make a poem of, even. But little by little now I am getting back my health, and here in this quiet place somehow it doesn't seem to matter whether it matters or not. You know what I mean.

Bunny, is it only when you're tight that you want to be friends with me? I suppose so. And I don't complain. I have no rights in you. But I do solemnly offer this pious pagan prayer: that one of these days you'll become a dirty inveterate souse, and bully your wife and beat your kids and kick your dog, and think of me with steadfast love.

That's all of that.

What sort of person is Elinor Wylie? I think I should like her. I saw a great deal of Anna Wickham while I was in Paris this spring.

She's an awfully interesting person, great big jolly, untidy, scathing, tender and brilliant. She's about thirty-eight now, and strikes you at moments in her conversation as curiously reactionary in comparison with The Man with a Hammer and the Contemplative Quarry, which she wrote ten years ago. She's the most *essentially motherly* woman I ever met. Would you expect that? It was an astonishment to me. I like her tremendously. She's a thrilling person. Beautiful in a way: Magnificent big head, and sweet, fine eyes. She writes ten thousand poems a day, writes them on the café tables, on the backs of menus, on the waiter's apron, anywhere, many very bad, naturally, but some splendid, and all interesting. She is married to an astronomer named Hepburn, and has three boys, the oldest fourteen, and lives in Hampstead. I remember that you told me about her poetry last year when you were in Paris, and were very interested in her.

Do you know the poems of Henri de Régnier? Probably you do. I am awfully keen on some of them. He seems to have more poetic sense, by which I mean poetic common sense, more sense of poetry as apart from oratory, than most French poets.

Well, goodbye, Bunny. I'd like to see you again sometime.

Edna.

Thine of the pittifull occasioun
Of John the Bishop's triste perditioun
In hand, and prayeres for hiss woful plyght
Sente uppe, this Thirtieth daye of June att nyght.

When thatte the sonne, aloftt in highest heaven,
Aroused me from manye a softe sweven,
Certes, hard bye my pillowe did I see
A doulce billet from ye fatte Bunnye.
And toe myne eyen the sillye dropes did lepe,
Thus joyously to be y-shooke from slepe!

Syn I from love escaped am, I wisse,
But to be wounded bye thy gentilnesse,
Hark my confessioun, good Sir Bunnye:
Thy courteois words have sleyn me sodenly.
Thy salty wit and eke they words of silke
My herde herte have fonded into milke;
Now fare I forth with modest speech and kynde
To beasts and briddies and the doulce blynde.

The poet synges and spylls abroad hiss breth
In prayse of prettye friends brought lowe by dethe;
Ah, me!—to lose a friend bye lyfe, I gesse,
Holds lesse of songe and more of bitternesse!

Prithee, in future houres, cher Bunnye,
Think on thy distant friend withe charytee,
That hath of thee, I sware bye the swete sonne,
No evyll thought, but manye a wystful onne.

To E. W.
From E. St. V. M.

---

[14] The accompanying Chaucerian lines (printed here at the close of the letter) were inspired by the news of the wedding of their mutual friend, John Peale Bishop, the poet, which Edmund Wilson had communicated to Miss Millay.

104　TO NORMA MILLAY

MY HUT
Shillingstone,
Dorset, England.
July 21, 1922.

Dear lickle Normie:

I am writing thik letter (as the Dorset people would put it) in my little white-washed and straw-carpeted hut up in the field under the down, out of sight of man but not of beast, there being at the moment two horses, seven cows and a large flock of sheep gracing my dooryard and the down beyond. The field has just been mown, and smells very sweet, but will, I fear, never live to be hay, with seven cows and two horses gobbling it up as fast as they can. It's almost time for mother to be bringing me my luncheon. I stay here all by myself most all day, and scarcely ever see a living soul except the animals, and once in a while a shepherd taking a flock across the down. It's beautiful. You'd love it, sister. And so would Wumpie. Sometime we all must be together again in the summer. Wouldn't that be nice? If you only knew how often my baby needs a new pair of shoes! I am getting better, though for the last two months I have been very sick with my old chronically petrified intestine. However, I am really getting better, and perhaps shall be quite well again if I stay here long enough. Mother's such a cute old sport. Three days ago we walked to Blandford and back, a distance of twelve miles, and bought a hammock for my hut, and two grape-fruit, for which we paid a shilling apiece (a shilling is nearly a quarter) and some Keating's Flea-Powder, to sprinkle on my straw (!) and picked some beautiful flowers from the hedges all the way home, poppies and honey-suckle and garden-heliotrope, the tall white kind (only here it's rather pink) all grow wild here. Mother is wonderful. Think of twelve miles! Every day we go for a long walk, either climb one of the downs or walk to some other little village and back. She loves it. And she loves being able to speak the language, too. The people we live with are sweet. He is an old army man, that is, he's only forty-four, but he's been in the army since he was eighteen and is now retired on a pension, has spent a lot of time in India and Palestine, and tells very interesting things, being very careful of his English, and frequently apologizing for not being able to speak correctly, though he speaks astonishingly well, making very few slips into the Dorset; and she, his wife, who has never even been to London, and who adores him and thinks him quite the most wonderful thing in the world. And they call me Miss Edna, and they say, "Yes, miss. Quite so, miss. I expects you know all about that, miss, being so educated." They are *so* sweet.

Later. Mother has brought me my luncheon, or rather, my dinner, —one has mid-day dinner here—and stayed with me while I ate, and then gone back again. She cooks me nice things, meat and most always baked potatoes, and salad and bread-pudding with cream or prunes with cream—anything to get the cream into me—and milk for me to drink. She doesn't cook the milk, thank God, but I mean she brings it. She brings everything up all piping hot in a little basket with a cloth over it.

You were such a darling to send me that money the moment you got it, Norma. I hope you didn't send it too soon, so that you are going to need it. If you get hold of any more royalties, dear, don't think of sending them to me before you've paid that twenty-five to J. Cog— that you sent me in Vienna; that is only right, sweetheart; it was wonderful of you to do it, and it certainly saved my life just at the time, but you can't afford not to get it back.

I'm so glad that you and Chas are playing in the same company. What luck that you could get together like that. I hope you'll have such good luck all along, dear kids, that it'll be like a fairy-tale.

Oh, there are such lovely larks and blackbirds here! You'll cry the first time you hear a lark's song, Normie, just as I did. They are little sort of brown birds that make their nests in ploughed ground, and when they're not on the ground they're way up in the air; they have never been known to alight in a tree even for a moment. When they sing they leave the ground suddenly and rise right straight up in the air, and then usually they just stand still in one place, fluttering their wings all the time, and sing the most wonderful joyous, rippling, trilling, drunken song, sometimes singing longer than three minutes without stopping, way way up in the sky, a tiny black speck, or out of sight altogether. There's nothing in the world like it. You'll hear it some day.[15]

Mother and I have dandelion greens all the time. And you'd die at mother. This is what she cooked one day all in a pot together and served up to be et: dandelions, mustard, dock, pig-weed, clover, nettles and thistles! I put the clover in myself, making fun of her for cooking nettles and thistles. Some of the neighbors had told her nettles were good, boiling takes out all the sting—when they're alive they are the most awful things in the world to get into, next to poison ivy, they burn just exactly like fire—and the kind of thistle she gathers is called milk-thistle, it's much gentler than the other kind, but that's not saying much. But I tell everybody how my mother feeds me on nettles and thistles, the heartless old thing.

I just heard a little lamb bleating. He is up on top of the down. You would be crazy about the down, darling. It is something like the dunes at Truro, like the big one opposite our house, only it's higher and bigger, and part of it is all barren and the rest is covered with little scrubby hawthorn trees and prickly gorse bushes. And flocks of sheep graze up the side of it all morning. Last night mother and I, on our way walking back from a little hamlet called Okeford Fitzpaine (isn't that too wonderful?) saw two little twin bullocks in a meadow, tiny ones, just exactly alike, with about six inches of white on the end of each tail, and their mother licked first one and then the other.

Well, after all this news, about calves and dandelions, the Bingville Bugle will draw to a conclusion.

But not before I tell you how beautiful I think your photographs are, and how sweet above all things you were to send me one of each kind. I think you posted them the 17th of February; I didn't get them until, I think, the twentieth of June, something ridiculous like that. Where they were all that time I can't imagine. I will send you a little photo of our sister Sefe as soon as I can find an envelope that it will fit in.

Goodbye, Lovid. So much love to you and to Charlie.

Vincent.

P.S.   It's just begun to rain, & on my tin roof it sounds "like firecrackers under a dish-pan." I'm so glad you liked "The Barrel."¹⁶ I like it, too.

                                                                    Sefe.

P.S. You remember once I stole some of your English lavender to burn & make a nice smell. Well, here's some English lavender on account.

> ¹⁵ This bird, "A dark articulate atom in the mute enormous blue," is the subject of a poem in the volume *The Buck in the Snow:* "On First Having Heard the Skylark."
> ¹⁶ One of the prose pieces which appeared under her own name in the July, 1922, issue of *Vanity Fair*.

105   TO ALLAN ROSS MACDOUGALL

                                        Shillingstone, Dorset
                                        July 22, 1922

Dearest li'l' Wisdim Toot',

Here I is way up in a hut in a field in Dorset, H'England.—*And* where is you, li'l' Savige Bres'?—Did you see the cullud lights in Virsailles? End was they beautifil?

———

Good luck to you, swittie,—have a swill times this summer.—End don't fergit to rimimbah thy littil aingil wot pelpertates fer thee here.

———

I carried the sweet roses like a child in my arms all the way to London. They didn't get sea-sick at all, and they didn't mind the rain at all, and I put them in a jug, & they lasted three days.

Love & kisses from both me & my ma.

                                                        Thine,
                                                        Edner.

106   TO ARTHUR DAVISON FICKE

                                        Shillingstone, Dorset
                                        August 8   [1922]

Sweet old Arthur,—

Am having a fine time.—Wish you was here.

———

I've thought of you a lot.—I've been thinking somewhat, too, of Mrs. Fate & Mr. Gord, & other star parts in this Hicktown mellerdrammer full of worn-out jokes entitled, "*Life,* or *Ain't it Hell to be Thirsty.*"

Gladys[17] is here, just down the road from me, & has a horse to ride, & looks handsome in her riding-things.—I have discovered that she paints damwell. Why didn't you tell me?

Oh, how ridiculous everything is!—One's conversation broken off in the middle of a sentence!—My dear, you know what I mean, all I mean, & when I send my love you know I mean that, too.

—Vincent.

[17] Gladys Brown, an artist, who on December 8th of the following year was married to Arthur Ficke.

107   TO ALLAN ROSS MACDOUGALL

> The American Women's Club,
> 41, Hertford Street
> Park Lane, W.1. [London]
> [September 6, 1922]

Darlink li'l' Wisdim Toot,

I hears indirect that youse is hard up & wantin' a job. I aint got no job, but it occurs to I that while waitink for sed job, inclosed might come in handy.—So tek it, its your very own.

Why dont you hire a hall like Harrison done & sing littil songs & mek monies offn the idil ritch? If I was there stid of where I is I would sell many tickets for youse: Krazy would do gret thinks were he only where he isnt, doubtless.

In the mintime mutch love like alwiz, to my dear Ignatz,

> from his faithfil
> Krazy.

108   TO EDMUND WILSON

> The American Women's Club,
> 41, Hertford Street,
> Park Lane, W.1. [London]
> [September 14, 1922]

Dear Bunny,—

You will have received by now the three articles sent by Mr. Wood.—If the one called *The Key*[18] is too long, please don't cut it,

or do anything to it, *or let anybody else,* but just send it back to me,
& I'll send you something in its place.—There were a couple of changes
made in *The Barrel,* & I was furious. Don't let Crownie do anything to
anything that's signed by my own name.—As for Nancy, that's a little
different.—But Crownie asked me once if, should he want to use two
Nancy Boyd things in the same number, I would be willing to have
him sign some other name to one of them. I replied that I should be
perfectly willing. But I must have been drunk at the time, because I'm
not willing at all. Don't even let him do that.

You might reply to my sweet letter I wrote you,—but suit yourself, old thing.

I'll bet the heading of this paper made you laugh.

I received *The Undertaker's Garland*[19] with its devilish inscription;
but I refuse to say a word about it until you write me.

Yours,
Edna.

[18] A prose piece published under the poet's own name in the
December, 1922, *Vanity Fair.*
[19] A book of prose and verse by John Peale Bishop and
Edmund Wilson.

109   TO MARGUERITE WILKINSON

Shillingstone, Dorset,
England.
Sept. 25, 1922.

Dear Marguerite Wilkinson:

Go right ahead and use Renascence and The Beanstalk.[20] As to the
possible reaction of Mr. Mitchell Kennerley,—we should worry. I
hardly believe that Mr. Kennerley is anxious to become involved in a
law-suit with me, in which he would, I should think, cut a rather
ridiculous and unpopular figure, since from one year to the next I
receive from him not one penny of royalties on any of the three books
of mine which he has published.

Some day I shall see about that, too.

But in the meantime, go right ahead and use the poems, with my
authorization. And if Mr. Kennerley nags you about them, tell him that
Edna Millay suggests that he go to hell.

(You would have received this restrained and elegant epistle some time ago, except that I never got the other letter of which you write. Although I did get the letter about New Voices, and was glad to know that you liked Second April, even though it was too late for you to use any of it.)

Very sincerely yours,
Edna St. Vincent Millay

20 The two poems were published in the anthology *Contemporary Poetry*, published June 19, 1923, a recasting of *New Voices*, which had previously printed only "Renascence." The new volume had also "Autumn Chant."

110 TO NORMA MILLAY

Shillingstone,
October 13 [1922]

Dearest Normie:

I see by the letters you forwarded to me that you are back in New York. I am so anxious to hear how everything went in Rochester. It seems as if I had not heard from you for a long time; and I know I haven't written you for a long time! Mother and I had the bright idea about three weeks ago of writing you and Wumps a great long letter, and with that great long letter on our chests, of course we haven't written at all. So this is just to break the silence between us, baby, as I am terribly busy, writing, and can't stop very long. It seems almost hopeless to try to write you at all, I have so many things to write about, so many thousands of little insignificant, but interesting, things to tell you. For example: that one day I saw A. E. Housman, who wrote A Shropshire Lad, and chased his retreating tall, thin grey figure and cotton umbrella for about half a mile through the streets of Cambridge, till he turned in at Trinity College[21] and was lost in the gloom. I caught just a glimpse of his face, a nice face. They say nobody ever sees him, that he goes along like a shadow and is lost before he's found.— Darling, I don't know if you know that I have an agent now for my stuff, Brandt & Kirkpatrick, New York. They have a London representative, and the London representative just wrote me that they have an offer from Martin Secker a very good English publisher, (he has published D. H. Lawrence's last books) for a volume of my selected poems, stuff selected from all my books that have been published in the States.

Won't it be nice to be published in London? I have written them that I will do it.—Charlie may be interested to know that while I was in Paris I met the sculptor, Brancusi, who did some things that Walter Arensberg had in his studio,[22]—do you remember?—notably, a great shining brass thing that might have been two breasts and a long curved neck and a round blunt head, and might have been a penis and two testicles. I am sure Charlie will remember, and I think you will.

Brancusi was giving a dinner in his studio one night, for one other person and me—he does his own cooking—and the other person didn't come until later, so the two of us had dinner all alone. It's the greatest, barest studio you ever saw, all white beams and white blocks of marble and everything covered with white dust like a flour mill, and we ate our dinner off a great round marble thing like an enormous mill-stone, and all full of little depressions and bitten-out places where he has pounded and banged at his work—no cloth on the table, and in the entire room not a square-foot of fabric of any sort, no hanging tapestries, no kimonos flung over easels, no pictures, nothing—only some beautiful, pure curving figures standing on pedestals, looking like nothing on earth that you ever saw, things complexly wrought into a simplicity that fools one,—and little Brancusi with his fine, shaggy, grizzly-dark head and beautiful black eyes, dressed in loose trousers and a shirt rather like a smock, and heavy rough shoes, which either *were* wooden sabots or looked exactly like them—a little Roumanian peasant and a great sculptor all at the same time, shuffling in from the kitchen with bowls of soup, and chicken that he had broiled himself, and poking up the fire in the big, rough white-stone stove, like a stove you build on the beach, that he had made himself, and the two of [us] chattering at each other in two different kinds of French, and eating big white radishes sliced across like turnips, and drinking sweet white wine.

Well, so much for that. It is beautiful weather in the country now, and we shall stay here as long as it holds. Then to London. Then, in the spring to Spain, I think, and on to Italy, and so home. It is almost two years since I said goodbye to my sweet brothers and sisters. My mother doesn't count, for here she is right here, jumping round me and barking and dragging at my skirt to get me to go beech-nutting.

I hope Gladys Brown has been to see you. She is the secretary, I think it is the secretary, of the Whitney Club, and herself paints charming things, things that give me, at least, the "aesthetic emotion." I should like her and Charlie to be friends. And if Tess Root hasn't been to see you, you look up Charles T. Root in the telephone-book,

2 West 67th Street, and call up the hussy, and make yourself known to her. She has a whole lot of snap-shots of Shillingstone, and me, etc.

Why didn't you write me a weeny note when you forwarded the letters? Was you house-cleaning, or was you mad at me?

Who is The Provincetown Players this season? I say "is" advisedly.

I'd give a lot to ride with you on a horse's back, two horses' backs, Normie. Some day we'll go to Camden and have three horses, and you and Wumps and I all go *widey*-widey-widey-*widey* just like the Ballard girls! I am crazy about it. And I know you are. I have been just twice, though, this summer, though the second time was a long ride, and besides, right in the middle of it, I got thrown on the back of my head in the asphalt road, which, like the cat in the window, counts fifty. Gladys will tell you all about that, she was my riding-master, and an excellent one. Needless to say, it was not in her general program of instructions that I should go off on the back of my head into the road. Howsomever, I done it, being too strongly an individualist by nature to follow any course of instructions too closely. And after I had done it, I sat up, rather slowly, and watched my horse disappearing up the road at a brisk trot, and put my hand to the back of my head, and took it away covered with blood, and wondered what had happened to my boot to knock the heel off, and thought what a nice, nice road it was, and that I would sit there a long, long time, in that nice, nice road, and not get up for anybody, not even for Gladys. But I did get up and Gladys went off after my horse and brought him back, and I climbed up again into the saddle, though one of my legs wouldn't work at all, which made the process rather involved, not to say difficult. Well, they say you have to be thrown one hundred and fifty times before you're an expert horsewoman! Suffice it to say that I had a wonderful time every minute of the time, even when I felt myself falling. That's what it is to be crazy about anything.

Now goodbye, darlink, Sefe must go to woik.

Love to you both. And *please* write me.

Vincent.

[21] A. E. Housman, the poet, was a fellow of Trinity College, Cambridge, and also occupied the Kennedy Chair of Latin in the University. He is reported to have remarked to an American reviewer some years later: "I get more enjoyment from Edna St. Vincent Millay than from either Robinson or Frost." In 1932, in a letter to the Director of the Fitzwilliam Museum at Cambridge, Sir Sydney Cockerell, Housman also wrote: "Some things of Edna St. Vincent

Millay which I have seen make me think her the best living American poet, but as she is said to be profuse and unequal, I have never tackled a book of hers; so I shall be grateful for a sight of the sonnets which you approve of, though I could wish that they were not sonnets." Two weeks later he acknowledged the receipt of the book, saying: "I am very much obliged to you for letting me see *Fatal Interview*, which is mighty good."

²² The Walter Conrad Arensberg Collection is now housed in the Museum of Fine Arts in Philadelphia.

111 TO KATHLEEN MILLAY

Shillingstone [England]
Oct. 13 [1922]

Dearest Wumpus:

Sefe sends you bad picture of hisself, just for fun, cause he wanted to send youse picture of hisself, and good ones aint forthcomin'.

By the way—don't know why I thought of it—did you ever get a handkerchief I sent you to give to Isobel for her birthday, and did you ever give it to her? I was afraid it might have been lost. Not that it was of much importance.

Kathleen, I wish you would get out of the public library, or buy, or in some way procure, some books telling all about Einstein's Theory of Relativity, etc. So that when I get home you will be able to talk to me about it. I have just read a book by a Frenchman, an astronomer of the Observatoire at Paris, called *Einstein et l'Univers*. The whole thing is fascinating. I longed for you to talk it over with. You would adore it. That is, always provided you don't already know all about it. I know I'm rather late. Do read up on it, darling. It stretches the mind. It's a wonderful cold bath for the imagination.

I've been chewing some of the spruce gum you sent mother from Maine. What a thrill! I can just see the tree you dug it from; I know just how the bark looked. You said in your last letter that you both were feeling well, better for your summer on the sea-shore. I hope you haven't lost any of the good of it, now that you are—as I suppose you are—back in town.

Now we're going beech-nutting. We'll send you some, if we get some good ones.

Goodbye, darling.

Your loving sister,
Sefe.

112 TO NORMA MILLAY and CHARLES ELLIS

Shillingstone,
November 10, 1922.

Dearest Normie AND CHAS:

Just got your wonderful letter. Couldn't believe my eyes, it was so lovely and long. And so clever and amusing!—You're getting to be a very bright girl, ole hoss. I'm so glad you got the money back for the flowers that weren't delivered. Must have come in handy. As for your dirty industry of forging my name on all Aria da Capo checques —more power to your Waterman, and more performances of Aria da Capo! Can you tell me who sent in my bit of biography to Who's Who? I get a note from them by this post, saying, "You kindly revised your personal sketch for us several months ago, and of course it appears in this new volume." They also remind me in a chiding tone that my order for the ten or twelve copies absolutely necessary to me in my business, is not yet in. Who revised the dam sketch, that's what I want to know! That was a nice little review of the Two Slatterns, wasn't it? How did Stewart Kidd happen to publish that?[23] I never told 'em to. Oh, well, why worry about trifles. No, I'm not writing much poetry. A bunch of all the stuff I had on hand I have just sent on to Brandt & Kirkpatrick to place for me, also a story about Paris, called "The Murder in the Fishing Cat".[24] I tell you, me and Eddie Poe,—there's no stopping us Americans. As for HARDIGUT, it's really going to be published next spring. Liveright has got my agents by the coat-tail, and I get a wireless from them every other day anent the matter. Now little Ediner is hopping to the south of France to write the dam thing. But don't tell anybody; Liveright thinks it's all ready but numbering the chapters. Darling, I'm so glad you liked the picture. I sort of liked it myself, although so many people assured me it doesn't do me justice. Perhaps I'm handsomer than when you last saw me, so that you are satisfied where my more recent acquaintance wouldn't be. By now you have received the heart-rending ditty of Flea-Bane Floss and Furze-Bush Fan,[25] and probably the nuts we sent. It was disgusting about the other box. I explained all that to Kay.

* * *

Yes, Nancy is going to write a play, she just told me so, but says she thinks it best to wait till she gets back to New York and talks it over with her foster sisters and brothers. Nancy is going strong in

Vanity Fair, isn't she? Isn't she a blessing? Almost two years now the woman has been well nigh supporting me. Floyd Dell sent me a copy of his book of plays—Sweet-and-Twenty is dedicated to me, as perhaps you know—and told me he loves The Poet and his Book. I'm so glad people are beginning to notice that poem. I'm so tired of hearing about Renascence I'm nearly dead. I find it's as hard to live down an early triumph as an early indiscretion; if Renascence had been an illegitimate child people couldn't have flung it in my face any oftener. Darling, sister misses you so, to talk over poems and stories with!

* * *

Mother tells me to tell you she was so sorry not to get the beautiful flowers [for] her birthday, but that she is awfully glad you succeeded in getting the money back, and that you can meet her on the dock with a bunch of roses when she blows in to New York again, which won't be so terriby, terribly long now. Half of November is gone now, and then there's December, January, February, March, April, May, and maybe by the last of June we'll be home. Maybe in seven months I'll see you again. That's really not so long, when you consider it's nearly two years since I sailed from Pier 57. It *was* cute of me to come over here and stay, wasn't it, and to bring mother over? I'm so glad you get a thrill out of that. I do, too, whenever I think of it. I'll never cease to be grateful that I was able to bring mother abroad, while she is still, to all intents and purposes, young. You can't know how she enjoys it, and what a wonderful time we have together. We are rather looking forward to leaving England now, it has been so cold and disagreeable nearly all summer, although the country is undeniably beautiful. Yesterday afternoon was perfect autumn weather for a few hours, and we went out to get the holly to send you. You can't imagine how beautiful a holly tree is. I took a picture of one we saw when we were walking through the New Forest (not so very new, as this was the name given it, I believe, by William the Conqueror, as mother has perhaps told you). The tree was as tall as some of the pines, not the tall pines, but anyway, it was as tall as a tall pear-tree, and thick to the ground with branches laden with red berries. I don't know whether the picture will come out or not, as it was rather dark, and also as I'm rather a new hand at the Kodak—I always was a dub at that kind of thing, as you probably remember. But if it's any good, we'll surely send you one. Darling, I must say goodbye for now. So much love from mother and me to you and Charlie! When you see again that nice Walter Fleïsher, give him my affectionate regards. And remember me to Remo [Bufano].

Your loving sister,
Vincent.

P.S.   Allan Macdougall, whom I love, will be in New York by the time you get this. If you see him, be nice to him, for my sake. You see, I forget whether you got to like him or not yourself. Though on second thought, it seems to me that you did.

[23] Published by Stewart Kidd Company, Cincinnati, in their Modern Plays series, November 5, 1921.

[24] This mystery story appeared under the poet's own name, in the *Century Magazine* for March, 1923. It was reprinted in the *Ellery Queen Mystery Magazine*, May, 1950 and was the subject of letter No. 258 to the editor of that periodical.

[25] Comic verses about the poet and her mother in England.

---

113   TO HORACE LIVERIGHT

[Shillingstone,]
November [1922]

Dear Horace:

All this is a devilish nuisance. I have worked on the book[26] in Vienna, and in Paris, and now in Dorset I'm finishing it. But don't ask me for a description of the book, and don't scold me. It's working itself out beautifully and I like it.

Name of the novel, Hardigut. Ready for publication in April. The circumstances of my story are laid in a country where people, otherwise perfectly sane and normal, do not eat in public, or discuss food except in inuendos and with ribald laughter; where for unmarried people to eat anything at all is scandalous; where young boys and girls struggle through a starved adolescence into a hasty and ill-assorted marriage; where the stomach is never mentioned, and if you have a stomach-ache, you tell people you have a head-ache or writer's cramp.

No, the book isn't too highbrow. It is a story and it has a real hero, and a real heroine, and a plot, and its characters are, of course, just the people you and I have known all our lives. The book will be amusing, satiric, ugly, beautiful, poetic, and an unmistakable allegory.

[26] This letter to the publisher constituted the text printed on the back page of the dust-jacket for *Hardigut*. The remainder of the letter is not available.

114   TO ISOBEL SIMPSON

> Hôtel du Panorama
> Cassis-sur-Mer
> Bouches du Rhône, France.
> Dec. 15, 1922.

Dearest Little Sphinx:

My instinct, of course, when you tell me to *come home*, is to *come home!*—But I have a mother with me who *won't come home* until she has seen Italy!—at any rate, we are leaving France very soon & going in to Italy. We are going slowly along the Riviera, to Cannes & Nice & Monte Carlo, & then on to Italy. In the spring we are going to spend a month in Paris, then a month in London, & then we are going to *come home*!!

Dear, there *has* been something wrong with me,—I have been very sick; but I am better now. I have been quite respectably, but very unromantically ill,—trouble arising from an improper diet, unfamiliar queer foods in Hungary & Albania, etc., which have played the devil with me.—Thank heaven mother has been with me, & has been getting me straightened out.—But I came within an ace of having peritonitis, which is not a tidy thing to have.

Well, so much for that.—Only now I am really better, & you mustn't worry about me any more, sweetheart.—I love you always, just as ever. And someday, before very long, I shall see you again,—and you will squeak such a silly little squeak, just as ever, & we shall both be so happy.—So goodbye, little sphinx, and Merry Christmas, and a Very Happy New Year.

> From your most loving serpent,
> Edna.

115   TO ARTHUR DAVISON FICKE

> [Hôtel du Panorama
> Cassis-sur-Mer
> Bouches du Rhône, France]
> Dec. 17, 1922.

Arthur, dear,

It's not true that I don't like the sonnets. I love them. You know perfectly well, you lying dog, that I think you write wonderful sonnets. The reason why I haven't said anything about them is this:—I have been sick, so that I can just drag about, & what strength I have must go into the novel which Liveright is to publish in the spring;[27] and I couldn't bear simply to write, "I received the sonnets; they are very nice;" I wanted to have time to speak of each one separately, go over & over them, telling you what I thought about each little thing. And I haven't been able to do that. So I've said nothing. And you know that what I'm saying is the truth. So there's that.—And you can just stop nagging me.

Isn't it funny about you & Gladys?—My God—it's marvelous.—You don't need to tell me what a nice girl Gladys Brown is—*"nicer than that!!!"* I know in my way, just as well as you know in your way, how nice she is.—I knew it the first moment I set eyes on her in Prunier's. You can't fool me. And you didn't think we'd like each other!—men don't know very much.

Is this a snippy letter, dear?—No, it isn't. I shall love you till the day I die.—Though I shan't always be thinking about it, thank God.—Yet I shall be thinking about it every time I think about you, that's sure.

As for Hal, there's not the slightest danger that I shall marry him: he has jilted me!

With love,
Vincent.

[27] After her return to America, the novel *Hardigut* was abandoned due to ill health.

V

New York—The Orient—Steepletop

1923 – 1925

Mount Airy
Croton, N. Y.
May 2nd, 1923.

Dear Miss Tietjens:

I was a mean scut not to have answered your letter ages ago. Perhaps if I had had a poem for you I might have had the energy to send it but I hadn't a thing. Also I have never written in a dream so much as a single dactyl—so I am afraid I am not of much use to you.

I remember too the night I met you at the Poetry Society, and have been sorry that I did not get even a minute to talk with you. Let me know the next time you come to New York.

Very sincerely yours,
Edna St. Vincent Millay.

[1] Author of *Profiles from China* and one of the editors of *Poetry*, Miss Tietjens had sent out a questionnaire asking contributors to the magazine if they had ever written any of their poems in a dream.

117   TO EDMUND WILSON

Mount Airy
Croton, N. Y.
May 2nd, 1923.

Dear Bunny:

I did read the poems you left and like them very much. Who is this person?[2] I never even heard of her. I was quite thrilled by some of the poems. Isn't it wonderful how the lady poets are coming along? "Votes for women" is what I sez!

If you want the manuscript back at once I shall have to arrange to have my flat broken into and the envelope stolen for you, because I left town in a great hurry, tired to death and thinking of nothing but getting away. Write me if you want the poems at once and I will arrange to have Norma or somebody get in and get them for you.

I know Crowny is terribly peeved at me.[3] He thinks, I am sure, that the reason why I have not been writing anything for Vanity Fair lately is because I am writing for the Saturday Evening Post or something. Truth is I have not put pen to paper for anybody—not even for myself—in months. Please tell Crowny that I really am very tired and ill and not to be angry with me. I will write him too.

My love to Elinor.[4]

Edna.

[2] Louise Bogan.
[3] After the sonnet "To a Dying Man" printed in the June, 1923, issue (Sonnet XIV in *The Harp-Weaver and Other Poems*) no further contribution from Miss Millay, in prose or verse, appeared in *Vanity Fair* until September, 1928, when the lyric, "The Road to Avrillé" was printed.
[4] Elinor Wylie.

118   TO MRS. CORA B. MILLAY

Croton-on-Hudson
(New York)
May 30, 1923.

Dearest Mother:

I have been a bad girl not to write you, or send you any money, or send the book to Aunt Susie, or anything. But you will forgive me when you know my excuse. Darling, do you remember meeting Eugen Boissevain one day in Waverly Place?— It was only for a moment, & possibly you don't remember. But anyway, you will like him very much when you know him, which will be soon. And it is important that you should like him,—because I love him very much, & am going to marry him.

There!!!

Will you forgive me?—My mind has been pretty much taken up with all this, & I have neglected my mummie.—We shall be married sometime this summer, I don't know just when. Anyhow, we are coming up to Maine to visit you, either before or after, it won't matter, because it's perfectly proper for me to bring a gentleman-friend to visit my mother. We are going to motor up. Gene has a beautiful big Mercer,—at least he had, but now he has given it to me, so I have one. Won't that be fun?

You must need money, dear, but I don't know where you are, so I don't dare send a money-order. Let me know as soon as you get this & I will send you some—I haven't at the moment a great deal (except my thousand bucks,[5] which I ain't going to bust for god or hero,—

going to start a bank-account with it)—but I will send you a little, & there'll be more coming.

The mayflowers & violets were beautiful, sweetheart. A few of them were a little bit faded, that's all. They were perfectly beautiful. And I was too thrilled for expression. If you're still at Aunt Clem's, send me some dandelion greens here!—I love 'em, & so does HE!

_____

Don't tell a soul yet—*not a soul, nor a body neither—on pain of excommunication!*

Vincent.

⁵ The Pulitzer Award.

119   TO MRS. CORA B. MILLAY

June, Two Days before the TENTH
[1923]
Tess' Room, Waverly Place
[New York]

Darling Mother:

I am in town just for a few days, motoring out to Croton again this afternoon. At last I am doing what I should have ages ago, having an excellent diagnostician examine me thoroughly, and board me out to all kinds of different specialists who examine me in their own particular line, and all that. Pretty soon I shall know something about the condition of my insides, and what to do about it, and then I shall get well, and feel every day the way I felt that day in Cassis—do you remember?—when I took a plunge in the Mediterranean and then we went for a walk together up the hills among the vineyards. For the last three days I have been going to an X-ray man two or three times a day, having my stomach and bowels X-rayed. I have six doctors at work on me for different things. Don't be the least bit alarmed, dearest. It doesn't mean that I feel any worse than I have done for the last two years; it just means that at last I am going about getting cured in a reasonable way. So much for that.

In a couple of weeks or so Norma and Charlie and Eugen and I (I hope you got my letter about him!) are going to motor up to Camden and spend maybe a month with you,—if you will invite us. But please don't say much about this, darling, because I don't want to see a soul. I am allowed to work only one hour a day now, and I have to be lying down fifteen hours out of the twenty-four, and I must be pretty quiet and see almost nobody. These are severe instructions, severely enforced. I must tell you again not to worry about me; I don't feel bad at all; I am just being helped to get perfectly well, you see.

I hope you get this letter Saturday afternoon before your birthday. It isn't much of a birthday letter, all about me and nothing about you, but I know that nothing would be so nice a birthday-present for you as to know that I am being taken care of, and am going before long to be well and strong again. Eugen has been taking me to these doctors; probably by myself I would never have done it. You will like him, mother.[6] I must go now and pack my suitcase to go back to the country. I have to see one more specialist, and then we leave. It's a wild life! Love and love and love and Happy Birthday, sweetheart, and see you soon

Vincent.

[6] Edna St. Vincent Millay and Eugen Boissevain were married at Croton-on-Hudson on the morning of July 18, 1923, Miss Millay entering a New York hospital later that day, as previously arranged, for a serious operation.

120   TO ESTHER ROOT

[Croton-on-Hudson
August 24, 1923]

Tess, darling,—

No, they were not withered & I did not laugh,—all my childhood is in those bayberry-bushes, & queen-of-the-meadow, or maybe you called it hardhack, & rose-hips. And cranberries—I remember a swamp of them that made a short-cut to the railroad station when I was seven. It was down across that swamp my father went, when my mother told him to go & not come back.

(Or maybe she said he might come back if he would do better—but who ever does better?)

I looked most lovingly at every separate stem of the fifty different weeds & shrubs—it is raspberry, not blackberry, isn't it?—& is the little branch of leaves from a birch-tree?—a white birch? The blueberries came in the most perfect condition, not one crushed—they used to grow like that—acres of them—on my uncle's farm—& there was a little black & white dog named . . . was it Charlie?—who used to eat them from the bushes.

I must lie down & rest before Gene comes home. I am much stronger, but I have still to lie down rather often.

Bless you, my dear. How sweet you were, & how wise.

—Edna.

121   TO MRS. CORA B. MILLAY

> Hotel Holley
> Washington Square West
> New York
> Nov. 7, 1923

Dear Mummie,—

Eugen & I are crazy about the blankets—the two white ones are the sweetest, softest, most darling things; & the green one is terribly smart & handsome, just right for the car, as you suggested.—We are staying here at the Holley until our house shall be done—this is a lovely hotel, & the prices are very reasonable. I don't think you would mind it here at all for a little while—I really like it a lot—

* * *

Here is $75, dear, I hope you can make it do till you get back to N. Y. It is wonderful to have the Camden bills paid,—but of course it has made quite a hole in my bank account, which I must get busy and fill. Of course my lecture trip in January & February will do wonders for me. I shall clear nearly two thousand dollars which will come in very handy.—I am thrilled, darling, that the Camden-Rockland bills are paid . . . It seemed to me it would be too bad to have anything hanging over.—I suppose it is a mean pride in me, but oh, I wish I could have done this before I got married!—because of course everybody thinks it is my rich husband who has done it, when in fact it is really I myself, every cent of it, with money that I made by writing,— nearly a thousand dollars, in all, since you went to Camden.

Oh, well, it doesn't matter.

You didn't see my glasses down there anywhere, I suppose. I imagine I left them in some hotel on the way down. If I read without them I get a headache, for my eyes are still weak after my operation. I must get some others at once.

I think you would better wait till you come to N. Y. to see about publishing your poems.[7] You may do better than that. See you soon, dear.

Love,
Vincent.

[7] Short poems in which a little boy, Otis, relates his adventures. Later published in book form under the title *Little Otis* by Norton, 1928.

122   TO MRS. CORA B. MILLAY

Holley Hotel
Wash. Sq. West
N.Y.C.
Dec. 27, '23

Dearest Mummie,—

Forgive my long silence.—I am just recovering from my annual bronchitis!—I "went up to London to see the Queen"—that is, I went down to Washington to see the President—with a whole bunch of suffragists—also to read a poem which I had written, at a conference thingumajig in the Capitol[8]—I enclose the poem—written a propos of Susan B. Anthony and two other women who founded the Women's Party seventy-five years ago, or so—& I caught cold on the train—& here I am,—I'm all right again now—but somehow, ever since my operation, I catch cold twice as easy, & the dentist hurts me twice as much, etc.—Of course it's just because I'm not at all strong yet.—Eugen & I are stuck here until Dec. [Jan.?] 1, when at last we get into our house. I haven't been able to do anything about anything,—about your poems, or about anything of my own—as you know, Arthur Ficke even corrected my *Harp-Weaver* proofs for me. *The Harp-Weaver & Other Poems* is out now, and so is my English volume of selected poems that Martin Secker did. I send you three little pictures, one for you, one for Aunt Clem, & one for Uncle Albert. Uncle Albert is to have first choice, (& don't you and Aunt Clem get jealous), Aunt Clem second choice, & you are just to take what's left!—See?

The big package came but is still in Eugen's office. When our house is ready we are going to have it sent straight there.

[8] The unveiling of a statue to three pioneer fighters for women's rights: Lucretia Mott, Susan B. Anthony, and

Elizabeth Cady Stanton, in Washington on November 18, 1923. The poem referred to was the sonnet "The Pioneer" p. 66 of *The Buck in the Snow*. In the reprinting in *Collected Sonnets* it is dedicated to Inez Milholland, for whose staunch fight for Women's Suffrage during the Wilson administration the poet had great admiration.

123   TO EDMUND WILSON

75½ Bedford Street[9]
New York City.
Jan. 8, 1924

Dearest Bunny,—

Am I a swine?—Oh, but such a little one!—Such a elegant and distinguished one!—So pink & white!—A truffle-sniffer, not a trough-wallower!

I love you just as ever. I would go driving with you in Central Park in an open Victoria in a howling blizzard in a muslin frock.

But, since there is so little snow-fall as yet, won't you come to see me here instead—at 4 o'clock this Thursday, or at 4 o'clock next Monday?

—I will offer you a cigarette, just to be playful; and then I will give you a fine, sound, rosy-cheeked apple,—because my heart is really in the right place.

———————————

Do come, Bunny, Or suggest some other time. Wire me. Soon I shall depart this life or leave for Pittsburgh & points west on a reading-tour. I want to see you before I go. Let not the light tone of this communication put you off. I do want to see you.

Edna.

[9] This is a narrow three-story brick house, 9½ feet wide by 30 feet deep. The place is still pointed out to guided tourists in Greenwich Village as "Edna Millay's house."

124 TO EUGEN JAN BOISSEVAIN

Chicago & Northwestern Station
10:25 A.M. Wednesday [January, 1924]

Darling:—

I have made my train, & here I sit. The thing is just about to pull
out. The conductor has just called *all aboard* in the most musical &
lovely way—sort of like this—

All   Bo-ad

I put this down here not because it's done right, but because I want to
remember how it goes, & this is near enough.

Did you ever go from Chicago to Cedar Rapids on one of these
Middle-Western so-called Parlor-cars?—Well, don't. The only difference I see between this & the day-coach is that in the day-coach you
have one person at your elbow, & you see the backs of several people's
heads, & if you are lucky you get a seat by the window & can look out:
—whereas,—in the Parlor-Car you have two people at your elbow—
one at the right & one at the left, you stare into the faces of a long
row of people, and your chair is nailed with its back to the window
so that you couldn't possibly see a thing, even if you should happen to
want to, which I should say is unlikely; you have no place at all to
put your luggage, because right in front of your feet is the aisle where
people walk back & forth; you are squeezed together as tight as in seats
at the theatre; you couldn't possibly lean your head on the back of
your chair, because it isn't high enough,—also, it has no white towel
on it—well, in fact it is just like the subway when the subway comes
up for air at 137th Street. And I am to spend six hours in this chair.
Though I imagine they have a diner. If it is as funny as this I shall die.
Ask Arthur why he never told me about these terrible trains.

My hands are so dirty it's almost theatrical. Everybody who looks
at me wonders why such a nice girl, with such a beautiful gold pencil,
& such expensive cuff-links, & such a refined & elegant address-book,
has such dirty hands.—I don't care. I'm tired of washing my hands. It's
a great waste of time. Besides, in the winter it's dangerous. It is likely
to roughen the skin.

The men's & women's toilets are directly opposite one another, at the end of the car. If a man & a woman started to come out of them at the same moment, & turned to shut the door, they would bump backsides.

I got through my two readings yesterday well enough—the one in the afternoon in Evanston was a great success—a crowded house, large audience, etc.—But the one in the evening was in a private house!—A bunch of wealthy people come together to see what I looked like, & bet with each other as to how many of my naughty poems I would dare to read.—My hostess herself & her children were sweet & real people, & intelligent. There were a few women who came up & talked to me who had really liked some of the poems besides the *Figs from Thistles;* & one man, who was motoring back to Chicago & brought me home, was really a delight, awfully nice & clever & amusing, & seemed to know all my books by heart.—He said his seventeen-year-old daughter also knows my poems by heart.—But on the whole—oh, Jesus!—If ever I felt like a prostitute it was last night.—I kept saying over & over to myself while I was reading to them, "Never mind—it's a hundred & fifty dollars."—I hope I shall never write a poem again that more than five people will like.

The two gentlemen opposite me have just decided to have a friendly little morning chaw of gum together.—The one on my right is following with much concern the fortunes of *Abie the Agent* in the Chicago Evening American.

————————————

It's wonderful to write to you, my dearest. It takes the sting out of almost anything, I find. I wanted you so last night. I was pretty unhappy. And of course I was tired, too.—I had to get up early this morning, because I made a sudden decision to check out of the Hotel Windermere & never look upon its face again,—so I had to pack & it takes an hour to get from the hotel to the station, & I had to take a 10:30 train. This is a hard-luck letter, so I'll just keep on, & tell you about the Windermere Hotel, which is the God-damndest place I ever set an unwary foot in. You know, it advertises itself as *Chicago's Most Home-like Hotel.* Well, that's it. It's so . . . home-like that if you want a cup of coffee you have to go down to the kitchen & make it yourself. —Yesterday morning my train was about two hours late getting into Chicago, & I was an hour getting from the station to the hotel, & when I finally got into my room & took down the receiver to order breakfast, this is the conversation which took place:

I:—Room service, please.

Voice:—Do you want it from the East or from the West?

I:—What?

Voice:—Do you want it from the East or from the West?

I:—How do I know?—I don't know what you're talking about. I'm a stranger here. I want a cup of coffee. I don't care where it comes from.

Voice:—Well, some people want it from the East. But of course it has to come through the tunnel then, & it's likely to get cold.

I:—Well, then, that settles it. I don't want it cold. So send it from the West.—Hello!—Hello!—Operator! (Silence.)

I:—(After a pause, taking down receiver) Operator, give me the West Room Service, please.

Voice:—There is no West Room Service.

I:—Well, but what am I going to do? I want a cup of coffee!—They told me—(sound of receiver being hung up).

Voice:—(after a pause) Room Service!

I:—Hello, this is Room 275 West speaking.—Will you kindly take an order for breakfast?

Voice:—This is the East, Madam. Do you want it from the East?

I:—I don't *know!*—I don't *care!*—I'm dying for a cup of coffee! Won't you please send it up?

Voice:—You want it from the East, then?

I:—(very calmly) Would you mind telling me what is the difference?

Voice:—Well, some people like to have it from the East,—but of course there's a difference in price—

I:—I don't care anything about the price. Will you please send me at once a pot of coffee, half a grape-fruit & some Kellogg's Bran?—(Yes, I did, U-geen).

Voice:—Coffee, one half grape-fruit, Kellogg's Bran. (Receiver goes up.)

I:—(a few minutes later)—Operator, will you give me the Porter, please. I want to enquire about trains.

Voice:—Did you give in a breakfast order to the East, Madam?

I:—I did.

Voice:—Well, I'll give you the West.

I:—I don't *want* the West. I've got it all fixed up with the East. The East & I understand each other perfectly.—Operator!—Operator!

Voice:—Kitchen!

I:—Is this the East or the West?

Voice:—This is the West.

I:—Well, I'm sorry. The operator has called you by mistake. I've already given my order to the East Room Service.

Voice:—Is this Room 275?

I:—Yes.

Voice:—Well, you see, Madam, you're in the West, and—

I:—I know—I know all about that. You have me there.—But, *please*, won't you send me up a cup of coffee at once! I've just come in on the train, & I'm dying for a cup of coffee! Never mind the rest!—Just coffee!—Will you send it up at once?

Voice:—Sorry. But we work by rotation. You'll have to wait your turn.

I:—How long will that be?

Voice:—I couldn't say, Madam. You see, you're in the West, and—

I:—No, God help me, I'm in the Middle West! (I fall on the floor in a cataleptic fit.)

(Curtain)

I've just been into the diner & had my luncheon. I feel a little better. They certainly eat a lot of pork.

It's amusing to think how entirely, *totally*, ABSOLUTELY different everything would be if you were in this chair beside me.—It makes me laugh, it's so funny that there could be such a difference.—Oh, it will be so lovely when we go around the earth together!—I told some people yesterday that we are going to Java & China in March.—Why not?—For we are, we are!—Aren't we?

I will let you know as soon as I find another hotel in Chicago. It will be difficult, for everything's full up. But I won't go back to that Christless Windermere West if I have to sleep in the stock-yard. In the meantime, in case you didn't get my wire, address me *care of Margaret Burns, 1209 East 60th St., Chicago.*—I have given this address to the Windermere for forwarding.

There's a man getting off at this station, which is called *Sterling*. The porter just brushed him off, standing just in front of me. This is the porter's little trick. He brushes the dust from the man getting off at this station, onto the man getting off at the next station,—& business flourishes.—Well, darling, I have poured out all my troubles.—None of them matters, when I think of you.—

Edna.

U-geen—

I have to take back all the nasty things I've said about the Pullman car.—I've just found the most human little writing-desk at one end of the car, with a little desk-chair in front of it, & pen & ink & paper & envelopes, and a blue blotter. And there's a table right opposite it with periodicals.—The desk is much too high for my arms, but I don't care. —But I do mind riding backward, so I'm going back to my chair before I get sea-sick.

Give my love to Hattie. And tell her to be a good girl, & never speak crossly to you.

Edna.

125   TO EUGEN JAN BOISSEVAIN

Hotel Montrose
Cedar Rapids [Iowa]
3:25 Tuesday Afternoon
[Feb. 5, 1924]

My dear,—

All your letters came, even the ones that forgot to say *Iowa:*— this is a great & distinguishable city.—It's curious that I have been so unable to write to you lately. It is not only that I am tired. I am sunk in a lethargy of boredom too deep for action of any kind. Once a day my keepers come & drag me forth, "with all my silken flanks in garlands dressed", to the miniature sacrifice.—That is all.—Except that in Chicago a man named Otto Schneider, a very clever etcher, did a drawing of me, for which I sat about five hours,—which tired me, but did not bore me, as I think it is going to be good.—And except for one other thing which happened in Milwaukee: I met the mother & father of the girl to whom I wrote *Memorial to D.C.*[10] I will tell you about that,—it was a lovely experience.

But otherwise, I am like a man who has to travel a hundred miles between daylight & dusk. Nobody cares in what manner he does it; there are no rules to the game; he must just get there, somehow. He may walk on his hands, if his feet get tired; he may crawl on his hands & knees; he may roll; he may, if fortunate, at moments hook a ride. As for me, I find it easiest to run up all the hills at a heart-bursting pace:—that is to say, I give my reading still with charm & spirit, though with an ever-increasing nervousness if a door bangs or a train goes by; and to roll down them:—that is to say, I sleep whenever I can kill an hour in that way.—This day has been wonderful—all rolling— and a chance to lie in a ditch at the bottom for a while—no hill to climb until tomorrow night.

I do not even miss you very much. And I haven't wanted you to be with me these last days. Can't you understand that? If you had a date with the Queen of Sheba, either tonight, with motor-oil under your finger-nails, & a three-days' stubble on your chin, & last week's B.V.D.'s—or tomorrow night, after a day in a Turkish bath—well, it's something like that; I don't want anybody, not even you, maybe least of all you, to see how foot-sore & dusty I am.

———————

You can see now why, even if I had not been too tired to write, I have been reluctant to write you, since this was the only kind of letter I could have produced.—It would not have done to write you this a week ago. I enclose a telegram which I thought better of sending. I was afraid it would distress you.—I dare write you this now, because so soon after you have received it I shall be with you again.

—Edna.

[10] In *Second April*. D.C. (Dorothy Coleman) a close college friend whose untimely death moved the poet to write the tribute mentioned.

126 TO NORMA MILLAY

S.S. Taiyo Maru
May 4, 1924

Dear Normie,—

I am sending you enclosed a pressed flower,—an hibiscus, which grew in Honolulu. You've read about native Hawaiian or South Sea Island beauties with hibiscus flowers in their hair—well, this is it.—We spent about eighteen hours in Honolulu—did you get a post-card from me?—Went bathing at Waikiki beach, 'n' everything. People, native boys in bathing-suits, or barefoot in overalls, really do go about strumming ukuleles.—It's the most *beautiful* place, tropical but not too hot, pineapples, bananas, dates, mangoes, papias growing all around, (this last a fruit I never saw before & don't much like) & flowers everywhere. Eugen & I almost decided to leave the ship right there & spend the rest of our lives lying on the beach, playing duets on the ukulele & eating mangoes.

This hibiscus flower comes from a garland I bought of a native woman. Always when a steamer is getting up steam to sail they come in hundreds to the dock, all hung with garlands of flowers which they have made to sell to the passengers about to embark. It is considered bad luck not to throw a garland of flowers overboard upon the water as you leave the port,—an offering to the sea-god.—For an hour before we sailed the water about the ship was black with the heads of native boys swimming about & diving for coins which the passengers threw into the water. As the ship began to pull out they climbed up the side—just scrambled up like monkeys, & one by one dived off—several from the very top deck of the steamer, an enormous height, & swam back to shore; some of them stayed with us a long time, & had a long swim back.

Must close. Will stick in hibiscus flower, & seal up. Maybe from Japan I send youse cherry-blossom, but I'm afraid it's too late—wisteria, maybe.

Lub to youse & Chas.

Sefe.

127   TO MRS. CORA B. MILLAY

The Ikao Hotel
Hot Springs
Ikao, Japan.
May 15, 1924.

Darling Mother:

This is the funniest little hotel, very much like the *Hôtel Panorama* at Cassis, except that here there are mountains instead of sea. We are about a week out on our walking trip—have a coolie along as a guide and to carry our pack. We have been spending the nights so far in Japanese inns, sleeping on the floor, eating on the floor,—rice, tea & fish; rice, fish & tea; tea, fish & rice, etc. This is the first place we've struck where we could get bread, butter, or coffee. We are the only guests, & have the dreadfully ugly dining room all to ourselves—(just like Cassis). We are sitting around now waiting for tiffin; Eugen is playing *Home, Sweet Home* on the terrible piano "Guaranteed for Extreme Climates." We have been reading back numbers of *Punch* left here by former guests. (I need not tell you it is a rainy day. Yet it looks as if it might clear. We are above the clouds here, above some of them, & watch them rising & moving about in the gorges of the mountains.)

In the theatrical notes section of the July 1923 issue of an English periodical called *Gaiety*, I find:

"Anna Christie:—Powerful drama of the Seven Seas."

You can have a hot bath here any time you like. The water comes steaming into the wooden tub all day long through a bamboo pipe stuck into the side of the mountain, water that, as Eugen said, is "heated in Hell."

This letter is written, dear, with the hopes that it will reach you for your birthday. I sent Kay a wireless for hers because there was no time for a letter, but youse can't have no wireless,—wirelesses cost a billion bucks from this neck of the woods.

Here comes the food—I am always ready for it these days.—We are getting drunk at this place as fast as we can—on water. This is the first place we have struck since we docked in Yokohama where we dare to drink water—except bottled mineral water. The water here comes straight from the hills, without stopping to water any rice fields on the way, or running through the open gutters of a couple of villages.

Japan is a beautiful country, much more mountainous than I had thought—mountains everywhere, almost. Lovely pines & firs & giant cedars—cryptomerias.—We were afraid we were too late for the cherry-blossoms. In Tokyo they were all gone, but we got to Nikko when the double ones were just in their prime, & the singles ones by no means over—oh, they are so lovely! There was a big double-blossomed one right in front of the hotel at Nikko, a lovely soft clean pink, the tree just *busting* with blooms, not a leaf in sight. The only thing prettier is a New England apple orchard.

Happy Birthday, my darling Mother! I have bought you a little birthday present, in Toyko, & one for Kay, too,—but it's such a dreadful nuisance to send things, both for me & for you, that I'm bringing them home with me when I come.

Love to you, & to my little sisters & brothers. —Vincent.

Tell Hunkus to stop crying—I bring him something pretty, too.

128   TO MRS. CORA B. MILLAY

Broadway Hotel
Chefoo, [China]
June 22 (more or less)
1924.

Dearest Mummie,—

By this time you will have received my cable. I sent it because I didn't want you to worry about me & I knew it would be ages before you would be getting a letter from me. We haven't written a letter for weeks, because we've been laid up with the flu again, both of us. Isn't that disgusting?—We had a marvelous time walking through Japan, beautiful mountainous country, awfully interesting funny little Japanese inns, where we ate & slept on the floor. I got very big & strong. But the moment we struck the cities again we got the flu. We went to Peking—a two days train trip from Shanghai, where our steamer docked—because we were crazy to see the place; it is the old capital where the empress lived, where the young dethroned emperor still lives, in a little walled Forbidden City within the city. And when we got there we went to the hotel & went to bed with the flu—picked it up on the train, probably,—& stayed in bed ten days. When finally we crawled out, we took a steamer to this place, which is a lovely little seaside village on the Yellow Sea. We have chartered a Chinese sailing junk with a crew of two, man & boy, & every day we sail to some island or other & build a fire & make coffee, & swim & lie in the sun. So now we are feeling pretty fit again. (Anybody who had ever been in a Chinese sea-coast village, seeing that phrase, "build a fire," would say, "Of what?"—for there *is* no drift-wood. They are the cleanest beaches in the world. There are no forests to send logs down river to the sea, there are apparently never any wrecks, & wood is so scarce in China that if a drifting spar appeared on the horizon, I am sure that the entire village would swim out to it, yelling & beating each other off, to drag it in. It is my boast that there does not exist a beach where I can't gather wood for a fire, & so far I have just held my own. I gather the fire-wood in my bathing cap. A dried walnut shell! I see it from afar & make for it. This is not a joke—it is the truth,—dried shells & the corks of bottles & bits of bark no bigger than my finger—these make the drift-wood fire. I have never yet found a piece of drift-wood as large as my hand.—We are having a beautiful time here, getting brown & well.—But wasn't it hateful we had to be sick?—We are very careful, & are not likely to catch any major disease. We were both vaccinated on the steamer before coming into Shanghai, & are very careful not to drink any water—except bottled water—or eat any green vegetables.

If we stay well we shall write you oftener now. You must be lonely at times, dear, with Norma in Italy & Kathleen, I suppose, in New York. Darling little Hunk,—isn't that wonderful?—I got a letter from each of you three & was so happy to hear from you. There may be a note from one of you waiting for us at Shanghai, where we shall arrive again in about a week on our way to Hongkong & Singapore. I won't write any more this time, because I want to get this down to the boat which will leave soon. Our own means of communication with the rest of the world is by steamers which arrive here once or twice a week. Lots & lots of love, Mummie darling.

I will write again soon.

Vincent

129 TO MRS. CORA B. MILLAY

T. S. S. "Anchies"
July 14th, 1924

Hong Kong Harbor (I ought to spell it *harbour* since it's a British possession, or concession, or something or other—although it's the most Chinese city I've yet seen).

Dearest Mummie, I will now begin in a more fitting manner. I am now aboard the good ship *Anchies* (as per above) out of Shanghai, bound for Singapore, & having the most *wonderful* time.—We are at anchor here, taking in cargo; it is seven o'clock in the evening, and we sail at daybreak. Eugen, (who, I forgot to say, is with me) & I have already been ashore once & had tiffin at the Hong Kong Hotel an excellent & very interesting hotel, really really smelling of the *East*, everybody dressed in white pongee, or flannel so thin that the stripes of their shirts show right through their coats, & sweating a little, & intent on some strange business. We left Shanghai about three days ago at daybreak, & missed the tide & were stuck in the yellow Yangtse mud for six hours, our bow afloat & ready to go, but our stern inert under its cargo of several million Chinese eggs. That night the wind came up smelling terrific & the ship, a big ship & steady, leaped about like a floating cork, and all my scents & unguents rolled off the wash-stand shelf upon the floor,—nothing smashed the carpets are too thick, (I would God they were not, this sweltering weather)—the next morning I learned (a) that I was about the only passenger aboard who had slept a wink, & (b) that we had during the night passed unscathed through the whiskers of a healthy typhoon. The captain had been wirelessed that it was on its way & could tell by the direction of the swell & the wind from just what quarter to expect it, & reckoned that we could get across its track in plenty of time,—which of course we did, but not without a taste of it. This is the season for them, & they are terrible, but not really very dangerous for a big ship, the captain told us,—you may lose most of your rigging, but you keep afloat,—at any rate, we are now out of their district, darling, else I should not have regaled you with the yarn!

All we shall get now is the monsoon, terrific downpours of rain, of which we had an hour today, & the humidity following something fierce. Oh, mummie, you know, day before yesterday all day almost, first on the starboard & then on the portside, the spray of the ship was full of beautiful bright rainbows! & last night the phosphorus made the edge of the waves all like green electric light,—& there was heat lightning, & I said "Oh, Eugen, rainbows by day & phosphorus by night,—I can hardly bear it!"—& he said, "If you should see a rainbow at night, I don't think you *could* bear it." And just at the moment he finished speaking there was a flash of lightning, & across the phosphorescent crest of the wave at which I was looking, a beautiful perfect rainbow appeared bright for a moment & instantly was gone.—And I *did* bear it. Little Vincent big strong girl now.—I think not many people have seen a rainbow made by lightning or phosphorus. It was marvelous beyond words. Oh, mummie, I am having the most *thrilling* time!

Must go ashore now for dinner & a little quiet fun. Goodbye till next time & *so* much love from us both.

Edna

130 TO MRS. CORA B. MILLAY

Grand Hotel Preanger
Bandoeng, Java.
July 28, 1924

Dearest Mummie,—

Here we are in Java. It is beautiful here in Bandoeng (pronounced *Bandoong*) (*a* as in *father*)—In Batavia it was hot as hell, but here it is really cold—at night two blankets—& *beautiful!*—This is just a tiny note to catch this steamer & let you know that we are well & happy. Got your letter in Singapore, but as we shall not strike Colombo for six weeks at least, are wiring them to forward our mail here. I enclose a little note I wrote you in the pitch darkness as we crossed the equator on our way from Singapore to Batavia.

Will *really* write a longer letter soon, but we rush about so, & there's so much to do every minute! ! !

Goodbye for now, dearest darling sweetie mummie,

from

Edna & Eugen

131   TO MRS. CORA B. MILLAY

August 28, 1924
Friday—after tea &
before dinner
On board S.S. Plancius
Out of Batavia—
bound for Singapore.

Dearest Mummie:

I have been spending five days alone with some friends of Eugen in Samarang, while he went to Soerabaya on business. Today I have left Samarang on this boat & tomorrow morning shall pick him up in Batavia. Until a week ago we were in the mountains, where it was cool, but Samarang is the anteroom of Hell. Still it is not so hot as the trains.—We go now to Singapore, & from there to British India— Rangoon, Calcutta, Benares, Agra, Delhi, Jaipoor, Bombay—& then direct to Marseilles. I hope we shall have a minute to run over to Cassis. ('member Cassis?) This is just a note to tell you our plans. We expect to be in Paris by the middle of October—just too late to see Norma & Charlie & Gladys & Arthur!—but we shall not spend long in Europe—probably by Thanksgiving time we shall be home. After you get this it won't be so *terribly* long before you see me, old sweet *darling*. Maybe on Thanksgiving day we shall all be together.

—Love,

Sefe.

132   TO THE MUSIC EDITOR OF THE NEW YORK WORLD[11]

New York,
4th February, 1925.

Dear Sir:

In some indignation and no little disapproval I address you concerning your criticism in this morning's World of Mr. Deems Taylor's

"Portrait of a Lady". "The audience", you say, in reviewing last night's concert given by the New York Chamber Music Society in Aeolian Hall, "probably composed of the composer's relatives, greeted the piece with what seemed to us highly disproportionate cordiality." Sir, I was a member of that audience. I heard with close attention and deep pleasure an unusually good program unusually well performed, not the least interesting and lovely number of which was Mr. Taylor's "Portrait of a Lady". Mr. Taylor combines as a musician two excellent attributes far too seldom found in combination: the art to expound a fine theme with power and clarity, and the good taste when that theme has been expounded, to stop. You reflected, you say, "a little bitterly, upon the cleverness and resourcefulness with which Juon had juggled the themes of his divertimento". But cleverness and resourcefulness are the indispensable equipment of a juggler: we do not require them from a musician whose work may safely expose itself to the consideration of an unbefuddled ear and mind.

I suggest in closing that last night's audience, far from being composed of Mr. Taylor's relatives, was made up of discerning and honestly delighted strangers, and that yourself, far from being "one of Mr. Taylor's warmest admirers," represented the only relative in the auditorium.

Yours, etc.,

Edna St. Vincent Millay

[11] Deems Taylor.

133   TO MRS. CORA B. MILLAY
      and KATHLEEN MILLAY

8¾ [12] Bedford Street

Monday, April 10, or

thereabouts I mean May.

[1925]

Dearest Mummie and Kay:

So many adventures since we last met! First Bowdoin, which went off beautifully, packed house, students sitting even on the stage behind me, etc. I send you these clippings from the Brunswick and Portland papers, which I just received from Aunt Susie. Please keep them for me. The conference with about twenty-five students the following morning was extremely interesting, a most animated conversation, myself feeling just like talking, and holding forth on all possible subjects. So that's that. Aunt Susie and George came over from Portland to hear me, and Norma spent the night with Aunt Susie where we picked her up the following morning and had luncheon. Aunt Susie has a very nice house there, and a lovely garden, and was awfully sweet to us. We motored home by way of Exeter, etc. getting into some frightfully muddy and messed-up roads, and getting lost about every other sign-post, but coming constantly upon the most beautiful scenery, and everybody perfectly happy. Instead of coming directly back to New York, we decided, on finding ourselves in Springfield, to continue west and show Norma our place in the Berkshires, which we did, spending the night in Chatham, where Eugen and I had stayed before. (We had spent the preceding night in Worcester.) Norma was crazy about the place. And we were even madder about it than before. The house is in really splendid condition, and we found a brook, an extra one, which we didn't know was there, very near the house, and flowing through a little valley so deep that all it needs is a fourth bank to make a perfect swimming pool. We expect to move in about the first of July. There is too much to be done to get in much before then.

Well, girls, here's for some news. Tess and F.P.A.[13] were married Saturday at the country place of a friend of theirs near Greenwich, Connecticut, a beautiful place. Eugen and I went out, and Arthur and Gladys [Ficke]. The house is half in New York State and half in Connecticut, and they had put a long white ribbon under the apple trees to show the state line, and when Frank and Tess came out of the house to the garden where everybody was waiting, they had to walk over to the further side of the white ribbon and be married in Connecticut, because Frank had got his divorce in New York and couldn't be married again in that state. She looked perfectly beautiful, in the sweetest white dress, and carrying an enormous bouquet of lilies-of-the-valley. I never saw her look so pretty. And I never saw Frank look so well, either, very serious, and quite pale. Afterwards, and after consuming rafts of caviar and oceans of champagne, Arthur and Gladys and Eugen and I all went over with Elinor Wylie and Bill Benét to their house in New Canaan and spent the night and all of Sunday with them, coming home late last night.

And TONIGHT we are going over to Brooklyn to see the opening of MARCH ON![14] Arthur and Gladys are coming, too, and Norma is coming over a bit late, because she must first report at the Greenwich Village [Theatre]. We are all sending out strong electrical currents for Howid's success. Wish you both were going to be with us.

Dear Mummie and Kay, please have a lovely time in the country and come back big and strong. It was very sad, parting with you. You looked so sweet, standing there together. I had forgotten until that moment that I was not to see either of you for months, maybe.

Lots and lots of love to you, from me and Ugin.

It is too late to go to the bank today. But tomorrow I shall deposit one hundred dollars to Mummie's account. Make it go as far as possible for a while, darling,—I mean for a couple of months—because just now we are having to pay out enormous amounts.

Goo'by.

Vincent.

[12] A joke about the size of the house.
[13] Esther Root and Franklin P. Adams. He was then the conductor of The Conning Tower column which he signed with his initials.
[14] A new play by Howard Irving Young, being given a tryout in Brooklyn.

134 TO MRS. CORA B. MILLAY

Box 53
Austerlitz, N. Y.
June 22, 1925

Dearest Mummie:

Here we are, in one of the loveliest places in the world, I am sure, working like Trojans, dogs, slaves, etc., having chimneys put in, & plumbing put in, & a garage built, etc.—We are crazy about it—& I have so many things on my mind at this moment that must be done before I'm an hour older,—you know how it is—that I hardly know if I am writing with a pen or with a screw-driver.—You & Kay & Howard are all invited to come to see us when next you are in these parts again—one at a time or all at once, but the most restful time to come would be after a couple of months—just now there is a little too much mortaring & tearing down of old building going on, & a guest is likely to be pressed into service laying a floor or digging a hole for the septic tank.—

I have written the Corn Exchange Bank to transfer one hundred dollars from my account to yours. You will probably receive a notice of it in a few days. Make it go as far as you can, darling. Our expenses are staggering just now. The furnace & bathroom alone come to a thousand dollars. It's terrible, simply terrible. But it's going to be a sweet place when it's finished—and it's ours, all ours, about seven hundred acres of land & a lovely house, & no rent to pay, only a nice gentlemanly mortgage to keep shaving a slice off.

We're so excited about it we are nearly daft in the bean—kidney bean, lima bean, string-bean, butter-bean—you dow whad I bean—ha! ha! ha!—I'm off!—(Now you understand what I have been trying to tell you, that I am very interested in & pleased with the place that Eugen & I have bought.)

Please write me at the above address *soon*. Much love to you all three, from us,

Ugin & Edner.

I shall come across your little kid's book presently & mail it to you. Just now Gawd knows where anything is.

Respectfully yours, Sefe, Litt. D.[15]

[15] On June 15, 1925, Miss Millay had the honorary degree of Doctor of Letters conferred on her by Tufts College.

135   TO THE MILLAY FAMILY and FRIENDS

Steepletop[16]
Austerlitz, New York
July 28, 1925.

Dear Friends:

Ugin has just gone off in the Egg-beater to Albany to sell a load of crated huckleberries, and Freddie has to do the dishes, because as you must know, Julia—no, no, not Mrs. Hitchcock: Mrs. Hitchcock insisted on our eating in the kitchen and drinking for our supper cold tea left over from her breakfast; Mrs. Hitchcock went some time ago, and paid an aimless passerby twenty-five cents to carry her hand-bag from the sidewalk to her front door because Ugin who had brought her home in state in the Maxwell was so ungentlemanly as to suggest that she carry her bag herself; no, no, this is the big Negro Julia, who went crazy last night and ran roaring out into the yard to confide to the masons that she had heard us plotting to hang her from a rafter.—Mr. Crosby very kindly pulled her off us and put her aboard a train for Philadelphia, so Freddie has to wash the dishes. And a hard enough time he has of it, too, poor lad, what with Vasco and Albino and

Angelo and Helena and Martina and Eunice and Alice and Gino and Gialindo and Emilio all the time running down the hill with great pails of berries to be measured and boxed and crated. (You will note that Joseph is no longer among them. Joseph pissed in the berries, so we don't employ him any more.)

We have very little gin left. It takes about all we can get from day to day to keep Crosby laying brick. Fortunately the chimney, the big one, is finished, and the three handsome fireplaces won't smoke so much—at least they say so, through their tears and thrusting their faces very close to the floor to get a nose-ful of draught from under the door—won't smoke so much when the cement is dry. But of course the chimney for the incinerator isn't even started yet, and the tiles haven't arrived yet for the bath-room, and though the septic tank was sealed last night at the precise moment when Julia lost her mind, there's a lot of work still for Crosby to do and the gin is very low. One is to be congratulated that Kline, who sold us this excellent apple-jack—he makes it himself—is himself a teetotaler, and is most industrious and capable, too, considering that one of his hands got crushed one day in a cement-mixer; Kline's only weakness is that he insists upon addressing Freddie as Freddie. Altair has a very cute bark now, which he tries out once in a while. He tried it out on me yesterday, but he is to be excused, for he had been asleep under my desk all the afternoon in my study up in the field, and I stepped suddenly through the doorway out of the soft grass and wakened him. He refused his cod-liver oil last night. When Ugin held out the spoon he turned his head away and gently threw up. Ugin says it was the smell of the cod-liver oil. I say it was because Julia had washed the spoon. At any rate, Smoky doesn't mind him any more so much as she did, though she still puts her back up a bit at the sight of him. Smoky is a great comfort. She follows me even to the privy, and waits for me, and purrs and purrs.

The kitchen plumbing, you will be glad to hear, is all connected, even to the set tubs, and the guest bath-room nearly so, and the servants' lavatory and seat—we decided after all to postpone the installation of our individual bath until the dormer windows are in and the installation of the dormer windows until the terrace is laid and the laying of the terrace until the swimming pool is dug and the digging of the swimming pool until we get money enough to buy some cocoa-butter against sunburn. The only trouble with our plumbing is that we have no water, Frank having left the ditch half plowed and the plow by the ditch, to run home on the first sunny day and start haying, and Timmy Callahan having deceived us shamefully concerning the four Italian workmen he was going to lay off this week from dumping gravel on the Great Barrington Road. So we all took a bath in the brook, at least all but Ugin, who got lost trying to collect fifty cents apiece from the dozens of people who come in motor cars and camp on our land and steal our berries. Anyway, Deems and Freddie and I took a bath in the brook, and I made them give me up-stream because I was cleaner.

* * *

We have quite a lot of flies. It's hard to keep the doors closed in a house that isn't finished yet. But the nine Polish dogs haven't broken into the spring-house for a long time.

Mother's last letter was the best letter I ever received in my lifetime. We read it over and over, so full of interesting things it was, about birds, and stars, and all kinds of things that ought to be in a letter, and never are. We both were crazy about it.

* * *

What a thrilling time you must be having with that telescope, looking at the stars. There is nothing, not anything, so exciting. We have here no telescope, and for the most part no stars, it having rained here nearly every day since we came. It was pretty dismal at first, with no stove even in the kitchen, except a stinking kerosene modernity. You couldn't step outside the door without getting into grass up to your neck, and there wasn't a dry foot among us for over a fortnight. However, that's all over now, we have three splendid fireplaces and a handsome new range in the kitchen, and all the wood we can burn just lying around cluttering up the grass,—and it hasn't rained today, so far. Have you seen Mercury in the west with Venus, just after sunset? We saw him for three evenings, and then it began to be too rainy. I believe that by now he must be nearly if not quite invisible again.

If it wasn't for Freddie I don't know what we should do. Freddie is Gene's nephew, Robert's son, such a darling boy, not much over twenty, who is a landscape gardener, and left a growing business in Long Island to the care of his partner for two months to come up here and help us out with gardens and orchards and things, of which we are dismayingly ignorant. His coming has put new courage into us; we were about gone with weariness and confusion when he got here. You see, we have had living with us for three weeks now six masons, four plumbers, two carpenters, two ineffectual and transient servants, and fifteen insubordinate and mischievous berry-picking children. They don't spend the night here, but they might as well, for they appear in the morning before we are dressed, and tramp through the bed-rooms without knocking, bearing ladders and bricks and trowels and buckets of cement. There's not a room in the house that one or another of them isn't boring holes in or something, and there's not a spot within a quarter of a mile where I can stand and brush my teeth except in full sight of some of them.

Well—I would dearly, dearly love to get a letter from you, any of you, all of you. And if any of you should be leaving there, do come here, do. From now on it will be getting better. At least, after a week or so more, the mess will be our own mess, at least,—our own pails of paint and different colored brushes and hammers and nails and yards of cretonne, etc. We have only one guest-room, so far; but Freddie sleeps in the pantry, which leaves the guest-room free, and there will be the big davenport downstairs for one, and the big wide couch in the library for two, and indeed quite a number of nice people could be fairly comfortable here, from the jiffy the water is turned on,—provided any water appears.

The strawberries are gone by. We had a lot of them, both wild ones and tame ones, as Gene calls the others. Just at present we have besides the overwhelming blueberries, currants and a big lot of delicious cultivated raspberries, and there are going to be blackberries, too. We have set out a few tomato plants and peppers, which didn't seem to hold it against us and we have about a dozen heavily bearing pear-trees. We have quite a large apple orchard, too, but they are bearing very sparingly this year, being frightfully in need of pruning. We have bought—we did it almost the first day, every kind of garden tool and household tool that one could possibly wish, in order to be ready for anything, among other things pruning shears and a pruning-hook about twenty feet long. And we have been at the apple-trees, but haven't been able to finish them yet, there are so very many things to do. I have pruned and cleared out the raspberry bushes pretty well. Everything one does is about five times as much work as it should be, because the place has been running wild so many years. We found rhubarb and asparagus, a few plants, entirely hidden under forests of tansy, and we were here a couple of weeks before I, hunting wild strawberries, came upon a big plot of tame ones. I am dying to show you everything.

I must stop now because I am tired. I have a headache all the time lately and spots before my eyes, and, as mother used to say, I don't feel so darned well myself. I have no idea what the trouble is, but have been taking Carter's Little Liver Pills just on a guess; they haven't changed my life so far, but I'll give 'em a little more time before I go over to Swamproot or Lydia Pinkham's well-known stirrup-cup. I imagine I got too tired just at first. I worked frightfully hard.

Let me hear from some of you soon. It is such a delight, among all my tiresome mail, to get a letter from friends. Of course I don't deserve any letters, because I don't write any, but I get frightfully sick of strange names and self-addressed envelopes all the time. Once in a while comes a letter from somebody I know, and once in a while an interesting letter from somebody I don't know, but mostly my letters fall easily into one or the other of the classes itemized below, the quotations being exact quotations from letters received yesterday:

Class A: "Dear Mrs. Boissevain—anthology—two of your poems—Brandt & Brandt—polite refusal—hope that you will intercede in my behalf."

Class B: "Dear Miss Millay: Will it be possible—Women's University Club—reading from your poems—February 1926."

Class C: "Dear Mrs. Milay: My classes in English composition—would like to hear from you, therefore, why one should learn to write well and whether your writing is a mere pastime done easily, under an inspiration, and without many revisions. And will you also tell them whom you enjoy reading most or whom you would recommend to students to read among past or contemporary writers—will you also designate or submit for study an example of what you consider your best writing with an explanatory or supplementary letter as to your methods, habits of writing, revisions, etc.—I am afraid this seems like a pretty big order."

Class D: "My dear Miss Millay: I have been ill for five years with an enlarged and leaking heart so have made autographs my hobby."

Well—can you 'magine what fun it is once in a while to pick up a letter in Kay's crazy hand or Normie's crazy hand or Mummie's great big large strong perfectly sane and grown-up woof-woof crazy hand? I don't mention the gentlemen, because Howard's letters are likely to be written on the backs of snap-shots and enclosed in envelopes addressed by somebody else's crazy hand, and Charlie, as everybody knows, is illiterate, and couldn't write a letter if he wanted to.

Meseems I hear the infernal whirring of the Egg-beater. Ugin will be back from Albany with presents for Ediner,—paint-brushes and loaves of bread and empty blueberry crates, and maybe if I'm very very good some white lead and linseed oil!

Next Day

Eugen read this letter, and he is frightfully jealous because he hasn't had a minute to write to *his* family. So he begs you to return this when you have finished with it or make a copy of it or something, so that he can ship it on to Holland. I tell him there are bad words in it; he says there are bad words in Holland, too.

I send you all much love from both of us.

Vincent.

16 This was the name which the poet chose for her house. The pink spires of the tall weed (*Spiraea tomentosa*)—also known as Hardhack—were to be seen all over the fields and meadows of the farm. When her old friend, Arthur Davison Ficke, some years later bought a house in nearby Hillsdale, he named his property "Hardhack."

136   TO MRS. CORA B. MILLAY

Steepletop
[Austerlitz, New York]
August 20th, 1925

Dearest Mummie:

I am sending you my personal check, instead of putting the money through your bank for you, because it's so much easier for me this way,—one letter instead of two! Let me know when you need some more, which will be before long, I imagine. I know you want your pass-book balanced and sent to you, and all kinds of things, but it's impossible in the midst of the pandemonium in which we live just now, to find anything, even if I had the time to hunt for it. Things are slowly getting done here, but we still have six workmen working in the house. Yesterday we got one room into fairly decent order, so that one could retire there and sit in comparative peace,—the only spot within a radius of a thousand feet where one could safely install one's harassed behind for a moment, without becoming firmly imbedded in a half-ton of cement—and today a hive of migrating honey-bees picked out that particular room to swarm in. We smoked them out finally, and nobody got stung; but it's so long since I dared sit, that when I again begin to sit, I shall have to go about it a few minutes at a time at first, as with any other unaccustomed exercise, in order not to get stiff.

I received Charlie's letter about the huckle-berry picking—wasn't it stunning? terribly clever, I thought; we were crazy about it. Since they got back to town, however, we haven't had a word from them, and as Norma will be beginning rehearsals in a couple of days now, I suppose they won't get out here at all until much later. When you come back from Maine you must come directly here, and stay with us until some one of us has found a respectable and attractive place for you. I'm so glad you're not going back to 8th Street. I always hated that whole evil-smelling house. Your July Geographic Magazine was forwarded to me here, why, God knows, except that everybody's mail just now, including Norma's, Howard's and Allan Macdougall's, is being forwarded to me. A little joke of the Postmaster General, perhaps; somebody has told him I have six workmen and a swarm of bees in the house, so he thinks he'll give me some letters and parcels to re-address. Anyhow, I'm not re-addressing 'em. There's been nothing of importance, by the look of the things, except your magazine, which will be here when you get here.

I am going to Pittsfield on Tuesday, it's only about seventeen miles from here, to have my eyes examined. I went to a general practitioner in Great Barrington, a very good man, I think, who assures me there's nothing the matter with my heart, lungs, kidneys, liver, lights, etc., so I imagine it must be my eyes. I've had a headache for two months now without an hour's respite, and dark spots before my eyes all the time, so if it isn't something else, it damn well must be my eyes, for it's damn well something. I'll let you know what the fellow says; it's probably nothing serious at all.

Let me know when you want some more money, even if it's by return mail. I can always go out and gather a few dollars for you; but it's been a very wet spring here, and it will be late in October before the dollars are really ripe enough to drop from the bough.

Goo'bye, darling, and ever and ever so much love,

Vincent.

Tell Kay to be sure to come & visit us on her way back—Howard, too, if he can come.

VI

Steepletop

1926 – 1930

Steepletop, Austerlitz, N. Y.
March 4, 1926

Dear Frank:

Nancy and I are awfully excited about the Conning Tower watch.[1] Only we'd rather have something else than a watch,—at least, I *think* we would. If we could have made up our mind earlier, we should have written you earlier, but you wouldn't have got it any earlier, so it wouldn't have mattered. Our house is an island in the snow; it's an expedition to go to Austerlitz; and when you get to Austerlitz you haven't got anywhere, except to the post-office and two little empty churches. Gene has to walk five miles on snow-shoes, coming and going, to post this letter, and fetch the mail!

Frank, what I *think* I want more than a watch is a silver candelabrum for my bedroom, one for five or seven candles. For all I know this costs eight hundred dollars. And there are several things I'd quite as soon have. I want awfully a set of Thomas Hardy. But maybe after all maybe a wrist-watch would be the greatest fun, especially if that is what you have always given, up to now; the one I have is awfully be-gemmed and be-nameled to be wearing at the typewriter. And you couldn't very well engrave a set of Thomas Hardy, and it must be engraved,—the bottom of the candelabrum could be engraved. Hell, I don't know! I pass the buck to you, Frank. Do what you think would be the most fun. You can't go wrong. WHATSOEVER will make me happy as a child.

I was crazy about your "Beside the street of Grove." It's the most perfect picture of Tess that could ever be. "A poppy by a mossy stone,"—oh, Lord! "Fair as a moon, when only one"—oh, God! I clipped it out, and read it aloud to Gene and mother, first reciting William's version,[2] then Frank's. I adore it.

I'm a little better. At least, I'm a lot stronger. My funny spotty eye-sight is just the same, and my headache hasn't let up yet. But it's so beautiful here, even looking at everything through a dotted veil, that I should worry.

Tell Tess, one of us will write her very soon, maybe right now.

Love, Edna.

It's to be inscribed to Nancy, isn't it?—Else she'll be mad.

P.S.—There was a word left out of "The Armistice Day Parade." I didn't notice till long after. Didn't matter much. I wrote it "Same as the clergy," & it was printed "Same as clergy." If I'd known it was to go into a book[3] I woulda told you.   E.

> [1] Under her pseudonym, Miss Millay had contributed a poem, "The Armistice Day Parade," to F.P.A.'s column in the New York *World*. It was awarded, in 1925, the watch presented annually by Mr. Adams for the best contribution of the year.
> [2] Wordsworth's "She Dwelt Among the Untrodden Ways."
> [3] *The Conning Tower Book*, an anthology of the best verse that had appeared in F.P.A.'s column.

138   TO EDMUND WILSON

Steepletop, Austerlitz, N. Y.
March 4, 1926.

Dear Bunny:

This is just a snow-ball at your window,—I *can't* write letters.

But I did think you a darling to give me the champagne, both bottles, too. And I was awfully excited about Leonie Adams' poems; I nearly went blind reading them that night. And after I had finished them, and read some of them to Eugen, we drank her health with the champagne. When I see you, we'll talk about them.

We have been snowed in,—I mean hermetically—four weeks today. Five miles on snow-shoes, that means, to fetch the mail, or to post a letter. And the thermometer at zero again this morning.

I have a shanty up in the field where I work,—did I tell you? (You'll smile at that, meaning I never told you anything) I'm in my shanty now, and have a scorching fire at my back, in the funniest little stove.

* * *

How did you guess that a lacquer serpent with a ruby eye was just what I had written Santa Claus please to bring me? I didn't have a single lacquer serpent to my name, Bunny, let alone one with a ruby eye.

I have to go down to luncheon now.

Yours as ever
Edna

139 TO FRANK CROWNINSHIELD

Steepletop, Austerlitz, N. Y.
March 17, 1926.

Dearest Crownie:

You will never know how your sweet funny little letters cheer me up. What a nice person you are! Eugen thinks so, too.

The etching is lovely.

As for me, I am getting stronger every day. Though my head aches still all the time, and I still look at the world through a veil of dancing dark spots, in spite of all that a thousand doctors have been able to do. All the king's leeches and all the king's men, Haven't put little Edna together again!

I have started to work at last on the book of an opera which I promised back in the dark ages to Deems Taylor and the Metropolitan.[4] It will be done by the beginning of the summer. And then,—a year late!—the articles for V.F. will begin to come in. You have been a darling, Crownie, as I believe I said before.

About the opera, it is supposed to be a secret; but I imagine it has begun to leak out a little.

We have been snowed in here tight exactly six weeks tomorrow,— no road to our house at all. But I saw a blue-jay yesterday. And maybe someday it will be spring.

As ever, affectionately yours,
Edna.

[4] The first book, according to Deems Taylor, was based upon the story of Snow White and the Seven Dwarfs. One act of this was already written by the end of November, 1925. But by Christmas she had scrapped it and begun to write the dramatic work she was later to call *The King's Henchman*.

140 TO DEEMS TAYLOR

Steepletop, [Austerlitz, N.Y.]
March 28. [1926]

Dear Deems:

Here is Scene II, first draft, much too long, nail that, but you know all that.—The scene plan thing I'll send in a day or two, as soon as I can hustle it together. Yes, *The Saxons* is a good title, & looks fine on the program, you cute old thing. I don't think it perfect, but am willing to keep it till we think of a better; & if we never think of a better,—we'll let it stand. I had hoped very much that Urban[5] would do the sets, & am thrilled that he's going to—he's the only one that could make it look the way I see it.—Out of my mind to hear your music for Scene I.

—Love,
Edna.

[5] Joseph Urban, famous architect (the Ziegfeld Theatre and the New School buildings, among others) and stage designer for the Metropolitan Opera House at that time.

141   TO ABBIE HUSTON EVANS

Steepletop, Austerlitz, N.Y.
Oct. 6, 1926

Dear Abbie:
    I am so happy to be able to tell you that Harper's, on two conditions which are not difficult to comply with, will bring out your book. —The two conditions are: that I make the selection of what poems are to be included; and that I write a short preface to your book. You told me in Bedford Street that you would not want anybody to write an introduction to your book of poems, & I quite understand how you feel—no one can introduce properly another person's work.—But I thought we could get around that, & please Harper's just as well, if I should write a preface not about your poems, but about you & myself, how we were friends in Camden, & used to climb Megunticook together, & read our poems to each other, & so forth.—I am sure that people would be awfully interested in that—they love so to know things about the people whose poems they read. Let me know what you think of this.—I would be only too glad to do this if you want me to, Abbie.[6]

As ever your friend,
Vincent.

[6] "I may say for the record, about the Preface," Miss Evans has written, "that (in answer to her suggestion that it take the form of a note telling of our personal friendship, etc.) I turned thumbs down on it, although I knew it was her attempt to meet my objection to any preface at all—I was that stiff-necked. But once I'd come round to the idea of a preface I felt that it ought to be about the poetry itself. Otherwise none at all. I must say she was patience itself with my New England independence!"

142   TO MR. and MRS. H. A. MILLAY

Steepletop
Austerlitz, N.Y.
Oct. 15, 1926

Dear Aunt Rose & Uncle Bert:

My visit to the doctors in Boston was so thoroughly unsatisfactory & depressing, that I hadn't the heart to write you about it.—The X-ray man in Boston said precisely the opposite of what the X-ray man in Augusta had said,—there was no trouble in the nose at all, or in any of the sinuses; a Boston nose-&-throat specialist examined me & said the same thing: that there was no trouble there at all, & that an operation would be ridiculous & criminal.—When I considered how near I had come to having the operation in Augusta I was thoroughly disgusted & fed up with the whole medical profession, & decided to get well all by myself & never consult a doctor again.—Which I am now proceeding to do, and although so far my headaches & my eye-spots are just the same, my general health is improving slowly.—So much for that tiresome & horrid subject.

I have been kept very busy correcting proof on *The King's Henchman*. It is nearly finished now. The singers are already rehearsing the first act: a few days ago I received from the publisher a copy of the first act entire, words & music, bound into a book. On the cover it says: "Solely for use at the first performances of the Metropolitan Opera Company, New York." It is awfully exciting.

Eugen & I are leaving in a few days for Santa Fé, to visit friends there for a few weeks. It will do us both a lot of good to be going somewhere to have a good time, instead of to consult a doctor.

Aunt Rose, my asters are still blossoming. Are yours? But I have none of that lovely delicate pink such as you gave me when we left Camden.—And the blossoms seem to be small & short-stemmed. I think I like the old-fashioned kind better, not so branching, and with larger blossoms. My clarkia did nothing at all. But we had a riot of sweet-peas until a fortnight ago, and there are still a few blossoms on the vines. I have potted all my geraniums, and a fuchsia and some rather special petunias, two ice-plants, and millions of carnations, which are blossoming splendidly.—We took some snapshots of a garden we made with the ruined wall of an old barn as a background. If they're any good, I'll send you one.—I've spent the last twenty minutes, as it is, hunting for a photograph of our place to send you, but can't find a good one, so I'll wait.

I put up some plums today, & some tomatoes, too, off our own place. I wonder if they will keep. It seems a miracle, doesn't it, that they should ever keep?—Mother put up a lot of things for us this summer, jelly & jam & lots of things. They look so pretty, I think, on a table in rows with the sun shining through them.

Gene is driving down for the mail now, so I must hurry this into an envelope.—We have no R.F.D. even, here. We are really in the wilds, you see.

Lots of love to you both, from your niece,

Vincent.

P. S. I have baked beans in the oven,—& on *Friday*! Do you suppose they will refuse to bake at all?—I am sure they are as indignant as anything.   V.

---

143   TO MRS. CORA B. MILLAY

922 Canyon Road
Santa Fé, New Mexico
Dec. 6, 1926

Darling Mumbles:

Goodness knows where you are, but I imagine this will be forwarded.—My manuscript of *Aethelwold (The King's Henchman)* is at last ready for Harper's, & lies on the stand in the hall, all wrapped & stamped & girded for its journey to New York.—I have made a lot of changes in it since you saw it, & I feel sure that I have improved it. It has been a terrible job, but it's done now. All that's left to do is a few odd jobs such as writing a synopsis for the front of the printed libretto, & correcting proof, etc.—dirty chores, but nothing more.

We go this week to see an Indian dance at a place called Zuni, a thrilling ceremony, they say. We shall motor past the Petrified Forest, through the Painted Desert, & home by way of the Enchanted Mesa (pronounced Maý-suh). Doesn't that sound wonderful? I am too tired and let-down to write a very long letter. But it has been so long since you heard from me,—& just because you were a good sport & told me I needn't write until I feel like it, is no reason you should be punished, old sweet thing.

If we have good luck we shall have some corking photographs to show you when we get back.—Though the Indians don't like you to photograph their dances—which are all deeply religious.

Sante Fé is the funniest little place you never saw—about as big as Rockland—but much more like a village.

So much love to you. I hope you are getting rested, & having a good time, & getting a little fatter!

—Vincent

144   TO MRS. CORA B. MILLAY

Steepletop, [Austerlitz, N.Y.]
Jan. 6, 1927

Dearest Mumbles:

Kay wrote me about the plan for everybody to send you thirty-five beans the first of each month—an awfully good plan.—So here's mine.—It's not exactly the first of the month, but I just heard about it yesterday.—You *must* go back to your chiropractor—get a nice, gentle, sympathetic person; if you get one & don't like him or her, go to another one. There must be several in Newburyport.—Does Aunt Clem think it all nonsense?—Most nurses do, of course.—That doesn't prove anything.—We know this one here helped you; and so can lots of others.

The opening of *The King's Henchman* is tentatively scheduled for Feb. 17.[7]—You will have to be in New York for that, darling. It will be a great night.—Gene & I shall be staying with Florence;—do you think Norma & Chas will have their little room empty then?— You'd better write & ask Normie if they can put you up.—There will be at least four performances, the 17th, the 28th, & two later.—But of course you'll want to be there for the premiere.—And Harry Dowd's Mozart opera, *La Finta*,[8] opens January 17, just a month before mine, & Norma is singing Serpetta,—Folly—She just wrote me. Isn't that thrilling?—If you come to New York for my opening, you can go to hear Norma in La Finta, too!—What a lovely life it is!—Isn't it, darling?—

I wrote the expressman about your things. They are all right, he replies.—We are trying to get him to send them on to State Line by train. From there we could fetch them with the two horses & the sled. —We had some more tomatoes & blueberries for luncheon, simply delicious, both!

—(Golly, the snow's getting pink. I must go!)

I had to run & look at the color.—It was marvelous tonight,—that deepest rose-pink that you get once in a while, you know, with bright blue shadows.—It's so beautiful here. *You* know.—It was four below zero this morning. You know that, too.—It has been down to fifteen this winter, but today there is a strong wind blowing as well.

I shan't be able to give anybody free passes to *The Henchman*, of course.—I'll be lucky if I get one for myself. But you're rich, you've got lots of money, & in February you'll have lots more; you can buy yourself a seat.—(Poor old sing, everybody 'fusin' her, & makin' jokes an' everythin') . . . You go with Kay & Howard, or Norma & Charlie —see?—You write & ask 'em about it now. I'll make you a present of the ticket, if they'll take care of you, tell 'em.

Lots of love, mummie. If anybody's being mean to you, you tell me. (This is just a joke. I'm not hitting at anybody.)

Vincent.

[7] World première at the Metropolitan Opera House.
[8] Harrison Dowd's poetic adaptation of the German libretto of Mozart's opera, *La Finta Giardiniera* which was produced by The Intimate Opera Company at the Mayfair Theatre in New York.

145   TO MR. and MRS. DEEMS TAYLOR and JOAN TAYLOR

[Steepletop, Austerlitz, N.Y.]
Jan. 12, 1927

Dear Deems:

It was dreadfully nice of you to write us with all the latest news about the Henchman.

Dear Deems:

Gene got that far, & then had to leave to milk our cow, whose name is Buttercup. So I take it up from where he left off.—I am more thankful than I can well express that the Henchman is going to be, apparently, a single bill.—The first rehearsal must have been yesterday. I don't suppose you were present—yes?—no?—if you were, & don't dish me the dirt, I'll be mad at you.

I haven't played a *bar* of the Henchman today—not a note. And yesterday I was unfaithful to you! I only did an act and a half of it, & then deserted to Chopin, who is child's play in comparison. My favorite motif for Wednesday & Thursday of this week is the Maccus motif.

What Wymetal's[9] *other* name?—Or when you have a name like Wymetal, don't you *have* another name?

Dear Mary: How is our Steepletop baby? If Joan would like to come again to Steepletop: we've got a room for her Mamma and Papa, and a nice sunny room for her R.H., also a bathroom for the crown-princess.—We have a certified cow which gives Grade A no. 1 milk, and cream.

Are you still as beautiful as when I saw you last? Or does that only last a few days after the great event.—

love, Ugin.

Dear Mary:—You *must* be well, you know, in time to help me come & clean the brook! We'll put Joan in a wood-pecker's nest—an old one, one that's for rent—& she'll be all right for hours.—Don't forget.— And don't back out. It's a date of long standing.—

love, Edna.

Dear Joan:

Don't throw it up!
Don't!
You can keep it down!
And it's *awfully* good for you!

Y'r aff't, Aunt Edna.

Dear Deems:

Listen,—listen, Deems: If you hear any more news—good or bad —out with it, see?—I'm a big girl now.—Do they still like it?—Did you hear the rehearsal?—Was it rotten?—How 'bout it?—Semme a pos' card.

E.

[9] Wilhelm von Wymetal, stage director of the Metropolitan Opera Company.

146   TO ALEXANDER WOOLLCOTT[10]

Vanderbilt Hotel, New York.
Feb. 19, 1927.

Dear Alec Woollcott:

This morning, much to my disgust, I find that a letter written by me to you some time ago—in fact, shortly after I first saw *La Finta* at the Mayfair Theatre—has not been posted; but at any rate, it was not in *my* coat-pocket that I found it.

I do not enclose the letter in full, for since I wrote it things have changed somewhat for the Intimate Opera Company. Many discerning people have seen and heard *La Finta,* and, struck by its loveliness and charm, have sent their friends in ever increasing numbers to the Mayfair Theatre.

This, however, was the beginning of the letter, & it still holds true. "It is of importance to you & to myself," I wrote, "& to many people in this city, that The Intimate Opera Company, now producing Mozart's *La Finta* at the Mayfair Theatre, be fostered & sustained." Now believe me, this is precisely what I mean; it is of importance to the city. Nothing is further from my intention than to say: "These young people have worked very hard, & should be encouraged." I am not at all in favor of hard work for its own sake; many people who work very hard indeed produce terrible things, and should most certainly not be encouraged. The Intimate Opera Company should be fostered & sustained not for its own sake, but for ours. It is giving us more than we can ever return. The exquisite *Finta Giardiniera* of Mozart, the beautiful *Orpheus* of Gluck,—where else shall we find them?—nowhere else. And there are many evenings when nothing else at all will do. As for yourself, do not be too busy to go to see & hear *La Finta* & *Orpheus.* It is not only the music that draws one back for the second time & the third time to the Mayfair Theatre. It is also the delightful voices, the sweet pretty faces, the graceful lyrics, the charming costumes & sets, & the general gaiety & fun & air of improvisation about it all. And it is all so delicate & miniature. And it doesn't hurt your head, & it doesn't hurt your eyes, & it doesn't wear you out in any way. You just sit there, contented and glad you came, while one lovely scene succeeds another.—

Edna St. Vincent Millay.

[10] Then Dramatic Editor of the New York *World.*

147   TO ELINOR WYLIE

Steepletop, Austerlitz, N.Y.
Day after Easter [April 18, '27]

My darling:

Enclosed you will find a letter from me to the League of American Penwomen. If the address is wrong or insufficient, change it—(on your typewriter!)—Please read the letter, then post it at once.—Be a good girl, & do as I tell you, & post it at once.

Vincent.

To the League of American Penwomen

[Steepletop, Austerlitz, N.Y.]

Ladies:

I have received from you recently several communications, inviting me to be your Guest of Honour at a function to take place in Washington some time this month. I replied, not only that I was unable to attend, but that I regretted this inability; I said that I was sensible to the honour you did me, and that I hoped you would invite me again.

Your recent gross and shocking insolence to one of the most distinguished writers of our time has changed all that.

It is not in the power of an organization which has insulted Elinor Wylie, to honour me.

And indeed I should feel it unbecoming on my part, to sit as Guest of Honour in a gathering of writers, where honour is tendered not so much for the excellence of one's literary accomplishment as for the circumspection of one's personal life.

Believe me, if the eminent object of your pusillanimous attack has not directed her movements in conformity with your timid philosophies, no more have I mine. I too am eligible for your disesteem. Strike me too from your lists, and permit me, I beg you, to share with Elinor Wylie a brilliant exile from your fusty province.

Very truly yours,

Edna St. Vincent Millay

148 TO LLEWELYN POWYS

Steepletop, Austerlitz, N.Y.
May 2, 1927

Dear Lulu:

What you must think of me for never having written about *The Verdict of Bridlegoose*, I hate to imagine.—Someday when I see you I shall tell you how it happened, how ill I have been for the past two years, & unable to use my eyes for reading, & how I put your book in a drawer of my dressing-table to read when I should get well, & how I never got well, so that I did not know until a few days ago, when I gave the book to Eugen to read aloud to me, that *Bridlegoose* is dedicated to me.[11] In pride & dismay I write you. It is a lovely book. Nobody can express as you can do how precious a thing is life, and how delicate & how to be cherished. I shall never forget the old janitress. It is incredible that she could die, who in her youth had seen wild deer with golden branches on their heads. You do write so beautifully, Lulu. —Please do not think too harshly of me. Please believe how happy & proud I am that you should dedicate this book to me.

                                                                Edna.

I am sending you my "King's Henchman."

> [11] "Dedicated to Edna St. Vincent Millay/ A leprechaun among poets." The book itself was the English writer's memories of his first years in America. On pp. 36-37 he tells of his first meeting with the poet.

149   TO DEEMS TAYLOR

                                        Steepletop, Austerlitz, N.Y.
                                        May 7, 1927

Dear Deems:

Please forgive a girl that's had a hard spring, what with tonsilitis & all.—It's such a beautiful book![12]—I cannot tell you how I shall always treasure it.—It means so much, somehow, I feel.—And the signatures gave me the strangest kick—& still do, every time I open the book to show it to somebody. I never thought autographs very interesting, but there is something about that bunch of names all together there that brings tears to your eyes. I couldn't for the life of me explain how it makes me feel.—

The book has the most handsome back—the ridgy part that shows when it is in the bookcase—(except that mine isn't in a bookcase, but in a drawer of my desk done up in cotton-wool & marked *High Explosive—Keep Off*.)—And the picture of you is extremely good, Deems, I think.

I loved the "To whom so much of it belongs"—of your inscription. —I gasped when I saw it—it is such an imposing big serious book—I suppose I had expected "to my esteemed collaboratress"—or some such thing.

Dear Deems, *please, please* forgive me for not writing before, & do not hate me, I implore you. I love the book.

I wonder what is happening about the Henchman on tour.—But if you are resting, as I hope, & getting well, but still very tired, don't bother to write me.—Perhaps Mary would send me a postcard sometime about it.—My love to you both & to Joan—lots of love, you understand. —Are you ever coming to Steepletop?

Edna.

[12] An edition de luxe of *The King's Henchman*, signed by all the principal singers and staff members of the Metropolitan Opera Company.

150 TO MRS. ESTHER ROOT ADAMS

Steepletop, Austerlitz, N.Y.
May 23, 1927

Dearest Tess:

Don't dare to forget that you're coming up here for your birthday,[13] & don't dare to say that I didn't answer your letter, & so you thought, & so you didn't think—

You wrote me such a lovely letter, the kind one doesn't get any more, & certainly doesn't write any more!—But we are, as my mother says, busier than the devil in a gale of wind.

I suggest that you come Friday the third, so that you can bring Frank with you if he'd like to come, and spend a week with us. If Anthony isn't weaned yet, you can perfectly well bring him along. We have a bathroom & everything; and can make you as comfortable as a feller need be in June. My wonderful cook got a stitch in her side & had to go home & rest,—doctor's orders—but we have a woman who comes every day to clean up after us, so it's not so bad. And anyway it'll be June. And you come, old Esther Root, or I'll be mad at you!

Darling, it occurs to me that there are people who really do get mad at people, so I hasten to say that if for any reason you can't make it, I shan't be mad at you, I shall just be very, very sorry.

* * *

Let me hear from you soon, as we have no telephone, & have to go three miles for our mail, & wires are sent out from Chatham with the postman! Sometimes we gettum & sometimes we don't.

Love,
Vincent.

(I sign myself Vincent to avoid confusion with Edna Ferber!)

[13] June 4th. This had become an annual celebration, started when the friends were together in Europe in 1922. It had continued in America, and especially at Steepletop.

151 TO MRS. CORA B. MILLAY

> Steepletop, Austerlitz, N.Y.
> May 25, 1927

Dearest Mumbles:

I wrote Kathleen ages ago about her book.[14] I told you I would, & I did. And that's that.

Now will you please stop worrying?

Kathleen is about to publish a book, as thousands have done before her. A person who publishes a book wilfully appears before the populace with his pants down. And there's nothing you can do about that.

Kathleen is not a baby. She is a grown-up person quite able to take care of herself. And she has been struggling for years to be allowed to manage her own affairs. If she knew the kind of letter you wrote me in her behalf, she'd froth at the mouth & spit brimstone.

Kathleen is about to publish a book. If it's a good book, nothing can harm her. If it's a bad book, nothing can help her. And all your stewing & fretting will accomplish just one end: it will make you very sick, & a nuisance to yourself, and a care to everybody,—so will you please forget it, & relax, & interest yourself in something else? If you don't, you're not the intelligent woman you have the reputation of being; you are just one more typical, sentimental, agitated *mother*!

Won't you please *R E L A X ?*

Kathleen is not a baby. She is six years older than I was when my first book of poems was published. Can't you let her attend to her own business?

You see, I *know* that it is worrying about Kathleen that is making you sick, & not another darned thing. And I tell you you are absolutely powerless to do a thing about it. And I ask you to *S N A P   O U T   O F   I T* and stop making yourself sick for nothing! Pul yourself together, & go to Maine, & start your garden. And I'll send you lots of plants, & help you all I can, with advice, & my own experience, & seeds, & money, & any darned thing you want. If you'll only be good, & STOP WORRYING ! ! !

> With a hell of a lot of love,
> Vincent.

[14] *The Evergreen Tree*, a volume of poems published in the fall of 1927. Later Kathleen Millay was to publish two other volumes of poetry, *The Hermit Thrush* and *The Beggar at the Gate*, and two novels, *Wayfarer* and *Against the Wall*.

Steepletop, Austerlitz, N.Y.
July 20, 1927

Dearest Mumbles:

I haven't written you for such a long time, darling!—But I don't feel so very strong yet, though it was just a tiny operation . . . I don't feel much of any change in my condition—but here's hopin'.

———

Lots of little pieces of news from Steepletop. Dolly Steepletop has a spotted calf born June 16, named Spotty Steepletop, a heifer. Blossom Steepletop has a beautiful calf that looks just like a young deer, born about July 1, also a heifer. We are going to raise them both.—We have a couple now to work for us. They live in the north guest-room for the present. The man does all the chores, which now includes milking three cows, & feeding two calves by letting them suck your finger in the milk-pail!—Picking about ten quarts of strawberries a day—the strawberries are wonderful, those we set out, you remember—& pecks of peas, & a million other things. The man is excellent; he seems really to like the work. His wife is very little of a cook & considerable of a slattern, but she'll do. For the sake of the man, we'd put up with worse than she. We also have Freida, the young school-teacher from up the road. She does the house-work, & serves at tea-table; between them they do the laundry. So you can see we are pretty well fixed.—Mumbles, we are not so interested any more in modern quilts; we have acquired a terrible crush on old ones, & are getting together quite a collection. You know the kind, anywhere from forty to a hundred years old, all quilted by hand, & beautiful formal designs, "Rising Sun", "Evening Star", etc. If you can get hold of a Rising-Sun or a Cottage quilt or a hand-woven counterpane, or anything like that, I'll pay anything up to twenty-five dollars, but we can probably get them here better than you can there. We are still just as keen on the rag-rugs. But if you ever come across a pretty hooked rug, grab it for me.—The roses from Dreer did splendidly & are nearly all in blossom.—You were sweet not to mind it that I didn't get around to sending the flowers. I'll send you some in the fall, if I can. As for your birthday paper, I have ordered it, hones' ta Gawd, at last. You will probably get it in about a fortnight.—

Love & lots of love,
Sefe.

The story of Nicola Sacco and Bartolomeo Vanzetti has already been told in detail in innumerable books and pamphlets. The murder trial of the two then obscure Italian anarchists, which began in 1920, lasted through much legal wrangling until the fall of 1927. The defendants—accused of the murder of a shoe-factory paymaster and the guard accompanying him, in South Braintree, Mass., on April 15, 1920—were finally executed a few minutes after midnight on August 23, 1927.

153   TO GOVERNOR ALVAN T. FULLER

August 22, 1927

Your Excellency:

During my interview with you this afternoon I called to your attention a distressing instance of the miscarriage of justice in a neighboring state. I suggested that, for all your careful weighing of the evidence, for all your courage in the face of threats and violent words, for all your honest conviction that these men are guilty, you, no less than the governor of Maine in my story, who was so tragically mistaken, are but human flesh and spirit, and that it is human to err.

Tonight, with the world in doubt, with this Commonwealth drawing into its lungs with every breath the difficult air of doubt, with the eyes of Europe turned westward upon Massachusetts and upon the whole United States in distress and harrowing doubt—are you still so sure? Does no faintest shadow of question gnaw at your mind? For, indeed, your spirit, however strong, is but the frail spirit of a man. Have you no need, in this hour, of a spirit greater than your own?

Think back. Think back a long time. Which way would He have turned, this Jesus of your faith?—Oh, not the way in which your feet are set!

You promised me, and I believed you truly, that you would think of what I said. I exact of you this promise now. Be for a moment alone with yourself. Look inward upon yourself. Let fall from your harassed mind all, all save this: which way would He have turned, this Jesus of your faith?

I cry to you with a million voices: answer our doubt. Exert the clemency which your high office affords.

There is need in Massachusetts of a great man tonight. It is not yet too late for you to be that man.

Edna St. Vincent Millay.

154 TO MRS. CORA B. MILLAY

Steepletop, Austerlitz, N.Y.
Oct. 5, 1927

Dearest Mumbles:

Thanks a million times for all your trouble. I wrote a letter to the World yesterday, quoting from several of the clippings you sent me, etc. If they publish it, I will try to get a copy for you. I am enclosing a clipping from the Musical Observer, an article by Eddie Johnson, who sang Aethelwold, you remember. Isn't it lovely?

I don't know the name of those darling small apricot-coloured gladiolas; wish I did.

* * *

Have you seen any nice new ragrugs—ragrugs looks funny, doesn't it? Mine are so faded that I can't put my stair carpet down till I get some new ones, sort of dark but bright in colour.

* * *

I wrote a swell letter to the World,[15] which ought to shut the raucous mouths of the whole darned bunch. So you can relax a little now. I sha'n't bring up the subject again; so my only interest now is my usual thirst for knowledge.

What made you think Eugen would be picking on me, or on you, about this matter? He has been perfectly magnificent through this whole thing, as you ought to know he would be. Don't be sill.

Much, much love,
Sefe.

[15] This letter, in answer to one from Mr. Edmund Pearson who had questioned the veracity of the story that Miss Millay had told to Governor Fuller, appeared in the New York *World* on October 6, 1927.

155 TO MRS. CORA B. MILLAY

[Steepletop, Austerlitz, N.Y.
Oct. 28, 1927]

Dearest Mother:

I will write you a real letter soon, but am too tired now. Have been working very hard writing. Just finished an article for the *Outlook*[16]—published next week probably—about the Sacco & Vanzetti case. Have been writing mostly poetry, though.—Just came back from Boston. Six of us were to be tried for "sauntering & loitering" on the 16th of Oct.[17]—but having got us there from all over the country, they put it off till the 21st of November. We shall plead "not guilty" & appeal to the Supreme Court—anything to keep people from going to sleep on the subject!—Expect to refuse to pay a fine & probably shall spend a fortnight in jail—shall do just what is considered best by our counsel—Art Hays[18] &, we hope, Clarence Darrow. Dos Passos & Jack Lawson (who wrote Processional) are two of the other defendants.

Bless you, darling, for working so hard for me. Hope you didn't make yourself sick.

* * *

Love & love & love,
Sefe.

[16] "Fear."
[17] Finally acquitted of the charge on December 3, 1927.
[18] Arthur Garfield Hays.

156 TO WITTER BYNNER

[November 1927]

Dearest Hal:
Thank you for your letter about the Outlook article. I read it over and over and over. It made me very happy. You were so sweet to write. It was a beautiful letter, dear Hal. I have kept it to read again, sometime when I am sad.

Love,
Edna.

157 TO ABBIE HUSTON EVANS

[Steepletop, Austerlitz, N.Y.]
Dec. 27, 1927.

Dear Abbie:
I am sending back to you your lovely poems, for you to arrange as you want them to go and send on to Harper's. I am afraid I have given you scant time, by taking so terribly long myself. If you will get in touch with Mr. Saxton he will tell you just how long you can have.

I have written a short Foreword for the book which I hope you will like. I have only a pencil-copy of it, or I would send it to you.

If, when the galley-proof comes in, there is anything about it you do not like, please kick and scream lustily, and I will change it.

I feel sure I have somewhere a second copy of many of these poems, the collection you sent me first, containing some which are not here. Isn't that so? Do you want me to hunt them up? Or have you the whole collection right at hand?—I rather imagine you have.

I have marked with a faint V the poems which I feel should certainly go into the book. I may have left out special favorites of yours, in which case you will just put them in; but would you mind letting me know which ones you wish to put back, that I have left out?

There are several which I like extremely with the exception of one stanza, usually the final stanza,—Cock-Crow, for instance, and the one about the Northern Lights. I am sure you won't mind my saying why, for I know how happy I always am when people whose opinion I value make suggestions about my poems. In Cock-Crow the final stanza seems much less beautiful than the others, more involved, somewhat awkward, less lovely in sound. The part about the fifty banded men back to back defying the spears is so triumphant—I always feel disappointed with the end. I don't suppose you could just leave off the final stanza, (always supposing you should agree with me a little!) or change the three stanzas about in some way? It is such a splendid thing, with the exception of the last stanza, I feel.

In the Northern Lights poem, I am sure that you weaken the beauty of the thing by saying suddenly, "Why waste all this on people who are asleep?" The ecstasy drops right there; the poem, too, goes to sleep right there. I believe that the first two lines of the final stanza should be the last two lines, and you should put in two new lines for the first and second, objective lines, not subjective.

These are the two poems I feel strongest about,—that they need some change, I mean. I have made faint penciled notes on the margin of several others, notes that you can easily erase.

Good luck, dear Abbie. I have had so much pleasure with the poems, and am looking forward eagerly to seeing them done into a handsome book![19] Be sure to tell them what kind of binding you prefer, what colour, and all that. They might possibly, if left entirely to themselves, give it a colour you wouldn't like, although I must say they are pretty good about this usually.

Affectionately your friend,
Vincent.

[19] *Outcrop*, published by Harper & Brothers with a Foreword by Edna St. Vincent Millay, March, 1928.

158   TO MRS. CORA B. MILLAY

Steepletop, [Austerlitz, N.Y.]
August 29, 1928

Dearest Mumbles:

It seems long, long ages since I heard from you, and I know it is even longer since I wrote. Please forgive me, if you can, for not having hunted up the Little Green Cheeses.[20] This has been a very upset place this summer. In the first place it has rained every day, with the exception of about six, since the beginning of April. Everybody's potatoes have been killed by the blight; ours not yet, but we are expecting them to be stricken any day now. We have had so few dry days that we have been able to spray them only twice. I believe there are about eight acres of them. Everybody's oats are rotted, many of the fields so flooded that the teams couldn't go in to cut them, even if there should be a dry day. Ours are still all right, but they must be cut at once or we shall lose them, and we can't cut them in the rain,—we have about twelve acres of oats. Of course this is not my department, but it means quite a big money loss, and besides it is so depressing to see the rain ruining everything that it quite takes one's pep away. Then Anna and Conrad left without giving notice; for a while Freida and her sister worked for us, but they had to go because Freida had to get ready to teach school. Then we got a Swedish couple from an agency in New York, very nice; they have just given notice. In the meantime I have been working very hard on my new book of poems, trying to get it ready in time. That is finished at last, and the page-proof, and they are at work printing it; it will be published September 21.[21] Right in the middle of everything I had to pick up the flu somewhere, or maybe it was only the grippe, but in any case it left me sort of weak, and I lost almost all the lovely extra pounds I had gained. Well, so much for all these lugubrious details.

* * *

I had to give my darling little Lupa away. We had a little black lamb named Rainy, and Lupa attacked her, and tore her leg frightfully. We took her to the veterinary, and we had to keep bandaging her wound for weeks; she recovered, and is perfectly happy now, except that she will probably always limp a little. Of course, I couldn't keep a dog that is a sheep-killer, so many people right around here have sheep, so I had to give her away, or else keep her chained all the time, which is no fun. But I didn't enjoy much having her go. I was fond of the bad little thing.

Darling, your lilac-bushes that you pulled up by the roots and drug home here by the hair, and we planted by the sunken-garden—'member?—are growing simply marvelously. They will very likely all blossom next year. They are going to be beautiful in a few years. And your little pine, the only one that was left, is still flourishing.

I was to have been in Boston last week, at the Sacco-Vanzetti memorial meeting, and read some poems, but I was still in bed with the grippe.

Aunt Susie sent me some lovely iris. She said she sent you some, too. They have been sitting here in the living-room for a week; I hope they don't die before I can get them planted. If they do, I am determined to send to Dreer and get the whole bunch duplicated exactly, and pretend they are the ones Aunt Susie sent me, and never let her know.

Arthur and Gladys are still with us. They have bought a beautiful place about fourteen miles from here, with a very good house on it, and are having the house remodeled. They decided it was much easier and cheaper and more practical to do that than to build an entirely new set of buildings on the land adjoining ours. And of course they are quite right. Max Eastman and Eliena have been up here several times, looking around for a place for themselves. Croton is getting pretty thick, and they want to sell their house and come here. They have not found the right place yet, however. Next year, God willing, we shall have a tennis-court, and have lots of fun. We want awfully much to have a swimming-pool, too. But if it rains as much next year as it has this year, we can just use the tennis-court as a swimming-pool.

Mumbles, dear, I am afraid this is not a very nice letter, so full of whining and sniffling. Next time I'll write a nicer one.

Lots of love to you, and to the kids. We turned the radio on one day, and there were three people singing in harmony, little cute and funny songs. I couldn't help thinking it was not nearly so well done as Kay and Norma and I used to do it.

Did I ever tell you my little rhyme about Jesus and Buddha?[22]—probably I did, but anyway, here it is, just in case.

> Said the little Lord Jesus to the little Lord Buddha,
> "The world is getting ruder and ruder."

Said the little Lord Buddha to the little Lord Jesus,
"They're only doing it to tease us."

Love,
Sefe.

[20] Children's stories written by Mrs. Millay when her girls
were very young.
[21] *The Buck in the Snow.*
[22] Sent out as a Christmas card in 1930.

159 TO WILLIAM ROSE BENÉT

Steepletop, Austerlitz, N.Y.
December 28, 1928

Dearest Bill:

You were so sweet to write me. You are so sweet anyway. Eugen &
I both think so.

Yesterday we were in the cellar, sampling the new wine which
Pierre our cook has made, and there on a shelf we saw the tiny keg
labelled *Seven Shires* which we had been keeping for Elinor.[23] It was
that wine we had that she liked so much, you remember. We were
keeping it for her; nobody was allowed to touch it. When you come
here we will give the little keg to you, and we will all drink to our
beautiful, brilliant, adorable one. She is not out of our minds or off our
tongue for very long. We talk of her for hours at a time, just as we
used to do. The other day we were with Arthur & Gladys, & we talked
of her, and Arthur showed us a marvellous letter she wrote him, in
answer to a letter from him about *The Orphan Angel*, or *Mortal
Image* as she preferred so much to call it. Such a thrilling letter it is.
I have still, of course, her few letters to me, & I am so happy that I have.

Bill, dear, don't torture yourself with thinking if only you had
been better to her. It was you just as you were that she loved, & loved
so truly. She was so wise, and though she was often hurt by thoughtless
or tactless words not meant to hurt her, I think that a few moments
later she understood & forgave, as she did once with me when I had
wounded her deeply without of course wishing to wound her at all.
People always torture themselves in this way; I could do it, too, remembering that I hurt her, but instead I remember the happy times we
had together, & how delightful she was, & how funny, so gay & splendid
about tragic things, so comically serious about silly ones. Oh, she was

lovely! There was nobody like her at all. I am grateful for all she gave me.

With so much love from Eugen & myself,
Vincent.

You must forget, dear friend, the little things that made her cry, or if you would rather remember everything about her, as I would, too, then be sure to remember oftenest the great things that made her laugh.

[23] Elinor Wylie (Mrs. William Rose Benét) had died the sixteenth of December.

160   TO STEPHEN VINCENT BENÉT

Steepletop, Austerlitz, N.Y.
Feb. 6, 1929

Dear Steve:

Can you forgive a non-union poet, who for weary months has been working twenty-two hours a day on her own stuff, for not writing to thank you for John Brown's Body, and to congratulate you upon a splendid piece of work? It made me so proud of you, Steve. And I don't know when I have been so happy about anything as I have been about the success of this book of yours—I mean its success from every point of view, not just that it's so darned good, but that so many people think so, and are buying it. What fun for you and Rosemary! What fun for all your friends, myself among them! And what fun for me to write to the Guggenheims as I had occasion to do the other day in answer to a letter such as they once wrote me regarding you: And what did I tell you once about Steve Benét—and wasn't I right?

Dear Children: I have just re-read the above, and I see that it sounds rather as if I were proud of myself, than proud of you. It sounds as if it were written with the thumbs in the weskit-armholes. And although you know that it wasn't written like that—since who could type with any fluency and his thumbs in his armholes?—still I feel that I must hasten to tell you that this is not the case. I haven't seen you for a long time. I wonder if you remember me clearly enough to be sure how happy I am for you.

Dear Steve and Rosemary, dear Children: This letter can't go on any longer without speaking of Elinor. How shall we bear it? How can we manage without her? There was only one of her. I was in New York at the time it happened. I was just at the end of a long and tiring reading-tour, reading from my poems. I said to myself, As soon as this darned chore is over, I'll rush to see her. And just as I was dressing to go to give my last reading in the Brooklyn Academy of Music, somebody who didn't know that I even knew her, casually mentioned that she had died. How do we bear these things? How do we manage?

I suppose you are hard at work on another big book now, Steve. I wonder what it is going to be. Whatever it is, I know it is something I shall love to read. I thought some of the lyrics in John Brown's Body were among your loveliest. I adored the one about the Hilders, and the one that says: Now listen to me, you Tennessee corn.

Good luck to you, and happiness, and all the things you want. And my love to you both.

Jerry.

161   TO EDMUND WILSON

Steepletop, Austerlitz, N.Y.
[Feb. 6, 1929]

Dear Bunny:

No, I'm not offended. I just have so many things I want to say about your book[24] that I couldn't seem to get time to write them. I'll do it soon.—In the meantime, if you value my opinion at all, please be persuaded not to publish your book this spring. It is really not ready to be published, & I swear that you will do yourself a great injury if you publish it just as it is—it is very uneven—I like much of it tremendously—but it is not a whole—it needs a whole lot of working on still. *Please* don't have it published this spring—no matter what your publisher says—your reputation is the principal thing,—& it really isn't good enough, yet, Bunny, I swear it isn't.—You can make a grand book of it, but it's not finished.

You'll probably be mad as hell with me—but I can't help it.—I want to talk it over with you. I'll write you about it later—unless in the meantime you write asking me to mind my own business.

Affectionately yours,
Edna.

[24] *I Thought of Daisy*, a novel, published by Scribners, 1929.

162 TO MAX EASTMAN

Steepletop, Austerlitz, N.Y.
Feb. 6, 1929

Dear Max:

Ugin and I, or Jo and I, I should say to you, have just read your review of the Buck in the Snow in the Nation. I want to write and thank you for it. I thought it terribly nice. You are quite right that it is fashionable here to be disappointed in the book. In England it isn't so; the British press has been wonderful. But you are one of the very few in our own great metropolis who has had a good word for it.

I am sending you a couple of new sonnets that I thought you might like.

How is Eliena? Her paintings of Rosie and the pigs are still sitting on top of the piano along with Ione's water-colour. We never seem to have time to do anything about anything. I want to hang the golden-straw one in the hall, but it doesn't get hung. Nor do our electric-light fixtures ever get put in. The Christmas mistletoe still dangles from a rather fly-specked and very decrepit naked bulb.

We are snowed in now. At least, we can get out, but are never quite sure of getting back up the hill. I wonder if you are still at $50\frac{1}{2}$ Barrow Street. I'm sure that was the number. I've never written it down, but I feel sure I've carried it correct in my head.

Love to you both. I was thinking of you, and I wanted to write you.

Edna.

163 TO EDMUND WILSON

Steepletop, Austerlitz, N.Y.
Saturday [Feb. 10, 1929]

Dear Bunny:

We're motoring into New York Tuesday, & shall be there several days. Can't I see you? Can't we do something together—have tea, or take in a cock-fight or something? I'm dying to see you. I'll bring your manuscript with me. When I was reading it I took a lot of notes—mostly little things, places which I think you could easily polish up—not so much in the character of Rita as in other characters,—just general remarks, really.—It was horrid of me to keep the manuscript so long. I might have known you'd think I was offended. Yet it hadn't occurred to me that you would think so, since I wasn't a bit.—I'm so keen to talk with you about it. I imagine that from my note you'll think I hate the guts of it. For of course I neglected to tell you that I think it contains much of the loveliest stuff I ever read.—But anyhow, I'll go into that when I see you.—I'll call up the New Republic when I get in town, & we'll decide where to meet. I'll bring you in a bottle of the loveliest red wine you ever tasted, & not until you're a little tight on it will I confess that it was made right here on the premises by my French chef Pierre. Could you have dinner with me Tuesday?—If not, *you* think up something bright. We shall be at the Vanderbilt, but probably shan't get in until about five o'clock Tuesday. You might call up & leave a message for me.—I've got some new sonnets to show you, but first I want to talk about your book—so maybe I'll just send them to you later. It'll give you a swell chance to get back at me for whamming your book the way I did in my last letter.—In any case I'll call you up as soon as I get in.

I never thanked you for the flower-seeds you brought me from California. I shall plant them with ceremony in April & doubtless by August I shall have a forest of redwoods on my hands.

With love,
Edna.

•

164   TO MRS. CORA B. MILLAY

Steepletop, [Austerlitz, N.Y.]
September 24, 1929

Darling Mother:

It's so terribly long since I heard from you, and so terribly long since you heard from me! Why are we both so lazy about letters? Usually you are not so bad as I am, but this summer you're almost worse, because you heard from me last! Ugin wrote you that I had quinsy. It was pretty bad, and I haven't got my strength back by any means yet. I get awfully tired doing the least little thing. I'm afraid you feel the same way, darling, after the terrible time you had here. I've heard from you through other people, Harry Dowd, Isobel Simpson, etc. so I have known that you were not really ill. Still, I'm thoroughly ashamed not to have written you before. Please let me know how you are.

We have had a most unusual summer here, perfectly beautiful weather all the time, but not a drop of rain for months. First all the wells in the village of Austerlitz began to go dry, and finally the spring that feeds our house went so low that the water no longer came through the pipe; for nearly two months now we have had to get our water from across the road by attaching a hose to the barn faucet; fortunately the spring on High Hill is still all right, otherwise I don't know what we should have done.

Pierre and Susanne are in the cottage now, and we are so much happier with them there. Pierre has made a chicken-yard and a little pool for the ducks, and for the first time since we came here the damned chickens are not scratching about in my flowers and dropping manure all over the lawn so that you don't dare sit down anywhere, or wish you hadn't dared. The old barns are all torn down, they pulled them down with the tractor,—a fine sight. And all the old beams and boards that were no good for anything else have been sawn up and stacked in the most beautiful wood-pile you ever saw. Everything has had another coat of paint, and the place is beginning to look pretty sweet.

We have another French couple in the house; the woman cooks, and very well, and is both neat and thrifty, which is a great change from most people I've had in the kitchen; the man, who is a darling, does the house-work and serves at the table; he is an excellent butler. They sleep across at the cottage, of course. This man's name being also Pierre, a difficulty presented itself at once, which I solved by saying that he should be called Pierrot. So he is called Pierrot, and since his wife's name is Colombe, and he often calls her Colombine, it is all rather cute. They are also young, have children in France, and are apparently serious about working hard with us for a few years and saving up money to buy a little place when they go back. So it really looks very well. Pierre and Susanne have been with us over a year now. So it *is* possible to keep servants in the country, even in a wild country like this. Susanne does all the laundry, which is enormous, tends the chickens and ducks, and makes the butter. Colombe is busy now canning tomatoes. We had a marvelous garden this summer, and haven't bought a vegetable for goodness knows how long. Let me tell you, just for fun, what we've had from our garden: Potatoes, cabbage, cauliflower, squash, peas, string beans, shell beans, lima beans, cucumbers, radishes, turnips, carrots, pumpkins, sweet corn, tomatoes, eggplants, fennel, parsley, garlic, and CANTALOUPES! And maybe even now I've forgotten something. And oh, mumbles, the mushrooms! The big field across the road, the one that's over to the orchard, has been full of them. Every time we gather them I think of you, and Ugin gets so jealous when I tell him that our field in England was even more wonderful, which I'm beginning to have to admit is not strictly true.

Mumbles, have you read All Quiet on the Western Front? If you haven't, you must. Do get it and read it. It's wonderful.

* * *

I am writing this in my study over the garage. Through my window I can see Pierre coming down from the oat-field on top of an enormous load of oats driven by Molly and Tom. It looks so pretty. It is so tall that he has to lie on his stomach when they go under the willows, to keep from being brushed off. This afternoon they will come back with two loads, one behind the other, Pierre driving one team and John Pinnie[25] the other. John Pinnie has been here for a couple of months, helping Pierre with all the extra work. It's the most thrilling sight to see the two loads coming up the road, enormous, one team behind the other.

Well, darling, I must go to luncheon. Please let me hear from you soon. It's awful not hearing from you for so long.

Lots and lots and lots of love from
Your Vincent.

[25] John Pinnie, who is now, and has been for over twenty years, caretaker at Steepletop.

165   TO ALLAN ROSS MACDOUGALL

Steepletop, Austerlitz, N.Y.
[October 3, 1929]

Dear li'l' Alling:

This house has been so full of wild Indians ever since your letter came that there was no sense in my answering you, there being not so much as an empty shelf in a medicine-closet to put you up on, & I being of those who never write letters except when blatantly necessary, & usually not then.

However, can you come here next Monday—the 7th—& stay till Saturday when another bunch of wild Indians will descend upon me? —*Please* come, & bring your mss.[26]—I'm dying to see you. Wire me

at once what train you expect to take to *Hillsdale, N.Y.*—We will meet
you there.— Wit luv.—Me.

[26] *The Gourmets' Almanac* (1930). Miss Millay went through
the Ms. with her usual thoroughness, read the proofs, and
then scribbled the following imprimatur:

October 23, 1929

Dearest Alling: This is all right just as it stands, as far as I'm
concerned. The whole preface is charming. Ugin likes it a
lot, too. Just one suggestion: Cut out "Tunisia" from the
list of places where you have been working on the book,
and at the end of the whole thing, instead of saying "Tunis,
North Africa", just say "Tunis". I think this is pretty important. There's something so uncosmopolitan, so provincial
in the sound of the added "North Africa" that it detracts
enormously from the ease & urbanity of your preface. Now
"though thou hast much to do, see to 't," etc.

Yr aff hbl svt

Edner.

166   TO MRS. CORA B. MILLAY

Steepletop, Austerlitz, N.Y.
Day after Thanksgiving [1929]

Dearest Mumbles:

You are quite right not to travel when you have a cold, and of
course this is not a very specially good time to be at Steepletop. But
Ugin and I are both awfully disappointed that we shan't see you this
fall. We were so looking forward to having you here. However, if I get
anywhere near you this winter, I'll try to make it to Newburyport. If
not, keep in touch with me, darling, from time to time. I shall leave
for the Coast about the first of January, but shall arrange to have my
mail forwarded in some way. I shall be too busy to write you very
often, but Ugin will write you.

So be a good girl, and don't take any chances with these hateful
colds.

I have been having an orgy of playing the piano lately,[27] several
hours a day—Beethoven, Bach and Mozart. It has been wonderful. I
seldom put my hands on the keys without remembering how you taught
me to play when I was a baby, and all the money you paid for my

music-lessons afterward. No one was ever more grateful for anything than I am to you for this beautiful gift you gave me, mother.

Goodbye for now. Give my love to Hazel. Poor, pretty little thing, when last I saw her she was a tiny child; and now she is a widow.

Love, Mumbles. Sefe is terribly happy that you are better.

Love from Ugin, too.   Vincent.

[27] It is not generally known that the poet made an appearance in Camden, Maine, at the age of seventeen as a concert pianist. Her program on that occasion, Friday, June 2, 1909, consisted of works by Bach, Haydn, Mendelssohn, Goddard, and Chaminade.

167   TO MRS. CORA B. MILLAY

Steepletop, Austerlitz, N.Y.
May 27, 1930

Dearest Mumbles:

Thanks heaps and heaps for the lovely presents. The silver things are just too grand for words; I'm crazy about them. And I am so happy with the German dictionary. I had a little one, but so incomplete it was a nuisance. We have been building in book-shelves, acres of them, and have lots of room at last for our books,—and to spare. So if you meet any more elegant volumes, knock 'em on the head and ship 'em south. (Or inelegant!)

Darling, you have one book, if you still have it, which I want awfully to borrow sometime,—it's the big Shakespeare with the pictures of "Sweet Phoebe, do not scorn me, do not, Phoebe," etc., from which I used to read when I was eight. I want to read all of Shakespeare all over again, and in that book. (I speak as if I hadn't opened a copy of Shakespeare since I was eight, but never mind.)

One of the little white lilacs that you dragged out of the ground by the hair of the head and we planted by the sunken garden IS IN BLOSSOM! I enclose a scrap of it. It is the first one to bloom. Next year maybe they all will blossom! Isn't that thrilling?

Also, your little pine is doing very well,—the only one that our bright-eyed hired help (help is euphemistic) didn't mow down; I transplanted it to the hedge out of help's way.

Also, every one of the cunning little yellow tulips that you carried around in your handbag for weeks and then we planted for Ugin under an apple-tree, every one of them blossomed this spring. Ugin thanks you again for them; and for the butter patter.

Norma and Charlie motored up to see us last week. I squealed so with delight when I suddenly saw them sitting in their car outside the window, that Ugin thought Altair had gone mad and was chewing me up or something, and came leaping downstairs white as a blood-root blossom.

Well, I must close, with many respectful salutations, and much love from Steepletop.

I beg to remain, as ever, yr most aff daughter and obdt hbl svt,

Vincent.

168   TO MR. and MRS. DEEMS TAYLOR

Steepletop, Austerlitz, N.Y.
June 10th, 1930

Dear Kids:

This is to invite you to a grand house-party to be thrown at Steeple-top July 21st to 24th or as long as everything—meaning hosts, guests and liquor—holds out. On the evening of July 22nd we are having the Jitney Players here to give a show for us: Gilbert's "Haste to the Wedding", I believe it will be, but we may decide on something else. In any case it will be something silly and amusing and very well presented and a hell of a lot of fun,—at least, if all the nice people we are inviting arrive on time and get filled up with punch on time. We expect to have about fourteen house-guests. Then Arthur Ficke will fill his house with people; and our friends the Branns and the La Branches whose new houses will just about be ready to be moved into by that time, and to smooth whose ruffled plumage we suddenly decided just like that to give this here party, will also fill their houses with people, so that there will very likely be about fifty or sixty souls, poets and musicians included, to see the show. Please tell me at once that you will come.

Thanks for the cheque. It came in lovely.

And say. We want to do our hall in slate like your drawing-room; you said you didn't mind; and we thought it might be nice to have a hall-floor for the party. Will you have Joan write me information on the subject,[28] what the slate is called, besides slate, and where you get it, and if there is any special way it must be laid, et cetera?

We have no servants. But we have a new colt, born this morning.

And our other mare, Molly, expects to be brought to bed at any moment.

> Hoping you are the same, I am, as ever,
>
> Yours, Edna.

P.S. If you want to come up *before* July 21st, *we* don't mind.

p.p.s. deems, is it finished?[29] (sh-sh-sh—, meaning *hush*, not what you think)

---

[28] Joan Taylor was then three years old.
[29] Deems Taylor's new opera, *Peter Ibbetson*.

169 TO MRS. CORA B. MILLAY

> Steepletop [Austerlitz, N.Y.]
> July Third, 1930

Dearest Mother:

I hope you got the letter and the wire we sent you for your birthday, and that the reason why you haven't written for so long is that you are busy and having a good time, not that you're not feeling well, or something.

I have three little mountain laurels for you, tiny, but in perfect blossom. We will bring them down to you later in the summer. The best time to transplant them, I now learn, is when they are in bloom, like the azaleas, so I am having them taken up now and potted in buckets. They are perfectly sweet and you will love them. Next year they will bloom like anything.

Please let us hear from you, darling, as soon as you feel like writing. We're a little worried about you.

> Lots of love,
> Vincent.

105 BRATTLE STREET
CAMBRIDGE, MASSACHUSETTS

August 23, 1930

Dearest mother

You will see me
long before this letter reaches you,
but I thought you might think it fun
to have a letter from this house,
which was Washington's headquarters
for nine months during the Revolution,
& where Longfellow lived so long
with his family. — we have
just finished luncheon, — Harry Dana,

170   TO MRS. CORA B. MILLAY

105 Brattle Street
Cambridge, Massachusetts
August 23, 1930

Dearest Mother:

You will see me long before this letter reaches you, but I thought you might think it fun to have a letter from this house, which was Washington's headquarters for nine months during the Revolution, & where Longfellow lived so long with his family.—We have just finished luncheon,—Harry Dana, whose whole name is Henry Wadsworth Longfellow Dana, Longfellow's grandson, Mr. Dana's aunt, Mrs. Thorp, who was the "laughing Allegra" of "The Children's Hour", & Ugin & I. It has been extremely interesting. We have spent two nights here.

Last night was the third anniversary of the execution of Sacco & Vanzetti. I spoke at the Memorial Meeting in the Old South Church, & read my poems inspired by the case.[30]—But I'll tell you all about that when I see you.

Much love to my Mumbles
from Vincent.

> [30] Part II of *The Buck in the Snow.* "The Anguish," "Justice Denied in Massachusetts," "Hangman's Oak," "Wine from These Grapes," "To Those Without Pity."

171   TO ARTHUR DAVISON FICKE

[Oct. 24, 1930]

Dearest Artie:

It's not true that life is one damn thing after another—it's one damn thing over & over—there's the rub—first you get sick—then you get sicker—then you get not quite so sick—then you get hardly sick at all—then you get a little sicker—then you get a lot sicker—then you get not quite so sick—oh, hell

Love from
Little Wince.

VII

Steepletop—Paris—Florida

1931 – 1935

Steepletop [Austerlitz, N.Y.]
Feb. 18, 1931

Dear Joan:

Here is the handkerchief you so graciously lent me one day, when
I was sorely in need of it, and you were in your bath. Don't you remember?—Mary said, "Joan, don't you want to lend Edna a handkerchief?"
—And you said—at least, I *think* you said, " 'With all my heart, but
much against my will'," misquoting Mr. Patmore.

Love and thank you
from Edna

173   TO LLEWELYN POWYS

Steepletop (Austerlitz, N.Y.)
April 20, 1931

Dearest Lulu:

I am sending you your manuscript.[1] (Whether under separate cover
or not remains to be decided.) I am sorry I couldn't go on to the end
with it in the way I started. It was such fun. But I couldn't. I haven't
even finished reading it. I can't seem to read anything serious. I haven't
read anything but detective stories for ever and ever so long. Poor Lulu,
what a frantic time you're having with your mangy publishers.

We were so touched to see how beautiful, Alyse dear, you left
the cottage. Nothing was ever so scrubbed and so neat,—even upstairs!
It must have been a big job, all those floors. What a darling you were to
leave it looking so nice for us. And such sweet little dishes in the
pantry. Were they yours, or were they perhaps borrowed from Phyllis?
If they are yours, may we keep them? We want to eat our breakfast
from the yellow ones every morning, they are so gay.

We have been back from New York only a few days, and nothing
could be more different than our life there and our life here. We get
up at six o'clock every morning here, sometimes earlier. Ugin works
in the kitchen garden all day. I spend half the day cleaning house, and
the rest out doors. It will be some time before I get the house clean and
in order, after three months of that French slut, but I adore to do it.
I adore to send everything in the house to the cleaner, and then scrub

the house and hang up the clean curtains and lay down the clean rugs. We have no servants, and we're going to keep going without them just as long as we can stick it, it's so marvelous to be free of them.

* * *

Darlings, I knew that you were sorry. But there's nothing to say. We had a grand time. But it's a changed world. The presence of that absence is everywhere.[2]

Edna.

---

[1] *Impassioned Clay*. Llewelyn Powys and his wife, the American writer, Alyse Gregory, were guests in the cottage at Steepletop during the winter of 1930–31. While there, Mr. Powys finished his book.

In the preface to a volume of her late husband's letters, Alyse Gregory says: "The beautiful and famous poet had always entranced Llewelyn's imagination, and her husband was, in his own way, as rare a character as she. . . . Between Llewelyn and such a free spirit there was naturally a strong mutual attraction, and it was especially appropriate that 'Impassioned Clay,' his 'trumpet call to youth', should have been dedicated: *'To Eugen Boissevain, under whose roof and in the presence of whose daring spirit this book was finished!'* "

[2] The poet's mother had died on February 5th of that year, and had been buried at Steepletop on February 12th.

---

174   TO EUGENE SAXTON[3]

Steepletop, Austerlitz, N.Y.
December 30, 1931

Dearest Saxton:

I was very interested to see the page of advertising in the English weekly. I have noticed with considerable fun that many of the English women writers like "Fatal Interview" and not so many of the men.

I don't think you quite see what I mean about the make-up of the little play "The Princess Marries the Page." Woodblocks won't do at all. The play is too slight to be printed so seriously. What I really want —and if it is too expensive just now to bring it out in this way, then I would really rather wait, I think, until everybody has more money— what I really want is a big, flat book perhaps 14 by 10 with many colored illustrations, pictures of the Princess, the Page, etc., or scenes from the play done by such an artist as Mr. Paget-Fredericks. As a matter of fact, I heard from Mr. Paget-Fredericks a few days ago. He is very anxious to get to work again on a book of mine. I think he would be just the person for this. I want the book to be a Christmas gift book and as gaudy as a Christmas tree. Have you seen Oscar Wilde's "Birthday of the Infanta" illustrated by Pamela Bianco? This will give you an idea of the thing I want. Well, anyway we will talk about this when you get back.

I hope you have a swell time in England. Please give my regards and those of Mr. Boissevain to Mr. Hamilton[4] when you see him.

Very sincerely yours,
Edna St. Vincent Millay.

P.S. I am enclosing a copy of the poem The Fugitive, as I remember it. It was published in Ainslee's, but was never published, I believe, in any of my books,—although as I write this it seems to me that I did see it once in some edition of Figs from Thistles; I'm not sure about this.[5]

As you may guess, I have about two sheets of paper to write two miles of letters with.

THE FUGITIVE

Thanks be to God the world is wide,
    And I am going far from home,
  For I forgot in Camelot
    The man I loved in Rome,

And I forgot in Kensington
    The man I loved in Kew;
  And there must be a place for me
    To think no more of you.
E. St. V. M.

[3] Editor-in-Chief of Harper & Brothers. Until his death in 1943, he handled all of Miss Millay's relations with the publishing house.

[4] Hamish Hamilton, the English publisher who brought out *Fatal Interview* and all other works of Miss Millay published in Great Britain after that.

[5] Published in the January, 1919, issue of *Ainslee's*. It was not reprinted in the first edition of "Figs" nor in any of the subsequent enlarged editions.

175   TO MARY KENNEDY

5, rue Benjamin Godard, [Paris]
Monday morning [June 20, 1932]

Dear Mary,

Can you have dinner with me tonight, or failing that, cocktails?
—My purpose in asking you is twofold: to pump you of information
regarding your production of *The Princess Marries the Page*,[6] and to
give myself the fun of seeing you.—I've been to see you twice—did
you know that?—My child, I live just around the corner from you, in
the very next street—it was as much a surprise to myself as it will be
to you!—Walk toward the Square Lamartine & when you get to the
end of your street just make a hairpin turn to the right into my street.
I shall be here any time after six. Please dress in taste but soberly; I have
to work all night on that damned preface, & can't step out . . . Please
come.

Love,
Edna.

[6] At the Cosmopolitan Club, Philadelphia, December 22, 1930.
Staged by the late Dudley Digges, who played the part of
the King. Mary Kennedy took the leading role. Two of the
lesser roles—the First Soldier and the Third Soldier—were
played by young men who have since won fame in other
fields than acting: Samuel Barber and Gian-Carlo Menotti.

176   TO MARY KENNEDY

[5, rue Benjamin Godard, Paris]
Thursday Evening. [June 23, '32]

Dear Mary:

Here are the cards for Miss [Natalie Clifford] Barney's tea tomorrow. But your telephone is so unable to wake anybody at your
place that I'm afraid you're all gone to the country or something & that
you won't come.—Never mind. You've met Miss Millay.[7] You certainly met her Tuesday night, & so did your poor friends. I'm afraid I
shocked beyond hope of ever re-establishing myself your pretty little
Mrs. Guenini. Couldn't you tell her I'm not always so bad.—Or am I?
—They are such darlings, I'd hate to think they hated me.—I was dog-
tired (milk-wagon-dog tired), and had a pain amidships, and something
on my mind besides. But who cares what tripped a fallen woman?

Love,
Edna.

[7] The cards of invitation to Miss Barney's famous literary

salon read: "To meet Miss Edna St. Vincent Millay." Translations of her poems by Madame Lucie Delarue-Mardrus were read by Rachel Berendt of the Comédie Française.

177   TO EUGENE SAXTON

5, rue Benjamin Godard,
Paris, XVIᵉ.   June 23, 1932

Dear Mr. Saxton:

If we ever get this book put together I'm sure that you will be glad, and I'm sure that Mr. Rushmore will be glad, and I'm darned sure that I shall be glad. With some luck it's going to be a sweet book, but it's going to take luck,—what with Mr. Paget-Fredericks way out there beside the Pacific, and me beside the Seine, and you and Mr. Rushmore both beside yourselves.—It was easier to write the play, as I remember it, than to write this preface. And it's a verminous preface even at that. But never mind. Nobody else will mind, I don't even mind, myself. All I mind, is having to get up at dawn tomorrow morning and gallop to the Gare St. Lazare with it to get it on the boat-train. I should have got it aboard the *Paris* if I'd not been sick in bed two days.

If you could get Deems Taylor's little tune into the book it would be adorable. He wrote it expressly for the page to play on his pipe, in the production by the Cosmopolitan Club. And if you could get the cast as it was produced by the Provincetown Players, it would be grand. (I remember only that I played the Princess, & Vadim Ureneff the Page). But you probably can't do either, & if you can't, we won't cry. I'm sure you consider yourself lucky to be getting the play into the book.

Good luck. It's nearly midnight & I'm going out to get some food. I've not had a scrap to eat since yesterday. I'll drink good luck to you. With love, Edna Millay (or how did I sign myself in the days when I kept in touch with my publishers? Was it "Yr hbl svt, Mister Saxton"?)

178   TO MARY KENNEDY

Steepletop, Austerlitz, N.Y.
April 5, 1933.

Dear Mary:

Enclosed please find (a) one one-hundred-franc note; (b) my personal cheque for twenty-five dollars to the Stage Relief Fund; and (c) a cheque for five dollars destined for the same cavernous maw.

The first represents fifty francs which I borrowed from you at the Grand Prix last summer, and which by now, what with interest, taxes, customs, bribes, boarding, inflation, and England's going off the gold standard, must amount to precisely one hundred francs. And if it doesn't, why, that's just too bad; because I haven't *got* a fifty franc note and I *have* got a hundred franc note. So here you are, baby, and if you're hungry, gnaw it, and pretend it's a dinner at the Reine Pédauque.

Like you, and like all the rest of the poor cusses engaged upon this enterprise of relieving the stage (and would God the stage would relieve itself, and be done with it) I am having the hellovatime disposing of those pretty little blue books. I never knew money so sticky as it is this year. Money this year is just a one-man dog. And so, just to show there's no hard feelings and that I'm still on the job, I've dug up (b) twenty-five gold moidores out of my own sea-chest.

The cheque for five dollars (c) represents one dollar each received from Margaret Cuthbert, Norma Millay and Rollo Peters,—innocent recipients, poor things, of three of the little blue books—plus two dollars which I got one evening out of a couple of drunken friends. I had placed another of the books, a sacred fourth, with another drunken friend; but when he woke up, he remembered that he was deep in the Stage Relief Fund on another angle, so he guv me back the book, and since I had no gun on my hip, having sent my only gun to the cleaners in my other suit, I took it.

If you know anybody who's mad at you for not having let him in on this job, and who'd do it much better than I do, just wire me. No, don't write; wire.

Love,
Edna.

179 TO MR. AND MRS. LLEWELYN POWYS

Steepletop, Austerlitz, N.Y.
April 11, 1933

Dearest Lulu and Alyse:

Don't hate us. We didn't give up hope of coming to England this year until just a little while ago. We thought we would try to get over if only for a few days, just to see you. But we couldn't make it. We didn't write because we were never sure.—You see, we couldn't go to Africa after all. I got a job reading my poems over the radio[8]—

eight Sunday evenings—which kept me so late into the winter & made
me so tired that when it was over we just rushed to Florida to get out
of the cold & into the sunshine—I needed it badly. We wanted to come
to you afterwards. But we decided that since it could only be for such
a short time—not longer than a week—since we had to be home by
April this year to attend to our neglected gardens—we decided that
we really couldn't afford the trip, and would better wait until next
year when we can have a long time.

—So there it is, darlings.—*Do* you hate us?—I'm sure you do. We
love you, anyway. Even if we didn't get to England this year. Forgive
this dull & horrible scrawl. I never was less in the mood for writing a
letter. But I had to let you hear from us. ("And about time!" you say.)
—Well, there it is.—Can we ever be friends again?

Edna.

[8] This marked a milestone in radio broadcasting in America.
For the first time an internationally famous literary figure
was given equal rating with artists of the stage and concert
hall. This series of broadcasts of Edna St. Vincent Millay,
reading her own poems over a nation-wide hook-up, was
arranged by Miss Margaret Cuthbert over the WJZ Blue
Network. The readings, which began on December 25, 1932,
were tremendously successful and brought an overwhelming
listener response to the network.

180   TO MARY KENNEDY

Steepletop, Austerlitz, N.Y.
May 6, 1933.

Dear Mary:

Will this do?[9] Or must you have something more ponderous? Must
I say there is nothing like this book to make the children eat their
carrots? Or what? I am yours to command.

Please thank your lord for the information anent my academic
kimona.[10] And tell him that the only Doctor's hood I possess was *mailed*
to me, because it didn't get to the party on time; so I couldn't make the
particular kind of fool of myself that he did. And Ugin says that, although a Dutchman, he knows perfectly well how to write Litt. D. and
Mus. D.; but he has a stenographer who always knows better. A youth
from Canaan, N.Y. He is not so much as a stenographer, but he has one
attribute which more than outweighs all his limitations, a negative

attribute worth more than much fine spelling: he has absolutely no sex appeal.

I'll bet you that if ever Deems really *does* begin to work in the garden, he won't begin by digging, or fertilizing, or sowing, or weeding, or setting out shrubs,—he'll begin by getting himself a BEAOO-TIFUL big chest, containing as follows: 3 trowels, one with a steel handle, one with white-pine handle, and one with handle of finest quality cedar, to keep away the cut-worms; 2 prs. Grass Shears, one for grass and one for quack-grass; 2 prs. Pruning Shears, one that gives you blood-blisters, and one that gives you just blisters; one patent collapsible Pruning Hook; one patent collapsible adjustable convertible Dock and Dandelion Annihilator; 300 yards of Mulch Paper; 17 Bales of Peat Moss; and 164 Mole Traps (i.e. one each of the 163 Mole Traps that have ever been patented, plus one whose patent is pending); and that while burning his monogram into the end of the chest he suddenly remembers that he's forgotten to get any Hedge Clippers, and that he thereupon jumps into the car and motors to Stamford.

Well, that is all for the present, that is, until I can think up some more dirty cracks.

Please tell Joan that I saw the pale-brown lamb yesterday and he wished to send her his love. At least, I happened to pass him as I was going into the barn to tie a pink hair-ribbon on Serena—her hair is always getting into her eyes—and he looked at me and said something which was either "Please give my love to Joan Taylor when you write," or "What the hell's the matter with this nipple lately?"—I couldn't make out which it was.

Yr aff hbl svt

E. St.V. M.

[9] A blurb for a children's book which Miss Kennedy was about to have published.

[10] In June of this year Miss Millay was to have honorary degrees of Doctor of Literature conferred upon her by both the University of Wisconsin and Russell Sage College.

181 TO MRS. ANNE GARDNER LYNCH

Steepletop, Austerlitz, N.Y.

Dec. 8, 1933.

Dearest Anne:

You certainly are being picked on, you poor child! What a terrible time you've had! Do you really think you are going to feel heaps better now, and get some fat on your skinny little bones? Perhaps by the time you get this you will be feeling just a little bit better. I do hope to God you will be.

* * *

Eugen and I are sailing for Europe on the twenty-sixth of this month. At least, I believe it is the twenty-sixth. We are going to the south of France for the winter. We have rented Eugen's brother's house at Antibes, right out on the end of the Cape, a perfectly lovely place. I am writing like fury now, shall probably have a new book of poems out in the spring, in the autumn, anyway;[11] and I want to be where it will be nice and warm, and I shall be able to keep all my energy for my work. Eugen, of course, thinks he's going to make a fortune at Monte Carlo, Cannes and Nice. Well, anyway, he can't *lose* a fortune! —that's one comfort.

Here are some silly verses, to make you laugh. Or mayn't you laugh yet, darling?

> This was on a Sunday.
> Dinner was at two.
> Vincie wrote a poem;
> And then what did she do?
>
> Vincie wrote another.
> The roast was nice and hot.
> Then she wrote another.
> Then the roast was not.
>
> Instead of eating dinner,
> Vincie wrote a verse.
> Then she wrote another.
> Then she got the curse.
>
> Don't say it and upset her—
> She's typed another sheet—
> But Vincie must get better,
> And wash her hair, and eat.

* * *

Lots of love, my dear. And a Merry Christmas in spite of hell! Please let me know before I sail, how you are getting along . . .

Vince.

[11] *Wine from These Grapes*, published November 1, 1934.

182   TO MRS. FRANK L. RICKER

Steepletop, Austerlitz, N.Y.
December the 8th, 1933

Dear Aunt Susie:

I thought I should be seeing you some time this summer, but it didn't work out that way.

Eugen and I early in the summer bought an island in Casco Bay not far from Brunswick.[12] We intended to spend August there, but I had to go and get flu or something like it, and have had it all summer,— and I haven't set eyes on my island since we bought it!

Isn't that too exasperating? We are sailing for Europe in about a fortnight now, going to spend the winter on the Riviera, where it will be warm, and I can work until I'm tired, and then go out and play tennis until I get tired in a different way.

Next summer we expect to spend a lot of time on the island, so we shall probably be dropping in on you sometime. We would let you know beforehand, except that we never know ourselves!

I am sending to Aunt Clem a copy of Mother's song, "The Good Ship Maud".[13] Have you a copy? If not, I have one for you.

Merry Christmas and lots of love to you and Uncle Frank,

Vincent.

[12] Ragged Island, "or Rugged Island as it was once known," according to Herbert G. Jones in his *Isles of Casco Bay*, is one of the outermost and least accessible of the group of islands in the lower bay. It is famous as being "Elm Island," the setting for a popular series of boys' stories written by Elijah Kellog, a Maine minister and writer. The house still standing on the island, renovated and improved by Miss Millay and her husband, was originally built by Kellog.

[13] A published song; words and music by Cora B. Millay.

183   TO ALLAN ROSS MACDOUGALL

Steepletop [Austerlitz, N. Y.] December 10, 1933

Dear Alling:

I have not answered your letter of August 30 for two reasons. One is, that I have been sick all summer with the flu or some other thing so weakening that I've hardly been able to stagger about; lots of times I've had to go to bed for days. The other is, that I've been writing poetry for about twenty-four hours a day, flu and all; and what little strength I had, has been used up in this most arduous of occupations.

I do not know whether Kay Boyle did finally apply for the Guggenheim Fellowship or not.[14] But just in case she may have done so, I have written to Mr. Moe[15] about her, and giving her a send-off which ought to get her the Fellowship even if nobody else vouches for her at all. Well, no, I don't suppose they ever take the word of just one person. Still, the fact that I don't know Miss Boyle at all, have never set eyes on her, on top of my estimate of her work, should have considerable weight.

I hope that her not hearing from me has not been a sort of last straw which, added to other considerations of which I know nothing, has dissuaded her from applying for the Fellowship. I should be very sorry to think that. But, dearest Alling, I can't tell you how many requests I get all the time, to help people in one way or another. I really do the very best I can about it, but I find that unless I wish to give up my own work entirely, I must resign myself to the fact that I cannot help all the people I should like to help. Of course in this instance, as sometimes happens, it is not a simple case of "helping somebody." I admire Miss Boyle's work so much that an obligation is involved of quite another sort. Still, as I hinted in the beginning, if one has a book of one's own to write, and the influenza for an incubus, one can't do a hell of a lot more.

I am as ever, sir, yr obt and hbl svt,

Edna M.

About "girdle" and "griddle": you find the same metathesis of the letter *r* in "bird" and "brid", "birdie" and "briddie."

[14] Kay Boyle was granted this Guggenheim Fellowship to enable her to write an *Epic of Aviation*. This piece does not figure in Miss Boyle's published works.

[15] Dr. Henry Allen Moe, Secretary of the Guggenheim Foundation.

184   TO FLOYD DELL

Steepletop, Austerlitz, N.Y.

Dec. 13, 1933

Dear Floyd:

Thank you ever so much for "Homecoming."[16] I enjoyed it immensely. It is a darned good job. It is earnest and sincere, without ever becoming ponderous or sentimental; gay, without ever becoming frivolous; and modest, without ever becoming humble (and what a straight and narrow path *that* was, my lad!) In fact, I was delighted with it.

In addition to your corrections made in ink in the copy you gave me, I noted two further *errata*: on page 157 the word *contemptuous* is mis-spelled *contemptious*; and on page 165 there occurs "maybe for neither you nor I." Also, I should think that "bout rimes" on page 227, should be either "bouts-rimés" or "bout-rimé." Unless this is an Anglicization of it with which I'm not familiar.

As far as the book itself is concerned, I have read it with extreme care, and have found only one flaw in it. And since you will not agree that this is a flaw, and since probably nobody else will notice it, it cannot be considered very important. However, just for fun, I append my remarks concerning page 337 of "Homecoming," middle of the page.

Love, and many congratulations,

Edna Millay.

I shall be at the St. Regis from the 20th to the 26th, when we expect to sail for France. If you're in town, do come in to see me.

[16] Mr. Dell's autobiography.

Appendix to letter to Floyd Dell, Dec. 13, 1933

Excerpt from an Unwritten Book Review
(concerning "Homecoming," by Floyd Dell)

But on page 337 we come upon a passage which distresses us. "Prohibition came," writes Mr. Dell, "and I was glad of it, for I thought the saloon a bore . . . I had no notion of the incredible ingenuity that would go into home-brewing, nor of the pride that respectable citizens would take in safe, popular and petty law-breaking (for which I, a law-breaker in the grand style, only despised them)."

Now to the reader of "Homecoming" it can come as no shock, on page 337, that wines and spirits and their accompanying amenities have no attraction for Mr. Dell. He has not kept this a secret from us. And, while we have deplored it, we have not condemned it. Nor should we ever attempt to coerce Mr. Dell into having a drink with us. Is he not as free to refrain from drinking as we are to . . . but alas! we forget; he is freer. For "Prohibition came," even as he says; and he was "glad of it, for he thought the saloon a bore."

We remember now that there was a passage somewhere earlier in the book which disturbed us slightly; but we passed it over. We go back and look for it, and here it is. Page 256. "In Greenwich Village, though there was a very general sobriety, I saw more drinking among presumably intelligent people than I had ever seen before." Why does the author speak of these people who drink as "presumably intelligent" —which, of course, is just another way of saying, "actually, in this respect at least, unintelligent"? He considers these people unintelligent because they care about something which means nothing to him.

The man who was prepared to go to jail for twenty years for having written, "There are some laws that the individual feels he cannot obey," et cetera (p. 315), is snugly intrenched in his boredom against the possibility that the "respectable citizens" who are brewing wines and distilling spirits in their own cellars, and whom he "despises" because they take pride in what he calls "safe, popular and petty law-breaking" are behaving as they do because to them the 18th Amendment, with its accompanying Volstead Act, is one of those very laws.

"I disagree with every word you say, but I will defend to the death your right to say it," wrote Voltaire. "I disapprove of every drink you drink, but I will defend to the death your right to drink it,"—so should have written, or so it seems to us, Floyd Dell. But he did not.

Uneasily we ask ourselves now, "Just what principle then, was our author defending, in the Masses trial?" Why, freedom of speech, to be sure. And freedom of the press. And very fine of him. But right here we are struck by two things, which we have known all along, but which up to this moment we have not considered in their possible relationship to Mr. Dell's splendid behavior in the affair of the Masses trial, namely: that Mr. Dell was a newspaper man; and that he was a man who loved beyond almost everything else in life, to talk.

Here was a man who loved so to talk, that even when he was on trial for a crime which might send him to prison for twenty years, he found "in cross-examination the distinct excitement of a primitive sort of game of wits . . . It is a strange, stimulating, and—or so I found it— an agreeable experience." (p. 317) "I was told to take the stand," he writes in the paragraph preceding this, "and I did so with pleasure. It was not only an agreeable break in the routine, but a chance to speak after an enforced silence that had lasted many days." Floyd Dell was defending the inalienable right of Floyd Dell to write and to say whatever he pleased.

"It was not thus (i.e. by drinking whiskey) that I liked to get drunk," he has said on p. 257. "I preferred to get drunk on ideas, on talk, on argument . . ."

Mr. Dell, (who was later to be so pleased when the 18th Amendment set out to take away from so many of his friends and fellow-citizens, who preferred to get drunk in quite another fashion, the means of doing so) was defending in the Masses trial, we regretfully infer,—oh, very innocently and with the noblest of emotions in his heart!—the right of Floyd Dell to intoxicate himself in his own way.

185   TO LLEWELYN POWYS

> S.S. President Roosevelt
> Just getting into Cobh
> April 20 [1934]

Dearest Lulu:

It occurred to me after we left Southampton, that here I am, committed for eight days to the care of a most capricious element, & under my arm my Black Note-Book, containing the only copies in existence of many of my new poems![17]—so I've had copies made of some of them & am sending them to you from Cobh, just in case, et cetera.—As you know, some of them are still being worked on, but there is something in all of these that I do not wish to be lost.—In case anything unpleasant *should* happen—Harold Cook, Avon Old Farms, Avon, Connecticut, U.S.A., has the rest of the *Epitaph* & could help you find some other things;—he's just done a bibliography of me.[18]

> So much for that!—Lots of love, my darlings!
> —Edna.

[17] Later to be printed in *Wine from These Grapes*. Part V contained the proposed sonnet sequence "Epitaph for the Race of Man," ten sonnets of the sonnet sequence first appeared in a special anniversary edition of the St. Louis *Post-Dispatch*, December 9, 1928.

[18] Mr. Cook contributed a fifty-page essay on the poetry of Edna St. Vincent Millay to the Bibliography of the poet's work compiled by Karl Yost and published by Harpers in 1937.

186   TO LLEWELYN POWYS

> Wahoo, Islamorada, Florida.
> March 9, 1935

Dear Lulu:

If you wish to hurt me beyond healing, refuse my gift. I swear to you that I can afford it perfectly well, that I do not need the money;

my new book has sold already more than forty thousand copies. But suppose I could not so well afford it, suppose I had meant to use this money for something which now I should be unable to buy—tell me, what could I buy with a thousand dollars so precious as the thought that perhaps I may be helping you to get well? I am ashamed of you, darling. And of Alyse, too. You are both being very naughty.

I know what it is, of course. It is that dingy law-suit, and the Two-Hundred-Pound-Look of Mrs. Nincom and her daughter that have made you two clear beings think about money in this smudgy way.[19] You must both send your wings to the cleaner.

* * *

We have been spending the winter in the Virgin Islands, on St. Thomas, one of the most beautiful islands in the world. Now we are slowly moving northward,—Puerto Rico, Haiti, Santiago de Cuba, Havana, Islamorado—from here to visit Mr. Brann in Boynton Beach, Florida; from there to Charleston, South Carolina, to see the great magnolia gardens in blossom; from there to Steepletop to say hello to the dogs and pick up the car; then on to Ragged Island, where we shall be entirely alone in our little house and entirely alone on the island, to gather driftwood, and haul our lobster-traps, and make fish-chowders, and sail, and read, and sit on the rocks, all through the month of April. As Eugen would say just here, "Yes, it's a hard life."

Our address until the first of May will be Ragged Island, Post Office Orr's Island, Maine. After that, Steepletop.

Love to you both, my dears. Your beautiful cable made us happier than you can possibly believe.

As for your letters, all about that silly money—as I said in the beginning, if you wish to wound me with a hurt I shall never recover from, persist in this drab madness.

Edna.

[19] Having circulated a petition against the treatment of delinquent girls in a home in his neighborhood, Mr. Powys, James Cobb, and two well-known women writers, Sylvia Townsend Warner and Valentine Ackland, were all convicted under the stringent libel laws then in force in England. They were each fined one hundred pounds and costs when the case came up on January 18, 1935. In the end Mr. Powys had paid out almost six hundred pounds to his solicitors and others in the case but was reluctant to allow his friends to help him.

187   TO WITTER BYNNER

Steepletop, Austerlitz, N.Y.
May 2, 1935

Dear Hal:

Yes, I did get the beautiful quilt. And you were a darling to send it me, and I was a pig not to answer. And there you are. I love it; it is extremely pretty; I remember your speaking to me about these quilts years ago when I was in Santa Fe; I am grateful to you; I think you a darling; but I simply can't write letters . . . I have made a name for the disease from which I suffer: I have named it EPISTOPHOBIA. I haven't written a letter all winter. I wish it were socially impossible to write a letter. I wish there were no post-office, no stamps, no facilities whatever for expediting the smug, intrusive, tedious letters that people write.

We called up the Hotel Seymour, being in New York for two days to see my brother-in-law Charles Ellis' show at the Montross Galleries.[20] But you hadn't come yet. Can you come to Steepletop sometime in May. Can you do it without bringing your mother? I know she's grand and all that, and besides she's your mother; but I'm going to die in a few days, and I have no time left except for people I'm crazy about. Please come.

Edna.

How dared you get my headache? And why must you be ill? Let them be ill who enjoy it—there are many. But for you to be ill—this is effrontery.

[20] An exhibition of his paintings.

---

188   TO PROFESSOR HERBERT C. LIPSCOMB[21]

Steepletop, Austerlitz, N.Y.
May 2, 1935

Dear Dr. Lipscomb:

. . . I never wrote to thank you for the mistletoe and holly which you sent me at Christmastime . . . I am very bad. It is painfully difficult for me to write a letter . . . the real anguish, the knowing that I must write a letter, and that I want seriously to communicate with somebody; and that I cannot bear even to think of writing a letter . . .

* * *

The Catullus you gave me I take with me everywhere—along with my tiny, shabby brown leather one; I could not decide which to leave behind so I took them both. Yet I have read very little Latin this winter. I don't know why. I have been extremely busy. But that was never an excuse.

. . . over Christmas the house was beautiful with the mistletoe and holly that you sent . . . I love the holly; it is beautiful. But I am afraid of the mistletoe; and I love it much more. I could not be more afraid of it were I stained blue with woad. I loved it so I could not leave it behind, so I took it with me. And then I was afraid to have it with me, so I burned it. And then I was really afraid.

Edna St. Vincent Millay

²¹ Professor of Latin at Randolph-Macon College.

George Dillon and Edna St. Vincent Millay had each translated selected poems of Charles Baudelaire's *Les Fleurs du Mal*, which were to be published by Harper & Brothers in 1936 under the title of *Flowers of Evil*. In her preface to this book, Miss Millay explains how she came to join Mr. Dillon in this work which he had begun.

189 TO EUGENE SAXTON

Steepletop, Austerlitz, N.Y.

Nov. 18, 1935

Dear Mr. Saxton:

I think the type extremely good-looking, and so does Mr. Dillon. The italics are the least alarming I ever saw,—usually when I first glance at a page of italics it looks to me like a page of the Odyssey. The two facing pages will look very handsome together.

Unless, that is to say, you really intend to print as many stanzas on the page as these sample pages seem to indicate—six stanzas on the page that bears the title; seven, I suppose, on the other pages. In which case they won't look handsome at all, except of course to pure artists like Mr. Rushmore, who are interested only in making up a thrillingly beautiful page, and don't give a darn whether or not anybody is ever going to read the words on it.

My first thought when I saw the sample page was, "My, what good-looking type!" My second thought was, "Good God, can there be all that poetry *on one page?* How much can there be in a whole book then? How much in the New York Public Library? How much in the whole world?" It was an awful thought. And seeing how tedious, how plodding, how discouraging and text-bookish my own poem looked, I could have cried, except that suddenly nothing seemed worth crying about any more, and I didn't care *how* you printed the book, since I, for one, was certainly not going to read it.

Mr. Dillon, when I first handed him the sample sheets to look at, said at once, as I had done, "Awfully good-looking type, isn't it?" Then he said nothing for a moment. Then he said, "Well, it just makes me feel the way I feel when I'm out walking, and turn a corner, and see miles and miles of perfectly straight road ahead of me."

Consider this: in every instance the left-hand page and the right-hand page are going to look exactly alike, the same length line, the same number of stanzas, etc. That was necessary, and it is interesting that it should be so; but at the same time, this fact will help to increase any sense of monotony, any sense of suffocation or just plain weariness, which the reader may well experience when he opens the book and sees seven stanzas of hexameter staring him in the face. If the lines were not for the most part so long, it would not be quite so bad; but hexameter-from-left-to-right multiplied by seven-stanzas-from-top-to-bottom equals one thick page of prose; and the person who reads it at all is bound to read it as he does prose, not a line at a time, as poetry should be read, but a whole bunch of lines at a time, a paragraph at a time, a stanza at a time.

Mr. Rushmore is by way of being a genius at this business of making books, I should say; he does beautiful things. But he is a hopeless Anglophile. And in this particular instance, if the sample sheet is really an indication of the way he wants to print the book, he has gone so Bloomsbury that he has almost gone Bloomingdale. And he may put all-the-love-of-his-deep-and-subtle-nature into choosing the type, etc; he might just as well send the whole job over to the Daily Mirror and let them print it up for him, because the book will be a flop, anyway. (At least, if *I* can't read that page, who can?)

All this sounds very light-hearted and cheery (or does it?), but you will observe that I have typed it double-space,—so that you can read between the lines!

The authors are fully aware that they have advised the publishers at least twice as to their preference concerning the number of stanzas to the page, even going so far as to set forth plainly in the English manuscript and in the manner in which the French original was cut and pasted on the sheet, their preference concerning the number of stanzas to the page; they are further aware that said publishers have paid not the slightest attention to said preference on the part of the authors; and the authors respectfully submit that not even those lovely bits of coloured paper which the publishers sent them to play with, have succeeded quite in taking their minds off the main issue.

Now: if you will print the pages five stanzas to the page-with-title, six stanzas to the page-without-title, it will be a great improvement from the reader's point of view over what you seem to have in mind. This will mean having somewhere between thirty to forty more pages, as I estimate it, in the book, possibly as many as forty-five. This would very likely mean that you would have to charge more for the book,— $2.75; possibly even $3.00. But it would be better to charge even as high as $3.00 than to cramp and disable every poem in the book.

(I have had to pound this point even at the risk of boring you to suicide or exasperating you to murder, because you seem not to have understood our other letters!)

Please give my compliments to Mr. Rushmore on the type, not only of the French and English texts, but of the page which immediately precedes the poems: "Selected Poems of Charles Baudelaire", with its two stars or flowers, or whatever they are; it is very good-looking. (Not that he'll care much for my opinion, after this letter!)

I am enclosing:
1. The samples of end-paper and dust-cover, with our choice marked; if you think us unwise in our choice, please tell us why.
2. A few more changes to be incorporated into my manuscript, if still possible; otherwise I can make the changes in the galleys.
3. Two aspirins.

Yours for a care-free winter,
Edna St. Vincent Millay.

190 TO MRS. ARTHUR DAVISON FICKE

Steepletop [Austerlitz, N. Y.]
Nov. 29, 1935

Dearest Gladdie:

Here is a flock of books for Artie; I've read most of them, and found some of them very interesting, others gay, etc. If he wants to take any of them along with him for the winter, tell him to go ahead. I have made a list of them, so it will be perfectly easy next summer to get them back from you. Some of them I've not read, and can't vouch for. Many people think *Butterfield 8*[22] very exciting. I didn't; but you'd better read it yourself before letting Arthur see it. When you leave, just leave the books you don't want in this same suit-case, or whatever I find to send them in, and write a little note to True Heline, Steepletop, Austerlitz, N.Y. to come and fetch them at any address you say. I hope both you and Arthur will find something worth reading among them.

Ugin is in Florida, and has found a house for us, I don't know exactly where, somewhere between Palm Beach and Miami. I am going down tomorrow with the servants. I wanted so much to get over to see you and our darling Artie, but I am so simply exhausted after getting the Baudelaire off to Harpers, that packing—even with somebody else to pack under my direction!—is taking all the strength I have, and there are so many things to attend to, closing up the place without Ugin. Ugin knows how tired I am, and is wiring frantically for me to get aboard the next train. So I shan't see you, kids, before I go. But I'll see you next summer; and we'll have lots of fun, because Arthur will be well again, and more like his cute, gay old self, and I shan't be working so hard, so perhaps I shall be a bit more like *my* cute, gay old self!

Lots of love to you both, and I hope you will have as happy a winter as you both deserve, after all the hard knocks you've had, you poor kids.

Vincie.

[22] A novel by John O'Hara.

191   TO EUGENE SAXTON

Delray Beach, Florida
Monday Dec. 9, 1935

Dear Mr. Saxton:

I hope you can read this scrawl. My portable is at the cleaner's.— First, I agree with you about suppressing that phrase in the Mardrus material.[23] I meant to suggest that, among other things, if I had had more time in New York & could have seen you; it would be very bad to use it; it would give the whole book an undergraduate air.—Second, please send me at once a copy of the *original* Mardrus letter, *or* the original letter—(I asked Miss Herdman to do this, but apparently she did not understand). The point is: I want the French text, because there are one or two points in the translation which you sent which I should like to discuss with you. For instance in the Valéry: I think we are perfectly justified in translating "Cette traduction" as "The quality of this translation",—this seems to me excellent rendering; but the literal translation of "lecteur Français" does not perhaps give quite the impression intended—I mean, "the French reader" might possibly be taken as meaning any person who reads French; I think we might better translate this as "the French reading public."—There are a few other points. Please send me the originals right away, if possible.

* * *

Sincerely,
Edna Millay

²³ Lucie Delarue-Mardrus had written a letter-tribute to the translators, which was to be used as a blurb for the book. A friend of Miss Millay, she herself was a poet and best-selling novelist in her own country. Madame Mardrus was known also for her translations into French of the poems of John Keats and Edna St. Vincent Millay, among others.

192   TO GEORGE DILLON²⁴

Delray Beach, Florida
Dec. 25, 1935

Dear George:

I am delighted with the "Sapho." It will be mid-summer before I get a chance to read it—I am giving myself time to get the final proofs of the Baudelaire back to Harper's and time to have a nervous breakdown—but I did take a peek at the illustrations and they are charming.

I am glad you still like the preface, and that you think the biographical stuff all right—you hadn't seen that before, had you? Things were finished up in such a rush. Finished up, did I say?

It is obvious that Harper & Bros. are trying to kill us, so that they'll never have to have anything to do with either of us again. You will have noticed that when they give us a week's extension they give the printers a fortnight; it's easy to see who is teacher's pet here. I say "extension", but it's really no extension at all; they're not giving us anything like the time we're entitled to; I'm perfectly furious with them. Only sent me one set of proofs, too—how many did they send you?—almost impossible to work with one set—and no return envelope, either, such as they always send me—and how the hell am I going to get hold of an envelope, out here among the rattlesnakes and the red-bugs?

* * *

And now for the business of the meeting—and I wish it could really be a meeting; I wish that the bang of a gavel could bring you here and bring you to order; it's so difficult doing things this way, especially with not a scrap of time (the hounds!); and you're going to *froth* when you read what I have to say next—probably roll about on the floor and put tooth-marks into things—possibly even stiffen into an arc. This is it: I think the arrangement of the poems very bad, very bad indeed; the book is all out of balance. I don't know what happened to it, because we tried hard to avoid just this thing, I remember; but anyway, the fact is that twenty-four of your poems occur in the first half of the book, leaving only twelve for the second half, the consequence being that the second half of the book gives the impression of being all written by me, and the first half by you. As I say, I don't know how this happened, because we were quite careful about it; but of course we were in a frightful hurry. I am enclosing a possible Table of Contents; personally I think it good; but of course you may not; if you don't like it, then I suggest since the time is so short—so nonexistent!—that we make the whole first half of the book yours, and the second half mine; this would be perfectly dignified, and simple.

In making up this new Table of Contents, I haven't changed the order of your poems at all; I have simply changed the order of my own, taking some from the back and inserting them more toward the middle and toward the front of the book. Also, I must have been crazy when I put that poem "The Unforeseen" right at the beginning of the book like that, the most irritating and unsatisfactory poem in all Baudelaire, starting out in such an exciting way and ending up with about as much punch as a wet sponge. I put two short ones in place of it. In making up this new list—and I've given the devil of a time to it—I've kept in mind the desirability of varying the meter from poem to poem whenever possible; of having no two poems close together repeat each other in any important way; and of not having their titles conflict (except for the fact that "The Fountain" is your fourth poem, I think I should have made "The Fountain of Blood" my second); also I have tried sometimes to have groups of poems that in some way seemed to belong to each other, and even to enhance each other; "The Fountain; The Fleece; Remorse Too Late; Heauton Timoroumenos; Semper Eadem; The Owls"; but of course in spite of all the care I've taken, you may find something glaringly bad in this arrangement; I wish you'd study it carefully, and then, if you think it good, send it right on to Saxton; if you think it bad, wire me, and we'll put all your poems in the front and mine in the back; if you like it for the most part but have certain suggestions to make, wire me what you object to.

You write that you are in a state of exaltation about my translations. Well—they're all right. They are good, honest, earnest, intelligent translations. But they have no sonority, no sensuousness; which so many of yours have; and which is so important. Oh, they're all right; I like 'em all right. I think your new translations awfully good; The Drunkard is excellent, very dramatic—which is what he meant it to be—a real tragedy, with the proper elements of tragedy, in a few stanzas. I still wish you'd say dog instead of log; old logs don't go to sleep in the road, but old dogs do; and besides who cares whether an old log is split by a wheel or by an axe; if it were an old dog, that would present a picture, that would be different. Anyway, it's a darned fine translation, even if you *are* a thick stubborn oaf.

Of course the most beautiful poetry in the book, aside from some lines written in French, and who cares about French, is your translation of La Chevelure".[25] I can't wait to see the rest of it. The first stanza and the last two are perfect. Now that's what I mean by sonorous, sensuous. In the second stanza, however, the fourth line comes to me as a definitely unpleasant thing, a line of prose, a line obviously translated; that line, I think, should begin with the words "My soul"—also the final two lines of this stanza happen too quickly, are too glibly run off, after the slow, rich, mouth-filling lines preceding them. I suggest something more in this pattern:

My soul, as other souls put forth on the deep flood
Of music, sails away upon thy scent instead.

You'd think I had no poems of my own to chew my nails about. But my own poems seem so set, so *there*, so inert, so hopeless to wangle into redemption!

Well, I'll baste all this together and get it off to you. Would you mind sending me a wire as soon as you've read this? I don't care what you say in it, just quote a couple of lines from the book of Job; all I want is a yellow envelope dexterously arriving on a bicycle, to make me feel efficient and alert and neatly capable of getting this amorphous mess off to Harper's on time.

Love,
Vincent.

[24] George Dillon, besides being co-translator of *Flowers of Evil* with Miss Millay, is the author of two volumes of poems: *Boy in the Wind* and *The Flowering Stone* and a Pulitzer Prize winner.

[25] Pages 23-25. This translation is signed by both poets.

VIII

Florida—New York—Steepletop
1936–1945

Delray Beach, Florida
January 6, 1936

Dear Mr. Saxton:

* * *

I am ever so grateful for the books you sent me at Christmas. Darling old Thurber just saved my life.[1] And what an extraordinary piece of work that Mussolini book is![2]—incredible—except that the time is almost at hand when the word *incredible* as applied to politics will be a smart-crack.

You will by now have received my telegram asking for three sets of page-proof. I cannot put it before you too strongly that this is not the time for your manufacturing department to become stingy with your authors. Certainly it cannot be very much more expensive to pull four, or even six, sets of proof, than two. Yet this is what happens: I receive my proof from you on a Saturday in Florida; you insist upon having the corrected proof back in your office in New York on the following Saturday; and you remind me to take into account that the holiday mails are slow. Since under the most favourable circumstance I must allow two days between the posting of a letter in Delray Beach and its delivery to you in New York, if I allow one day extra in consideration of the slowness of the holiday mails, I have just four days in which to read, study, re-arrange, re-assemble, correct and dispatch to you the unwieldy and cumbersome proof of a large and complicated book, the co-author of which is in Virginia. Yet, instead of trying to make things as convenient as possible for me in the exiguous circumstances, your manufacturing department proceeds (a) to pull page-proofs at once, without giving the authors the usual and of course expected galley-proofs, and without giving them the slightest warning of this arbitrary and high-handed act beyond a letter which arrives only a few days before the page-proofs; (b) to divide between two authors, already painfully handicapped by the geographical difficulty of communicating with each other, the two sets of proof which every author since King Solomon wrote the Proverbs and King David wrote the Psalms has been accustomed to receive for his single, un-collaborating self alone. I don't know who is responsible for this niggardly behavior—but I can assure you that whoever it is is very short-sighted: you wish to bring out a beautiful book; you have not as much money as you wish you had in order to enable you to do so; therefore you skimp, stint, press for time and endeavor to bully—whom?—the printers?—no, the authors. Let me point out to you that all the discreet and handsome bindings, all the subtle and distinguished type in the world will not advance you, if you are in the end obliged to carry six pages of Errata in the front of the book.

You wrote on December 18th that if you could have the finally revised proof back in your hands by January 9th, you would publish on March 5th. You telegraphed on December 20th, that if you could have the finally revised proof back in your hands by January 16th, you would publish on March 19th. You wrote Mr. Dillon on December 24th, and sent me a copy of your letter, "We have chosen the date of April 1st for publication. That decision in no way affects the dates we have set down for the return of the proofs."

Now it is a matter of record that I never received higher than *C minus* in arithmetic; but do not for a moment on that account fan yourself with the cooling thought that I fail to see what is going on here, and how gradually you have managed to sneak two weeks extra, then three weeks extra, to your presumably competent and unruffled manufacturing department, while doling out an inflexible and adamantine one week extra to the long-haired authors.

It all comes down to this: you have your troubles; I have mine. I expect you to hold me to as close a schedule as possible, while at the same time allowing yourselves as open a schedule as possible. This only is important, so far as I am concerned: refrain from treating me as if I were either a child or a mental defective; I have ceased to be the one, and I was never the other. Tell me what you expect from me, what you hold me to; but refrain from swathing your honest angular stipulations and exactions in disingenuous cotton-wool.

As far as the publication date is concerned, you may publish whenever you get around to it, except that I won't be published on April Fool's Day.[3]

Yours sincerely, and a Happy New Year to us all, in spite of each other.

Edna St. Vincent Millay.

[1] *The Middle-Aged Man on the Flying Trapeze.*
[2] *Sawdust Caesar,* by George Seldes.
[3] The book was published on April 2, 1936.

194   TO PROFESSOR HERBERT C. LIPSCOMB

Delray Beach, Florida.
Jan. 7, 1936

Dear Dr. Lipscomb:

Will you be so kind as to answer the following question for me?
—and so especially kind as to answer it very soon?

In the following stanza which is a translation from Baudelaire, do
you think I could use, instead of the fourth line I have here, the Latin
fourth line which Baudelaire himself uses? I should so much prefer to
use the Latin line, but fear that the accents, which in French don't
matter, since no Frenchman ever pays the slightest attention to the fact
that certain languages have strong tonic accents, would be all wrong in
English, and spoil the rhythm of the stanza, etc.

This is the first stanza of Baudelaire's poem *La Prière d'un Païen;*[4]
following is my translation of it.

> Ah! ne relentis pas tes flammes,
> Réchauffe mon coeur engourdi,
> Volupté, torture des âmes!
> *Diva! supplicem exaudi!*

> Ah, damp not yet the living coals!
> Heat once again my heart in thee!
> Voluptuousness, thou scourge of souls,
> Goddess, incline thine ear to me!

You can understand how much I should prefer to use the Latin
line, if possible, in place of

> Goddess, incline thine ear to me!

but I couldn't, could I? Wouldn't the accent of *exaudi* throw the whole
thing out? Doesn't *exaudi* rhyme with rowdy?

I am bringing out, together with George Dillon, a book of translations of selected poems from *Les Fleurs du Mal;* that's what it's
all about . . .

Thank you for the Christmas card, and for your good wishes; it
was kind of you to couch them in Latin that I could read at sight,—it is
always so exciting to me to read even a few words of Latin.

Sincerely, and wishing you a beautiful and exciting New Year,

Edna St. Vincent Millay

---

[4] Page 220 of *Flowers of Evil.* The English version is on the
opposite page. In Miss Millay's rendering her translation of
the Latin phrase was printed. See also page XX of her Preface
to the Baudelaire translations.

195   TO GEORGE DILLON

> Delray Beach, Florida,
> January 9, 1936

Dear George:

You have probably just received a proof of the jacket of the book from Harpers'. In my opinion, it couldn't be worse. And it's not their fault; it's our fault; the whole trouble is with the title. And with the jacket like that they're not going to sell ten copies. Anybody who sees that name BAUDELAIRE in large letters like that, and everything else in small letters, will take it for granted the book is a biography, and run like hell. "Selected Poems of CHARLES BAUDELAIRE" may be a scholarly title, but that's all you can say for it. "Selected Poems" in itself is unattractive; "Translated by" in itself is unattractive; "CHARLES BAUDELAIRE" in itself is terrifying, to the average reader; and the combination of the three is suicide. I don't know whether or not it's of the slightest interest to you whether or not this book is a financial success; but if it is, then study carefully the suggested title-page which I enclose, which would also be the upper half of the jacket. After all, Baudelaire himself published his book under the title "Les Fleurs du Mal"; we have every right to publish our translation from it under the title "Flowers of Evil",—an extremely attractive title, arresting to the eye, exciting to the imagination, et cet., et cet. Yet we deliberately left it out, and crammed the title-page with stodgy information. I don't know what ailed us. We couldn't have been cock-eyed; if we had, we'd have done something brighter, or at least more imaginative; we had probably just had a very ample breakfast of doughy pancakes and greasy sausages.

I am sending a copy of this suggested title-page to Harper's; will you let them know what you think of it, and let me know at the same time?

Also, I think that the paragraph of Llewelyn Powys should be on the *white* part of the jacket, which is the most conspicuous part. Don't you? Also, I think they are foolish to say "Member of the French Academy." There's nothing grand-sounding about that. They should say, "de l'Académie française". Anybody who doesn't know what that means, wouldn't be impressed by "French Academy" anyway.

Please let me know *right away* what you think of all this. Good God, shall we never get this book off our laps and published?

> Vincent

196   TO GEORGE DILLON

Little America
Friday, August 13th, 1948
[Delray Beach, Florida,
January 1936]

Dear George:

It never occurred to me that they wouldn't have sent *you* a proof
of the jacket, too. What ails them?—hardening of the arteries or
softening of the brain? Let's clear out and the hell with them. Let's send
them a corrected copy of the Bronx and Queens telephone directory
and skip. Let's go to the Galapagos and gather boobies' eggs.

In the meantime I am sending on to you the jacket-proof which
by mistake, instead of being mailed to Edna Ferber, was mailed to me.

The time, as the feller said and was promptly crowned for it,
is short.

Now you've been in the advertising business, and I haven't; so
perhaps you know more about the advertising power of this jacket than
I do; but I've been buying longer than you've been advertising; and
I know that if I went to Brentano's with money to buy just seven books,
this book would be the eighth.

Think it over. You have just one hour before Sharper and Smothers
(alias Harper and Brothers) come in with the confession, a fountain-
pen, and a piece of lead pipe. Think it over. Think it over. What shall
the title be?—I suggest: "POSTCARDS FROM HAPPY-DUST CHARLIE TO HIS
LENOX AVENUE MOLL".

Love and all that,
Vincent

197   TO ARTHUR DAVISON FICKE

Box 787, Delray Beach, Florida
Feb. 11, 1936

Darling Arthur:

So *that's* where you are, you poor sweet thing! What a wild time
you must be having! Well, this is where *we* are. We've been here since
the first of December, in a cute little furnished house with all the con-
veniences except one—the water for one's bath is heated on the roof by
the sun, and since there's never any sun, but only fog and wind and
clouds and pouring rain and icy cold weather, there's never any hot
water, except that which one heats on the kitchen stove.

And speaking of the kitchen stove: Sophie has just spilled grease on it, and the whole house is full of the smoke and stench of burning fat. (Yes, we brought Sophie and Marie down here with us. And in spite of things like burning fat, it's nice to have people around who know from experience just what particular species of cock-eyed, crazy idiot you are, and to whom you don't have to be explaining yourself and excusing yourself all the time!)

I've just got off to Harper's my final corrected proof of my Baudelaire translations, together with a thirty-page preface on the art of translation, facial massage, Roosevelt's second term, the Hay diet and the sex-life of little G. V., which last summer and autumn I had the giddiness and effrontery to write, and which all winter I have been busy re-writing, pruning, grafting, fertilizing and ploughing under. Well, the book will be published sometime late in April. And that's that. Except that even with two hot-water bags at my feet, I have bad dreams, and shall probably try to sell what is left of my honour, in order to buy up the whole edition.

I am happy and excited to hear that a book of your new poems is to be published soon.[5] I hope you haven't cut out any of my pets. *Have* you, Arthur? Don't be too clever now. This is the time when we all get so clever and cynical that we are capable of doing more harm to our own book than the Commissioner of Police could do!

I'm glad you got the flowers I sent. They were supposed to get there for your wedding anniversary, but probably they didn't.

I hope Gladys is with you now. It must have been pretty awful, being there all alone. I think you've got plenty of pluck, Artie.

Well, there are lots of things I want to say, but I think I don't need to say them, because I think you know what they are.

Love to you, and to Gladdie, from us both.

Vincent

[5] *The Secret & Other Poems*, Doubleday-Doran, 1936.

198   TO PROFESSOR MARGARET GILMAN[6]

Box 787, Delray Beach, Florida
Feb. 18, 1936

Dear Miss Gilman:

* * *

I am enclosing a copy of my translation of *Les Litanies de Satan*, together with a copy of that part of my Preface which deals with the

passage from it about which I wrote you. This was my original translation of the couplet—I have five or six others, and then returned to
this. My rendering of the passage is rather close to your conception
of it; with this difference; that instead of making the irony of the
passage lie in the theory that prostitutes are prone to feel love and pity
for the sick and poor, i.e. those who are unable to support them, I
translate the couplet as having relation to the couplet which preceded
it: that is, Satan, seeing that the banker, the respectable man, the
Croesus, has a cold and hard heart, brands him as "impitoyable et vil,"
and puts into the hearts of the prostitutes, God's outcasts, that pity for
the afflicted and sick which God *should* have put, but did not, into the
heart of the wealthy, the well-cared-for, the well-thought-of man.

I do not know what you will think of this. I hope you will think
I have some justification for it.

I am greatly obliged to you and to your colleagues for your
courtesy, for your prompt and thorough response to my appeal. Please
tell Miss Schenck and the others of your department who were so kind
as to interest themselves in this question, why I have been so tardy
in replying.

Sincerely yours,
Edna St. Vincent Millay

[6] Professor of French at Bryn Mawr College. Miss Millay had
already telegraphed a request on January 6, asking for a
prose translation of two lines in Baudelaire's *"Les Litanies
de Satan,"* pages 114 to 120 in *Flowers of Evil.* See also pages
XXVII to XXIX of the Preface. Miss Millay also consulted
the French professors of Vassar, Barnard, Harvard, and Yale
on obscure points in the Baudelaire poems.

199   TO LILIAN HUGUENIN[7]

Box 787, Delray Beach, Florida
March 16, 1936

Dear Miss Huguenin,

The delicious subtlety of this second lovely gift, following at a
discreet distance the first inexcusably unacknowledged one, gave me
almost as much delight as the gift itself. You not only made me happy;
you made me gay!

How else could you ever find out whether or not your beautiful
little salt and pepper set had gone astray and never been received?
You could not very well write me, "See here, did you ever get that

present I sent you for Christmas? If you didn't, all right; that lets you out; I'll look it up from this end and see what was the trouble. But if you did, why couldn't you have the common decency to let me know you did? You might even have thanked me for it, you so-and-so!"

Now, however, if I write thanking you for the handkerchiefs and do not mention the salt-and-pepper, you will know that I never received them. If I acknowledge neither, then the next thing you send me had best be held to the ear before it is opened!

I said "inexcusably & unacknowledged," yet the truth is that I have been working so hard this winter, and so many hours a day, that I have been forced to neglect everything else; and another truth is that although you could not know it, the charming little crystal things have been before my place at dinner every night, and have given me much pleasure. If some night they should not be there, I should be seriously annoyed, and would not be able to eat a mouthful until they were brought on. And fine linen, cunningly worked by hand, is one of my most special delights.

> Sincerely, with these belated thanks,
> Edna St. Vincent Millay.

[7] An admirer of the poet and one of the rare few, outside Miss Millay's immediate circle of family and friends, who received a letter from her.

200   TO LLEWELYN POWYS

> Delray Beach, Florida
> April 24, 1936

My darling Lulu:

Of course you would put the most important news in the world, that you are getting better, in a scrawly marginal post-script where I might perhaps not have seen it at all! Really, you are too absurd. What do you think I care about anything else you could possibly have to say, in comparison with the fact that you are getting better?

Will you be very discreet, my dear, and take no risks? Will you be rigidly scrupulous about not tiring yourself? The temptation will be so great!—you will want to see, all in one day, every polished bit of flint there is, so miraculously clean, like a cat, in spite of the mud; you will want to see the two ears of every hidden hare on the downs, all in one day. Will you please try to remember, sometimes when you want to walk just a few steps further, that Edna wants you to turn back, instead, and go quietly home?

I am so sorry about your brother.[8] I think about it, and I say to myself, "There is nothing to say". Yet perhaps there *is* something to say, only I don't know what it is. I am the last who could teach you how to fit into the pattern of your life the death of someone you love; I have no skill at this.

Of course I knew you would not like my preface to the Baudelaire translations. Sometimes when I was working on it (and I never worked so hard on anything in my life) I thought, with a wry and sad smile, "Lulu will be pained by this." I knew that you would consider flippant and in bad taste many things which were not flippantly conceived or written, and which, if I had considered them in bad taste, I should not have printed. It is our old quarrel. It is not that you would like me to write ponderously because the subject is a weighty one, but that, naturally, you wish me to be lighthearted and human in your way, not in mine. I wonder how you can *stand* Shakespeare, (perhaps you can't; I never asked you) Shakespeare, who permitted Mercutio to die as Mercutio *would* have died, did not force upon him in the end the extreme unction of a traditional solemnity, permitted him to die cracking jokes, and with a pun on his lips,—and this, mind you, not in The Merry Wives of Windsor, or any other rollicking piece of horse-play, but in a proper tragedy. I suppose you agree with the French that the "Knock, knock" scene from Macbeth is most regrettable; unless perhaps the archaic flavour of the words and illusions makes it acceptable to you. If you had been present on the opening night of "Macbeth", and had yourself been wearing a pair of the fashionable and very tight and scanty "French hose" for stealing from which the English tailor is sent to hell, you would have been shocked, I think, by the guffaws of your elegant neighbors. Not that there is anything Shakespearean about *my* writing—would God there were!—but that in temperament I am rather close to him. And it is my guess that you would much prefer Racine to Shakespeare, supposing that they both were bringing out their plays today.

And what of your revered St. Ealdhelm, about whose "attitude to literature" there was "something debonair"?—who "carried his scholarship with lightness"!—who taught the King of Northumbria "to make Latin verses by composing a series of amusing riddles"! Alas, how frivolous an approach to how serious a structure! Fie, fie upon St. Ealdhelm! And a fig, a dried fig, for St. Lulu.

Enough of this! (Too much of this, I dare say!) But it's such fun having a swipe at you for once,—you've had so many at me.

Oh, God, how lovely it will be to talk with you again!

I loved your Dorset essays,—I am not sure that you have ever done anything better.[9] I do so love the way you write. (Even when you are scolding me, I love the way you scold me . . . and might, perhaps, in conversation, provoke a small scolding purposely . . . though not, of course, in a book.)

Do you know what mushroom it is that is so cleverly photographed in the book you sent me? Probably you do, but you may not. It is the *Lepiota procera*, the "parasol mushroom." My mother and I used to gather them on the downs between Shillingstone and Blandford. She would dry them, and make beautiful panels of them, sewing them to a dark cloth; and once she trimmed a hat for me with them . . . it was charming. Eugen and I find them sometimes at Steepletop, too. They are edible, and sometimes we broil them in butter, and eat them. But although they are said to be one of the most delicious mushrooms, we have only once had them when they tasted truly superior to others,— and ever since then we are in despair about them, because we are unable to remember just how we prepared them on that day. If you are unacquainted with them, I beg you not to eat them; I am identifying them only from a photograph.

I have so many things to write you. But I have poems to write, too; and they keep teasing me.

Will you please give my love to Alyse? How you can give it her, when she already has it, and knows that she has it, I do not know. Nevertheless, greet her for me; she will know how much love is in the greeting.

As for yourself, you say that you are better. Perhaps I helped to make you better, caring so much whether you are better or not. You could not know how often you are in my mind.

                                                                Edna.

[8] Albert Reginald Powys ("Bertie"), a beloved older brother who died in March of 1936.
[9] *Dorset Essays*, published in England by John Lane in 1935, with forty photographs by Wyndham Goodden.

201　TO DANTE BERGONZI[10]

Steepletop, Austerlitz, N.Y.
Sept. 30th, 1936

Dear Dante:

Please let me know soon how the operation came out, and if your eyes are all right again, and quite strong. I am sending you a book of mine, which I hope you will like; but you mustn't even glance into it unless your eyes are quite well again.

I would have written you before, but my arm is still bad,[11] I can't practice the piano at all, and I've played tennis only once since you left, and then I had to stop, because it hurt; and of course my typewriter had to choose just such a time to crack up under me. This is a new typewriter. It hurts my arm to type, too, but not so much. They say what ails my arm is bursitis, which is the same as tennis elbow, or tennis shoulder. Strangely enough, about a week after you left, Eugen strained *his* shoulder, practicing hard serves, and since then he's been laid up, too. It seems that the very worst thing for it is MASSAGE! Poor darling Eolo, don't let him know, but he must have nearly killed me that day of the last rehearsal of our ill-fated quartette. Isn't it too hateful, after so longing to have a tennis court, finally to get one, and such a beautiful one, and then to be laid up for three months or so with bursitis? For it takes about three months, they say, and by that time it will be too cold to play until next summer. Couldn't you utter a nice round vindictive Italian curse for me?

We wanted to see you again before you left for the south; but we've both been so crippled, and so cross; and I couldn't see you without thinking both of music and of tennis, and then I should probably become perfectly frenzied, and start tearing out fistfuls of your adorable hair.

Goodbye. And come back.

Eugen sends his love. And so do I.

Edna St. V. M.

[10] One of the students attending the summer school of Blanche and Alexander Bloch in Hillsdale, N.Y. With his friend Eolo he lived one summer in the studio at Steepletop.

[11] The trouble with her arm was the first evidence of serious injury caused by an accident in the summer of 1936 which was to give the poet increasing pain. In a letter to Alyse Gregory, her husband described the accident as follows: "When taking a sharp turn in the Station wagon, the door

flew open and Edna was thrown out and rolled down the embankment. She had a big bump on her little red-head, scratches and bruises all over, and her right arm was all bunged up so that she cannot play the piano or use the typewriter. She's getting better now. But we are not pleased with God, although he might have done worse."

Several years later in September, 1940, she wrote to a friend: ". . . for something over a year now I have been very sick,—or, rather, not sick, simply in constant pain, due to an injury to certain nerves in my back (referred to by the ten or twelve different doctors and surgeons who have tried to cure the trouble, as nerves 4, 5, & 6 of the dorsal spine— referred to by me as that place up under my right shoulder-blade). The nerve injury is the result, it seems probable, of my having been thrown out of the station-wagon one night— not by the driver, as you are probably thinking, but by the sudden swinging open of the door against which I was leaning; I was hurled out into the pitch-darkness—a very strange sensation it was, too—and rolled for some distance down a rocky gully before I was able to grab at some alders or something and come to a halt. I have had three operations and should be quite well now, I think, if I were not still, naturally, rather weak.

202   TO C. NORWOOD HASTIE[12]

Steepletop, Austerlitz, N.Y.
October 5th, 1936

Dear Mr. Hastie:

Can't you come north when Mrs. Hastie comes? I do wish you could. I would so like to see you again.

You must not say that I forget my friends in Charleston. It was just because I remembered you so well that I didn't want to stop there, because by the time we got near Charleston I was such a complete mess and such a sight. Did you ever drive thirteen hundred miles in a car with a loose bearing, plodding north at thirty-five, thirty, twenty-five, twenty miles an hour, to the accompaniment of an increasingly inter-ested populace, swathed in something which once had been a white linen suit, and wrapped in a rug in lieu of a coat, because every scrap of your luggage, your hat and coat included, had been burned up in a hotel fire.[13] We were so painfully unpresentable that we slunk into hotels late at night with our arms over our faces, and sneaked out before daybreak. And do you suppose I wanted you to see me in a state like that?

Please say that you do not think unpleasant things of me. And please, if you can, come to Steepletop.

Sincerely,

Edna St. Vincent Millay.

[12] Mr. and Mrs. Norwood Hastie were the owners of "Magnolia" in Charleston, S.C., the garden of which, according to John Galsworthy, "consigns the Boboli at Florence, . . . Versailles, Hampton Court, the Generaliffe at Grenada . . . to the category of 'also ran.' "

[13] "I arrived at the Palms Hotel [Sanibel Island, Florida, Saturday, May 2nd, 1936] an hour or so before sunset, engaged a room, and had my luggage sent up. I did not go up to the room myself; I went out at once upon the beach to gather shells. Looking back up the beach a few minutes later, I saw the hotel in flames."

Foreword to *Conversation at Midnight*, May 1937.

203 TO ALYSE GREGORY

Steepletop, Austerlitz, N.Y.
October 6th, 1936

Dearest Alyse:

I am so distressed by this bad news. Poor, poor Lulu!—Poor, poor you.

Oh, my dear, who *is* it that is trying to kill him?—for indeed anyone who comes to see him too often, and stays too long, and excites and wearies him, is either trying to kill him or is so profoundly an egoist that he is truly insensitive to Lulu's condition. Is it one of those romantic and diabolical relatives of his? I wish to God he were far removed from England for a while! He wrote me that he hoped to go to Switzerland soon; I suppose now he is too sick to be moved.[14] Oh, dear, besides being so alarming, it is so infuriating! Is there *nothing* that can be done to keep people from stalking, or breezing, or gliding to his bed whenever they feel like it, and remaining for interminable periods, either agitating him into a fever, or boring him to exhaustion?

My God, you are not characters in a play, you and Lulu! this is LIFE that you are living all this time, the only life you will ever have!—and a life which should have been heroic; and which is only courageous.

Does anybody ever think about that? What if people *have* come all the way to see him? What if they crawl on their knees all the way from Dorchester, and would weep with disappointment if they must depart without a glimpse of him?—it is a matter without consequence or even meaning. Let them crawl back.

Oh, my dear Alyse, I should think you would be so discouraged you could hardly drag your bones about the house. For Lulu, it is terrible; but for you, it is less and more than terrible; for you are not even in danger of dying, you are just in danger of never living any more.

I think you'd better not show Lulu this letter; it is too depressed, I fear, and too depressing. It is because I am so angry that I write like this, and because I don't know whom to hate.

How I wish I could see you, and talk with you. But then, I so often wish that.

Edna.

[14] On December 2nd of that year, Llewelyn Powys, his tubercular condition greatly aggravated, left England with his wife to go to Clavadel, Davos-Platz.

204   TO PROFESSOR HERBERT C. LIPSCOMB

Steepletop, Austerlitz, N.Y.
October 6, 1936

Dear Dr. Lipscomb:

* * *

You asked me in your most kind and very welcome letter if the Conversation at Midnight poems were burned.[15] Yes, they were all destroyed. Fortunately, I have a very good memory, and have been able to recall all those that were completed; but with those on which I was still at work I have been having an exhausting and nerve-wracking time.

My cherished little seventeenth century copy of Catullus, Propertius, and Tibullus (containing the Pervigilium Veneris . . .) also was burned; it was in my suit-case. The loss of this book was the only truly *emotional* loss I suffered from the fire. All my luggage went, and an emerald ring I thought very handsome, and, of course the entire manuscript of what was to have been my next book. But the only thing that touched me emotionally, the only thing I mourned for, was this book. Poignantly enough, or so it seemed to me, the only thing that could comfort me at all when I got to thinking about it, was to say over and over to myself, "Desinas ineptire—desinas ineptire, desinas ineptire— . . . et quod vides perisse perditum ducas."[16]

It is interesting that you should have said what you did about Propertius, I had often thought that I should like to translate some of his Elegies. What beautiful poetry he wrote!

And I have often thought how I should like to be a true scholar, truly and deeply learned.

* * *

How lost indeed I should have been when I got home from Sanibel Island, without the beautiful Catullus you gave me.

Sincerely yours,
Edna St. Vincent Millay

[15] The first part of the Foreword to *Conversation at Midnight*, published July, 1937, tells in greater detail of the rewriting of this work.

[16] "Cease this folly . . . and what you see is lost set down as lost." From the 8th Lyric of Catullus.

205 TO EUGENE SAXTON

Steepletop, Austerlitz, N.Y.
October 10th, 1936

Dear Mr. Saxton:

* * *

I am sending you enclosed my foreword for Mr. Cook's essay; I hope you will like it.[17] As for the photograph frontispiece; this presents real difficulties. I remember that I did not much like any of the photographs done of me by Doris Ullman, certainly not enough to have one of them reproduced in such a conspicuous position. And of course you would prefer something that had not been used before. I can seem to find nothing suitable. I may have to come to New York in a few days ("have to" is the exact expression, it is so beautiful here now!) to get a tweed skirt and a pair of oxfords that I can walk in; you have no idea how many clothes can be packed in a half dozen suit-cases, until you see yourself coming down to dinner attired in a necklace of jumbie-beads and a bath-towel swiped from the Francis Scott Key Hotel. It seems to me sometimes that I lost about everything I had in that fire, with the exception of a handsomely-polished piece of petrified wood, and an old copy of Punch with the round mark of a whisky-glass on it.

Anyway, if I come to New York, and you want to have me finger-printed, or tattooed, or photographed, I suppose I'll submit.

Submissively yours,

Edna St. Vincent Millay.

P.S.   I get a proof of these forewords, don't I?

P.P.S.   In typing my foreword I discovered that I had used the word "considered" four times in ten lines; something must be done about that; I will clean it up and send it to you tomorrow.

> [17] Essay in appreciation of Miss Millay's poetry by Harold Lewis Cook which comprises the first section of *A Bibliography of the Works of Edna St. Vincent Millay*, by Karl Yost (Harper, 1937). The poet also contributed a Foreword to the bibliographic section of the work.

206   TO ROLFE HUMPHRIES:[18]

One Fifth Avenue, New York.

April 28, 1937

Dear Mr. Humphries:

I am going to try to do the lovely and touching "Llegada" of Emilio Prados. But I shan't be able even to look at it with translating it in mind for at least a week; I'm frantically busy just now correcting the proofs of my new book and trying to write a sort of preface for it.[19] In a week or so I will take up the poem and try to do it. If I have good luck and it comes fairly easy, I shall be able to do it. But if I find after a few days that it is going to be extremely difficult for me, then I shall send it back to you, though I should be sorry to do so. I realize that this would leave very little time for the poor translator who followed me. But I don't dare promise it you, I am working so terribly hard as it is this spring.

Sincerely yours,

Edna St. Vincent Millay

> [18] Poet, translator, and Latin scholar. At that time he was editing, with M. J. Bernadette, an anthology of Spanish lyrics which were to be translated into English by various American poets.
>
> [19] *Conversation at Midnight*.

207 TO ROLFE HUMPHRIES

One Fifth Avenue, New York
May 17, 1937

Dear Mr. Humphries:

This is bound to be a long letter, and I hope it won't wear you out. It is not about the Spanish poem; I've done some work on that, and hope still to be able to finish it for you, although I'm still not sure. It's been difficult, surrounded as I have been for the past five weeks by a pack of baying publishers and printers, and far from my own earth and my Spanish dictionary. Also, it started out by being far too typically early-Millay, and all that must be changed.

I am writing you about your own Latin versions of the three Fatal Interview sonnets.[20] You sent them to me, you wrote, for my amusement. It might interest you, perhaps, to know that they have been my salvation.

I never, except through mischance, go anywhere, if it's only for so short a time as a week-end, without taking with me some book of Latin poetry. When I become so exhausted by my own work that I can neither think nor see, or so twisted and entangled by anxieties, either about personal matters or about the awful mess the world is in, that it seems that if I ever extricate myself at all, it will be with at least a double curvature of the mind, the only thing that can straighten me out is to read Latin poetry.

Not that I read it easily. I don't. I read it slowly and often with extreme difficulty. Yet I read it always with delight, and with no sense of strain, so that when I lay the book down, even if I am tired, I am at the same time serene and exhilarated.

All this would sound pretty phoney to most people, I know. I don't say it to most people.

Last December I came to New York to spend a few days only. I meant to bring along my Virgil, because I wanted to memorize the "Ducite ab urbe domum"; for one thing, it has so many words in it that I should like to add to my slender without being elegant Latin vocabulary. I left it behind. And in December I came down with the flu. And in January something else happened, and I am still here. I have been working all winter and all spring on my new book—not like a dog, not like a slave; dogs and slaves must be relieved and rested from time to time, otherwise they crack up; like a poet, let's say. And not a syllable of Latin, with the exception of the few lines which I have in my memory, to click my vertebrae into place.

You may think I could have gone out and bought myself a book. I couldn't. In the first place, I was probably attired in an ancient evening-gown, a steamer-rug, and a pair of beach-sandals. In the second place, I didn't want the book later, I wanted it right then. I was like the farmer in the Arkansas Traveller, who never mended the leak in his roof,—because when it rained he couldn't, and when it didn't rain it didn't need it.

Then one day I opened a letter from you, and out dropped those lovely Latin poems. I took them in my teeth and scurried under the couch with them, and nobody could tease me forth for hours.

It is wonderful enough, to me who can't do it at all, to be able to write poetry in Latin. But to be able to write Latin poetry, is quite another thing. I imagine that you are one of the very few people writing today who can really do it. The requirements are too many: you must know your Latin; you must know and love your Latin poetry, be sensitive to its music which is not our music, be so inside it that you write it from the inside out, shaping your lines and planning your effects naturally and directly in terms of Latin, not in terms of Latinized English; and besides all that, you must be a poet yourself.

In illustration of what I mean, take the first of the three poems you sent me:

"At, morose, dies veniet cum, murmure nullo", (I am quoting from memory; the poems are in another room, and my typewriter is on my lap and heavy to drag about. So perhaps that's wrong, though I don't think so.) Your "—cui nunc in caespite verna suavia vilia sunt, con-cubitusque nefas" makes me think of the "desinas ineptire" poem of Catullus, of the part in the middle—I think it begins "Soles olim tibi", though probably it doesn't, where he says that "the girl doesn't like it any more". You are saying something quite different, of course, and the circumstances are so different, yet it has something of that feeling. Then when you say, "Nox perobscura, mea lux,"—that interpolation of yours of "mea lux" is not only beautiful in itself, set against "nox" like that but it has precisely that quality of ironic and angry tenderness which, in the very midst of his despair, Catullus often showed.

The second poem begins, I think, "Prospera gemmata mane vestita corona". I don't understand the "mane". If it were "manu", I could understand it,—"gemmata manu". But probably you mean something which I don't get at all; without a Latin dictionary to fall back upon, I am very insecure. In this poem you do a thing which is purely classic,

not modern at all, except when consciously imitated from the classics
(Elinor Wylie did it beautifully in her

> "The trumpeters of Caesar's guard
> Salute his rigorous bastions
> With ordered bruit; the bronze is hard,
> Though there is silver in the bronze.")[21]

(Again I am quoting from memory, always a dangerous thing to do.)

When you describe the uproar of the men in the house and of the
horses outside you do it: "Quadrupedantes gravi sonitu quatit ungula
pontem"—the first word must be misquoted, never mind; in the next
line where you have the word "serena" everything is serene, even the
luxurious serenity of "iste fragor", to say nothing of the line, I think
the next line, which is humming like bees with domesticity and peace.

I must stop this; you'll be worn out. I want to say, though, that
the "crede mihi" in the first poem, placed just where it is placed, has a
charming flavour of "believe *me*"; also that the repetition of "languida"
and of "trita" in the last poem is very effective, as is the use of "Hes-
peris" at the beginning and "Lucifer" at the end; and the last two lines
beginning "Lente, Luna" and "Lente, Sol," where you get your effect
upon the *ear*, before the mind grasps that the constructions and mean-
ings of the two are going to be different.

Please forgive me for running on so. I never write letters. I just
wanted to thank you for the poems. And it turned out to be this.

[20] Sonnets VIII "Yet in an hour to come, disdainful dust,"
XXIV "Whereas at morning in a jewelled gown," XXVII
"Moon that against the lintel of the west." They were later
published in Mr. Humphries' volume *Out of the Jewel*,
Scribners, 1942.

[21] From "Bronze Trumpets and Sea Water—On Turning Latin
into English" (*Nets to Catch the Wind*).

208 TO THE SECRETARY OF NEW YORK UNIVERSITY

One Fifth Avenue, New York
May 22, 1937

Dear Sir:

This letter contains the answers to the questions which you asked
me in your very clear and most considerate letter of May the fourth;
it contains in addition some remarks concerning one aspect of your

Commencement activities, regarding which you raised no question, but regarding which nevertheless I feel compelled to speak.

First let me reply to your questions:

Thank you, it will not be necessary for you to send an escort to accompany me to Mrs. Chase's dinner.

There are no gentlemen whose names I should like you to put on your invitation list for the men's dinner at the Waldorf-Astoria that evening.

My address in New York for the period of the Commencement Exercises will be the Hotel St. Regis, Fifth Avenue and Fifty-fifth Street; telephone Plaza 3-4500. My address until the eighth of June will be Steepletop, Austerlitz, N.Y.

I should be pleased if you would send to Mr. Eugen Boissevain, Austerlitz, N.Y., and to Mr. and Mrs. Charles Ellis, 323 West 112th Street, New York City, cards of admission to the Commencement Exercises.

I will bring with me my own doctor's cap and gown.

I shall be pleased to attend the Commencement luncheon; Mr. Boissevain will be with me.

I have just had some photographs taken, and will send you one in a few days.

Having answered your questions, I come now to that aspect of your Commencement activities regarding which, I said, I felt impelled to speak.

I received from Mr. Chase, your Chancellor, in a letter dated April 26th, the information that New York University wished to confer upon me on the occasion of its Commencement on the ninth of June, the honourary degree of Doctor of Humane Letters. In the same letter Mr. Chase informed me that Mrs. Chase would be pleased to receive me as guest of honour at a dinner given for a small group of ladies at the Chancellor's house on the evening before Commencement.

I answered at once, accepting the award of the degree with happiness and pride, and the invitation to dinner with pleasure.

In your letter, dated May 4th, I was told for the first time that on the evening of the dinner given in honour of me by the Chancellor's wife, a quite separate dinner is to be given at the Waldorf-Astoria in honour of the other recipients of honourary degrees, that is, the male recipients.

On an occasion, then, on which I shall be present solely for reasons of scholarship, I am, solely for reasons of sex, to be excluded from the company and the conversation of my fellow-doctors.

Had I known this in time, I should have declined not only Mrs. Chase's invitation to dinner, but also, had it appeared that my declining this invitation might cause Mrs. Chase embarrassment, the honour of receiving the degree as well.

It is too late to do either now, without making myself troublesome to everybody concerned, which I do not wish to do. I shall attend Mrs. Chase's dinner with pleasure; and I shall receive the degree the following morning with a satisfaction only slightly tempered by the consciousness of the discrimination against me of the night before.

Mrs. Chase should be the last, I think, to be offended by my attitude. I register this objection not for myself personally, but for all women.

I hope that in future years many women may know the pride, as I shall know it on the ninth of June, of receiving an honourary degree from your distinguished university.

I beg of you, and of the eminent Council whose representative you are, that I may be the last woman so honoured, to be required to swallow from the very cup of this honour, the gall of this humiliation.

> Very sincerely yours,
> Edna St. Vincent Millay.

---

209 TO ROLFE HUMPHRIES

> Steepletop, Austerlitz, N.Y.
> June 14th, 1937.

Dear Mr. Humphries:

Here it is.[22] I hope you won't hate it.

I tried for a time to make a more literal translation of it, but found that for some reason in doing this I seemed unable to get any of the feeling of the original into my lines. I discovered that in some places the only way I could even approximate the mood of the Spanish poem was to soak myself in the mood and then let myself go and write my own stuff . . . that is why it is important to me to say "freely translated".

I don't know who your editors or who your publishers are, so I am depending on you to make sure that no change whatever, not even so much as the change of a comma, is made in this poem. Of course if I have misunderstood the original in some passage and am giving a wrong impression of it, I should be grateful to you for letting me know, and anxious to make any necessary changes.

Sincerely yours,
Edna St. Vincent Millay.

[22] The poet's rendering into English of "Llegada," by Emilio Prados. Printed in *And Spain Sings*, an anthology collected and edited by Rolfe Humphries, Vanguard Press, 1937.

210   TO ARTHUR DAVISON FICKE

Steepletop, Austerlitz, N.Y.
Sept. 23, 1937

Arthur darling:

This will be one of the most unpleasant letters you ever received, and I'm sorry. But it's time I got this matter off my chest and onto yours, where it belongs,—for it's all your fault, my dear, for persisting in asking such shockingly indiscreet questions. The sonnet was not written to you.

When you came at me like a prosecuting attorney the other night in the La Branches' gun-room, asking me so casually—and I at least six cocktails off my guard,—"To whom did you write that sonnet, Vince?"[23] I glibly and immediately countered with the only name which in the circumstances it would not be indiscreet to mention: your own. To keep my loosened tongue from folly.

That's all. Except that this is by no means the first time you've done that sort of thing to me. I remember your saying to me once, in exactly the same off-hand way—only with a little chuckle, too, that time, suggesting that whatever my reply might be the thing was just a joke,—"Vince, was Lulu ever your lover?"

My only reply was to rebuke you for your indelicacy in asking such a question. But the rebuke must have been a gentle one.

Knowing as you so well know, my dear friend, how reticent, both by nature and by taste, concerning my own private affairs and the affairs of other people, I am, it is wrong of you to do these things to me. But quite aside from that, and looking at it from your own angle, if you love me as you say you do, it is very foolish. For don't you see, Artie darling, that in the circumstances it is impossible for me to feel at ease with you, and that eventually just out of self-protection I shall avoid being with you whenever possible?

I know that I must have hurt you. I'm so sorry. But it was no good letting it go like that. Because it couldn't stop there. Our two distinct and incompatible memories of that moment in the gun-room, would have twisted out of shape every word we ever said to each other again.

With love,
Vincent

²³ Sonnet VIII in *Second April.*

211   TO JAMES WELDON JOHNSON²⁴

Steepletop, Austerlitz, N.Y.
Sept. 28, 1937

Dear Mr. Johnson:

I am sending you your books by this post. I am so glad you like Conversation at Midnight. You know, I find that I like it, too, even after all the gruelling work it has given me, what with one thing and another. Nothing could please me more than the two adjectives with which you describe it, "magnificent" and "delicious." (Of course, I'm not at all sure that it's either, but your letter tempted me for a moment into that hashish dream.)

We seem always to be going in opposite directions, like the two buckets in the well. This afternoon, for instance, I'm going down to New York; I suppose that when I get on my train at Hillsdale, you'll be getting on your train at the Grand Central, coming up! I hope it won't always be like that.

This summer has been so short, so small. I think that like "Alice" it ate the cake that said "Eat Me", and dwindled and dwindled until it was so tiny that it ran out through the crack under the door. If only just once it would nibble at the other cake!

Best wishes to you both,
Edna St. Vincent Millay.

²⁴ Poet and Hillsdale neighbor of Miss Millay.

212 TO AGNES YARNALL[25]

Steepletop, Austerlitz, N.Y.
April 18, 1938

Dear Agnes Yarnall:

I am dictating this letter because I am so busy that it will be, I am afraid, a long time before I am able to write you in my own illegible short longhand and because I want to thank you for the shells and to tell you how happy I was to hear from you.

As for the shells, I have nothing resembling any of them. Some specimens of the Florida shells, of course, I should have, but my collection, while really fine in some departments, is full of gaps. As for the shell from Siam, I have never seen a specimen of this. How strikingly handsome it is—that shade of yellow is rare and the black stripe is stunning. You were very good to give me this.

My good wishes to you whatever you are doing. Perhaps we shall meet again.

Edna St. Vincent Millay

[25] A sculptor friend who, in 1931, had modeled a head of the poet.

213 TO ARTHUR DAVISON FICKE

Steepletop, Austerlitz, N.Y.
May 25, 1938

Dear Arthur,

More dirt about the Pulitzer Prize!

After you had left the other day I kept on thinking about what you had said; that is, was it possible that this prize is being given or with-held more for moral than for aesthetic reasons? I decided finally that you were right about this: that it was not only possible but that it was the case. But I arrived at my conclusion in a rather round-about way. I thought first of Elinor Wylie. It seemed to me extraordinary that she had never received this prize; that even her posthumously published "Collected Poems" containing every line of poetry she had ever published, should be passed over by them, was puzzling. I thought they must have had something against her, but what could it be? Even a group of doddering octogenarians could not fail to be aware of the unusually high-class quality of her work. She was an aristocrat, a lady, and her grammar was faultless. The subject matter of her poetry was the furthest thing from erotic. What could they have had against her? Then it came to me. They knew, as everybody knew, that she had left her husband and her child to run off to Europe with a married man. That was why *she* never got a Pulitzer Prize. This suddenly was plain to me.

Then I thought of you. Why had you never received the Pulitzer Prize? Why did even your selected poems get no attention from this group? I thought as I had thought of Elinor: he is a gentleman and a graduate of Harvard, his grammar is faultless, the subject matter of his poetry has never been such as to cause either Professor Bliss Perry of Harvard or Governor Wilbur Cross of Connecticut to turn his face aside and take snuff out of embarrassment. I recalled that at one time you had been curator of Japanese Prints at Harvard; then suddenly I remembered something else. I remembered why you thought it advisable to resign from this position and all the circumstances attending the resignation. "Of course," I said to myself, "that's it, why certainly."

Then I thought of Robinson Jeffers. Why had he never received it? This was easy. In his case, it is the subject matter of his poetry. Rape, incest, homosexuality and other forms of plain and fancy fornication are the subject matter of all his books. No chance for him.

I wondered why I, having been once awarded this prize in 1923, never received it afterwards, although Robert Frost and E. A. Robinson seemed to be taking turns at receiving it year after year. I remembered that not so very long after "The Harp-Weaver" was published I went to Boston and walked up and down before the State House and carried a placard protesting against the execution of Sacco and Vanzetti, suggesting that President Lowell of Harvard was withholding evidence which might have freed these men; that I was arrested and taken to jail for this and that the whole country knew it. With how much affection following this action of mine would an aged professor of Harvard look upon my subsequently published volumes? With how much affection would any aged and conservative governor of a New England state look thence forward upon the published works of a person who had agitated as I had done against the governor of a neighboring New England state? That became at once pretty plain.

Now take Robinson and Frost. What a relief these two poets must have been to the harassed judges of the Pulitzer award. If their private lives, both sexual and political, were not thoroughly blameless, I have never heard about this. The judges must have felt entirely happy and at ease in their minds the moment either Robinson or Frost published a new collection of poems.

You hit it without any doubt when you said the prize was awarded, probably, or withheld for moral rather than other reasons.

Well, this is a long letter, but I thought my findings on the subject might amuse you.

By the way, did you know that the third member of the triumvirate was that poet whom I once met in your house in Sante Fe and a good poet, I thought, too—Leonard Bacon? What is he doing limping with that pack?

Love,
Vincie.

214   TO HAROLD LEWIS COOK

Steepletop, Austerlitz, N.Y.
July 6, 1938

Dear Peter,

You are right. I have wondered many times about you. Not so much what you were doing as how you were. I am very much distressed to hear that you have been so ill and that you are even sicker now. You must try to forget all this Guggenheim hooey and everything else that's on your chest like an incubus and on your brain like a red-hot stove lid and just get well.[26]

The fact is, I never should have tried to get a Fellowship for a person like you. You are excruciatingly conscientious and you haven't, if I may say so, a heluva lot of imagination. You were so overcome by the obligation to do something noteworthy for the Guggenheim and also, and this far more, for me, that you simply stalled and couldn't go anywhere. Listen, toots, nobody who ever had this Guggenheim Fellowship for poetry ever did a darned thing with it. This is speaking broadly. Some people have got along very well. Some people have kept on working just about as they would have worked if they hadn't got it and some people have been entirely dried up by getting it.

* * *

All this doesn't matter at all. You can't write a poem tomorrow just because you promised somebody today you would write a poem tomorrow and if you are obsessed by the feeling that you must come across with something pretty high-class in a pretty short time, naturally you get jittery just as you have done—start dropping ink bottles and all that sort of thing. Nothing is more natural and nothing is more unimportant. Very likely some day you will write beautiful poetry again; as beautiful as the poetry for which I recommended you. If you don't there is nothing whatever to be done about it and you know this quite as well as I do.

In the meantime, what *does* matter is that you are so very sick. That is serious. That distresses me. Will you please, like a good boy and because I have liked you so much and liked your poetry so much and tried so hard to help you, forget all this cluttered mess, try to relax a bit when the pain is not too bad, and try to get well?

Love,
Edna.

[26] In 1937, Mr. Cook, author of *Spell Against Death*, sponsored by Edna St. Vincent Millay, Ridgley Torrence, and Max Eastman, was granted a Guggenheim Fellowship in Creative Writing. A major operation and a long, serious illness subsequently prevented him from carrying out the project for which he had received the grant.

215   TO PROFESSOR ELIZABETH HAZELTON HAIGHT

Steepletop, Austerlitz, N.Y.
July 9, 1938

Dear Elizabeth,

Forgive me for dictating this letter. My right shoulder is all lamed up with too much tennis.

Isobel Simpson was here the other day and we talked a great deal about Latin poetry as we always do when we are together, always reading it aloud to each other. (She was on her honeymoon as it happens, but that's entirely inconsequential.)

I have always wondered whether or not the Horace "Otium divos rogat in patenti" was snitched from Catullus's "Otium, Catulle, tibi molestum est." Of course, the Catullus stanza has always seemed to me merely an exercise in the Sapphic strophe, (although the "perdidit urbes" came out pretty well) anyway, it has nothing whatever to do with his translation from Sappho which precedes it. Indeed, in one edition of Catullus which I have, this stanza is separated entirely from the preceding three and numbered LIb. Yet although possibly inspired by it, somehow the Horace poem seems less light, seems to me to have more feeling in it. Still, he might have got the idea from a stanza of Catullus and then written from that start a better poem than Catullus's poem. It is striking that both poems use the word "otium" (in one form or another) three times and that both are in the Sapphic strophe. This would hardly seem to be pure coincidence. I wish someday when you are not too busy you would tell me what you think about all this. Probably you will tell me you explained it at length to me in class long ago and that I have simply forgotten all about it; in which case, refresh my memory. I am curious.

After reading a great many other things together, Isobel said that her pupils at the Brearley School preferred the Eclogues of Virgil to all his other poetry. I said that I preferred the Georgics. In spite of the beauty of the Aeneid, I never really quite liked it, and I think for a purely feminine, unaesthetic and ignoble reason. I have always thought that Aeneas was what is vulgarly known as a "heel," walking out on Dido, the way he did. True, he said at the end that he never had promised her anything.

> "   nec coniugis umquam
> praetendi taedas aut hacc in foedera veni."[27]

He's so dumb, too, saying to her,

> "   si te Karthaginis arces
> Phoenissam Libycaeque aspectus detinet urbis
> quae tandem Ausonia Teucros considere terra
> invidia est?"[28]

As if he were proving a point; as if that had anything to do with it! I am all with her when she says,

> "nec tibi diva parens, generis nec Dardanus auctor,
>   perfide,"[29]

Still, it is awful how a woman can make a man want to go—go anywhere.

You have no idea how much Latin poetry I still read and how much it means to me and how much of this happiness (far and above one's everyday happiness, natural happiness because the sun is shining, etc.) I owe to you. My Latin is no better now than it ever was and you, God knows, know how bad it was. But it is still as fervent.

Please write me someday.

Love,
Vincent

Do you hate me for this? I haven't time any more to read Virgil without a translation on the opposite page. I never in my life until last year bought or even looked into a translation of any Latin poet—that

was the sin against the Holy Ghost. But last year I think I grew up
about it. (Though I *should*, of course, have written and asked you first.)
I am no longer a student in college trying to pass an examination.

[27] "I did not, ever, claim to be a husband,/ made no such vows."
[28] ". . . If the towers of Carthage,/the Libyan citadels, can
please a woman/ who came from Tyre, why must you
grudge the Trojans/ Ausonian land?"
[29] "You treacherous liar! No goddess was your mother,/ no
Dardanus the founder of your tribe,—"

216 TO MRS. ALEXANDER BLOCH[30]

Steepletop, Austerlitz, N.Y.
July 13, 1938

Dearest Blanche,

Might we possibly again this coming Friday evening repeat the
pleasure we have had so often before of having you bring the quartet
(quintet it is I believe this time, in the Mozart) over here for the dress
rehearsal?

It could not be quite so big a party as it was before because I am
not yet quite up to my gigantic and invulnerable stature, but I think
we could have a lot of fun and God knows, I am dying to hear the
music. There would be you bringing Allie (although I feel quite sure
this would be a bad way to put it to him) and the married members of
the quintet (heavens, how they do keep on marrying) are invited to
bring their wives if they want to and if their wives are not so bored by
music by this time that they would rather go to the movies. In addition
there would be just Eugen and myself and possibly Eolo since he sort
of lives here.

I do hope you can arrange to do this. We are both longing to have
you back again.

Forgive me for dictating this letter. My right arm is in a sling too,
like yours. I told the doctor I got my bursitis from over-doing it at the
piano two years ago. I presume you told your doctor the same thing.
My doctor smelled my breath and said, "nuts." Your doctor, I presume,
since you drink nothing stronger than ginger ale, took your word for
the outrageous business. In any case we shall be able to compare dis-
abilities so let's don't. I am crazy to hear some music and perhaps I can
persuade my cook, who is a pretty good one, to fix up something that
will be fun to eat after the servants have gone across to the cottage
to bed.

The room is very much as it was when you played here before, but if you think that Allie, whom I love with a real passion, is going to get temperamental and start taking the rugs off the floor and harpooning them to the walls or something like that I wish he would come over early and get that part of it done. As for the 'cello, it can punch holes anywhere except in the pianos, but you know this already.

Lots of love and please send an answer as soon as possible by Dante. We are anxious to know.

Edna.

[30] Musician, who with her husband, Alexander Bloch, conductor and composer, directed a summer music school at their place in Hillsdale, N.Y. With the poet she often played music for two pianos.

217   TO MRS. CASINA BERGONZI[31]

Steepletop, Austerlitz, N.Y.
August 8, 1938

Dear Mrs. Bergonzi:

Thank you for the garnets. I held some in my hands once for a long time, once in Italy, when I had been working very hard—and it seemed to me they rested me. They were not mine.

Dante will tell you—but only if you ask him, probably—how badly I play the piano.

Perhaps, with Bergonzi garnets about my throat, I shall play better. (They are as quiet as velvet; I noticed that.)

Sincerely yours,
Edna St. Vincent Millay

[31] Mother of one of the Bloch pupils. She had sent a necklace of garnets as a token of her thanks for the poet's hospitality to her son.

218   TO GEORGE DILLON

Steepletop, Austerlitz, N.Y.
September 5, 1938

Dear George:

I am very happy that you liked the poems I sent you. Of course, particularly happy that you liked the new ones. You say you would like a group of seven. I am sending you five more from which to choose the extra three. Two of these, "The Fitting" and "Fog off the Coast of

Dorset" (under a different title then though) you have seen before. In "The Fitting" I have made two changes which I think are good. I have changed "secret eyes" to "guarded eyes" and "quiet body" to "secret body." The second change you yourself suggested if, perhaps, you remember. I should like very much to have you use this poem as one of the three. Possibly you will find "Sonnet in Tetrameter" a bit too early Millay for your purpose although the end, of course, is not so. [Marginal note:] I suggest leaving this out—but let me know. I should like *The Fitting* to go in, if you still like it—partly because most of your readers will understand French. [Letter continues:] I hope you will like the "Song for Young Lovers." I rather think the fog poem is the one that really should be struck out. I hope my feeling about this does not rouse your stubborn nature to a point where you wish to include this one at all costs even at the cost of sacrificing "The Fitting" which I should love to have appear in *Poetry*. If you have any suggestions to make, for God's sake, make them.

* * *

Harpers Magazine has "The Ballad of Chaldon Down"; it will appear in the November issue. I am dismally aware that I should have kept this poem for you because I know how much you liked it. But Harpers wanted a bunch of things and as I was hard at work at the time, they were all sent off without my giving the matter much thought; all that I did was to look over them carefully to be sure that I still liked them all and off they were hustled. Harpers will print eight poems of mine in their October number, four in the November.

This is a long and rather bumpy letter and I shall have hardly time to go over it before it is rushed off to the airplane for Chicago. I hope everything is clear. If not, please let me know. Please let me know anyway. It is great fun having some of my poems in *Poetry* again, especially now that you are its editor.

I have been for a long time without anybody to talk with about my poetry, any other poet I mean. Most of the other poets who are my friends or good acquaintances dislike my new stuff and loathe the work of most of the new poets I think highly of. I know so well how you feel about poetry and about me as a poet and about me, that I put these things into your hands a little blindly. If you do not really think them good you will tell me.

As always,
Vincent

Steepletop, Austerlitz, N.Y.
September 21, 1938

Dear George:

Herewith is the corrected proof. There are only two changes to be made, as you see. I hope you will be able to fit the closing parenthesis into the line. Through an oversight this was omitted from the typed copy sent you.

* * *

As for the word "aghast" in "Sonnet in Tetrameter", since you feel as you do about it, I would give a great deal to have more time to think the question over. I have spent several hours, since your letter reached me, trying to think of another word better or even as good, and I can think of nothing. The simple word "bereft" might be good except that I cannot, I think, use "bereft" followed so closely by "buried brief" and I am unwilling to sacrifice the phrase "buried brief Eternal." As I wrote the poem I did not mean the word "aghast" to give the impression of violent emotion which it conveys to you, but rather as meaning "struck with amazement" which is the second meaning given it in the Oxford Dictionary. Perhaps, after all, the violence of the emotion shown in the opening of this poem is balanced by the quiet philosophical quality of the close. In any case, I would be scared to death to make a change too quickly in a poem I have worked over so long and with so much care.

I am very glad that they are to appear in *Poetry*. I imagine that, although you like these poems, you might very well have preferred poems less early-Millay in character; poems more concerned with, apparently, things going on in the world outside myself today; poems more, if we may still use that old-fashioned word, "modern"; but some of your other contributors will probably supply the revolutionary element (there is no crack of any kind meant here, even suggesting one could be construed from it, but you said that Stephen Spender and Malcolm Cowley would probably be among your contributing poets for October).

I hope the whole thing will be a great success and that your second year as editor of *Poetry* will start under the happiest of auspices.

When I think of my reading engagement in Chicago, it makes me happy to remember that you will be there. I think I should feel lonely in Chicago without you.

Love,
Vincent

P.S. If anything goes wrong, even at this late date, with these poems of mine,—I mean to say, that if even now you come across something which you urgently feel should be changed, telegraph me at once and I will see if I can help.

220   TO GEORGE DILLON

Steepletop, Austerlitz, N.Y.
Dec. 29, 1938

Dear George:

You asked me to send you some of my new poems to read. Well, here they are, cords of them. And you will probably not have time even to glance at them, especially if you are busy being urban, or putting the magazine to bed (do magazines go to bed like newspapers, or just sit up all night dozing in day-coaches?) Anyway, if you cannot find time to read them, particularly the two groups called Theme and Variations and Sonnets from a Town in a State of Siege, please let me know at once.

I am bringing out a book on about the twentieth of May, that is, if I think it fit to print when I once get it pinned together.[32] It will have been nearly five years since my last book of lyrics was published, not long, but a long time for me. "Une vache à ecrire"—was it Chopin who called George Sand that?—And of course I want your Imprimatur on it.

(I can really type much better than this, if I go about it properly. But my sweet noisy Helen of whom I am so fond is at home with her family for Christmas, and I have been forced to do all my own clerical drudgery, carbon-papers and all; and now that I have chipped off— for ever, or so it seems—three beautifully manicured finger-nails—I have taken to striking the keys with the flat of my hand.)

Harper's Magazine wants to publish one, possibly two groups of my new poems before the book comes out. If you have time to read the two groups I am sending you and let me know fairly soon what you think of them, I shall be immensely grateful. I must also try to place a few single poems with some of the smooth-browed, bridal-satin periodicals, although I have estranged many of these by insulting their editors.

I wrote to the editor of the Ladies' Home Journal—to whom I twice had sent at his enthusiastic request groups of my poems, and who twice after an interminable delay had returned them, saying they would not be understood by his readers, and who for the third time had the effrontery to write saying he would like to read some of my new poems,—that I begged him to refrain in the future from troubling me with frivolous requests for poems which he had no intention of printing, and that the simplest way of getting hold of my new poems to read them would be to buy my new collection when it should appear. So I imagine that henceforth the doors of the Curtis Publishing Company are closed against me.

There are other magazines, though, that pay just as well. And I must make some more money rather quickly somehow—for just guess what I have gone and done, the most outrageous thing—I have bought a painting by Walt Kuhn, one of the clown ones, a beauty, the terms being one million dollars down and a ball and chain about my ankle for the rest of my life. I had thought that my reading-tour was over, except for one appearance in Worcester, an old friend which doesn't bother me much—; but now poor Ugin, much against his will (because he wants me to take it easy for awhile) is entering into unsavory correspondence with Lee Keedick, who has been anxious for a long time to sign me up for some more engagements late in January and early in February, and whom we have both turned down with a perfunctory polishing of the monocle. Well, so we retract our honour and imperil our health, and all for the sake of a not very bright-coloured painting on a not so very large piece of canvas, and a frame as ugly as hell made of gilt-smudged almond-paste too dirty to eat.

Ugin is in despair, for it pretty well appears that I have sold myself down the river for good (or rather up the river, which is so much harder to swim); and I never make a penny on these tours, because although I get very big fees for each reading, I have to travel so expensively that I never have a penny left when I get home, because if I didn't travel like that I shouldn't be able to give the readings. Now. I have talked so much about money that you will without a doubt suppose me very rich indeed, and try to persuade me to become the Maecenas of POETRY: A MAGAZINE OF VERSE.

As for the other poems I enclose, several of which are among my favorites—such as Rendezvous, Anxious to the Wood,* etc. if you wish to use some of these in your magazine I should love to have you do so.

And you needn't think you must print me out in front (unless for the magazine's sake in that particular issue I should happen to be the best name you had to advertise with) I shouldn't mind at all being stuck between the Book Reviews and the Notes on Contributors.

Well, that's all. What a stolid yet exuberant letter, rambling all over the landscape, Tudor, Georgian and Victorian.

Please read the poems if you have time. Otherwise wire me that you have no time.

Love, Vincent.

* These two I will send later, at least the first one. This was so badly typed it is impossible. The second was so badly written, it is impossible. At least, I think it lousy. Perhaps I can delouse it, in which event I will send it.—In fact, I don't like any of them. If you do, for God's sake let me know right away.—I wrote this letter about ten days ago—but then I couldn't make up my mind whether or not to send the poems, they all seem so verminous.

> [32] *Huntsman, What Quarry?* There appeared in the May, 1939, number of *Poetry*: Sonnet: "My earnestness which might at first offend," "Rendezvous," "Modern Declaration," "The True Encounter," "The Plaid Dress," "'This Dusky Faith,'" "The Snow Storm," "Two Voices," all of which were included in the new book.

221　TO GEORGE DILLON

One Fifth Avenue [New York]
March 23rd, 1939

Dear George:

Enclosed please find a bunch of writing. Whether or not there's any poetry in it, I have no idea. I know that whatever it is I'm curst sick of it. I remember that you didn't much like The Snow Storm, but you didn't actually hate it, and I think that if you use the others you ought to use that, too, for whatever else it may be, it is a lyric, and otherwise it seems to me there'll be a sort of top-heaviness of those long loose irregular jagged lines that Edna Millay is that way about.

My new book is off, and the galleys are corrected and returned.[33] It's the first book I ever got to the printer on time, and I feel pretty squirmy about that: may be a left-handed omen. Anyway, it's going to have one good poem in it; I mean, besides "The Rabbit"—which everybody (Eastern Standard Time) is crazy about. The new poem is a sonnet called "Czecho-Slovakia". I can't send it to you, because it's out walking the streets.

I'm in a vile temper this morning. Ugin's gone and contracted the flu, or something; and we can't go to Cass Canfield's to dinner tonight to meet John Gunther. I don't know whether to be sorry for poor Ugin, or furious with him, or simply relieved that I don't have to go to dinner tonight, even to meet John Gunther.

In the sonnet you liked, which I am sending, I tried my best to get the gag out of the guy's mouth, but couldn't; and anyway, nobody but an exhausted editor of a poetry magazine would ever have the slightest trouble over that sestet. It is perfectly obvious, especially with all those semi-colons, that the scenes described take place at different times. The trouble with you is, you don't like poetry and you disapprove of it; and you're just trying to find a loophole in the law which will enable you to send it up for life.

Never mind. I send you my love.

Vincent

[33] *Huntsman, What Quarry?*

222   TO LLEWELYN POWYS

[Steepletop, Austerlitz, N.Y.
Fall, 1939]

Lulu, my poor, poor darling, if I wait to write you in ink, a proper letter, that a man out of his happiness dashed down again, with his tired eyes might read, I shall again be so overwhelmed by all I want to say to you, that again as so many times in these past months I shall not write you at all.—And that must not be; I must say something to you, simply speak to you, even if I say nothing.

So here I am, half an hour later, just thinking of you, saying nothing.—How senseless to try to say something to give you courage when you have already so much more of that than anybody I know, except Alyse.—Oh, Lulu, I do so hope that by the time you get this you will be better![34]

My love, Edna.

[34] Llewelyn Powys died at Clavadel in Switzerland on December 2, 1939.

223   TO ALYSE GREGORY

The St. Regis, New York.

[December 1939]

Alyse, my dear and lovely Alyse, my heart's friend;—if only I could be with you now, this afternoon, just for the length of time it takes to drink three cups of tea, quietly, saying hardly anything—

There is nothing that I can write; there would be nothing that I could say. But oh, if only I could be with you, my dear, just for an hour or two.

Edna

224   TO FERDINAND EARLE

Steepletop, Austerlitz, N.Y.

August 3, 1940

Dear Editor . . .

I am sorry that I was too ill to write you; oh, so sorry that I hurt your feelings. I am still too ill to write you,—even to dictate as I am doing now, a letter to a stenographer; that is to say, it is against doctor's orders that I do it. But I am somewhat stronger than I was a month ago, and I cannot bear to have you continue to think me forgetful and ungrateful. I remember too well that day, years ago, when I came back from the pasture carrying a pailful of blueberries which I had picked, and my mother was waiting for me on the doorstep with your letter in her hand.

* * *

I think of you always with the same affectionate gratitude I felt at the time when you were trying so hard to make the other judges see my poem as you saw it, trying so hard to obtain for me that prize of $500, a fortune then. (Almost a fortune to me now, in fact. Though in the meantime there have been periods when I could have paid $500 for an evening gown. My life has always gone abruptly and breath-takingly up and down, like a roller-coaster!)

I am still too weak from months in hospitals to be able to give any strength at all to anything but my own work; I can do nothing to help you now; and I wish, more than you will believe, perhaps, that I could help you. But you, who were the first, outside the little village where I lived, to think my poetry of some consequence, would be the first now, I think, to consider that I should give to it all the strength that I have.

I am, believe me, with the same grateful heart as on that day long ago when I learned that somebody beside my mother, a person whose name I later learned to be Ferdinand Earle, liked a poem of mine called "Renascence".

Sincerely yours,
Edna St.Vincent Millay

225   TO MRS. FRANK L. RICKER

Steepletop, Austerlitz, N.Y.
Sept. 14, 1940

Dear Aunt Susie:

I am sending you a little present of no value whatsoever except sentimental value, but I think you will be pleased to have it. It is a face towel, as you will see, with hemstitching on two ends and a piece of the worst crocheting you ever saw in your life on one end. The hemstitching was done, I am almost sure, by mother when she sewed on the piece of crocheting, which is, if you please, the only piece of crocheting I ever did in my life, and I did it at the age of nine. I can remember the date very well, because it was done while we were living in Rockport before we moved to Ring's Island, and I had my tenth birthday on Ring's Island, so I must have been either eight or nine when I did this masterpiece.

The towel, which has been lying around for a long time, waiting to be sent to you, is, as you will see, in need of laundering, but I was afraid that in having it laundered, the tear in the lace, if one might call it that, if one might call it lace, I mean, might become bigger and I thought you might prefer to mend the tear before having the towel laundered.

I hope you will think it fun to have it. It amused me to think of sending to you who do the most beautiful crocheting in the world the most awful piece of crocheting ever done in the world.

Lots of love to you, dear Aunt Susie, I think of you often. Eugen sends *his* love, too. (This is a horrible new pen—I'm going to send it back.) But there's nothing wrong with our love, dear, and we send you lots of it.

Vincent

226   TO GEORGE DILLON

Steepletop, Austerlitz, N.Y.
Nov. 29, 1940

Dear George:

I am sending you my new book of—not poems, posters;[35] there are a few good poems, but it is mostly plain propaganda. If some bright boy reviews it for *Poetry*, *please* remind him that I know bad poetry as well as the next one, and that this book—whose sub-title is "1940 Notebook", which I thought would make the matter plain enough to anybody, but doesn't seem to (although almost all the reviews have been wonderful, far beyond my expectations)—that this book is a book of impassioned propaganda, into which a few good poems got bound up because they happened to be propaganda, too.—I hope you will like some of it.

Love,
Vincent

[35] *Make Bright the Arrows.*

227   TO SISTER STE. HELENE[36]

Steepletop, Austerlitz, N.Y.
December 3rd, 1940

Darling Sister Ste. Helene:

I have been working so hard that I have had no time to write a letter; and I have been very sick, too—three times in hospital—an injured nerve under my right shoulder-blade, the injury received no one knows how, but plain to the X-ray—I think it happened one very dark night when the door of the station-wagon suddenly swung open just as we were going around a curve, and I was thrown out into the darkness and rolled down a rocky gully—I think it must have been then although nothing showed up for a long time, but a bad bruise on the head and very lame right shoulder.—I have tried everything, even nerve surgery, which did not help, but now I have a very famous and good doctor in charge of me, and I think I am getting better.—Anyway, never mind all that. It is not important, although I have been in unremitting pain for well over a year, it does not matter, because I have been able to work.

I am sending you my new book: "Make Bright the Arrows". (The phrase is from Jeremiah; perhaps you recall the passage.) It is sub-titled

"1940 Notebook", and that is what it really is, a piece of propaganda, acres of bad poetry, but perhaps you will forgive it, and me, for what I am trying to do, what I am trying to help save.

The lovely nun in the little play "The Crooked Cross" is of course named for you.

I will send you a photograph as soon as I find one I think you will like. It is disgraceful that I never gave you a photograph of me. And besides, you asked me for one in your letter. . . .

Merry Christmas and all my love,

Vincent

[36] Then Dean of the College of St. Catherine, St. Paul, Minn. On one of her reading tours, Miss Millay and her husband had been guests of Sister Ste. Helene.

"While giving readings from her poems in Minneapolis recently, Edna St. Vincent Millay received a telephone call from the Mother Superior of a convent in St. Paul, deploring the fact that since the rules of the convent prevented the sisters from going out at night, they would be unable to hear the author of 'The Harp-Weaver and Other Poems'. Miss Millay's response to this call was to go to St. Paul and give a special reading within the walls of the convent." From the *New York Times*, March 9, 1924.

228   TO MRS. CHARLOTTE BABCOCK SILLS

400 East 52nd St., New York

January 2nd, 1941

Charlie, my dear:

I am more distressed than I can tell you to learn that my Christmas gift, which I hoped might give you pleasure, gave you instead pain, hurt you and made you angry. But my dear girl, when we were in college together, were you (this is a joke) either fairly bright or pretty dumb?—because the reason why this book hurt you is because you utterly and thoroughly and from cover to cover misunderstood its meaning.

Think back, did I ever once, so far as you can remember, do anything, even a little thing, to hurt you, even a little bit, knowingly? And don't you realize that I know perfectly well that you have three grown boys? And if this book had really been the book you took it to be (being so convinced at the outset that you were right about this, that you were unable afterwards, no matter what you read in it, to learn that you were mistaken) would I have done the insolent and cruel thing which it would have been to send to you and Mac a book of poems trying to incite this country to send American boys into foreign lands to fight?

Please read once more, I beg you to do this, and this time with a reading mind, not with a mind which is quite naturally frightened and shrinks from what it considers is trying to send your boys to war, at least the very first poem in this book. I mean the small poem at the very beginning of the book; the poem which starts "Make bright the arrows". I beg you earnestly to read this with great care, giving particular attention to the phrase, "The bowman feared need never fight", and to the phrase further on, "O peaceful and wise". See if you then cannot understand that what I am trying to do with every bit of my strength, and being very ill all the time I am working, is not to get this country into war, but to keep it out of war.

Is it not unjust of you, my dear friend, to accuse me of trying to incite this country to send an army to fight on foreign soil just because my idea as to how best to keep this country out of war differs radically from yours?

Perhaps I am mistaken in my viewpoint, which is shared as you must know, by thousands of other good United States citizens who love their country and its democratic ideals, its freedom, its individual liberties quite as much as you possibly can. If I am mistaken, and if those who think as I do are mistaken, it will indeed be a terrible, an unthinkable error to have made. But if you and those who think as you do should prove to be mistaken and this country, because we have let Britain collapse, should then be crushed between Germany and Japan with the help of certain sections of South America and of certain Nazi infiltration there, that too will be a terrible, an unthinkable error to have made. Neither of us can know which is right. Each of us can only do his utmost to further the cause which he believes to be right.

You say that if I had three grown boys as you have I would feel differently about it. There is little doubt probably that I should *feel* differently about it, but I do not for a moment believe that I should *think* differently about it. And though I have no sons to be caught in this war, if we are caught in it, I have one thing to give in the service of my country,—my reputation as a poet. How many more books of propaganda poetry containing as much bad verse as this one does, that reputation can withstand without falling under the weight of it and without becoming irretrievably lost, I do not know—probably not more than one. But I have enlisted for the duration.

Have you the slightest conception of what this reputation means to me, who have been building it carefully for more than twenty years, taking a long time, months, sometimes as long as several years before permitting a poem to be published because I felt that in one line of it, one syllable was not as close to perfection as I might be able to make it? You see by the dates on the poems in this book that they were written in furious haste and published as soon as they were written. They are, with a few exceptions, considered as poetry, faulty and unpolished; and whatever the final verdict of our generation or the next may be upon me as a poet, there are already, I know quite well, thousands of people, true lovers of pure poetry, and who have—for I am humbly proud of this and feel no arrogance in saying so—in past years thought very highly of mine, who will, no matter what I may write in the future, never forgive me for writing this book.

Thus, you see, the dearest thing in life I possess which might possibly be of help to my country, has already gone over the top, in the hope that your sons need never go to war.

Affectionately,
Vincent.

229   TO EUGENE SAXTON

400 East 52nd St., [New York]
March 10, 1941

Dear Gene:

Once again I must ask my publishers to come—come running—to my aid. (Do not be deceived by the half-hearted facetiousness of that opening line into thinking that either the aid or the haste necessary in getting it to me is superficial. I write like that because I am so damned sick of having to ask Harper's for one advance after another on my royalties, that if I don't try to make the transaction sound at least faintly funny I simply can't go on with this letter. The matter is really far from funny.)

It seems to me that I never get you finally paid up, with a few hundred dollars to spare, but I have to start right in borrowing from you again.

And this, particularly during the past two years, when the outrage of unalleviated pain has been coupled with the infuriating obligation of

laying one sweet luscious grand after another between the self-com-
placent and condescending teeth of one officious and inefficient hospital
after another; and of one after another frivolous blood-pressure-taker
of a surgeon or physician, surrounded each by his own personal rake-off
racket of: X-ray man; infra-red-ray man; eye-specialist; sodium-salicy-
late specialist; etc.; including pet pharmacist and masseuse,—and this, as I
started to say, this just getting paid up in time to start borrowing again,
is, as you can readily believe from the above wild outburst, beginning
to get into my hair!

I did think, this time, however, that I was going to be able to
manage. My new book suddenly appearing the way it did was a happy
surprise to publisher as well as to author, I am sure. And of course it
does bring up my author's-morale quite a bit, and make this always
unfestive occasion less funereal, to recall that at the time last year when
Harper's so kindly grub-staked me for such a large amount, nobody
naturally had much hope of getting any sort of book from me until I
should be reasonably free from pain,—and so far the answer to *that*
had not been hit on.

Now, however, I think it *has* been hit on,—by Dr. Timme, of the
N. Y. Neurological Institute. For about eight months I had been following his what-seemed-to-be-absolutely-cock-eyed regime with no
result whatever, when suddenly, about a fortnight ago, all the tons of
calcium gluconate and assorted minerals and vitamins-sometimes-w-
and-y which I had been patiently swallowing and often managing to
keep from chucking up again—GOT TO WORK! Every day I got better.
One whole day I was almost entirely without pain. (I am telling you all
these details, Gene, because we talked together for quite some time one
day last year about the strange case of Miss M., and you were interested;
do you remember how you told me to go sleep on a plank?!!—I slept
on a plank for five months.)

What it comes to is this: Eugen has lost everything he had. At
least, for the present. There is not a penny he can get at. So for the
time being it's up to me.

* * *

But if only I can be kept for a time from worry over money-troubles,
I shall probably get well soon, be able to get back to work on my
autobiographical preface to Three Songs, and from that go on to
certain other things in which I am intensely interested but which I have
been for the most part not strong enough and far too uncomfortable to

bring off. (I have really been working very hard a great part of the time—but the business of cutting, cleaning, polishing; of documenting, of correlating; of fitting into place; the masonry of art, has been too heavy for me.)

I am writing this very long letter because I could not bear to write simply asking Harper's once more to advance me money on royalties, and asking you to do your best to help me get it; I wanted to tell you not only the fact but also the nature of my predicament, for I felt sure that you would understand it,—you who also have been in several kinds of distress at once, with the mental and spiritual kinds of pain twisting and tightening the knots of the physical.

Whether the above sounds more like Mrs. Shelley talking about Shelley or Gerard Hopkins talking about himself, I couldn't say. But in any case an example of what I mean comes too pat to hand not to be recorded here—a sort of ironical underscoring of every word in this letter: since my inexcusable folly of nearly two years ago—for which I dearly paid with this nerve injury under the shoulder (I presume I told you all about my bright idea of pulling six thousand plantains per day out of the door-yard, lawns and surrounding landscape until by and by there should be no more plantains?) since then I have made one or two attempts to do a little typewriting, but have always had to give it up after half a page or so because of the sudden sharp increase in the pain. This time, though, I really thought myself sufficiently improved to be able to go through with it. But the anxiety which was my reason for writing you this letter suddenly tightened up on me, and made the posture, (so close to the plantain-pulling posture!) of typing (as also of eating with knife and fork, which is invariably painful) something close to excruciating. Seldom has the morphine seemed so slow in getting to me; although poor Ugin, who naturally hates like hell to have to give it me, is quicker with it than the doctor by now.

Can Harper's help me as per enclosed list of my needs?

Affectionately,
Edna.

230   TO ALYSE GREGORY

Steepletop, [Austerlitz, N.Y.]
June 10, 1941

Alyse, my darling,—beautiful person, belovèd friend:—all during this dreadful winter you have been constantly in my mind and heart, and oh, how often we have spoken of you, and always with deep love for you and deep anger and scornful reproach for ourselves, because we have not written you. But, Alyse, I have been very ill, and Eugen has been desperate about me. Day & night he has nursed me. He has written no word to any one. His face has been gray with anxiety.

But now, I am beginning to have moments, even hours, when I am not in pain. He will be more like himself soon.

Edna.

231   TO ARTHUR DAVISON FICKE
[Sept. 16, 1941]

Dear Arthur, I am as sure as I am of anything that you sent me *two books only* this time: one your own poems; the other the poems of Tuckerman, which I am returning. Your *Selected Poems* I am *not* returning, because in the first place you gave it to me, and in the second place (although the copy you first gave me, while too dog-eared, knock-kneed, out-at-elbow and generally threadbare to grace—so far as one can see without opening it—the Library of Steepletop) it will do splendidly for me to spatter clam-juice on while opening clams for chowder on Ragged Island and at the same time checking up on the parts I don't know by heart in the poems I do know by heart.

As for Masefield, if you want Masefield for a while, I'll lend you my Masefield (collected) or the *Lollingdon Downs*, whichever you like—but dearie, I ain't got yourn—at least I'm pretty sure I haven't. —However, on my Shelf of Borrowed Books (a swell idea, by the way,) there may very well be some book of yours, which I borrowed when I just learned to read and have probably decorated with coloured chalk, —I think there is something, I'll look. Sorry, I haven't either of the other two you mention.

—Love   V.

232   TO WITTER BYNNER
            The Night before Christmas when all
            Through the House
            Not a creature's a-stir
            But a little deer-mouse

Steepletop, [Austerlitz N.Y.] 1941

Dearest Hal,—I *am* well enough to check the copies—well enough to check a whole Nazi motorized division simply by butting at it with my forehead! (There now! Isn't that a nice pun for Hal's Christmas?)

But darling, I am so very busy,—yes of course, writing more verses for my poor, foolish, bewildered, beloved country.—I have written four poems already since the outbreak of this war—which of course was not an outbreak at all, but simply a visible manifestation of something already in existence for a long time. A great part of the work on these poems (for I really think they are poems) was done long before the attack on Oahu, a fact which made it possible for me to send to Mr. Markel of the New York Sunday Times Magazine a poem for his Christmas number, containing obvious allusions to our entrance into the war, so short a time after war was declared. (This piece got held up in the post, though, and will appear instead in the New Year's number, next Sunday, Dec. 28.) I hope you will see it. And I hope you will like it.[37]

I am working very hard now on the three others, in order to get them off as soon as possible and at the same time have them really poems. *Make Bright the Arrows*, of course, did no good at all. The American who read it didn't even know why I had written the verses; or why, having written them, I should be in such haste to publish them.—Professor Irwin Edman, in a review of the book, expressed regret that I had not seen fit to "wait a year longer" before presenting it to the public!—And some of the reviews were insolent to the point of being really "actionable", I think. Not that any of this mattered at all. What mattered was that in spite of all that so many of us tried so hard to do, the Professor Irwin Edmans of the country, as well as the Charles A. Lindberghs and the Senator Wheelers, let Pearl Harbor happen.

Oh, well, I suppose what the Japanese can take, the Americans can take back again, if they ever get their hands out of their pockets long enough to load a gun.—Yes, I mean this in both ways.

Anyway, in the meantime, it is all pretty nasty, and a handful of rather brave boys are now busy trying to wipe the spit off their faces of a horde of thoroughly unpleasant conquerors.

Hal, I haven't time, just now, to read over the letters.

Love,
Edna.

I am really cured of the pain under my shoulder, it seems. You are glad!

[37] "Not to Be Spattered by His Blood. (St. George Goes Forth to Slay the Dragon—New Year's 1942)."

233   TO MRS. FRANK L. RICKER

Steepletop, Austerlitz, N.Y.
Dec. 30, 1941

Dearest Aunt Susie:

I have just received your letter.[38] My first instinct of course, was to get as close to you as I could, in the quickest way I could—which would be, of course, by long-distance telephone—just to tell you with my own voice that I am waiting and watching with you. But I realized at once that to do such a thing might cause you more excitement, (thinking that here at last was news—perhaps good news), or more unnecessary alarm, than any comfort you might perhaps receive from talking with me. For of course I have no news of any kind.

I had heard nothing of the disappearance of the plane until I got your letter. But I cannot help thinking that the old "no news is good news" is particularly true in a case like this. The pilot may for some reason have been obliged to change his course, and to make a forced landing at some point farther away than anyone would think at all likely, and they may quite possibly be all safe, yet unable so far to communicate.

If their radio was damaged in landing, this would be the case. If they came down safely, then wherever they are, they will have matches to build fires, to keep them warm, and of course they were warmly clothed for the flight, and, being officers, they would be carrying revolvers, and are good shots, and the small game in such a wild place as they probably are (since they have not yet been sighted) should be plentiful.

Also, highly trained as they are, they will be much more resourceful in many other ways, and so have a much better chance to come out of it safe and sound, than the average citizen would have.

So we will wait together, darling!

I know that I do not need to tell you to keep up heart; I know of what stuff you are made, and a fine thing it would be, if George returning home from a pretty harrowing experience, found his mother in a nervous breakdown!

Enclosed is a letter for Gladys, I haven't her address, so sorry, darling, please address it for me, and read it, of course. And I don't know whether George is a Major or Lieut. Colonel.

Enclosed is a poem of mine from last Sunday's New York Times Magazine—which might have been written for my dear cousin George.

Love to you from both Eugen and me.

Love—you know how much—from *Vincent*.

[38] With the news that the plane in which her cousin Lieut. Col. George Ricker of the U.S. Army General Staff on a mission with Major-Gen. Herbert Durque, Commanding General of the 1st Air Force, was missing somewhere over Southern California. The plane, with seven officers and men aboard, had left Phoenix, Arizona on Friday, December 12, 1941.

234   TO ARTHUR DAVISON FICKE

Saturday, Feb. 14 [1942?]

Arthur, darling,—it is wonderful and beautiful to me that at this moment in our history somebody is studying ancient Chinese art—and I am glad that that somebody is you.—If I were in New York I would take a course at Columbia, too, I think; I don't know what, but something lovely and satisfying like that, and full of peace and majesty—to take my mind for several hours a day away from the ugliness and hypocrisy and greed that is like a stench under my nostrils all the time.—Have you ever read James Hilton's "Lost Horizon"? Very likely you have, and perhaps you hated it. I loved it, and I am going to read it again,—read about a world where people have time to study without haste and deeply all the things they long to study, where people live long enough even to acquire a little wisdom, or at least to value it. —If you haven't read it, please do.

Forgive this scrawl. Lots of love from us both to you and Gladdie.

Vincent.

235   TO LEONORA SPEYER

Steepletop, Austerlitz, N.Y.
March 18, 1943

Dearest Nora,—It was a shame!—I did so want to see you again!—But you were beautiful that night—radiant.[39] I don't remember a word you said—I day [sic] say it was very wise, and I'm sure it was very witty. But sitting there beside you I didn't even try to listen, except to the sound of your voice,—and for the rest, just looked at your face.— *Nobody* has more beautiful eyes than you—although they are really and always blue; the color of the sea sometimes, they make me think of these two lines of Matthew Arnold's, whose poetry I love so much:

"Eyes too expressive to be blue
Too lovely to be grey."—
Since this is apparently a love letter, I sign myself

Yours with love,
Edna.

[39] At the annual dinner of the Poetry Society of America, on January 31, 1943, where Edna St. Vincent Millay received the Society's Gold Medal, Mrs. Speyer made the presentation speech.

236 TO ARTHUR DAVISON FICKE

[1943]

TO ARTHUR!

Dearest Louse:
            I came upon this preposterous document while cleaning out a desk drawer. God knows how it got there in the first place, instead of into the dust-bin (dust-bin being the quaint, historically-geographically interesting all-hope-lost yet somehow euphemistic word for "garbage-can". "God knows", I say. Substitute "God knew, but has forgotten."

—V.

Facsimile of egregious—no, help! help!—gregarious and wolf-upon-fold-descending hordes of spoiled ignorant arrogant (yes, unconsciously arrogant twerp-squirt-brats of this newest generation) whose indolence is exceeded only by that of their teachers, only too glad to pass the buck of toilsome teaching to busy poets and authors.

—Vince.

            These notes are penciled on the back of the letter which follows.

March 23, 1943

Edna St. Vincent Millay
C/o Harper Bros.
New York, New York.
Dear Miss Millay:
            The English III Class of the C—— High School, has just begun to study poetry. We thought it might be interesting to ask a famous poet a few questions.

One of the things we should like to know is your reason for becoming a poet. It seems that a person must be Gifted to do any outstanding writing. What are your other interests? Some people have
hobbies, others enjoy sports; but we would like to know just what your
other activities outside of writing are. (!)

Surely everyone has some childhood experiences that are fun to
hear about or that are interesting to others. Have you? (!)

How long does it take you to write a poem? Is it necessary to have
some definite inspiration or can you sit down and write on the spur of
the moment?

There are many things that poets enjoy writing about. Do you have
a certain subject you like to write on in particular?

Of all your poems, the Class would like to know which one you
consider best? Why?

Hearing these questions answered by the person whom we are
studying, will make our lessons much more interesting.

We are hoping to hear from you soon.

Sincerely yours,

B——— C———

(Correspondent of English III Class)

The exclamation points are Miss Millay's.

237   TO AMY FLASHNER[40]

[July, 1943]

Dear Miss Flashner:

There seems to be nobody at Harpers to whom I can go now with
my troubles, now that Gene is gone. He was always there, to talk to
and explain things, always so sweet and kind to me, with his white
face and sad, unhoping eyes—happy only when we were quoting Latin
poetry to each other, or something like that—Of course I can't write
about him or even think about him without crying, and of course I
am crying now—only fortunately the paper held in the typewriter
does not get splashed by tears the way a sheet of notepaper on the
desk does—I don't see how any of you get along without him—I should
think that the whole building would be like a mausoleum—it seems
strange that it is so hard to believe, really to believe in the death of so
fragile and suffering a person . . . and besides really missing him, I
miss him also in a very and simple childish way: he always helped me

out of my troubles, and he isn't there any more, and I don't know what to do. If I don't get some money I can't go on writing, can't go on doing anything. It's all very well doing things for the government, things that might help a little to win the war, but I spent all last year doing that—Writers' War Board, Red Cross, New York Times Conference of Women (no, that was this Spring, but anyway, the N.Y. Times didn't even pay my expenses for it) but the point is that I'm stone-broke. Can Harper's help me, Miss Flashner?

Sincerely,
Edna St. Vincent Millay

⁴⁰ Assistant to Mr. Eugene Saxton.

238   TO ARTHUR DAVISON FICKE

Steepletop [Austerlitz, N.Y.]
July 9, 1943

Darling Arthur:—I have wanted so often to write you—not that I like writing letters—I loathe it—but just that I have wanted to write to *you*. About what, I don't know, in particular.—Perhaps to ask the advice of the Sage of the Hill—perhaps to tell you that the young wrens in the house under the peak of the ice-house are flying this morning (and what a to-do! and what beautiful singing from their father!—as if to say: some day you will have as handsome feathers as I, and a tail that sticks up straight behind your rump, and a song as beautiful as mine—you boys, that is,—and even you girls will have fun, engineering long twigs through small doorways!)—this is just to say Hello, darling Artie.—

Love, Vincent

239   TO DANTE BERGONZI

Steepletop, Austerlitz, N.Y.
October 26th, 1944

Dan, my dear, I think so often and with so much pleasure of one night here at Steepletop when, because I felt sick and sad and nothing could cheer me up, you and Eolo suddenly departed to the studio and as suddenly returned, sternly marching into the drawing-room with fiddle and cello and the music of that lovely Mozart trio, which you insisted that the three of us play together and at once, I to play the piano part at sight!—And it did not go so badly, either; there were even moments ————

It was 9:45 in the morning when I wrote the lines above. It is now nearly one o'clock. 10:45—11:45—12:45—it is now more than three hours that I have sat here, still as a statue except for the outwardly imperceptible movements of my remembering mind, thinking of that moment, that great moment which happened to the three of us, happened even to me, that moment above all earthly moments exalted— when all at once the music took things into its own hands,—so hard to express it—disregarding even its composer who had conceived, contrived, and set it down—the music, emerging, coming forward, speaking at last not through several instruments, but with one clear, beautiful voice.—

Edna.

240   TO ARTHUR DAVISON FICKE

Sept. 9, 1945

Dear Arthur,—

I used to think that I knew something about pain, both physical & mental. But when I think of you—as I do constantly, my dear, with a heart full of tenderness and a mind full of furious rebellion against the Gods for what they are doing to oh-so-darling you—I realize that I have never suffered at all, that I cannot even imagine what suffering might be.

I would give you my love, but I did that long ago, sweet and true friend.

Vincent

241   TO ARTHUR DAVISON FICKE

[Fall, 1945]

Dear Arthur:

I *did* write that sonnet to you, the one you asked me about.—I denied it at the time,—but what a hell of a time, and what a hell of a place, to ask me about it!—A cocktail party in George La Branche's gun-room! Of course, you spoke in a voice so low that no one could possibly have overheard you. But anyway. And besides, you sprang the question on me so suddenly, without the slightest warning, in the course of a conversation we were having about something entirely different, that it almost caught me off guard. And I loathe being caught off guard; it makes me furious. (A devil's-trick that is of yours, too, Angel-in-all-else.)

Perhaps, also, I didn't want you to know, for sure, how terribly, how sickeningly, in love with you I had been.

And perhaps, also, I was still in love with you, or I shouldn't have cared.

Well, anyway. The sonnet was the one beginning: "And you as well must die, beloved dust".[41] In case you've forgotten. Which you haven't.

Vincie

[41] Arthur Davison Ficke died on November 30, 1945. At his burial, at "Hardhack," Hillsdale, N.Y., Miss Millay read this sonnet and passages from one of his favorite poems: Milton's "Lycidas."

IX

Steepletop — Ragged Island

1946 – October, 1950

Steepletop, Austerlitz, N.Y.
January 8th, 1946

Dear Cass Canfield:

It occurs to me with something of dismay, that, if I were dead—instead of being, as I am, alive and kicking, and I said *kicking*—the firm of Harper and Brothers (Est 1817—and how good is your Latin?) might conceivably, acting upon the advice of a respected friend, alter one word in one of my poems.

This you must never do. Any changes which might profitably be made in any of my poems, were either made by me, before I permitted them to be published, or must be made, if made at all, someday by me. Only I, who know what I mean to say, and how I want to say it, am competent to deal with such matters. Many of my poems, of course, are greatly reduced in stature from the majesty which I hoped they might achieve, because I was unable, as one too often is, to make the poem rise up to my conception of it. However, the faults as well as the virtues of this poetry, are my own; and no other person could possibly lay hands upon any poem of mine in order to correct some real or imagined error without harming the poem more seriously than any faulty execution of my own could possibly have done. (I do not, of course include here such hastily-written and hot-headed pieces as are contained in "Make Bright the Arrows", "The Murder of Lidice", etc. I am speaking of poetry composed with no other design than that of making as good a poem as one possibly can make, of poetry written with deliberation and under the sharp eye of an ever-alert self-criticism, of poetry in other words, written with no ulterior motive, such as, for instance, the winning of a world-war to keep democracy alive.)

As for Sonnet XIV from "Epitaph for the Race of Man", let me assure you now (because I know that you are deeply troubled about this matter and in a mood to accept from a friend whose learning you respect, a suggested alteration in one of my poems) let me assure you that your friend has brashly leaped to an ill-considered conclusion, and that in this instance he has made a complete ass of himself.

This particular sonnet is guilty of a serious fault, but from the point of view of sonnet-structure, not from the point of view of either fact or mythology. The octave is written in the pure Italian form, whereas in the sestet the rhyme-scheme (ccddcd) is improper. This is very bad, of course. Yet I do consider this particular bastard sestet to be sometimes, as in this sonnet, for instance, not ineffective.

As to what this sonnet actually *says*,—well, it seems to me that any bright boy in the eighth grade, who cared for poetry, and was not too lazy to look up a few words in the dictionary, would have little difficulty as to its literal meaning. If this poem makes any statement at all, which it does, then the substitution of the word "Ixion" for the word "Aeolus" would render the whole sonnet utterly ridiculous, confusing and meaningless.

Let me go back for a moment to sonnet XV which begins:
        "Now sets his foot upon the eastern sill
        "Aldebaran, ..."
When I say Aldebaran, I mean Aldebaran; I do not mean Arcturus, and I do not mean Antares. And when I write concerning Aldebaran, that:
        "And tracks the Pleiades down the crowded sky,
        "And drives his wedge into the western hill;"
I mean that the reddish star Aldebaran does seem, if watched through the night, to track the Pleiades; and when I say:
        "And drives his wedge into the western hill";
I am speaking of the constellation Taurus of which Aldebaran is the principal star and which is wedge-shaped. And so I mean that Aldebaran in Taurus drives his wedge into the western hill. I do not mean that Regulus in Leo is hacking at the hill with his sickle.

Likewise, also, when (in sonnet VI) I say:
        "See where Capella with her golden kids
        "Grazes the slope between the East and North!"
I am speaking, not of Vega, nor yet of Spica, but of Capella. I, looking with my own eyes, see this beautifully-coloured star as followed not by two lesser stars, as she classically is stated to be, but by three stars; and so in the closing lines of the octave of this sonnet I write:
        "The risen She-Goat showing blue and red
        "Climbed the clear dusk, and three stars followed her."
This is to say, I am speaking of something which I personally have observed, concerning which as a plodding amateur astronomer, I have some acquaintance, and with which as to the classical treatment of these subjects I am not entirely unfamiliar.

Now let me advise you as to sonnet XIV, concerning which you are distressed, because some acquaintance of yours, whose scholarship you admire (although I might say that from my own one example of it, this scholarship would seem to have—although in places possibly it is profound—at mean low water, a depth of something less than half a fathom) has urged upon you the idea that not only is my own scholarship, if indeed it exist at all, a scattered and flighty thing, but also that in the executing of my own craft I am so careless and indolent as not to care at all whether the words I write have any meaning whatsoever, so long as they string along together in a fairly pleasant way. Has your friend ever read this sonnet? Have you?—If either of you had done so, then all this painful and tiresome balderdash and bilge would have been avoided. For in this sonnet, as in all the other sonnets of this sequence, I am not concerned with the domestic intrigues of the gods amongst each other. Their constant contriving, and deceits, their easy adulteries and capricious revenges do not interest me: I am as bored with their household concerns as they themselves are. All throughout the Iliad it is apparent that the only personages who show courage, who play fair, are mortals, not gods. Despite the great strides and the majestic proportion of the goddess Pallas Athenae, it is she who by the dirtiest trick in fiction, if not in history, delivers over Hector to his death at the hands of Achilles. But in the same book, Achilles, a Greek engaged in a desperate war against the Trojans, makes a gentleman's agreement with Priam, the King of Troy, and sticks to it. (And if you wish to point out that Achilles, being the son of the goddess Thetis, is half god, your point would be blunt indeed, since Achilles, being half human is mortal and must die, does not want at all to die, yet is, as he says of himself, "the bravest of the Greeks".)

In sonnet XIV, I am in no way concerned with, or distressed by the plight of Ixion, who because he has been impulsive enough to commit the act of fornication with a goddess, who was not his wife, was chained hand and feet to a wheel: his torture does not interest me. I am concerned in this sonnet, with the attacks of the several gods, not against each other, but against Man, in an effort either to destroy him entirely or at least to subdue his proud spirit, a thing which, as this sonnet declares, the gods with all their force and all the weapons and disguises at their disposal are quite unable to do.—At the end of this sonnet Man does succumb, but not before the onslaught of all the might which the gods have been able to bring to bear against him; Man gives up, as the last phrase of this sonnet states:

"Before the unkindness in his brother's eyes."

As when I said Aldebaran, I meant Aldebaran, as when I wrote

Capella, I meant Capella and no other star, so when I wrote:
                "Whirling Aeolus on his awful wheel"
I meant Aeolus, not Ixion (nor for the matter of that Catherine) I
meant the god of the Winds Aeolus, who has under his control all winds
from the lightest Zephyr, to the most frightful typhoon and that the
god of the winds has launched in vain against mankind a terrific whirl-
wind. After all the line does begin: "Nor whirling Aeolus".—

Now if you say you saw a man on a motorcycle, you mean that
the man was riding and directing that motorcycle, you do not mean
that he was bound hand and feet to the wheels of it.—Your friend being
acquainted with these myths, when he looked at the sonnet, saw at once
words which were familiar to him and after that cared for nothing else:
if I speak of someone whirling on his awful wheel, I must of course to
his mind mean Ixion, although the sonnet in that case would have no
sense of any kind whatever.

I would not, if I were you, in the future, pay much attention to
any suggestion made to you by this acquaintance of yours on the
subject of poetry, for which, it would seem, he really cares little, and
concerning which, even more seriously, he knows even less. He is not,
in any case, a thorough going student: he is a pouncer upon details, and
his scholarship—if indeed it exist at all—is bumpy and uneven.

Sincerely yours, and with every good wish for the New Year,

Edna St. Vincent Millay

243   TO PROFESSOR HERBERT C. LIPSCOMB

Steepletop, Austerlitz, N.Y.
January 17th 1946

Dear Dr. Lipscomb:

. . . there is practically nothing under the sun or moon which I
would not rather do than write a letter, (and in particular begin it; I
don't mind it so much after I have really made a start: Gerard Hopkins
felt much the same way; so I read in one of his letters to somebody)
than write any letter to any person whatsoever on earth: I would
rather wash dishes all day; I would rather do a big washing on an old-
fashioned scrubbing board; I would rather lay a pipe-line; I would
rather dig a grave. The reason I never write a letter to anybody, is not,
as you might think, that as a child my nurse stabbed me with a pen, or
that my typing is verminous—no; as for pens, I use them rather often

in my own work, and my typing is usually pretty good. But enough of that . . . much too much.

The only reason I *ever* write a letter to anybody is out of desperation, a fear that some person, whose friendship I esteem and cherish, not understanding my continued silence, may become lost to me.

* * *

I have just finished learning by heart the beautiful "Si qua recordanti".[1] I can't imagine why I never learned it by heart before. I think it the most beautiful short poem in any language I know. The Iliad is the most beautiful long poem!

My earnest friendly greetings to you,

Edna St. Vincent Millay

[1] The 76th Lyric of Catullus.

244 TO EDMUND WILSON

Steepletop [Austerlitz, N.Y.]
[August, 1946]

Dear Bunny:

It is two years now since I received your letter. You had bad news to tell me: the death of John Bishop.[2] Even now, that seems unlikely. How you must have missed him that summer, and how you still must miss him, is something that I would rather not go into in my mind. For it would make me ache, only to think of it. And I don't like aching, any more than anybody else.

You told me also, in that letter, that you liked my recorded readings from my poems. That pleased me enormously. I had felt pretty sure, myself, that they were good. But your verdict was like an Imprimatur to me.[3]

Your letter reached me at a time when I was very ill indeed, in the Doctors' Hospital in New York. I was enjoying there a very handsome —and, as I afterwards was told, an all but life-size—nervous breakdown. For five years I had been writing almost nothing but propaganda. And I can tell you from my own experience, that there is nothing on this earth which can so much get on the nerves of a good poet, as the writing of bad poetry. Anyway, finally, I cracked up under it. I was in the hospital a long time.

This does not explain, of course, why, when I got out and came home, after I got well and strong again, still I did not write you. But here, happily for me, and for you, I can save ourselves the cumbersome explaining, by reminding you of a letter of Gerard Hopkins. In this letter he makes apology—I forget to whom; possibly to Robert Bridges, although, somehow, I think not—for having been so slow in answering. And he states—not in these words at all, but this is the meaning of it—: that the driving of himself by himself to make the beginning of a letter, is almost more than his strength can support. When once he has forced himself to begin the letter, he says, the going is not so bad. Well, I, too, suffer from that disease. For it is a disease. It is as real, and its outlines are quite as clear, as in a case of claustrophobia, or agoraphobia. I have named it, just in order to comfort myself, and to dignify this pitiful horror with a name, epistolaphobia. I say, "I, too, suffer from that disease." But I think I have it very much worse than he had. For after all, he did write many letters. And I don't. It is sheer desperation and pure panic—lest, through my continued silence, I lose your friendship, which I prize—that whips me to the typewriter now. I don't know where you are. But I think, and I think it often, "Where ever he is, there he still is, and perhaps some day I shall see him again, and we shall talk about poetry, as we used to do."

I have just finished learning by heart Matthew Arnold's "Scholar Gypsy",—such a lovely poem. I had wanted for years to know it by heart, but it had always looked a bit long to me. It is not at all difficult, however, to learn by heart, stanza by stanza; it is so reasonable. I have also learned by heart "The Eve of St. Agnes" and "Lamia". Lamia, let me tell you, is a very long poem. And Keats, in both these poems, makes it as tricky as possible for you, by shifting all the time from "thou" to "you", and by whisking you suddenly from the past tense into the present tense. To get these passages into your memory, and exact, is really quite a chore. I have learned by heart, of Shelley, not only "To the West Wind"—and surely the second stanza of that poem is as fine a thing as ever was written in English—but also the "Hymn to Intellectual Beauty"— a devil to learn by heart. Anyway, I have them all now. And what evil thing can ever again even brush me with its wings?

With love, as ever,
Edna.

Bunny: I am sending you, here-enclosed, three new poems of my own.[4] I hope, of course I hope very much, that you will like them, but don't— oh, for God's sake, don't for one moment—feel that you must write me something about them, or, indeed, in any way acknowledge this letter at all. I would not put so great a burden upon the shoulders and upon the brain of the person that in all the world I hated the most. I do not need your answer. I am happy enough as it is. For I have at last, after two years of recurring spiritual torment, been able to flog myself into writing a very simple letter to a dear and trusted friend.

E.

I forgot to tell you, even though I was speaking of Father Hopkins, that I have also learned by heart at least one third of his published poetry. Have you ever tried to learn him by heart?—It is great fun, very exciting, difficult.

[2] John Peale Bishop died on April 4, 1944.
[3] In April and August of 1941, the poet recorded for RCA Victor a group of her poems which were issued on four records and are sold in an album. The poems are: "Renascence," on three sides of two records; "The Ballad of the Harp-Weaver," one side; "Recuerdo," "Biologically Speaking," "Portrait by a Neighbor," from *A Few Figs and Thistles;* "Elegy" and "Travel" from *Second April;* "To Pao-Chin" and "The Anguish" from *The Buck in the Snow;* Sonnets 2, 11, 30, 33, 52, from *Fatal Interview;* "Childhood is the Kingdom" and "Where can the heart be hidden" (one of the two sonnets written in memory of Sacco and Vanzetti) from *Wine from These Grapes;* "I must not die of pity," and "The Maid of Orleans," from *Make Bright the Arrows.*
[4] "Ragged Island" (printed in the November issue of *Harper's Magazine*); sonnet: "Tranquility at length when autumn comes" (*Harper's Magazine*, April, 1947); "To a Snake" (*Atlantic Monthly*, August, 1947).

245   TO EUGEN JAN BOISSEVAIN

The House, Ragged Island
September [1947?]

Dear Ugin:

You have just gone down to the harbour again. It seems really only a moment since we both came up from the harbour, you drenched to the skin, I shining and excited almost to—what is the French word?—not "translution"—certainly not transport—what the hell is it?—anyway, watching it, at a safe distance until you called me to help you with the ropes (and what a silly knife you have, it doesn't cut at all, a sharp-edged stone would have done better—I could have done better with my teeth—but things that you do with your teeth, do things to your teeth in return—

Darling, come up from the harbour—the sea is making—at least it looks so, and anyway the wind is coming up N.W. by N.—I think—I don't know.

Don't go out, please.

We have everything here. There's no need to tackle it.

Alexander said this morning, when he put into our harbour, because his engine was on the bum—"If I'd heard the radio this morning, I'd never have come out,—I'm not going to haul my traps—not off this island—I'm just going to leave 'em—& put for home."

> Meen Liefje:
>
> Ik gaar naar top-side.
>
> Misschien slaap ik.
> Misschien niet.
>
> Oy sey nooit t'huis.

> [Dearest:
>
> I'm going top-side,
> Maybe I'll sleep.
> Maybe not.
> You are never home.]

246   TO CASS CANFIELD

Steepletop [Austerlitz, N.Y.]
October, 1947

Dear Cass:

First of all, I want to thank you for your kind and thoughtful letter of last spring. I took you at your word, at the time, and did not write to thank you then. But I was deeply touched, and very grateful, and I still am. I admire you, too, for the easy manner in which you led me round that really muddy puddle, without letting me get splashed at all: it was chic, what you did.

———

As to your proposition that Harper's publish my Collected Dramatic Works, I am afraid I must disappoint you here, although I hate most dreadfully to do so. The fact is, I have too much pride and too much faith in myself as a dramatist, to permit the publication in one volume of seven dramatic works of mine, of which only three—*Two Slatterns and a King; The Princess Marries the Page;* and *Aria da Capo,* are good plays, and only one of these, *Aria da Capo*, of any significance.

Two Slatterns and a King does exactly what it sets out to do. It is very light and slender, but it is carefully constructed, and plays well.

The Princess Marries the Page is romantic and sentimental. This, too, is well constructed. It is easy to act, and pretty to watch and listen to. It is a good little play, but of no importance.

Aria da Capo, of course, is something else entirely. It has its imperfections, but they are not heavy enough to drag it down. A person reading it might think it too complicated for the stage, but he would be mistaken. It was written for the theatre, and on the stage all its intricacies move into place in a clear and terrible pattern: to see it well played is an unforgettable experience. (*Aria da Capo* is being played all the time, in little theatres, colleges, high schools, clubs, all over this country and Great Britain, and in other countries. I saw it a few years ago in Paris, done in French, of course. If you ever get a chance to see it, please go. You will be astonished at the power of it, when, actually seen before your eyes, as it was meant to be seen. Eugen, when he first read Aria da Capo, said, "I understand that this play is a great success on the stage, but I find that hard to believe. If I were a producer, I wouldn't touch it." But one night he saw it played. It was at Avon Old Farms; the young boys of the school were giving a performance of it as their Christmas play. He was very deeply moved, as was everybody else in the audience. You have no idea how good this play is, until you see it on the stage. I hope you will see it someday.)

Well, as you have gathered, I am very proud of *Aria da Capo*. I wish I had a dozen more, not like it, but as good. *Then* we could bring out a book!

The King's Henchman is a bad play. It was written in the first place as the libretto for an opera. Later, I tried to make it into a play. But it was hopelessly contaminated. It smells of libretto; and has other grave faults as well. This is a pity. For some of my very best poetry is to be found in *The King's Henchman*,—to be found, that is, by a reader tough enough to struggle through acres of ostentatious and pedantic drivel in order to get to it.

The Lamp and the Bell was written as an occasional piece, and shows it. It was written to be played at Vassar, on the fiftieth anniversary (I think) of the founding of the college. It was written to be played by girls, and shows it. This play is well constructed. It is not, like *The King's Henchman*, diffuse, crowded with detail, and verbose (verbose in Anglo-Saxon!) But whereas *The King's Henchman*, considered not as drama but as dramatic poetry, is often full and rich, the blank verse of *The Lamp and the Bell* seldom rises above the merely competent. Five acts of uninspired writing, with only here and there a line, or two or three lines at most, to light up the page—and by no means every page—this is not good enough.

The Murder of Lidice, of course, was and is, merely propaganda.[5] I tried to make it as good as I could in the time I had. It has some good lines, but not very many, and not very good. This piece should be allowed to die along with the war which provoked it. I only hope its death will not be so lingering as that of the war itself.

Conversation at Midnight is an interesting book: I like it. But the published version is not nearly so good as the original manuscript, which was destroyed by fire. I was able to remember the greater part of it, but there were many passages which I had to re-invent, and others which I was forced to leave out entirely, so that the result is patchy and jerky. However, if I had a half dozen or more really high-class plays to be printed in a collection, I might wish to add *Conversation at Midnight* to the group. I don't know. It is not really a play, and might suffer in the reading, if the reader were tacitly instructed to consider it as a play.

We are left with only *Aria da Capo*, one really good, serious play, and two other one-act plays, both skilfully wrought, but both inconsequential. We have nothing to work with. We have no book.

I am very sorry to have to disappoint you. Naturally, Harper's wants, and needs, to bring out another book by me. But it will do no good to me, or to Harper's, when I bring out a book of new lyrics, good lyrics, to have this book preceded by a book of bad plays.

I am writing. I have not many poems finished, but those that I have are good. The effect of writing so much propaganda during the war—from the point of view of poetry, sloppy, garrulous and unintegrated—is to make me more careful and critical of my work even than formerly I was, so that now I write more slowly than ever. But there will be a book. I am afraid even to suggest a possible date, lest I be caught again in that paralyzing nightmare of writing against time, which I so often experienced when writing for the radio during the war. If Harper's can be patient with me still, there will be a book.

Sincerely,
Edna.

[5] On June 10, 1942, the Nazi government announced to the world that it had razed the tiny village of Lidice in Czechoslovakia, killed every man and fifty-two women, driven the remaining women off to concentration camps and herded the

children into "educational institutions." Two days later in America, the Writers' War Board asked Edna St. Vincent Millay to immortalize this martyred village in a poem. She responded with a long verse-narrative work. This was dramatized and, with a distinguished cast and music specially composed, was broadcast by the National Broadcasting Company to American listeners on the evening of October 19. At the same time Spanish and Portuguese translations were broadcast to South America. It was also short-waved to England and other countries. Among the millions who heard this work over the airwaves was Dr. Eduard Beneš, President of the Republic of Czechoslovakia, who wrote the poet to tell her how moved he had been.

The work in its original version, "one of the finest pieces of true propaganda to come out of the war," according to the Writers' War Board, was published in pamphlet form by Harper & Brothers to coincide with the international broadcasting of the radio version.

247 TO FRANK CROWNINSHIELD

Steepletop, Austerlitz, N.Y.
December 20, 1947

Dearest Crowny:

You will have decided by now and at last that I am a dreadful person. And I dare say I am, in more ways than one. But not in the way you have decided I am. For, the reason why I did not see you at Steepletop this summer, is that I was not at Steepletop myself. I did not get your telegram until we returned from our island, Ragged Island in Casco Bay, where we spent the summer, and where for a time it looked as if we should have to spend the winter as well. We had stayed on there much later than usual, and got caught in the autumn storms, the sea becoming so rough that it was impossible to cross the four miles of open water to the mainland. There is a well on the island, and luckily we had plenty of provisions, and the surf of course was magnificent, so we had great fun. But we didn't get back to Steepletop until darned near time to slide the Thanksgiving turkey into the oven.

Of course, I should have written you at once, and if I had had a secretary I would have done so—the secretary to attend to business while I fooled around with you. Indeed, if I had a secretary, I would do a great many things at once which now I never do at once and often do never. It is not that life is so complicated, it is that it is so unmanageably simple.

Anyway, I still love you, even if you do hate me, and I wish you A Happy New Year.

And I wish myself a happy new year, too,—a year in which I shall see you and talk with you.

Edna.

248   TO DR. ALBERT F. BLAKESLEE[6]

Steepletop, Austerlitz, N.Y.
December 20, 1947

My dear Mr. Blakeslee:

The Thorn Apple of my poem is the purple thorn apple, the Datura Tatula, not the Datura Stramonium. I may quite possibly have seen it in England, and have learned the name Thorn Apple. However, the one time I *know* I saw it—and smelled it! for the revolting smell of it made me very ill, and was one of the most distressing experiences of my childhood—was when I was very young, and therefore must have been in Maine, where I was born, or in Massachusetts, where we lived for a time when I was nine.

I am almost certain it was in Massachusetts (at Ring's Island, near Newburyport). I remember that I was wandering about alone, as I usually did, when I came upon this flower. It was growing in a barren, naked stretch of ground, not very far from the sea (a few miles from the sea, possibly, but I think nearer). I saw it from far away; it was the only flower growing anywhere about, and there was no grass there, either—I remember a yellowish-brown, dry, hard earth—and I ran up to it, it looked so beautiful. And then I smelled it. Perhaps to my grown-up nostrils the odour of this flower would be less offensive, although I doubt this, as my sense of smell is very keen, but at the time, the experience of smelling it was so shocking and revolting that when I got away from the plant feeling very ill, it seemed to me that I myself had been made in some way indecent and unclean by what had happened to me, and I was so ashamed that I had been so close to such a horrible thing that I never mentioned the incident to anybody, and so, of course, did not learn the name of the plant at that time. Perhaps I learned the name of it in England, perhaps from a flower book. It is a pity to call it Jimson Weed.

Sincerely yours,
Edna St. Vincent Millay

[6] Director of the Smith College Genetics Experiment Station,

who had written Miss Millay after having read her poem
"In the Grave No Flower," where she speaks of
> ". . . the rank smelling
> Thorn-apple,—and who
> Would plant this by his dwelling?"

Dr. Blakeslee had been working with the *Datura stramonium*,
"the very best plant with which to discover principles of
heredity," and did not agree with the poet's adjective. He
was also interested in her use of the term "thorn apple," he
using the common name applied to the plant in this country—
Jimson Weed.

249   TO BASIL O'CONNOR[7]

Steepletop, Austerlitz, N.Y.
January 14th, 1948

Dear Mr. O'Connor:

I cannot describe to you with what a sense of shock and dismay
this morning, I came, quite by accident, upon your letter of November
4th, still unanswered.

Most of the letters I receive remain, and must remain, unanswered.
For I have no secretary, and I have no servants, and if I spend such
leisure as I have in writing letters, obviously I shall write nothing else.

There is one kind of letter, however, which I try always to answer,
and answer promptly. It is a letter in which some responsible person,
or group of persons, asks me to do something for a specific occasion:
read a poem; write a poem; be a judge of poems entered in a poetry
contest. Though the requests are different, all these letters have one
thing in common: that if I do not reply within a short time the writer
of the letter is left in a predicament, wondering just how long it takes
this particular poet to answer a letter, wondering just when he may
properly turn to another poet for help. Since I am by nature neither
uncivil nor inconsiderate, this kind of letter I do usually manage to
answer.

Yet, had I received your letter in time—or, rather, had it not been
mislaid and had I read it in time—I should have felt obliged to write
you that, as much as I should like to write the poem you wanted, I
could not undertake to do it. There is something about the writing of
a poem for an occasion, and the consciousness that a definite time-limit
to the exercise of one's imagination and one's self-criticism has been
imposed, which paralyses all my creative powers except one—the tech-
nical ability, the skill of the artisan, which every writer who has written

for many years, at length acquires. I could, of course, have produced a competent piece; but it would not have been good enough.

There are writers, I know, who are stimulated and impelled forward—not oppressed and inhibited, as I am—by the consciousness of a time-limit and of an occasion. I hope that some other poet has been able to write, for the birthday of The President, a fine and moving thing. The whole world misses him so much.

I speak of him still, I see, as "The President". I realize that I always do. I still think of him as The President; and I shall continue to do so, I suppose, for a long time to come, no matter who, in his absence, in his regrettably enforced absence, may preside,—taking his place, not filling it.

The imprint of so powerful a personality is not a mere mark made by a casual pressure, gradually fading, once the pressure is removed; it is more in the nature of an intaglio, cut into the mind.

I am more sorry than I can say for the inconvenience I have caused you, and for the embarrassment, and—most of all, in a time when we should spare each other all the nervous strain we can—for the exasperation.

Sincerely yours,
Edna St. Vincent Millay.

[7] President of the Franklin D. Roosevelt Birthday Memorial Committee.

250   TO MAX EASTMAN

Steepletop, Austerlitz, N.Y.
[January 28th, 1948]

Dear Max:

Enclosed is my letter stating why I must decline to serve on the Board of Chancellors of the Academy of American Poets, Incorporated.[8]

Please excuse *errata et alia*. (Since reading the legal documents which Mrs. Bullock sent me, I catch myself ever so often lapsing into Latin, my native brogue.)

So far, I have typed only three of my eleven letters, and already I have neuritis, bursitis, arthritis, and encephalitis. Now there I go, babbling in Greek, instead! (It's just a touch of my old schizophrenia.)

I also have double curvature of the spine and a bad squint.

Forgive my silliness. It is four o'clock in the morning, and I am hilarious with fatigue.

The enclosed letter itself, as you will see, is not a joke.

My love to you, and to Eliena. Please tell her that I want very much to write her about her completely charming libretto, and about the newspaper cutting which she sent. Tell her that I will do so as soon as my Russian comes back to me: at the moment I am in a bad state of aphasia *in re* my Russian.

Edna.

[8] For a copy of the communication sent to all the Chancellors of the Academy of American Poets (of which this to Max Eastman was the covering letter) see the second letter to Mrs. Hugh Bullock, President of the Academy.

251   TO MRS. HUGH BULLOCK

Steepletop, Austerlitz, N.Y.
February 2nd, 1948

Dear Mrs. Bullock:

I cannot tell you with what distress I write you this letter. The letter will seem to you to be late in reaching you, I know. But that is not because I have been careless, or unthinking as to your natural eagerness to learn my decision, in order that the Board of Chancellors, should I decline to serve as one of them, might elect as soon as possible someone to take my place.

Indeed, I have been uncomfortably aware, during the past few days, that you must be looking for a letter from me in every post.

But my decision was not a decision which might be made in haste. I had to read, to re-read, to study with much care all the legal documents you sent me. And then I had to think the matter over, having regard for every aspect of it that I could see. And, when my decision was made, I had to write a letter which should justify it, if possible, in the consideration of the chancellors who had elected me. For I would not have it appear that I could take lightly so grave a matter as to refuse to serve on this board.

I think I know something of what this project means to you. But I wish you had not, in your earnestness, got yourself all embroiled with a firm of lawyers who in their bossy dustiness have made it so difficult for you to do the beautiful thing you want to do.

This is only my opinion, of course. And it is a fagged and four-o'clock-in-the-morning opinion.

I had not intended, when I wrote the enclosed letter, to send it to you. It will seem very harsh, I am afraid, and I do not mean to be unkind.

It was written for the Board of Chancellors, to which, since it is this board which has elected me, I must present, as clearly and as forcefully as possible, my reasons for declining to serve.

But it seems to me now that I should make a copy of this letter for you.

Can you not, in some way, persuade the Board of Directors to bestir themselves, repeal a few articles, drop a few lawyers out of a few high office windows, do something to make more simple and more acceptable this marvellous and shocking award.

Sincerely yours,
Edna St. Vincent Millay.

252   TO MRS. HUGH BULLOCK

Steepletop, Austerlitz, N.Y.
February 2nd, 1948

(Dear Mrs. Bullock: This is my letter to the chancellors)

Since it is a serious thing for a poet to refuse to help another poet when he is in need of help, I am writing this letter to the Board of Chancellors of The Academy of American Poets, setting forth my reasons for declining to serve on this board, to which with such warm pleasure I learned that I had been elected. I am sending this letter to each of the chancellors.

The By-Laws of The Academy of American Poets, Incorporated, are not in themselves, of course, any business of mine. Nor is its Certificate of Incorporation. Since, however, my decision that I must decline to serve on its Board of Chancellors is based upon my objection to Article VII of its By-Laws as combined with the sections numbered *Second* and *Eighth* of its Certificate, I feel that I have the right to discuss these documents as critically as may be necessary in order to explain my action, and defend a position which badly needs defending.

The passages I mention are quoted below, for your convenience and my own. I have underlined certain parts of them.

BY-LAWS—ARTICLE VII

"1. Every fellow of the corporation elected by the chancellors to receive a fellowship shall, at least three (3) times during the year of his fellowship and each time within thirty (30) days prior to the time fixed for the payment of his next quarterly installment of the stipend, communicate with the Secretary of the corporation in writing as to the general nature of his activities in connection with the purposes of the fellowship.—"

CERTIFICATE OF INCORPORATION

"*Second:* The purposes for which the corporation is formed are: To provide fellowships for American *poets of proven merit* through the creation of a trust fund for the purpose, with a view to fostering the production of poetry through suitable *rewards for poetic achievement* as well as enabling individual poets of inadequate pecuniary means to devote themselves to poetic production;

"*Eighth:* The following persons shall be eligible for fellowships: *poets of proven merit,* either natural born or naturalized American citizens, not possessed of a regular income in excess of five thousand dollars (5,000) lawful money of the United States of America, per annum. *No holder of a fellowship shall engage in any gainful occupation for the whole or any part of his time other than such occupation as may be approved by a majority of the chancellors of the corporation as not incompatible with poetic production.*"

The impulse of any artist to help another artist who is in distress, is natural, and the satisfaction experienced when he feels that he has done this, is great. Therefore, and since your chief duty as a chancellor of this board is to determine whether or not a poet is worthy of the fellowship, you may not have inquired as closely as I have done into the matter of whether or not the fellowship is worthy of the poet. For I am one of those people who read with dark and heavy suspicion all contracts, deeds, affidavits, insurance policies and driving licences. And I have looked this wooden gift-horse in the mouth.

It is not what it appears to be.

It is not, as stated in the leaflet entitled "The Academy of American Poets", an award "made for a term of one year"—"carrying a stipend of $5,000." It is in fact, as a study of Article VII of its By-Laws will show, an award made for a term of only three months, carrying a stipend of only one quarter of the amount stated. If the distinguished person who has gratefully accepted this award (and he must, according to the second section of the Certificate of Incorporation, in order to be even eligible for consideration as a possible recipient of this award, be a "poet of proven merit")—if this distinguished person does not "at least three (3) times", and at stipulated intervals, during what is referred to as "the year of fellowship", apply for that very fellowship of which he is said to be a fellow, then the fellowship and the stipend which it carries are revoked. Three times, "at least three (3) times" during "the year of his fellowship" this "poet of proven merit" must "communicate with the Secretary of the corporation in writing as to the general nature of his activities in connection with the purposes of the fellowship." Here is no "reward for poetic achievement". This poet must sing for his supper. The pen with which he has written poetry of conspicuous merit, must now be employed in writing letters to a secretary of a corporation, explaining "the general nature of his activities".

Is this mature artist being treated as if he were a talented child of undeveloped capacities? No. He is being treated worse than that. For this is not the sum of his onerous and humiliating obligations. Not only three times during the year, but every day of the year, during "the year of his fellowship", he must be circumspect that he engage himself in no "gainful occupation" "for the whole or any part of his time", which might, in the opinion of a board of judges, be "incompatible with poetic production." In return for his freedom, his freedom from poverty, this "poet of proven merit" must conduct himself, throughout the period of his fellowship, precisely as if he were a prisoner on parole.

My reasons for declining to serve on such a board as this, assembled for the purpose of trying to help poets who are in need of help, must be in my own opinion not only adequate: they must be strong. Five thousand dollars is a lot of money.

But pottage is pottage, even when it is five thousand dollars' worth of pottage. And I can have no part in seducing any poet into accepting this award, under these conditions.

I think of what Shelley said, in "An Exhortation":

> "Yet dare not stain with wealth or power
> A poet's free and heavenly mind.
> ....
> Spirits from beyond the moon,
> Oh, refuse the boon!"

Sincerely yours,
Edna St. Vincent Millay

The By-Laws were amended, April 22, 1948, and Article VII omitted. The Certificate of Incorporation was amended on January 10, 1949 and now reads: "Eight: The following persons shall be eligible for fellowships: poets of proven merit, either natural born or naturalized American citizens, not engaged in any gainful occupation incompatible with poetic production."

In 1949 The Academy of American Poets voted to award Miss Millay a fellowship with its accompanying stipend of $5,000. She, however, refused the boon—despite the long-distance telephonic insistence of her friend, Chancellor Max Eastman, who explained that the above changes had been made.

253   TO CASS CANFIELD

Steepletop, Austerlitz, N.Y.
May 10th, 1948

Dear Cass:

Enclosed is a copy of my letter to Arthur Rushmore, in reply to his of several weeks ago. I cannot do what he suggests. So, once again, Harper's makes me a proposition which I must turn down. I feel very bad about it, always turning you down.

*   *   *

I think it only fair to tell you, fair to my publishers and to myself, that if only you and Rushmore and all the rest of you nice people down there at Harper's, would just for a little while stop nagging me, I might be able to get some work done. It is perfectly natural and understandable that you should try to think up schemes for making people buy more of my books,—new combinations, new material combined with old, etc. I do not blame you; I sympathize fully. But on the other hand it is a fact, that you harass me so, you run me so ragged, with your one proposition after another, propositions which, more often than not, I feel unhappily obliged to turn down, that you destroy all my serenity of mind. And surely this is unwise: you do not get anywhere; and you impede me. If you really want a book from me, why not stop worrying me for a while, and give me a chance to write it?

On which genial and diplomatic note, I close.

Trusting, however, in closing, that for one year more it may be said of me by Harper & Brothers, that although I reject their proposals, I welcome their advances.

Sincerely,
Edna.

254   TO ARTHUR RUSHMORE

Steepletop, Austerlitz, N.Y.
May 10th, 1948

Dear Mr. Rushmore:

As a result, perhaps, of the recent making-public of Max Eastman's to-the-minds-of-some-better-kept-private affairs, is not the venerable firm of Harper & Brothers running just a few degrees of fever?

If so, it is a fever to whose contagion I am immune. Your proposition, that Harper's bring out a volume of "The Love Poems of Edna St. Vincent Millay", containing a "mellow *Foreword in retrospect*" written by their author, in which foreword she confides to the public "when, where, and *under what impulsion*" (the italics are mine) these poems were written, leaves me strangely cold.

(I did get a grin out of it, though. Pretty hard put to it, weren't you, dearie, to say it with flowers, and yet say it?)

Of course, you have no possible way of knowing how very reticent a person I am, since I am far too reticent ever to have told you. You might, however, just by accident, have come across the knowledge that I am the only poet in America (at least, I believe this to be true) who consistently and in all circumstances refuses to make in print any statement whatever regarding any poem whatever that she has published. In all the years during which my poetry has been in print, there has been, I think, only one exception to this rule, and that of little importance, except that even so, naturally, I regret it. My discussion of the sonnet printed in my foreword to the Collected Sonnets does not count, of course, since this piece was merely a juvenile exercise in sonnet form, something which obviously I did not take seriously as a poem, for I had never published it.

A glance, for instance, at the anthology entitled "This is My Best",[9] would show you that it was not I, but William Rose Benét, who made the selection from among my poems which this book contains, and who wrote the accompanying comments. I refused to have anything to do with the project.

You state that, in your opinion, such a book as you describe would "make new readers" for me. I do not doubt it. People who never in all their lives, except when in school and under compulsion, have held a book of poems in their hands, might well be attracted by the erotic autobiography of a fairly conspicuous woman, even though she did write poetry. The indubitable fact that, even as I was winning my new readers, I should be losing entirely the good esteem of the more sensitive and by me the most valued, of the readers I already have, does not seem to have occurred to you.

"It would make a lovely book", you say. In so far as your own part in it was concerned, it would, I know. But even you, with all your exquisite skill, could not make charming the indelicacy of such a fore-word as you suggest.

I am not saying, and of course not implying, that you yourself are insensitive: I know the opposite to be the fact. Nor do I mean to say that indelicacy is less shocking to you than it is to me. It is simply that your enthusiasm over the proposed volume from the point of view of format, paper, cover, size, etc., has pushed other aspects of the book from your mind, and you have never really once quietly considered just what it is that you are asking me to do. Is not this the truth, my friend?

Sincerely,

[no signature]

> [9] Edited by Whit Burnett, Dial Press, 1942, *This Is My Best* contained fifteen sonnets by Edna St. Vincent Millay, selected and introduced by William Rose Benét.

255   TO AUSTIN PERLOW[10]

Steepletop, Austerlitz, N.Y.

June 18th, 1948

Dear Mr. Perlow:

I should have written you long ago to thank you for the delightful album, but spring is a busy season for us farmers; and a spring like this one, so consistently rainy and cold, leaves us even fewer hours of leisure than in more normal years,—we have to spend so much time cussin'.

Much of the pleasure which the album has given me, you can well imagine. But there are three photographs in particular—and although you might guess which ones they are, I think you could not possibly know, since Norma does not know—which have given me a very special happiness. I will tell you about that presently.

But first I want to tell you this: quite apart from the significance to me of every picture in this book, I am more deeply touched than I can say by the fact that you made the book for me. How many hours of thought and patient search and nice care went into the making of such an album, would be obvious at once to anyone who even glanced through it. But the thing which touched me the most—and "touched" is a pretty feeble word for it, since the truth is that it nearly made me cry—is the *kindness* which the book gives forth like a physical warmth, the strong well-wishing, the desire and the determination to give me pleasure.

Do you know that lovely sonnet of Gerard Hopkins which begins,
      "I remember a house where all were good
        To me—"?

I know the sonnet by heart, but I'll look it up anyway, for I couldn't bear to misquote it. (Misquote *it* or anything else, for that matter.)

IN THE VALLEY OF THE ELWY

I remember a house where all were good
  To me, God knows, deserving no such thing:
  Comforting smell breathed at very entering,
Fetched fresh, as I suppose, off some sweet wood.
That cordial air made those kind people a hood
    All over, as a bevy of eggs the mothering wing
    Will, or mild nights the new morsels of spring:
Why, it seemed of course; seemed of right it should.

Lovely the woods, waters, meadows, combes, vales,
All the air things wear that build this world of Wales;
  Only the inmate does not correspond:
God, lover of souls, swaying considerate scales,
Complete thy creature dear O where it fails,
  Being mighty a master, being a father and fond.

I quoted the sestet, too, because it drives me crazy when people quote only part of a sonnet. It is the octave, though, which I specially like, that and the last line of all; and it is the octave, of course, which your album makes me think of.

And now I will tell you about the three photographs. They are the photographs of the three houses where I lived in Camden, and they are the only pictures of these houses which I have.

If my childhood and girlhood had not been so extraordinarily happy, I could not, of course, study with such pure delight every aspect of these pictured houses; but the fortunate truth is, that I can and do. And one exciting memory after another fills my mind as I look.

I remember the nasturtiums, climbing ones, which grew every summer over the trellis of the porch at 80 Washington Street,—higher than the roof of the porch they always grew, and Mother was proud of this, and would make everybody who came there look at them and admit that this was so. She loved nasturtiums, the smell of the blossoms, and the velvety feel of them, and the rich colors. (And I do, too, and I still can't abide the double ones!) But I think most of all, perhaps, she loved the planting of them. For no matter how busy she was—and I suppose she was about as busy every minute of the time as it is possible for a person to be—she always planted them herself; and yet, the planting of nasturium seeds is a thing that could well be trusted to any fairly intelligent child: they sprout easily and grow well, no matter how you plant them; they are not poisonous to eat (though they are rather hot on the tongue, as I remember it,—anyway, we used to put them in pickles); and if you spill them you can easily find them to pick them up, for they are as big as gooseberries. What has happened to gooseberries, by the way? I know what has happened to ours here at Steepletop, and our currants, too: they have all been dug up and destroyed, because they are the host of the white pine blister rust, and our hills here are heavily wooded with white pine.

But some people's hills are wooded with red pine, and some with yellow, and still no gooseberries; I don't understand it. I wish I could see a gooseberry bush again; and an orchard, a very small one, of quince trees; and a russet apple tree. If I ever see a russet apple tree, I shall climb it. And with a book in my hand. Or, if I find that I must use both hands now when I climb an apple tree, then with a book in my mouth, like Fido bringing home the newspaper. And I shall sit in the tree for hours, hidden by the leaves, reading *Hero and Leander*, or *As You Like It*, or the *Essay on Man*.

Oh, don't you see what your enchanted album has done?

Why, this morning, I do not know at all whether the rain has really stopped and the sun is actually shining, or whether it is just my childhood that I see!

For, as Aethelwold says in *The King's Henchman*:

"Meseems it never rained in those days."

Sincerely yours,
Edna St. Vincent Millay

---

[10] A journalist and an admirer of the poet, who spent one of his vacations up in Maine taking photographs of various places where Miss Millay had lived during her childhood and adolescence, and of scenes identified with her poems.

256   TO NORMA MILLAY

Steepletop [Austerlitz, N.Y.]
March 2, 1949

Hunk:

Your little silver ring came on my birthday. I would have written you a letter at once in answer to that, except that I had done something queer to my shoulder—wrenched it, strained it, pulled a ligament—I don't know—one of those things you do when you are so busy doing something that you don't notice what else you're doing—and my shoulder hurt and I couldn't write. I can type only a few lines now, though I'm much better; but I must get some word to you. Not only about the ring, and all that it meant, all that the three rings meant, when the three of us were children—Sefe, Hunk and Wump, and so engraved (Oh, poor little Wumpty-Woons) I can't go on about that—I want to write you about your poem, that fine poem you sent me—later I will—but in the meantime, how many poems as good as that have you written? Get them together, in case you haven't, work over them in case you need to in some instances, write more, in case you haven't enough, bring out a book. There's no doubt at all that you have the talent, the imagination and the technique. Any publisher would publish the book, if this poem is a sample of its quality. So get on with it, and don't let anything stop you: you're good.

Love,
Sefe.

257   TO CASS CANFIELD

Steepletop, Austerlitz, N.Y.
6/22 '49

Dear Cass:

Must you do this to me—must you make me break down and cry, when I am so tired out from writing poetry that I am nearly killed, as it is?

I was astonished by your letter and deeply touched. I would never again have written asking for this loan—for it had become truly a loan: it could no longer be regarded as an advance on royalties, since no book by me, in so far as you could properly expect, after so long a silence, would ever be forthcoming. You must have known, after my letter of last year, that I would never ask for it again.

I accept, however, with gratitude, your offer, which I now truly may consider again an advance on royalties.[11]

I have been working very hard, all day and during a great portion of the night also, for, I think, about seven months. A few poems are finished to my satisfaction, but on others I am still at work. I cannot give you a date line. Please say nothing of this to anyone else at Harpers. If you did tell them that there might be a new book by me pretty soon, they might all go crawling about in my hair again, and I should start scratching my head with both hands, and no hand left to write with.

Quite apart from my new poetry of which I was speaking, I have been recently engaged in writing—after having read a thoughtful review by Lewis Gannett concerning a late book by T. S. Eliot,[12] and, more recently after reading the brilliant and truly witty, although sometimes I thought, in some ways overstressed articles by Robert Hillyer in the Saturday Review of Literature,[13] against the awarding of the Bollingen Award to Ezra Pound,—a satire in verse against T. S. Eliot. In this collection of poems, of which I think there will be about twenty . . . there is nothing coarse, obscene, as there sometimes is in the work of Auden and of Pound, and nothing so silly as the childish horsing around of Eliot, when he is trying to be funny. He has no sense of humour, and so he is not yet a true Englishman. There is, I think, in these poems of mine against Eliot nothing which could be considered abusive: they are merely murderous. I am enclosing copies of several of them, including the first one and the last one, which I should like you to see.

* * *

As I asked you before, do not speak of these poems to anybody at Harpers.

Come here some time. Steepletop would love to have you come here. We have no telephone any more, because we got sick and tired of its insistence and its inefficiency, so we up and yanked it out. But come anyway, if you are ever in Stockbridge or Lenox or anywhere about there. It is only a short drive and almost anybody can tell you how to find us. Just drive up.

I should like to see you and there are many things about which I should like to talk with you; for instance that marvellous book about Baudelaire, "The Midnight Gardener",[14] which you sent me about a year ago. When I saw the words on the truly fine dust-cover: "A novel about Baudelaire" I was afraid to pick it up, because I thought that nobody possibly could write a novel about Baudelaire, bringing him in as a moving and speaking character, in a way which would not greatly offend me. I took up the book finally and began to read it, because it seemed only fair, although I was unacquainted with the works of Max White, to give the book a chance, since you had thought it would interest me. I picked it up and I never once laid it down until I had finished it. I was enthralled by it. On every page and without ostentation, there was presented to me the very Baudelaire with whom I was so well acquainted. After reading the book, I felt not so much that I had been reading a book as that I had been sitting, quiet and unobserved, at a table in the Tabourey in Paris, and that at a table near me Baudelaire himself had been talking with his arrogant brilliance to Poulet-Malassis and Asselineau and to several others of his friends.

Thanks for sending me the books at Christmas. I have not yet read the book of Thornton Wilder:[15] it seemed when I started it very involved and I was busy writing at the time.

* * *

Affectionately,
Edna.

[11] In his reply to this letter Mr. Cass Canfield wrote: "I appreciate your kind words about the renewal of the monthly payments for another year, but you should realize that the continuing sales of your books make these payments possible without your being in debt to us. In other words, we are merely providing you with an accommodation and should not be given the credit for doing you any special favor!"

[12] *Notes Towards a Definition of Culture*, reviewed in the New York *Herald Tribune*, March 14, 1949.

[13] "Treason's Strange Fruit," and "Poetry's New Priesthood," *The Saturday Review of Literature*, June 11 and 18, 1949.

[14] By "Max White" (Charles William White), Harper & Brothers, 1948.

[15] *The Ides of March.*

258   TO ELLERY QUEEN[16]

[Steepletop, Austerlitz, N.Y.]
August 4, 1949

Dear Mr. Queen:

I know that is not your real name, but it is your real name as far as I am concerned.

I am sorry to have kept you waiting so long for an answer to your question. I should indeed be conscience-stricken—for I did promise you an answer—except that I have the best possible excuse, and one which you will understand: I have been working very hard, writing.

As to "The Murder in the Fishing Cat,"[17] I wrote it in Paris. I was sitting alone having lunch outdoors at just such a restaurant as I describe. I was not only alone at my table; there was nobody else at any table. I turned my head and saw over my left shoulder, and very near to me, just inside the window of the restaurant, a large glass tank containing water in which eels were swimming. I wished they were not there.

The rest was all imagination. Except, of course, that when you have lived in a place for a long time, you are able to describe things about it in a fairly accurate way.

The restaurant called "Le Chat qui Pêche"—at least, the only one I know—is in quite a different part of Paris from where I put it. I used that name because it seemed to make a good title for the story.

Sincerely yours,
Edna St. Vincent Millay

[16] Pseudonym of the mystery writers, Frederic Dannay and Manfred B. Lee.

[17] Reprinted in Ellery Queen's *Mystery Magazine*, May, 1950.

259 TO EDMUND WILSON

Steepletop, Austerlitz, N.Y.
[August 9, 1949]

Dear Bunny:

This is awful; but I can't see you; I can't see anybody on earth just now; I am working seventy-two hours a day; and I don't dare run the risk of being deflected.

This is an ironic and hateful thing: I have so often longed to talk with you. I shall feel very sad about this—and I know that I shall—as soon as I am able to feel anything at all beyond the periphery of my intense occupation.

I liked your longer poem; I liked it very much.[18] But don't use the word—if it is a word—"gals". Not even although it makes a fine Janus-faced rhyme for "slag". Don't do it. "Slag" is a fine word. "Gals" is cheap, common and indecent. Don't use it; don't for God's sake, use it, in a poem which has so much elegance.

Love,
Edna.

[18] "The Pickerel Pond: A Double Pastoral." Elegiacs, with amphisbaenic (backward-rhyming) endings. *Furioso*, winter number, 1949.

260　TO MANUEL MARIA MISCHOULON[19]

Steepletop, Austerlitz, N.Y.
August 10, 1949

My dear Mr. Mischoulon:

Yes, fortunately for me, I do read Spanish: otherwise I should have missed many hours of great enjoyment in my life.

I should have missed, for one thing, the pleasure of reading your excellent translations of three of my sonnets.

I, too, have had some experience with translating poems out of a foreign language which does not seem foreign at all when one is reading it, but which becomes difficult and at times impossible, when one tries to render it into another tongue. The only translations that I ever published were some English renderings (about thirty-five, I think) of Les Fleurs du Mal of Baudelaire. I, too, as you have done, kept the original metre, and kept as strictly as possible to the text. So I know how you must have sweated and swooned over these translations of my sonnets which you sent me: in most instances they are so exact that, quite apart from the lovely shout and savour of the line in Spanish, I am full of admiration for your skill, your zeal, and your talent.

I have several remarks to make; and one or two suggestions. I will consider your three translations one by one. And you, of course, will take into account the fact that my knowledge of Spanish is, although enthusiastic, very faulty.

In your translation of my sonnet beginning "Well, I have lost you," your first line could not be better—"limpiamente" is perfect—and in the second line I get a beautiful subtlety and ambiguity in the phrase "en propia ley": Perhaps it is an ordinary phrase, and you meant it to be very simple; but the mixed meaning of the word "ley" lifts it out of the law-courts into a different "law", a "law" which can mean fidelity, loyalty to an ideal—at least, so I think—and the word "propia", if the mind sees it suddenly not as an adjective but as a substantive, makes the whole phrase mean (mean in a sort of over-tone, that is) "I am relinquishing my property out of allegiance".

How lovely that "calido llanto" . . . I have always thought "llorar" such an expressive word. Do you know that wonderful poem of Ruben Dario: "O juventud, divino tesoro"? I am quoting it from memory, and I hope to heaven I am not misquoting it. I can't get the next line straight. But the next two lines go like this: "Cuando quiero llorar, no lloro; Y a veces lloro sin querer". I love his poetry; I hope I haven't got it wrong.

I must get back to work: so the rest of what I say will probably be jumbled. And it may sound severe: for the reason that it is severe. In the sonnet beginning "Bien, te perdi", you have no possible excuse for substituting, after "secaba", a full-stop, in place of my semi-colon. It is not the exigencies of translation which cause you to do this: it is some other reason, which I do not understand. Can't you see that in your version (and although it is perfectly permissible to translate "wing" as "canto") you give the impression that it is my own "canto" that I am setting free, and not—and this is what the whole poem is about—the wings of some other person? You must change your period after "secaba" to a colon. I used a semi-colon; but by changing "wing" to "canto", you incur an obligation to be even more explicit.

Is it impossible to say "y soy hombre" instead of "soy un hombre"? Unless there is some Spanish reason against this, it seems to me closer to the meaning, and not so startling.

Also, and this is very important, and you must answer it. I do not understand your use, in two of the three sonnets, of the word "mas", when I should have thought that "pero" would have been the correct word. The word "mas", in the last few years, may have broadened its meaning to the point where it may touch a shading of "pero"; I don't know a thing about that. But it seems to me that, classically at least, the proper translation of my "but"—and "yet" used in the sense of "but"—would be "pero"; and that you ruin in translation two of my three sonnets by saying "moreover", when what I said is "but" or "yet".

Also, you may not use the word "engano" in a sonnet which has in it not the slightest hint of "engano". This word defeats the whole translation. Can you not say "que al ser mas fiel, mas infiel soy, mi amada,"? or is that bad Spanish?

Your translations are so very good that I wish you would translate more of me some time. If I sound cranky and dictatorial, it is because I am very much interested, and feel as if I were having an argument with you.

Also—and this is the third and last "also" in this letter—I wish to goodness you would clean the type on your typewriter. A foreign language is hard enough to read, anyway, even for a person who thinks she understands it pretty well, without the *a*, the *c*, the *o* and the *s* looking exactly alike. An old toothbrush and a small saucer half-filled with petrol—the wonders they can do!—with, of course, a watchful and industrious supervision.

Good luck to you. Of course you may use the sonnets.

Sincerely yours,

Edna St. Vincent Millay

[19] An Argentine poet who had translated seven of Miss Millay's sonnets. The translations were later printed in a volume titled: *24 Sonetos Magistrales de le Lengua Inglesa*, published in the Argentine, October, 1950. Other sonnets were by Shakespeare, Spenser, Sydney, Christina Rossetti, Elizabeth Browning, W. S. Blunt, and Santayana.

Eugen Jan Boissevain died on August 30, 1949, at Deaconess Hospital, Boston, Massachusetts. His death was attributed to shock following a critical operation. He had learned of his condition suddenly, having suffered no apparent illness.

261   TO MRS. MARY V. HERRON[20]

Steepletop [Austerlitz, N.Y.]

Dear Mary:

Thank you for all your kindness. I don't know how I should have managed, without your help.

Yes, it must indeed seem impossible to you that he will not be coming down the hill to fetch the mail, this lovely autumn day.

He never comes up the hill, either, any more.

[20] Mrs. Herron, Postmistress of Austerlitz, friend of Miss Millay and Mr. Boissevain, aided the bereaved poet at this time by answering for her the many letters of sympathy.

262   TO CASS CANFIELD

Steepletop, Austerlitz, N.Y.

Nov. 21, 1949

Dear Cass:

I am terribly sorry to have kept you waiting so long. It was a tough assignment: if I had realized quite how tough, I should not have attempted it.[21]

I have felt so hurried all the time, knowing how impatient I was making everybody at Harper's, that it was very hard not to get too nervous to think straight. And then—and this was the toughest part of all—the realization, not constant, but intermittent, which made it worse, that I had no authority at all, except in two instances, to put into execution a single one of the revisions on which I was working with so ardent a zeal. (I suppose that when I get the proof of a manuscript into my hands, I just can't help it.)

If you ever again want me to look over something like this, let me have it while it is still in galley form: I shall not feel so hustled, and you will not feel so frantic.

Quite apart from the things in this Introduction to which I properly, as a person, can object: the too familiar (and, to the reader, puzzling) use of the name *"Vincent"* (too familiar for a formal piece of writing, I mean to say: Bill Benét has always called me Vincent, as did Elinor Wylie); and the bit of gossip beginning, "I think I know of whom", (which also would prove distracting to the reader, who would say to himself, "This might be juicy, if only I could squeeze it")— quite apart from the two changes I can insist upon—I hope that you will hold up the publication of the book until the Introduction can be whipped into shape and if not cleaned up, at least tidied up. If this is a sample of what Benét has been turning out lately, he must be accustomed to having his stuff cut and revised by editors.

As the piece stands, it must not come out under the Harper imprint. In so far as I am concerned, it does not matter much,—except that bad writing always makes me feel sick and embarrassed. I am responsible only for the poetry which follows. But Harper's is responsible for the Introduction, as a contractor is responsible for an insecure bridge built by workmen he himself has hired.

Sincerely,
Edna

[21] The Introduction written by William Rose Benét for an edition of *Second April* and *The Buck in the Snow*, which Harper & Brothers were bringing out in one volume in the Harper's Modern Classics series. After reading the four pages of critical notes on his Introduction enclosed with the above letter, Mr. Benét wrote Cass Canfield: "I think Vincent improved it . . . She's fitly a laurelled poet! God bless her! . . . My stuff's not sacrosanct—though I don't like my *poetry* changed!"

263 TO MARGARET CUTHBERT AND ALICE BLINN[22]

Steepletop, Austerlitz, N.Y.

December 10, 1949

Dear Margaret and Alice:

If you chaps are determined to give me a Christmas present, nothing I can say will stop you. Not that I want to stop you! Yet it does occur to me, and by no means for the first time, that for years and years and years the two of you have been so occupied in carefully selecting, efficiently dispatching or in person to me bearing, so many baskets and salvers heaped with varied and delightful gifts,—that the wonder is you can find time even to sign your letters.

However, if I *must* accept a Christmas present from you, I must. (Goody, goody, goody!)

———————————

Whatever you send me, though, please do not send either newspapers or magazines. There follows a list of those which I already receive: The Atlantic Monthly; Harper's Magazine; The Saturday Review of Literature; The Saturday Evening Post; The National Geographic; The New Leader; The Herb Grower; American Forests; The Audubon Magazine; the illustrated Bulletin of the Metropolitan Museum; The Rural New Yorker; The Chatham Courier; Punch; and The Herald Tribune.

Time was when I would read, or at least glance through, all of these. Now, except for The Herb Grower and the Museum Bulletin and Forests and the Audubon Magazine, I lug them all upstairs the moment they arrive, without even removing the wrappers, and leave them on the library floor in stacks, someday to be sent to Holland.

(It was a good scheme, kids,—darned cute. I'm too Out of Touch with People!—I ought to know What's Going On in the World!—it would Take Me Out of Myself! . . . Well, well, well. Too bad.)

(Don't mind my ragging, darlings. I love you very much.)

———————————

And now I'll tell you what I *should* like for Christmas:

a.—3 Typewriter Ribbons. (One for a Remington Portable; one for a full-size, mature but very well-preserved Underwood; and one for a before-the-war-before-the-war L. C. Smith, which is in the best condition and types the most distinguished script of them all.) Plain dark-blue or black. Very likely they all take the same size ribbon. (I don't use these three typewriters simultaneously, like three telephones on a desk. Each has its proper place and function: one is for business; one is for typing out poems to go into a loose-leaf notebook; and one is just for the hell of it.)

b.—6 Composition Books. (The kind that used to cost ten cents. (!)—I want them with stiff covers, so that I can pick one up and prop it against my knee and scribble in it, informal-like, and not have to precede my exertions by exerting myself to find a tin tray or a collection of Peter Arno to make it stay flat. I can buy Composition Books in Great Barrington, but they are all the *bendy* kind!—before I can write ten words the darned book is winding itself about my leg as if it were a bandage.)

Query: Does *a* plus *b* indicate creative cerebration on the part of the poetess? In a way, yes. I have set myself to curry and braid and polish by hand for the Fair (to saying nothing of the Market) some poems I was working on last year. But first I must get the burdocks out. And if there is anything more stimulating to such activity than a brand-new typewriter ribbon, it is a brand-new Composition Book. (With stiff covers.)

c.—(For the time when the battery gets weak and needs recharging.) Some Who-dun-its and Westerns, in the Pocket Book, Avon, Bantam, Penguin, Dell,—any of those editions. I think the ones I have mentioned are always unabridged. I don't like the ones that are cut "to speed up the action". These will have to be the very latest ones out; otherwise I shall have read them at least twice.

My sweets, I'd be ever so grateful for any one of the three items above. I don't want you to spend a lot of money on me; I just don't know the price of things. The typewriter ribbons are the most important. But they may be three dollars apiece, or more, by now,—in which case send nothing else. Oh, I should feel so rich, so reinforced, so sassy!—with a new ribbon on each of my three typewriters.

The degelation of the Home Freezer has been accomplished. (And thanks very much for the bulldozer and the elegant, elegant putty-knife.)

John helped me for a while. But it is, of course, pretty hard work for a hired man. So when John staggered out and collapsed in the middle of the kitchen floor, I scooped up the shovel from his hand, dashed a bucket of frost in his face, and finished the job alone.

(It is well to wear gloves, I found.)

Heavens, what an interminable letter!

Love, quickly,
Edna

(P.S.—wouldn't you know?) I am renewing my subscription to the Herald Tribune: all the pine-cones are deep under snow. (Modern poem.)

---

[22] Respectively, Director of Public Affairs Programs for the National Broadcasting Company, and an associate Editor of the *Ladies' Home Journal.*

---

264   TO MANUEL MARIA MISCHOULON

Steepletop, Austerlitz, N.Y.
Dec. 10th, 1949

Dear Mr. Mischoulon:

You feared that I might be ill. I am far worse than ill. My husband has died.

I cannot write about it, nor about anything else. And I cannot answer questions. But I wanted to get some word to you, you were so distressed by my silence.

The books came, early in November. I have not yet been able to read them. But I thank you very much.

Good luck to you.

Sincerely,
Edna St. Vincent Millay

("Miss Edna")

---

265 TO NORMA MILLAY

Steepletop, Austerlitz, N.Y.
January 27th, 1950

My darling little Sister and 'Loved:

I wanted to write you the minute I got Charlie's letter, but all I had time for then was the telegram, which I do hope you received. I have been so bedeviled with taxes to make out and bills to pay—and having not the faintest idea where to look for the necessary documents, so that I can check up on things—that what with stuffing myself with all the best proteins and taking my stinking vitamine capsules and my loathsome Liver-Iron-and Red Bone Marrow Extract, I haven't had a minute for my Brave Big Girl of a Little Normie.

You know very well, of course, even without my writing, how happy I am for you and for Charlie and for myself, and for all the people who love you, that you are making such a splendid recovery from such a very serious operation. Still, a letter saying that, is more fun than just sitting on your butt and knowing it. You are going to be better than you have been in years and years, you poor little thing that have been sick so long—and with Indigestion, of all tyrannical things! Talk about the control of mind over matter! Or, rather, let them talk about it who have never suffered from Indigestion. The supreme example of the control of matter over mind, is the way in which when Indigestion moves in, everything else moves out: nothing but grey skies all the day long; Fate and one's fellow-man malevolent; all values distorted.

Well, baby, I must go now, and lift a three-inch beefsteak out of the deep-freezer to thaw for my luncheon; and, for my breakfast (I am writing this at 6 A.M.) squeeze the juice from five oranges and one lemon; boil the two eggs which my chickens were boasting about all yesterday afternoon and, as I think I mentioned before, take my vitamines, et cet.

In order to help me feed myself properly and take my nasty medicines, I have devised a scheme which really works. I have artfully developed a beautiful case of schizophrenia: The strange case of Miss M. and Mrs. Somebody-Anybody. (I will explain her name presently.)

Soon after I returned to Steepletop from the hospital in New York, I found that whenever I was cooking food for a person with no appetite —myself—I would frequently sigh with boredom or twist my head about in exasperation; and that when I was setting out my various smelly vitamine capsules and spooning out into a glass Mr. Armour's obscene concoction, I would wrinkle up my nose in disgust, shrinking back from the moment when I should have to swallow the stuff—in other words, that I was using up a considerable amount of the very energy which the medicine was trying to build up, in a perfectly futile resistance to preparing it.

So I hit upon the bright idea of splitting myself into two personalities, one the patient, one the nurse. The nurse, now, cooks my meals, and sees to it that they are not only nutritious, but also appetizing and attractive. And she prepares my medicines with no repugnance, just as a matter of routine, almost automatically, while her mind—except for that small part of it required to check on what she is doing and be clinically accurate—is occupied with more interesting matters: she is thinking forward to this evening, when at last she is going to see and hear "South Pacific"; or she is thinking back to last evening, and staring again at that incredible Pure Canasta, those seven enchanted Aces.

As for the patient, she obediently, and also absent-mindedly, swallows and swallows and swallows: she is wondering if perhaps Shelley *invariably* wrote "as if", whereas Keats, also perhaps invariably, wrote "as though"; she decides to look into the matter.

Mrs. Somebody-Anybody got her name in this manner: when in Doctors' Hospital, I made known to several friends who visited me there, my decision to return to Steepletop and live here all alone, they were appalled, and begged me not to try it. They all said, "But you *must* have *somebody* with you! You simply *can't* be there without *anybody*!"

I knew, beyond any doubt, that to be here alone, was the only way I could go through with it. But I could not convince them.

When, finally, by getting the doctor on my side, I prevailed; when I was here alone, and thought up my pretty schizophrenia; I named my nurse Mrs. Somebody-Anybody. She doesn't know that I called her that; she wouldn't like it. So to her face I call her "Mrs. S.A." She thinks I mean Mrs. Sex-Appeal! And she *bridles*, my dear, she actually *bridles*!

Well, my darling, Mrs. Somebody-Anybody must really go and squeeze those oranges.

Don't worry about me at all, either of you. To pretend that it is not agony, would be silly. But I can cope.

Please thank Charlie again, as I did in my telegram, for his thoughtfulness in writing first that you were in good condition, and only after having set my mind at ease, telling me about the operation. Ask him to write me how you got home, and how things are with you now.

So much love, dear Normie. And to my Charlie, too.

Ediner.

266   TO MARGARET CUTHBERT

Steepletop, Austerlitz, N.Y.
March 3, 1950

Dear Margaret:

I might as well break down and confess—I might have known that I couldn't really fool you and Alice for very long—! Well, the reason why I don't telephone you is because I have no telephone, I have been without a telephone for two months.

When the weather began to get cold, the wires began to make such a noise that I couldn't stand it. I tried everything—I had them make the wires more slack—I had them change the point of entry into the house (so that the noise wouldn't come right into my ear when I lay in bed)— time after time I got up out of bed in the middle of the night, and sighed, and picked up a couple of blankets and a pillow, and trudged up to my cabin in the pines, and tried to sleep there. But there is no bed there, not even a couch, just a rather small chaise-longue. So—I haven't had much sleep this winter.

I did not have the telephone instrument taken out—they are hard to get—I had the wires taken down, but arranged so that I could keep the instrument itself & pay for it at the minimum rate—until warm weather should take the humming out of the wires and I could have the blasted thing installed again.

Love,
Edna

267   TO CASS CANFIELD

Steepletop, Austerlitz, N.Y.
April 4th, 1950

Dear Cass:

I meant to write you at once, after sending you that telegram. For I realized, the moment it had gone, how abrupt and chilly it might sound, unless it were followed at once by a letter explaining it. But I have had little time for writing letters.

The reason I wired you not to come that Friday, was because it suddenly occurred to me that that day would be the day after Thanksgiving day; and I was not at all sure how I should get through that day, the first Thanksgiving Day I had ever spent all alone. I got through it all right, and all the other happy holidays, too, by simply by-passing them. (I love that expression.) The only thing I did by way of observance, was to sit at the piano on Christmas Eve, and play and sing some Christmas Carols. And on New Year's Eve, I rang up Eugen's family in Holland. None of them had received any word from me at all, since that one shocking cablegram. And New Year's Eve, which they call Old Year's Eve, is a very solemn occasion with them, not like our gay and rowdy drunken tooting. The family assembles, and talks about what has happened in the year that has passed. And I knew that they would talk of Eugen with heavy heartache; and that they would be worrying about me. For they love me as if I were their own kin; as I do them.

I should like very much to see you, and I will let you know as soon as the roads are open. The weather this winter has been phenomenally bad. Spring is at least six weeks later than usual, and the roads are just now beginning to thaw, and are like quicksand. John Pinnie has to walk here every morning, to do the chores. Please forgive me for not writing sooner.

Affectionately,
Edna.

268   TO MRS. MARY V. HERRON

Steepletop, Austerlitz, N.Y.
April 5th, 1950

Dear Mary:

Enclosed is a little Easter book-mark. Isn't it sweet? I had a feeling you might love it. My aunt sent it me several years ago, and I kept it in a copy of Keats, so that it would open at The Eve of St. Agnes, while I was learning The Eve of St. Agnes by heart. And even after I knew the poem by heart, the little book-mark stayed there, so that the string and tassel part of it look just a bit grubby, I'm afraid. Not very, though.

I'm going to write out my own cheques from now on, and attend to my book-keeping myself. You've been a marvellous help to me: I don't see how I could possibly have managed all these different kinds of business without you. But it's time I stopped being such a baby.

If you will please still read my mail, though, and answer for a while still the kind of letter you have been answering for me, I shall be very grateful.

You can't have any more Steepletop butter until the roads are in better condition. Poor John has to walk every day to and from his work here. And I can't ask him to carry anything more than a few letters. I'll send you a nice big piece next time.

Edna

269   TO MRS. MARY V. HERRON

Steepletop, Austerlitz, N.Y.
April 20th, 1950

Why, you horrid little thing, you! I'm *giving* you the butter!—It's a *present*! Why, I never was so shocked in all my life! You make me sick.

Anyhow, it won't work: I refuse to have my arrogant, aloof, pure-Guernsey butter all computed in U. S. Gov. stamps. So if you want it, you'll have to take it as a present, and charge me for the stamps. (And no funny business.)

After all that you have done for me, and are constantly doing—no sister could have given me more tender care—and I mayn't even give you a greasy little present! You make me sick.

More later. John must start splashing down for the mail. Enclosed cheque is for the American Cancer Society. Make the contribution an even fifty.

E.

Dear M. (this continued from yesterday—I had no time to finish)

I want to give much more than two dollars to the American Cancer Society. Hence my cheque for fifty. Good God, I gave *five* dollars to the Infantile Paralysis drive! And what is Hecuba to me, or I to Hecuba? (Hamlet would forgive me: he was a bit upset, himself.)

My own sweet wonderful darling died of cancer.

As did, a few years ago, our good friend, that fine poet, Arthur Davison Ficke.

As did, a few years ago, Eugen's brilliant young nephew, Dr. Charles Boissevain, well known in medical societies for his research not only in tuberculosis, but also in cancer.

To me, long before any of these deaths occurred, cancer was the most horrible and the most to be dreaded of all diseases.

The American Cancer Society doesn't know how to advertise itself. This is a pity. Infantile Paralysis is all over the radio and all over everything else with its tricky slogans—March of Dimes, and what not—; and Heart Disease has gone and spoiled St. Valentine's Day with its National Heart Week—as if it weren't bad enough to have heart trouble, without having St. Valentine's Day all ruined as well. But all that the American Cancer Society ever does, is simply to announce, in a dignified way, that it exists, and is not averse to contributions.

I hope I didn't neglect to enclose the cheque. No. I remember. I did enclose it.

You wonder how I am going to stand the spring. I'm wondering myself, I can tell you. And I'm plenty scared. Not scared that I shan't muddle through in some way or other. Just scared. Shrinking from being hurt too much. Scared the way I used to be as a child, when I had to go to the dentist. In the days before they gave you novocaine.

I have already encountered the first dandelion. I stood and stared at it with a kind of horror. And then I felt ashamed of myself, and sorry for the dandelion. And suddenly, without my doing anything about it at all, my face just crumpled up and cried.

How excited he always was when he saw the first dandelion! And long before the plants got big enough for even a rabbit to find them, he had dug a fine mess, for greens. He used to say "pick dandelions"; and I would say, "Not pick,—dig." And he would say, "Oh, don't scold poor Uge—he does so his best."

Alas, alas, and alas.

270   TO MRS. FRANK L. RICKER

Steepletop [Austerlitz, N.Y.]
April 30, 1950

Dear Aunt Susie:

This is just a note to say that I'm sorry you didn't get a note from me for your birthday.

One of the reasons why you didn't get it, is because I didn't write it.

One of the more unsatisfactory things about me is, that the only dates I know are 1066 and 1492, and I never can seem to fit them in anywhere, lately.

My own birthday I should never in the world remember, except that it also happens to be George Washington's birthday, and there is always a great to-do and fanfare about it, and a national holiday and all, and so it is somewhat forced upon the attention.

Last-Minute-News:

It hasn't snowed today. At least not quite. At least not yet.

Daylight-Saving-Time!—*What* daylight?

Love, anyhow,
Vincent

271 TO MARGARET CUTHBERT

Steepletop, Austerlitz, N.Y.
May 1st, 1950. 6 A.M.
DAYLIGHT SAVING TIME

("Eh?—what say, stranger?"
"Daylight Saving Time."
"*What* time?"
"Daylight Saving."
"Saving *what?*"
"*Daylight!*"
"Excuse me, stranger: I reckon I must
be gittin' jest a leetle mite deef. Yuh
know what I thought yuh said?—I
thought yuh said—he! he! he!—'DAY-
LIGHT' ! ! ! ")

Dear Margaret:
This is just a weather report.
Letter follows.
As spring follows winter.
That is to say: not immediately.

WEATHER REPORT

ANNOUNCER: Ladies and Gentlemen, I regret to say that Mr. Steele,
who usually at this time gives you his Weather Report, has just—
UNIDENTIFIED WOMAN IN AUDIENCE: Weather *what?*
ANNOUNCER: Report.
UNIDENTIFIED WOMAN: Oh, yes, *report.* I *thought* I heard a pistol
shot.

I have always disliked that line of Swinburne, "When the hounds
of Spring are on Winter's traces": it always seemed to me such a silly
and awkward metaphor,—especially, coming as it does just three lines
before that "lisp of leaves and ripple of rain." (And if I am misquoting,
I don't, for once in my life, give a darn.)

Speaking of hounds, and of spring: The Annual Spring Meet of
the Columbia County Yoicks-and-Gone-to-Earth Club, has got off to
an extremely bad finish. All the hounds have laryngitis, as well as a
cold in the head, so that even if they could pick up the scent, which
they can't, they would not be able to utter a whimper concerning it.
The M.F.H. has chilblains and can't get his boots on. The Gamekeeper
is in "THE QUEEN'S ARMS" (I beg your pardon, Your Majesty) playing

darts; and not an earth has been stopped. But all of this, really, matters very little, as the fox is nowhere in the vicinity. The fox is in the hen-house. And the farmer doesn't care.

Well, toodle-oo. I must button up my organdy and go out and dance around the May-Pole; with a sprig of mistletoe in one hand and a snowball in the other; singing dirty songs, like Ophelia.

I am, dear madam, as ever, resentfully yours,

E. St. V. M.

Edna St. Vitus Millstone

272   TO NORMA MILLAY

Steepletop, Austerlitz, N.Y.

May 3rd, 1950

Dear Norma:

I nigh splat over your "The Stones of Gaul".[23] If I had time, I would go over it and tell you the parts that sent me into stitches. (By the way, I trust that your own stitches remained intact while you were writing it.) What a dirty trick—to take away not only your gall-bladder, but also your coffee. I have no way of knowing how attached you may have been to your gall-bladder, for I never asked you. But I do know that you and your coffee were practically inseparable.

I thought that the enclosed might interest you.[24] Good old "Me-gunticook"! . . . Was that a long time ago? . . . Or not?

Can you, by any chance, acquaint me with the habitat (as of the next few moments) of that rara avis, that warbler of many tunes, whose migrations are more unpredictable than those of the Evening Grosbeak —the Macdougallus Al(l)ae Ros(s)ae? (Not, of course, to be confused with the Nachtigallus, although such confusion has occurred, and is, to be sure, understandable.)

N.B.   This bird has never been banded.

Love,

Edna

P.S.   How are you coming along, honey?

[23] During her convalescence, Miss Norma Millay amused herself by writing this Gilbertian playlet.

[24] A rare book dealer's offer of two issues of the hard-to-find Camden, Maine, high school magazine, *Megunticook*: one dated March, 1909, has E. Vincent Millay listed as Editor-in-Chief, the other, dated December, 1910, contains a story by Norma Millay.

273 TO BERNICE BAUMGARTEN

Steepletop, Austerlitz, N.Y.
June 23rd, 1950

Dear Miss Baumgarten:

I am writing to you instead of Miss King, because you and I have known each other for years, and I do not know Miss King. It is about this business of the OXFORD BOOK OF AMERICAN VERSE.

They intend to print, it seems, nine poems by me. I have no objection to their printing any of the poems which they have selected. It is to their selection, as a group, that I object. I not only object: I will not permit them to use this group of poems as being representative of my poetry.

I have never interfered in matters like this before,—never interfered with you, I mean. You had the good sense to question me as to the inclusion of a poem of mine in that Communist anthology. But in instances like this, you cannot possibly know what the anthologies are doing to me. They do not do it purposely, of course; and what they do cannot harm me: it can, however, annoy me intensely. And I am getting sick and tired of it.

What the anthologists of poetry do, naturally, since they are not interested in poetry, interested only in selling their books, is to include the poems which they think will have the most popular appeal. Of my poetry they like to print such simple and youthful poems as "Afternoon on a Hill" and "Recuerdo", both of which are on the Oxford list; and if they use any of my sonnets, their preference is to use only love sonnets, and written in the Elizabethan form, two of which are on their list. (How on earth such a mature poem as "The Return" ever got on their list, I cannot imagine, unless, perhaps it is because it is the first poem in the book—Wine from These Grapes—and the first poem is about as far as they have time to read in a book.

Letter unfinished but continued in another, August 2, 1950.

Dear Miss Baumgarten:

It is probably too late now to do anything about the matter about which I was writing you nearly two and a half months ago. I was interrupted, and then I got to work on my poems, and had no time to continue. There is much more that I want to tell you about this anthology business, from the point of view of the poet, naturally; but there is no reason to take the time for it just now, unless I hear from you that

the Oxford University Press has not yet gone out of the galley proof
stage in its American Verse publication, and that it would be willing to
substitute for certain of my poems which they have selected, poems of
my own choosing. Will you let me know if there is still any chance of
this. The changes which I have in mind would make my group very
much more interesting, and certainly more representative of my work.
I should consider it a fine courtesy on their part, if they would oblige
me in this.

Sincerely yours,
Edna St. Vincent Millay

274   TO IRENE POIRIER

Steepletop, Austerlitz, N.Y.
July 19, 1950

Dear Madam:

Some years ago, the Lennox Library helped me out of a bad predicament. You had a book which I needed, and which I could find nowhere else in the vicinity, and which you were kind enough to lend me.

Now, I need your help again.

The Saturday Evening Post has commissioned me to write a
Thanksgiving poem for them.[25] You can imagine that, at a time like
this, to write a poem full of thanks, and hope, and cheer, is a hard
assignment. At first, I did not see how I could do it; I could not see
from what angle to approach it. And yet, I wanted to do the poem.
I shall, of course, be well paid for it; and that is always pleasant. And
yet, there was more to it than that.

Finally I hit upon the scheme of describing, as if I had been present,
that first Thanksgiving Day, in 1621, and showing, by implication only,
that the early settlers were in more constant and immediate danger than
we are today; and that yet, by their courage, they came through, and
proceeded to build a country.

I am telling you all this in detail, so that you will understand exactly
the sort of books I need to help me. I want everything you have, in a
more or less popular style, about the Pilgrim Fathers,—the landing at
Plymouth Rock,—their early hardships,—what sort of houses they built,
—when the Mayflower sailed back to England (or did it sail for Delft?)

whether they discovered cranberries (cranberries grow near there!) Will you do what you can for me?

Sincerely yours,
Edna St. Vincent Millay

²⁵ The poem was published in the Thanksgiving number of the *Saturday Evening Post*, 1950.

275 TO MRS. ESTHER ROOT ADAMS

[Steepletop, Austerlitz, N.Y.]
Aug. 14, 1950

Dear Tess:

Ragged Island is not for sale.

As soon as I can bear it, I shall go back there. Possibly next summer. I don't know.

Tell John [Johnson] to board things up as best he can, and carry on. I long ago stopped bothering about its being broken into. I will write him as soon as I have a little time (if and when). I am working terribly hard, writing. The Thanksgiving number of the Saturday Evening Post will have a poem of mine.

No, I can't visit you, darling; and even if I could, I would not— thanking you very much, however. When I go to Maine again, I shall go straight to Ragged.

Love,
Edna

P.S. I suppose you know the tax collector, Gladys Thurston. Will you please ask her to make a note to send me the tax in future *under my own name*? As you know, I never used Eugen's name: *(Miss)* etc. is my correct and legal name. And it is not only annoying, but in this instance it is downright painful, to see the tax for Ragged written out in his name (with just a Mrs. before it)—he did so love the Island.

276 TO HELEN ADAIR BRUCE²⁶

Steepletop, Austerlitz, N.Y.
August 27th, 1950

Dear Helen:

What an adorable baby!

But oh, what a great big name for a tiny little girl to carry!

I don't know what impresses me the more—the "Bruce" or the "Robin Adair"!

Did you notice that I said, all without thinking: "the Bruce"? Perhaps it is an omen: perhaps, one day, she will not only make the assembly shine,—she will be THE BRUCE.

With love,
Edna

[26] Before her marriage, Mrs. Bruce had once acted as secretary to the poet and had accompanied her on a reading tour.

277   TO CASS CANFIELD

Steepletop, Austerlitz, N.Y.
August 27th, 1950

Dear Cass:

I am glad you like the Thanksgiving poem. It must have startled you to read it, and find that it was quite a different poem from the one I outlined to you here at Steepletop, and of which I read you passages. I worked very hard on that poem—the first one—and it was going along well, I thought; but as things got worse and worse in Korea, I began to see that it was not the right poem for the occasion. "What," I asked myself, "would a few Indian war-whoops mean, and a neighborly little scalping-party,—to a nation dreading and awaiting the atom bomb?" "Fun and games, that's all; just good, clean fun."

So I scrapped the poem, as of that instant; and sat there, scared frozen; the deadline only ten days off; my promise to deliver the poem long ago given to the Post; and not an idea in my head.

What finally happened is as follows: when I got so scared that I was fair frantic, there was nothing to do but relax, and start all over; and so I did. And almost at once the first lines of the new poem came into my head.

Oh, I know that I am making a big fuss about a small piece of work, —but it is so wonderful to be writing again! (My only hope, just now: this is a bad time of year for me.)

Thank you for continuing the advance payments. I was so busy writing that I did not even notice, until the August slip came in. But this is a great help to me. And it was kind of you to do it, without even speaking about it.

Sincerely,
Edna

278   TO MARGARET CUTHBERT

Steepletop, Austerlitz, N.Y.
Sept. 6th, 1950

Dear Margaret:

I should love to see Marian. And I want dearly to see you and Alice. So come when you can, and as soon as you can, and stay as long as you can. Let John know, the night before. (Sevenish) That's all that's necessary.

I should tell you, I suppose, that in the circs, you'll have to pig it a bit. The circs are approx as follows:

Not only has the guest-house geyser gone to pot, so that the dear old h. and c. no longer funcs; but there are bees in the studio.

These bees, mind you, are the best bees: they are Italian bees. But—well—how good is your Italian?

As for the stitch at the Manor House,—oh, bother!—Oh, damn and blast! It's the vicar!—And, yes,—my God! All five of them!

Why, hello, Daisy! Hello, Pansy! Hello, Violet! Hello, Iris! Hello, Rose!

I say, this is most frightfully jolly!—Tea'll be ready in a jiff!

Margaret, you and Marian, being the tallest, will sleep in my bed; Alice and I will sleep on the two couches in the living-room. It is a simple matter of mathematics.

Speaking of mathematics: A lady in up-state New York ordered from a stationer in a town in western Massachusetts, two wire trays, one for Incoming Mail, the other for Outgoing Mail. What was the lady's dismay when, on opening the parcel, she found that the two trays were exactly alike! "How on earth," she thought, "shall I ever be able to tell them apart?"

The lady had no difficulty whatever in telling them apart.

How was her problem solved?

—Love, Edna.

279   TO HARRISON DOWD

Steepletop, Austerlitz, N.Y.
Sept. 9th, 1950

Dearest Harrison:

I wish I had the time to write you all the things I want to say about your fine book.[27] I expected it to be good; I did not know it would be

as good as it is. Only a very musical person could have written it. Not
that there is anything at all obviously *musical* about it! I refer to changes
of key, changes in tempo, that sort of thing, beautifully done. I get so
awfully tired of books that sit down to the typewriter in the key of C
Major and in 4/4 time and plod right along like that to the end.

* * *

Congratulations, my dear!

Love,
Edna

[27] *The Night Air*, a novel.

280 TO MRS. ESTHER ROOT ADAMS

Steepletop [Austerlitz, N.Y.]
Oct. 9, 1950

Dear Tess:

I should love to see you; but (and this is one hell of an invitation,
as I know) can you arrange to come after lunch and leave before
dinner? (!!!) I have no time to explain now; I want to get an answer
to you into this mail.

No, my dear. Don't bring me any lobsters. And don't bring me any
sea-weed.

John is ready to leave for the post-office.

Love,
Edna

281 TO MRS. LENA RUESCH

The following note was left one morning in the autumn of
1950 for Mrs. Ruesch, a neighbor who helped keep the house.

Dear Lena:

This iron is set too high. Don't put it on where it says "Linen"—or
it will scorch the linen. Try it on "Rayon"—and then, perhaps on
"Woollen". And be careful not to *burn your fingers* when you shift it
from one heat to another.

It is 5:30, and I have been working all night. I am going to bed.
Goodmorning—

E. St. V. M.

Index

Only the names of those to whom letters are addressed and names of persons mentioned in the letters have been indexed. Numbers appearing in boldface refer to letter numbers. Numbers in regular type are page numbers; when followed by the letter "n." reference is to a note.

Set in Linotype Janson
Format by Robert Cheney
Manufactured by The Haddon Craftsmen, Inc.
Published by HARPER & BROTHERS, *New York*